THE
PHYSICAL
PHENOMENA
OF MYSTICISM

WITH ESPECIAL REFERENCE
TO THE
STIGMATA, DIVINE AND DIABOLIC

By

FLORA ANNIE STEEL

First published in 1947

British Library Cataloguing-in-Publication Data
A catalogue record for this book is available
from the British Library

Revera ubi tuta firmaque
infirmis securitas et requies,
nisi in vulneribus Salvatorisí

ST. BERNARD,
Sermo lxi in Cantica Canticorum

Dieu parle; il faut qu'on lui réponde

ALFRED DE MUSSET

Montague Summers

Augustus Montague Summers was born in Bristol, England in 1880. He was raised as an evangelical Anglican in a wealthy family, and studied at Clifton College before reading theology at Trinity College, Oxford with the intention of becoming a Church of England priest. In 1905, he graduated with fourth-class honours, and went on to continue his religious training at the Lichfield Theological College. Summers entered his apprenticeship as a curate in the diocese of Bitton near Bristol, but rumours of an interest in Satanism and accusations of sexual misconduct with young boys led to him being cut off; a scandal which dogged him his whole life. Summers joined the growing ranks of English men of letters interested in medievalism and the occult. In 1909, he converted to Catholicism and shortly thereafter he began passing himself off as a Catholic priest, the legitimacy of which was disputed. Around this time, Summers adopted a curious attire which included a sweeping black cape and a silver-topped cane.

Summers eventually managed to make a living as a full-time writer. He was interested in the theatre of the seventeenth century, particularly that of the English Restoration, and was one of the founder members of The Phoenix, a society that performed neglected works of that era. In 1916, he was elected a fellow of the Royal Society of Literature. Summers also produced some important studies of Gothic fiction. However, his interest in the occult never waned, and in 1928, around the time he was acquainted with Aleister Crowley, he published the first English translation of Heinrich Kramer and James Sprenger's *Malleus Maleficarum* (*'The Hammer of Witches'*), a 15th century Latin text on the hunting of witches. Summers then turned to vampires, producing *The Vampire: His Kith and Kin* (1928) and

The Vampire in Europe (1929), and then to werewolves with *The Werewolf* (1933). Summers' work on the occult is known for his unusual, archaic writing style, his intimate style of narration, and his purported belief in the reality of the subjects he treats.

In his day, Summers was a renowned eccentric; *The Times* called him *"in every way a 'character'"* and *"a throwback to the Middle Ages."* He died at his home in Richmond, Surrey.

CONTENTS

CHAPTER ONE

CHAPTER TWO

CHAPTER THREE

CHAPTER FOUR

CHAPTER FIVE

CHAPTER SIX

CHAPTER SEVEN

ILLUSTRATIONS

INTRODUCTION

T HE important and very remarkable general revival of interest in the subject of Mysticism, which has been so widely in evidence in England during the past fifty years, and which shows every sign that it is no mere passing phase or transitory mode of thought, but a vital permanency since it has proved of real practical help and a source of strength and enlightenment to very many, is attributed to a large number of causes, the varieties of which I do not propose to discuss in detail. I will content myself with observing that I can hardly believe the impetus to be purely literary, although (as I suppose nobody would dispute) there is no doubt at all that valuable and sympathetic, and above all knowledgeable, Studies of Mysticism from able pens have done much, very much, to stabilize and help the movement. But seeing how deeply Mysticism has entered into and leavened people's lives, I hesitate to suggest that these Studies have actually *created* the great revival. For my part I would prefer to say that the time was ripe, and the "Spirit breathed where he will; and thou hearest his voice, but thou knowest not whence he cometh and whither he goeth".

It appears to have escaped notice, or at any rate it has not been sufficiently remarked, that in England throughout the nineteenth century, there existed a very lifesome, if indeed a rather reserved school of mystics, that not a few mystical works of rare quality were published and eagerly perused. It is true that the flower of these were, perhaps, translations. Contrariwise, the writings of the Oratorian, Fr. Faber, had a wide circulation and exercised much influence. Translations, inadequate maybe in the view of modern searching scholarship, of the writings of St. Teresa of Ávila and St. John of the Cross were made by David Lewis. Earlier in date, the "Oratorian Series", as it is generally known, of the Lives of the Saints, presented a number of volumes of mystical hagiography. To the first volume of *The Life of S. Alphonso Maria de Liguori*, five volumes, 1848–9, Fr. Faber prefixed a very ample Essay of one hundred and forty pages, *On Beautification and Canonization*. This is of great importance to the student of Mysticism.

The bulk of the *Oxford Book of English Mystical Verse* is occupied by poets who date from 1801, the birth year of John Henry, Cardinal Newman, to the work of Arthur Shearly Cripps, who was born in 1869. It is true that in those pages, 133–516, Mr. D. H. S. Nicholson and Mr. A. H. E. Lee admit a few names and some verse which cannot be called "mystical" at all, but even with this proviso a number of poems are there to prove that the nineteenth century was by no means so spiritually sterile as many suppose.

In their introduction (1921) Mr. Nicholson and Mr. Lee emphasize that the world appears to be "undergoing a spiritual revitalization", that Mysticism "has emerged from the morass of apathy which characterized the eighteenth and the greater part of the nineteenth century". I believe that this morass or slough has been thought of as far muddier, far more lethargically engulfing than really was the case. To turn to the eighteenth century, I will mention no more than two names, William Blake (1757–1827), and William Beckford (1760–1844). The latter may cause surprise. I reply, read *An Excursion to the Grande Chartreuse in the Year* 1778.

In the nineteenth century, wherever in England there was a cloister, there was a centre of Mysticism.

One may quote even an old Georgian divine in defence of Mystical Theology. William Law (1686–1761) in a letter to Dr. Trapp, says that mystical writers "there have been in all ages of the Church, but as they served not the ends of popular learning, as they helped no people to figure or preferment in the world, and were useless to scholastic controversial writers, so they dropt out of public uses, and were only known, or rather unknown, under the name of mystical writers, till at last some people have hardly heard of that very name . . . they were deeply learned in the mysteries of the Kingdom of God, not through the use of lexicons, or meditating upon critics, but because they had passed from death unto life". This letter of an eighteenth century cleric is of considerable interest, as being evidence from outside. Law's observations, moreover, are limited to England. In France, Spain, Italy, to name no other countries, Mysticism was always vigorous, fadeless and beautiful.

This is why I think that Dr. A. Allen Brockington has misunderstood when in his *Mysticism and Poetry*, 1934, he writes (p. 158): "This revival of interest (in Mysticism) in English-speaking countries coincides with a revival of interest in France". There could not in France be "a revival of interest", because the mystical tradition never lapsed. The Abbé Henri Bremond's *Histoire Littéraire du Sentiment Religieux en France depuis la Fin des Guerres de Religion jusqu' à nos Jours* did not *initiate* a rejuvenescence of Mysticism in France. The ten volumes of this great masterpiece were the effect not the cause.

This is not to suggest that the Abbé Bremond's work is not of the greatest value and the influence of so vast a Study must be widespread and enduring. In England Professor Allison Peers is doing something of the same kind for the Spanish Mystics, and we cannot be sufficiently grateful for his translations of St. Teresa and St. John of the Cross. We may especially look forward (I hope) to a study from him of the Venerable Sor Maria Coronal de Agreda, concerning whom we hear nothing in English save a very few superficial articles, of which all are nugatory, and one at least is positively offensive.

A systematic survey of the great Italian mystics is much to be desired. Baron von Hügel's intensive study of St. Catharine Adorno Fieschi of Genoa has notably enriched our mystical literature, but beyond this, with the exception of St. Francis of Assisi and St. Catharine

of Siena, in England the Italian mystics are practically unknown. We
have not a translation, selected passages or excerpts at least, from the
Spiritual Diary of St. Veronica Giuliani. Professed students of mysticism
have barely heard of St. Maria Maddalena de' Pazzi, of whom it has
been finely said by a famous French writer: "Elle converse directement
avec le Père, et bégaie, dans l'extase, les explications des mystères
que lui divulgua l'Ancien des jours. Ses livres contiennent une page
souveraine sur la Circoncision, une autre magnifique, construite toute
en antitheses, sur le Saint-Esprit, d'autres étranges sur la déification de
l'âme humaine, sur son union avec le ciel, sur le rôle assigné dans cette
opération au plaies du Verbe."

We have not even in English, an adequate and complete translation
of the *Opere*, the *Works*, of St. Catharine of Siena.

Frequently I have been asked, which are the best general surveys
of Mysticism? This is a question not easy to answer. To attempt to list
the old masters of the spiritual life would be to compile a bibliography.
There are, for example, such standard works as the *Instructiones Theo-
logiæ Mysticæ*, of Dom Dominic Schram, O. S. B. (1658–1720), and
Il Direttorio Mistico of Gianbattista Scaramelli, S. J. (1687–1752), Schram
has been translated into French. Scaramelli's work, of which there are
many editions, was posthumously published, Venice, 1754, and has been
translated into Latin, French, German, Spanish and Polish. An abridge-
ment of *Il Direttorio Mistico* which appeared, London, 1913, as *A Handbook
of Mystical Theology*, 168 pp., is altogether too drastically curtailed to
be of any real use.

La Mistica Teologia, 1623, of the Minim Fray Fernando de Caldera;
Terzago's *Theologia Historico—Mystica*, Venice, 1764, and Gaetano
Marcecalea's *Enchiridium Mysticum*, Verona, 1766, are books difficult to
find. The same may be said of Lopez Ezquerra's *Lucerna Mystica* which
appeared towards the end of the seventeenth century. The *Lucerna* is
actually the work of Dom Agostino Nagore, a Carthusian of Saragossa,
who did not publish it. The MS. came into the possession of Ezquerra,
who printed it at Bilbao, under his own name. Very valuable are the
mystical studies of the Discalced Carmelite, P. Michel de la Fuente, who
at the beginning of the seventeenth century died in the Odour of Sanctity.

Of more recent volumes, Dr. Ludwig's Noack's *Die Christliche Mystik*,
Königsberg, 1853, must be used with considerable caution. Far more
reliable and solid is Abbé Migne's *Dictionnaire de Mystique* in the third
Encyclopédie Théologique, 1885. The works of such authorities as Dom
Maréchaux, Mgr. Farges, Père Poulain, Canon Auguste Sandreau, Fra
Juan G. Arintero, O.P., all the Teresians, Léon Boré, Dr. Lefebvre of
Louvain, are classics in the history of Mysticism. If I have seemed to omit
some important names it is merely because one must perforce limit a
catalogue of authors.

Two works which I judge to be the essential text-books so to speak, of Mysticism, are *Die Christliche Mystik*, Regensberg, 5 Vols., 1836–42, of Johann Joseph von Görres (1776–1848); and Canon J. Ribet's *La Mystique divine, distinguée des Contrefaçons Diaboliques et des Analogies Humaines. Les phénomènes Mystiques, la contemplation, les phénomènes distincts de la contemplation, les causes des phénomènes mystiques*, first edition, Paris, Poussielgue, 4 Vols., 1879–1883. Albert L. Caillet in his authoritative *Manuel Bibliographique* gives unstinted praise to both these encyclopædic studies.

During the past fifty years a number of excellent books have been written by English scholars and students upon the various aspects of Mysticism, yet since these aspects are almost infinite, it is plain that there is room for many more studies of the supernatural and contemplative life. In fact, one may say that Mysticism is an exhaustless well, *"fons aquae salientis in vitam aeternam"*.

It can hardly escape remark that the more recent English writers on Mysticism almost sedulously avoid certain particular aspects of the subject, although such are integral to their theme, and of the very first importance. That the matter is difficult and needs most careful examination affords no excuse for this pusillanimity of approach. Many authors have here quite possibly taken their cue from Dean Inge, who in the Preface to his *Christian Mysticism*, 1899, very definitely emphasizes that he will not treat of and has nothing to do with "Supernatural phenomena".

None the less, a Mysticism without supernatural phenomena is a starveling. At best it is limited and lopped, however interesting it may prove within its own set bounds. A study of Mysticism which ignores so vital a constituent can but be, so to speak, introductory, and who would linger in the narthex when he may approach the Altar? The Supernatural Phenomena of Mysticism must be studied by English scholars with sympathy and respect, which by no means preclude a keen judgement and the critical spirit, as is amply proved by the many weighty volumes acknowledged masters have written in Latin, in French and Italian, in German, Spanish, and many another tongue.

I know of only two books in English which have as their definite theme supernatural phenomena: *Levitation*, published by Burns Oates & Washbourne, 1928; and *The Testimony of Blood*, by Captain Ian R. Grant, Burns Oates & Washbourne, 1929, actually not dated, but the Preface contributed by Mgr. Barnes is 16th October, 1929. The former of these, *Levitation*, is a translation, moreover, from the *Lévitation* of Professor Olivier Leroy.

There are, of course, in various journals and magazines a number of articles dealing with mystical phenomena. But then it is by no means easy to track down old magazines. As anyone who has undertaken such research well knows to his cost, it involves much time, and much patience. since at best it gives a considerable amount of trouble. One has to be quite certain of the year and the month of issue of the journal in which the article appeared. Files of these journals are seldom available except in the largest Libraries. Very often, too, when one has found the article in question it proves of little value, which is rather disheartening as the outcome of a long and difficult quest. One cannot help feeling that if a writer's articles and essays are important they should not be allowed to be *extravagantes*, but deserve to be collected together in book form,

In this present study, dealing with the Physical Phenomena of Mysticism, I have grouped these phenomena around Stigmatization, upon which (so far as I am aware) no book has been written in English. In saying this, it is, I think, quite legitimate to exclude *The Stigmata: A History of Various Cases Translated from "The Mystik" of Görres*, Edited with a preface by the Rev. H. Austin, one volume, Richardson, Derby, 1883. This is, truth to tell, a very thin, abridged, and attenuated version of two or three chapters from Görres' monumental work. In any case, since it was published in 1883, it obviously cannot discuss the many recent pseudo-problems which concern, and "explanations" of, Stigmatization; I mean hypnotism, autosuggestion, psychoanalysis, and other pathologies.

There is no work in English which corresponds to the immense investigations of Dr. Antoine Imbert-Gourbeyre of Clermont-Ferrand. His books have taken their place as classics, and must remain authoritative for all time. At least, humanly speaking, it is impossible to see how they can ever be superseded. The most important of Dr. Imbert-Gourbeyre's studies are: *Les Stigmatisées*, 2 Vols., Palmé, Paris, 1872; *La Stigmatisation*, 2 Vols., L. Bellet, Clermont-Ferrand; and the monograph *L'Hypnotisme et la Stigmatisation*, Bloud et Barral, Paris, 1899.

It is with a full consciousness that these problems are very many, very intricate, and very profound that I have written this book.

It is my pleasurable duty to thank Professor Allison Peers, Gilmour Professor of Spanish in the University of Liverpool, who has done so much to give us in England the Mystics of Spain, for his kind permission to quote from his many works, especially from those dealing with St. Teresa of Ávila, and St. John of the Cross.

I also have to thank the Editor of *Argentor*, the Quarterly Journal of the National Jewellers' Association, for kind permission to reproduce the illustration of St. Gregory the Great, Palazzo Ducale, Urbino. This illustration appeared in my article "Papal Tiaras", *Argentor*, January, 1947.

The remaining illustrations are all from my own collection.

MONTAGUE SUMMERS

26th July, 1947.
IN FESTO S. ANNÆ, AVLÆ DÑI.

CHAPTER ONE

The Question Mysticism answers—Derivation of the Word—The Mysteries of Eleusis —Dionysos—Orpheus and his Mysteries—Mystical Theology and the Areopagite— St. Gregory the Great—Contemplation—The Categories of Mysticism.

WHENCE? Why? Whither? The answer to these three questions is at once the explanation of and the reason for all religions. From the earliest dawn of conscious human intelligence to the very moment of penning or reading these words man is everlastingly asking himself, and always will be everlastingly asking himself, three questions. Where do I come from? Why am I here? Whither am I going?

The high philosopher grows old through long years of concentrated study and intensest thought, not only researching into written records, the lofty message bequeathed by the greatest minds of all time, but more, unsparing of himself whilst deeply delving into the most hidden and complex recesses of his own brain, analysing his own abstruse speculations, painfully codifying his own actual experiences, and his reward comes when he triumphantly gives his reply, albeit voiced in terms which to the man in the street seem just bemused and fogged, idle prattle upon stammering lips, but which are (as he himself knows full well) crystal clear and pregnant with profoundest meaning. The business man, the man of affairs, in a general way has little inclination and less opportunity to follow up even trite but primary inquiries [1]. Yet he cannot altogether escape. Willy nilly, these problems force themselves upon him, maybe whilst he lies upon a bed of sickness, or in a day of depression and bereavement. And they are none the less importunate for their infrequency. He will evade them by a stupid agnosticism, or if he be foolish enough shirk the issue more brazenly and more contemptibly by a blank denial. More wisely, ignoring the pitiable bankruptcy of science—falsely so-called —he will have attached himself to, or perchance luckily have been born, and, as it were, naturalized into some set school of religious thought. And if he is sincerely convinced of the truth of, and so acts consistently in accordance with, the moral and spiritual precepts of his religion, so far, so good. But it is not very far after all. Even the ale-house sot must have his hour when his dreams are least drunken, least fevered and crapulent. Even the lowest, when his sodden senses rouse dimly, will sometimes come face to face with the question—What is the meaning of it all? The finer the brain, the keener the intelligence, the more insistently does the riddle press for an answer. And as the Sphinx slew the man who could not solve her enigma, so a more awful death awaits those who refuse to attempt to find any answer to life's riddle, who counter the mystery with blank faces and sluggard denial.

The Before, the Now, the Hereafter. Only religion, that is to say the spiritual history of the human race, can answer these questions, and the only religion is "a religion of veracity rooted in spiritual inwardness" [2], based upon a Divine and infallible authority. God, having winked at the times of ignorance, has brought mankind to the knowledge that "in him we live, and move, and have our being" [*3*].

The religious impulse is active conscious life, and, as Professor Leuba says, "conscious life is always orientated towards something to be secured or avoided immediately or ultimately". It is a very common error to mistake conversion [*4*] for religion, whereas it is hardly the first step—it is more exactly an inclination to take the first step—on the way. Professor Starbuck defines conversion as "a process of struggling away from sin rather than of striving towards righteousness" [*5*]. Religion is not a conscious "struggling away from". But it is a "striving towards" God. It is true that the "striving towards" inevitably involves the former, but this is almost *per accidens*, and it involves a very great deal more, until eventually and in its more perfect form it necessitates, as St. John of the Cross teaches us, a detachment from self. "Desire to possess nothing," [*6*] says the great Carmelite Doctor, "the mystic's mystic." But in possessing nothing man finds that he has gained everything. Mysticism is the very life-blood of religion. Before attempting any definition of this word *Mysticism*, it will be well to consider it stymologically, and incidentally to avail ourselves of what hints or help we may glean from its semantics and historical associations.

Traditionally, and by very nearly the whole concensus of authority the word Mysticism is regarded as a derivative of the Greek μύω, I ritually close my eyes and my mouth; hence, I keep an absolute silence [*7*]. There is a close connexion with μυέω, I give secret instruction, I initiate. The *mystes* (μύστης) is one who has been initiated into profoundly esoteric knowledge of divine things, concerning which he is bound by a solemn vow to maintain an inviolable secrecy [*8*].

From the beginning then, the word is intimately related to the Greek mysteries [*9*]. It would hardly be too much to regard it as a purely technical, I might almost say a liturgical, term.

There were several great Greek festivals during which divine emblems were shown under a veil of metaphor, and sacred symbolism was dramatized and enacted, the ceremonies sometimes taking a very grotesque form, as when young girls in honour of Artemis Agrotera, Artemis, Lady of the wild open places, the steppes and wolds, danced a "bear-dance", and were ritually known as bears [*10*]. This would certainly seem to point back to some far distant totem-cult when the tribe who worshipped the local goddess claimed some kind of spiritual kinship with the bear [*11*]. Originally, indeed, Artemis came from the cold bleak north, that is before later poets fabled her to have been born of Leto at Delos, and before at Ephesus she was identified with their Oriental deity, the nature-power, Mother of fertility and abundance. Again, Artemis of Brauron, an Attic village (now Vraona) near Marathon, was ruthlessly savage and cruel, delighting in blood, whilst in the Tauric Chersonese (the Crimea), "land of murderers", the horrors of human sacrifice lingered long [*12*]. In later days Artemis was Hellenized. She became human and tender and fair, and was regarded as one with Diana, the chaste regent of the moon.

Among the Greeks the chief Mysteries, that is to say solemn festivals with a profoundly esoteric significance, which was, however, often lost sight of although the ritual acts persisted, were the Thesmophoria, the Arrephoria, the Skirophoria, the Stenia, which were women's feasts [13], and in many respects almost identical. The Scholiast on Lucian [14], on the Hetairæ (Dialogues of Courtezans), not altogether unlike a late Greek Ragionamenti), regards the Arrephoria and the Skirophoria as parts of the Thesmophoria, the Arrephoria being a carrying of things not named, that is to say male sexual emblems, an ancient fertility rite. The Stenia is a ceremony of lesser importance, which, Photius [15] says took place at night.

The mysteries of the Haloa, not celebrated by women alone, were according to Eustathius [16], who cites Pausanias, "a feast of Demeter and Dionysos", which is to say the conjunction of corn and the grape. Here the Hierophant presented the offerings, although priestesses solemnly attended. This is all most significant, and it is hardly too much to see a dim, and doubtless very vague foreshadowing, that sort of prototype of which ancient religions are full, of the one true Great Mystery, in which Bread and Wine are offered [17].

The Eleusinian Mysteries—which must be distinguished from the festival Eleusinia [18]—were a Ceremony so solemn, so sacred and august, as to stand away from (as it were) all other Greek Ritual rites, and they are well and wisely regarded as something altogether apart [19]. Their spiritual influence was enduring and immense. In fact it may be said that together with Orphism, with which occult philosophy they were largely infiltrated, the Eleusinian Mysteries were long the one spiritual influence of Greece. The other Mysteries—I except the Mithraic Mysteries which belong to a later period—the other Mysteries of Greece, at any rate, are no more than a fumbling in the dark, an endeavour, often praiseworthy enough within its limits, often pathetically childish and feeble, sometimes definitely twisted awry. At Eleusis we breathe a purer air, we sense the spiritual. Even now, after long centuries, anyone who has thoughtfully spent but a few hours at Eleusis can hardly fail keenly to realize the solemn associations of that place. Such was my experience during my own visits to the spot.

Eleusis lies about fourteen miles west of Athens. It was an immense sanctuary, comprising buildings of all kinds, the enclosure containing numberless altars, shrines, chapels and ex-votos. The Hall of Initiation, Telesterion, itself measured one hundred and seventy square feet. The sacred precincts were destroyed in A.D. 396 by Alaric the Visigoth. To discuss the ritual of the Mysteries in fullest detail would demand much space, and is, moreover, a subject proper to the antiquarian and mythologist. None the less, a sufficient outline of the significant ceremonies must be essayed.

The first and earliest stratum, so to speak, was no doubt the cult of the lady Demeter and her daughter, Korē, the maiden, whose worship contained the live seeds of aspiration which blossomed into full fruit and flower with the inrush of Dionysos. The sad winter months, the fall of the year, were renewed with the viridescence of young life, the springtide. It needs no very great preception to see how the Divine ordering of the universe thus in some sort pre-symbolized St. Anne, Our Lady, and the Birth of Our Lord.

Dionysos, who is commonly regarded as the wine-god [20], is primarily the Spirit of Ecstatic Rapture (however induced), he is no mere physical inebriation. As Father Martindale strikingly writes: "He goes back to something deeper in human nature, more akin to Asia, whether nearer or more distant (I mean, India), where dreams and ecstasy are congenital, you would say" [21]. "Dionysos," says Dr. Gilbert Murray, "has given man Wine, which is his Blood and a religious symbol. He purifies from sin." "The religion of 'Dionysos' as Euripides found it, already mysticized and made spiritual . . . was exactly that kind . . . which lends itself to dramatic expression" [22]. The Bacchae of Euripides, probably produced at Athens in 405 B.C., which might be called The Triumph of Dionysos, is a sacred Mystery Play.

Certain of Calderon's dramas at once recur in this connexion. Says Archbishop Trench [23]: "He took a manifest delight in finding or making a deeper meaning for the legends and tales of the classical world, seeing in them the symbols and unconscious prophecies of Christian truth. . . . Now it is the True God Pan, or Perseus rescuing Andromeda, or Theseus destroying the Labyrinth, or Ulysses defying the enchantments of Circe, or the exquisite mythus of Cupid and Psyche. Each in turn supplies him with some new poetical aspect under which to contemplate the very highest truth." Not the least lovely of these is El Divino Orfeo, the Divine Orpheus who descends into Hades to fetch back the soul He has wrested from Satan.

Originally Dionysos came from the north, from Thrace [24], where his oracle-shrine was upon the heights of the mountains [25]. Late in the sixth century B.C. he is an Olympian, that is to say he has taken his place in the pantheon of the great Deities. In the Bacchae, however, he is born of Semelê, the Theban princess, and comes back to Thebes [26], having journeyed far and taught the world his choric ritual and dances. Strabo [27] notes that his orgiastic cult was Phrygian, and closely resembled the Corybantine rites of the Great Mother. The fact is that in his essentially spiritual signification Dionysos—the Romans called him Liber, he who sets men free (in the highest sense, from sordid cares)— belonged to all peoples; his titles, Bacchos, Iacchos, Euios, Sabazios, and the rest are many; his activities manifold; and his mother Semelê is the Earth.

Before proceeding to a consideration of the ceremonial of the Eleusinian Mysteries it may be convenient here to devote some attention to the figure of Orpheus, whose Ritual and Mythology are so inextricably mixed and intertwined with those of Dionysos. As early as 450 B.C. at least and probably long before, the liturgy of Dionysos and that of Orpheus were considered to be identical. The historian Herodotus in his description of Egypt remarking upon the ancient traditions of the country observes that it is accounted profane for any to be buried in woollen

16

cerements and, he says, in this they agree with Bacchic and Orphic rituals which, in sooth, are really Egyptian and Pythagorean [28]. In the *Hippolytus* of Euripides acted at Athens, 429 B.C., at one of the tensest moments of the tragedy when Thessus upbraids his son, the old hero cries:

> *"Go revel in thy Bacchic rites*
> *With Orpheus for thy Lord and King"* [29].

Later, Appollodorus has no doubt that Orpheus "invented the Mysteries of Dionysos" [30].

The poetic fable of Orpheus is well known. He is the master musician, the lord of sweetest harmony:

> *Orpheus, with his Lute, made Trees,*
> *And the Mountain tops, that freeze*
> *Bow themselves when he did sing.*

He loves the nymph Eurydice, who at her nuptials is bitten by a venomous snake, and dies. Broken-hearted and bereft, he seeks his bride in the nether world, and by the magic of his music charms even the monsters and horrid powers of Hades, singing:

> *Such notes as warbled to the string,*
> *Drew Iron tears down Pluto's cheek,*
> *And made Hell grant what Love did seek.*

So it is conceded him that he shall lead Eurydice back to life on condition that he does not look behind him, not even a moment's glance, whilst they go. Just before they reach the upper air his longing is so intense that he turns, only to see her vanish into mists and darkness. The gate is shut, no more to be opened. Thus far the poets, Vergil, Ovid, and the rest. The legend is continued in various ways. All forlorn, Orpheus withdraws to Rhodope (to-day called Despoto Dagh), a mountain range in Thrace, a part of the Haemus (Great Balkan), and here he charms even inanimate nature, and the wild untamed animals become gentle and loving as he sings. A change takes place in him. Poliziano in his exquisitely beautiful "Fable" or melo-tragedy *Orfeo* [32] makes Orpheus sing:

> *He who would seek my converse, let him see*
> *That ne'er he talk of woman's love to me!*
> *How pitiful is he who changes mind*
> *For woman! for her love laments or grieves!*
> *Who suffers her in chains his will to bind,*
> *Or trusts her words lighter than withered leaves,*
> *Her loving looks more treacherous than the wind!*
> *A thousand times she veers; to nothing cleaves;*
> *Follows who flies; from him who follows, flees;*
> *And comes and goes like waves on stormy seas!*
> *High Jove confirms the truth of what I said,*
> *Who, caught and bound in love's delightful snare,*

Enjoys in heaven his own bright Ganymede;
Phoebus on earth had Hyacinth the fair;
Hercules, conqueror of the world, was led
Captive to Hylas by this love so rare—
Advice for husbands! Seek divorce, and fly
Far, far away from female company!

We here meet with an extremely ancient tradition, and it would seem to indicate that in some districts, and at some time, women were not without difficulty rigidly excluded from the Orphic Mysteries. It is significant that Ovid in the *Metamorphoses X*, follows up his account of the retirement of Orpheus to Mount Rhodope with the stories of Cyparissus, Ganymede, and Hyacinthus [33]. The legend continues that the Thracian women, the Maenads, the Bassarids, celebrating in wildest fashion the orgies of Dionysos, in fury at his sentiments—*spretæ injuria formæ*—tear Orpheus in a thousand pieces, most horribly mangling his limbs. But Dionysos, sore grieved at the death of the bard of his sacred rites, Ovid tells, terribly punishes his frenzied votaries for the evil they have done. He transforms them slowly into oak-trees and fearful are their agonies as their bodies cruddle and harden into knotty wood. It is no exaggeration to say that a whole library of studies and monographs has collected around the death, and debated the reason for the death, of Orpheus, which generations of scholars regard as of cardinal importance.

There are few gaps, in Greek literature, to be more regretted than that lost play by Aeschylus, whose subject was the slaying of Orpheus by the Maenads. We know little even of his Dionysian trilogy, *The Edonians*, *The Bassarids*, and *The Young Men*, with a satyric drama *Lycurgus* as the supplement. The first piece showed the advent of Dionysos in Thrace, and the third with a Chorus of youths, votaries of the god, exalted the triumph of their deity. One tradition related how Orpheus had been slain by Zeus, because he prematurely revealed the Mysteries to man. This legend, however, won little acceptance and is generally disregarded. This, at least, is certain, that the death of, and the subsequent divine honours paid to, Orpheus were closely connected with the worship of Dionysos.

In all its complexities and implications the legend of Orpheus—he was in early days made a Sun-god, Helios himself, or a high-priest and heirophant of the Divine Sun [34], who is inextricably combined with Dionysos, and, again, at other times a separate deity or hero, was indelibly stamped upon the imagination, and permeated the religion of Greece.

Dr. Gilbert Murray well says that the Religion of Dionysos, "already mysticized and made spiritual", "is hard to formulate or even describe, both because of its composite origins and because of its condition of constant vitality, fluctuation, and development".

Professor Lewis Campbell admirably sums up the importance of Orphism in the following sentences: "The Orphic ritual may be credited with two great contributions to religion—the belief in immortality, and the idea of personal holiness." Each contribution was made more valuable by the fact that both were combined, so that without holiness blessedness could not be secured hereafter. A third contribution was "the idea of redemption or of atonement which entered largely into this religion" [36]. The idea of survival after death as expressed in the Homeric poems is very feeble and unreal. There was a survival, and that is practically all that can be said. The soul is a mere wraith. "The living heart is not in it," it is "strengthless" [37]. The ghosts, whom Odysseus calls up, are empty shadows, until they have drunk of the spilth of new blood they cannot speak. They are "the thoughtless dead, the phantoms of men whose life is dead". Thus when Odysseus addressed the wispy shade of Achilles, he straightway made answer: "Console me not in death, noble Odysseus! Would rather that I were a bondman of the glebe, the serf of a master hard and harsh, of some poor man, whose living was but scanty and sparse, than thus to be king of all the nations of the dead" [38]. Even in the *Æneid* when Æneas tried to embrace the "infelix simulacrum" of his lost Creusa he clasps the empty air, her figure is unsubstantial as the breeze and vanishes away like a swift dream fleets at morn. Precisely the same passage occurs when Æneas in the underworld would clasp in his arms his father Anchises [39]. The poor ghosts gibber and wail like a thin wind. It is all very depressing and rather grim.

How entirely different the glorious vision of St. Rose of Lima, when she appeared to Diego Jacinto Paceco, a copyist who earned his livelihood by engrossing legal documents, but who was seized with agonizing writer's cramp so that his right-hand and whole arm were paralysed. Starvation, or the most abject beggary, seemed his fate. But there entered his room a Dominican nun, who smilingly sat down at his bedside, took the arm in her hands and stroked it gently. There was a spasm of pain, and the arm and hand were perfectly cured, and remained so until the day of his death. He was, in fact, able to write more clearly and with greater speed than ever before. This was not many years after Saint Rose's death, and seeing her portrait he at once recognized his visitant. After her death, Blessed Colomba of Rieti several times appeared in her convent and spoke with various sisters. She embraced the Prioress, Mother Cecilia, who said that the fragrance of her habit was like that of lilies, and the Mother distinctly felt upon her forehead a warm and loving kiss. Blessed Colomba also appeared in a Dominican convent at Mantua, where the sisters took her for one of the community. Here she talked with and affectionately embraced that astonishing mystic Osanna Andreasi, whose life has been written by the Bishop of Ceneda, Monsignor Corradino Cavriani. Similar examples might be almost endlessly multiplied.

Greek religion generally, then, could only glimpse a very indefinite and vague sort of survival, but the teaching of the Eleusinian Mysteries, and herein lay an inexhaustible source of strength, utterly rejected this false spectral phantomry. The future life offered to the mystics was rich and real—in one sense more real than this life—it was a state of supreme happiness and full content. That the Eleusinian Mysteries were an intensely spiritual and permanently elevating influence the greatest thinkers and gravest minds of Greece proclaim with one accord. Sophocles, most ethical and dignified of ancient poets, hymns the sublime felicity of the Initiated, both in this life and in the life beyond. Plato, in his highest flight of contemplation, his most transcendental wisdom, takes the liturgical phrases and consecrated words of the Mysteries as fittest vehicles of his inward vision. Plutarch, again, writes that to die is to be fully initiated into the Great Mysteries, that then man is truly restored to liberty, has complete mastery over self, and crowned with myrtle holds communion with holy and pure souls, while the profane, worldlings, besotted and blind, the uninitiated, find their own level, lapsing into utter darkness and blackest night. The devout Marcus Aurelius, who reigned A.D. 180–192, a man in whom it has been well said "natural religious philosophy reached its brightest"—his letters are full of references to prayer—during his visit to Athens was solemnly initiated into the Eleusinian Mysteries.

The ritual, in one or two details may seem to us a little crude, even grotesque, but it has to be borne in mind that, hallowed by antiquity, primitive elements which could not be discarded, enter in.

There was a period of nine days preparation, a novena, since the Great Mother, Demeter, bearing torches in her hands, wandered for nine days. Porphyry says that "at Eleusis a public proclamation is made that the mystics must abstain from barn-door fowls, from fish and from beans, and from the pomegranate, and from apples. To touch any of which utterly defiles."

The solemnity commenced on the thirteenth day of the month Boedromion, that is to say about the end of September, when the Epheboi (the Young Men), marshalled by the Kosmeter, went in procession to Eleusis, to return to Athens escorting the *Sacra* (ἱερά), which were carried, carefully veiled from view, by priests, whilst occasionally it would seem that priestesses assisted. The *Sacra* were taken to the Eleusinion at the foot of the Acropolis, and here they remained, strictly guarded until the nineteenth day of Boedromion. What were these Sacra, Holy Things? In the first place, they could not be seen by the worshippers, at any rate without terrible profanation, until the votaries had undergone certain ceremonial purifications, and had been duly instructed in the occult meaning and esotery of these objects. They were, in fact, extremely significant symbols.

The fifteenth day of Boedromion was occupied with the assembling of the Neophytes, youths who were candidates for initiation. In a solemn address delivered to the gathering in the Painted Chapter-house (Stoa Poikilē) at Eleusis, the Hierophant admonished all present to observe the ritual with most rigid punctilio, and proceeded to interdict and debar any with hands unclean, any who spoke an uncouth savage tongue.

A ceremony of essential importance took place upon the sixteenth of Boedromion, a day popularly known as Ἅλαδε μύσται, "To the salt sea, ye mystics all!" from the liturgical cry that heralded the act of purification in the sea. Clement of Alexandria says: "With good reason amongst the Greeks in the Mysteries a Ceremonial Purification takes the first place."

The Mystics went in procession to the sea, and it is curious to find that this procession was technically known as ἐ'λασις, a driving forth, in other words a driving out of evil. Each man took with him a young sucking pig. When they arrived at the sea, which is six miles from Eleusis, the votaries bathed therein to cleanse themselves, morally not physically, and the pig also was washed and purified. This ceremony of the animal purification is one of the primitive elements in the Mysteries, a detail which to us seems extraordinary, and, it maybe, unbecoming the solemnity. We can only compare it with the ritual of the scapegoat. "And when he hath made an end of reconciling the holy place, and the tabernacle of the congregation, and the altar, he shall bring the live goat; And Aaron shall lay both his hands upon the live goat, and confess over him all the iniquities of the children of Israel, and all their transgressions in all their sins, putting them upon the head of the goat, and shall send him away by the hand of a fit man into the wilderness. And the goat shall bear upon him all their iniquities unto a land not inhabited: and he shall let go the goat in the wilderness." Leviticus xvi, 20–22, (*A.V.*). And so in some sense the "caper emissarius" parallels the pig of purification. The pig was so important that when Eleusis minted her autonomous money, 350–327 B.C., the pig of purification is stamped upon one face of her coins.

Purification in the sea was symbolic, but (it cannot be too strongly emphasized) not merely mechanical. This point has been widely misunderstood, and whilst abuses may have existed, these were guarded against so far as was humanly possible, and the idea of an automatic purgation repudiated. The Roman poet Ovid in his liturgical poem the *Fasti* comments upon the primitive belief that murder, or the stain of blood, can be deterged by ablutions.

A! nimium faciles, qui tristia crimina caedis
Fluminea tolli posse putetis aqua!

A couplet which old John Gower, "Master of Arts, and sometime of Jesus College", Cambridge, in his version of the *Fasti* quaintly renders:

Ah, too, too silly, who imagine water
Can wash away that heavy crime of slaughter.

At the same time it must not be forgotten that pure water is a holy element, that certain natural things are in a very real sense hallowed of themselves, purifying and protective. The learned Bishop Binsfeld in his *De Confessione Maleficarum* has much to say very profoundly on this point. Divine Providence has given us, for example, herbs of virtue and healing, and from one point of view all that the Creator has made is worthy of respect. It is, of course, a very particular instance, and one in which the water has received a supreme sanctification, but the water of Lourdes (without, humanly speaking, any curative property *per se*) has restored to health hundreds of crass unbelievers. The Greeks believed in the cleansing power of "Waters at their priest-like task", and, myself,

I am extremely sceptical of this notion of a "mechanical purgation". To gauge an intention or even feelings at any given instant or in any given instance is scarcely possible.

The purification was followed by a sacrifice, which was a sacrament as well as a gift-offering to Mother Demeter.

Upon the 19th–20th of the month Boedromion (September–early October) came the Solemnity of the return of the *Sacra* to Eleusis with the ritual carrying of the statue of the fair boy-god, Iakkhos, from Athens to Eleusis. "The procession which set forth at sunrise did not come to Eleusis until a late hour of the night, a night made day by the thousands of torches borne by the Mystics." Iakkhos was identified with Dionysos, and is in fine the rapture, beauty, and inspiration of youth. Strabo [*48*] quite clearly says: "They call Dionysos, Iakkhos who is the live spirit and glad inspiration of the Mysteries of Demeter." At Eleusis, under the golden stars which spangled heaven's dark blue dome, the Mystics celebrated high festival. There followed very many ceremonies, sacrifices, prayers at shrines innumerable. Of priests, ministers and acolytes there were no less than twenty grades, and it is notable that the Supreme Hierophant and the High Priestess, when once they had been appointed, were never again known or alluded to by their secular names.

A fast followed [*49*], the sacramental *Kykeon* was drunk. Eustathius says that *kykeon* meant a food between meat and liquid, a kind of rich broth, we may suppose. The initiated then solemnly took the Holy Things from the chest, placed them in the appointed repositories, and after a short space replaced them in the chest. The handling of the Sacred Things, venerating them, and returning them to their original coffers, must have had some significance we do not know, or at best can but partially guess at [*50*]. Meanwhile the hierophant delivered a homily. There is a passage in Tertullian *Adversus Valentinianos*, which throws considerable light upon this mystery. It is hinted that there was in some cases a further, and more occult initiation by the Epoptes, the master mystic. There seems to have been, we might venture to say, an inner circle whose teaching and cult was Orphism. Upon the second night of vigil were presented what may perhaps be best described, or at least thought of as Mystery Plays. Only a select number of those who had been initiated, not less than a year before, were admitted to these, and, even after a most careful scrutiny, entrance could not be obtained without showing a secret token and replying to the pass-words. We must be careful not to think of these sacred plays as anything in the nature of a theatrical performance, but rather as an act of worship.

In some romantic and exquisitely poetical manner, we do not know how, they presented the legend of the lady Demeter and Korē the maiden, her daughter. There was, no question, elaborate and most effective liturgical symbolism. The ceremonial of a mimetic marriage, the celestial union of Heaven and Earth, Zeus and Demeter; the birth rites of Dionysos Zagreus; the adolescence of Dionysos the bridegroom; and other myths were shown. The god was slain by the wicked, and it would seem dismembered, as Orpheus was torn to pieces by the raving Maenads of

Thrace. But for all his death he was immortal, and he appeared triumphant, radiant with glory, to confirm the faith of his votaries. The history of the soul in the after-world was shown. Meanwhile the choirs chanted litanies and hymns, sweetest frankincense was burned, and from time to time the solemn voice of the hierophant declaimed rhythmic invocations. The Mystics were wrought up to the highest pitch of ecstasy. As Father Martindale admirably sums up the effect of the whole: The Mystics "were subjected to a series of thrills, of violent alternations of light and darkness, of exhibition of symbols, of abstinence followed by rhythmic movements and processions. No one can fail to see how profound a nervous impression could thus be administered to a very unsophisticated, or again, an over-sophisticated clientèle."

There were many other Mysteries besides the Eleusinian Mysteries. Smaller Mysteries, imitative Mysteries, local Mysteries, Mysteries which centred round the cults of tribal deities or even of heroes. There were too, in the course of time, Mysteries celebrated by vagrom priests and seers. The itinerant charlatan faquir had his following. Lucian in his *Alexander* draws a full length portrait of one of these pseudo-mystagogues and his quackeries. Abuses crept in and scandals. Apuleius of Madaura, who lived and wrote under Antoninus Pius and Marcus Aurelius (roughly, A.D. 160–192), draws a vivid vignette in his *Metamorphoses* of the votaries of the Syrian Goddess and their depravities, and the old high-priest who curses by Sabazios (a Phrygian Dionysos [*52*]), and Bellona, and the Idaean Mother (Cybele), and Venus, and Adonis. On the other hand this must be balanced by the exquisite rapture of the description by Apuleius again of the true Mysteries, chapters in which, it has been well said, "a pure mysticism and sublimity of emotion . . . an ecstatic adoration of God is manifested in language and thought never equalled, still less surpassed save in the inspired writers of the Church" [*53*]. Rome was horrified when Publius, the profligate Publius Clodius, profaned the Mysteries of the Bona Dea, and Juvenal [*54*] is never more scathing than when he denounced the "perverted Rites" of the Baptae, "polluted priests" of the Thracian, afterwards Athenian, goddess Cotytto.

Corruptio optimi pessima! Lilies, that fester, smell far worse than Weeds. "Later on the Mysteries became a money-making affair; and no one who observes the normal reactions to fierce religious nervous strain can be surprised that Christian Fathers rail bitterly at the obscenities accompanying, or following, these (lesser) rites" [*55*].

The Eleusinian Mysteries, however, and this is a most important point, preserved their pristine purity of intention, their solemn and august ceremonial. Had it been otherwise, that chaste and single soul, Marcus Aurelius, would not have been initiated.

There is, however, ampler proof of the unblemished virtue and high morality of the Eleusinian Mysteries, of—I do not hesitate to say—their hallowing (within their own natural limits, be it strictly understood) than this. Fathers and Saints of the Church, not without a purpose, have sanctified and legitimatized many terms and phrases used in the Mysteries by applying them to the Divine faith and inspired practice

23

of the Catholic Church. That they were guided to do so, nobody can doubt. The shadow has become a living substance. This is indeed a very beautiful and wonderful thing. It is a Divine testimony to the Catholicity of the Church. Dean Inge has admirably said: "A doctrine or custom is not necessarily un-Christian because it is "Greek" or pagan. I know of no stranger perversity than for men who rest the whole weight of their religion upon "history", to suppose that our Lord meant to raise a universal religion on a purely Jewish basis" [56]. St. Paul said: "Ex hoc ad gentes vadam" (Acts, xviii, 6).

When the clearer light dawned, Mysticism acquired a fuller and profounder signification than could possibly have been conceived by even the greatest minds of Greece and Rome, than could have been grasped by the most single and purest of Eleusinian or Egyptian occultists. Their rituals, exquisitely beautiful and deeply symbolical as they were, a quittance of earthly taint, a spiritual cleansing, a gazing up to the golden stars, fall and must necessarily have fallen far far short of the Divine Ordinances, when the Way to the Absolute God was manifested infallibly, most truly and unmistakably, once and for all ages of ages. But the Divine Spark was not quenched; it was rather kindled into a Living Flame.

One of the great problems discussed by Clement of Alexandria in the *Stromata*, written about A.D. 200, is the value of Hellenic philosophy to a Christian. This great thinker does not hesitate quite boldly to say that Hellenic philosophy is one of God's gifts and salutary. The part which it plays in the world's thought is most assuredly secondary and preparative, but none the less it is beneficial. "In philosophy there is philosophical truth, and so in Hellenic philosophy there is Hellenic truth. But there is only one great truth, beyond human conception, that is the Son of God Who Himself and none other teaches it to us and makes us understand." (*Strom.*, I, xx, 97, 1–100, 1.) "The truth which is manifested in Hellenic philosophy is but partial truth." (*Strom.*, VI, x, 83, 2.) Christ is the Truth. What is, within its own limitation, true of philosophy, is even more true in the case of the Mysteries. It must be remembered that St. Jerome, *De viris illustribus*, xxxviii, St. Cyril of Alexandria, *In Julianum* VI, and other Saints and doctors praise Clement very highly.

At this point it is essential to make quite plain and precisely define, even to meticulousness, the meaning which is connoted in this study by the words "Mysticism", "Mystic". It is safe to write that no vocable in the English language has been misused in such variations and vagaries, so misunderstood, so distorted in endless, question-begging, irrelative, and often meaningless contradictions as the term "Mysticism".

Dean Inge in his *Christian Mysticism* gives an Appendix (A), culled from authors of many centuries, of no less than six-and-twenty explanations. This proves a valuable comment and illuminating [57]. It is unexaggerated to say that a clear nineteen of these enucleations, particularly the more garrulous and verbose, display an almost incredible misapprehension of the subject and term; many are just ignorant, some perverse, some actually mischievous and travestied.

The word "mystic", as we have seen, was originally used in connexion with the Greek Religious Mysteries, particularly the Eleusinian Mysteries. The Christian use of the word is due to the author known as Dionysius the Areopagite, who was long traditionally identified with the convert [58] of St. Paul, by apostolic authority consecrated Bishop of Athens, and afterwards Bishop of Paris. Under the ninth Day of October the *Roman Martyrology* has: "At Paris, the *natalitia* of the Holy Martyrs Dionysius the Areopagite, Bishop; Rusticus, a Priest; and Eleutherius, a Deacon; of whom Dionysius, being baptized by St. Paul the Apostle, was consecrated First Bishop of Athens, after which, coming to Rome, he was sent as a missionary by Blessed Pope Clement I into France to preach unto the heathen folk, the Gauls, and having his see at Paris (Lutetia Parisiorum) for many years he most faithfully fulfilled the office of a good and vigilant Prelate, after which he suffered martyrdom, being beheaded by the sword together with his companions, all of whom had endured the most exquisite tortures. This took place under the prefect Fescennius" [59].

The Christian use of the word "Mysticism", then, is due to St. Dionysius the Areopagite, whose teachings on this subject are presented to us by a religious writer, probably of the earlier part of the fifth century, who gave the title *Mystical Theology* to a little treatise of five chapters, brief but most profound, in which he sets forth and formulates his teaching upon this subject. He claims to have derived much from the teaching of St. Bartholomew, and although no writings of this Apostle are extant, it is more than probable that Dionysius is actually deriving from the original source. We know from the Scriptures that St. Bartholomew was a contemplative and mystic of the highest order [60].

St. Dionysius in his very first chapter, at the outset, insists that the mystic, or he who aspires to tread the mystic way, "in the concentrated and wholly intent practice of mystical contemplation", must abandon the things which are merely intellectual and the conceptions of the intellect, all perceptions, indeed, conveyed by the senses, "all things which are not and likewise things which are", and thus, human understanding being wholly laid to sleep, he must with mighty effort and not without travail and toil strain upwards to union with Him, Who is above all understanding and beyond all knowledge. So the mystic will attain to that divine Darkness which is radiant Light [61].

St. John of the Cross, the mystic of mystics, writes: "The soul must not only be disencumbered from that which belongs to the creatures, but likewise, as it journeys on, it must be annihilated and detached from all that belongs to its spirit" [62]. This is a hard saying, and it may be as well to emphasize here that these experiences and aspirations and completest self-emptyings are only for those who dwell on the most rarefied heights. As in heaven, so in mysticism, there are many mansions.

Tauler the Dominican speaks of the mystic being utterly emptied by God, so that he may be completely filled with God.

According to Dionysius, who, as Abbot Butler says, being "the Father of scientific Mystical Theology, is rightly given the first place", according to the Areopagite, then, as essential (we might say the essential) of mysticism is "the intent practice of mystic contemplation", a striving, in which, as Blessed John Ruysbroeck makes clear, "two spirits strive together; the Spirit of God and our own spirit".

In the West for centuries the word which was in use was *Contemplation* and not *Mysticism*. Even when *Mysticism* became a current term, the old word "Contemplation" still held. Consequently, " 'Contemplation' is the word that will be met with in St. Augustine, St. Gregory, and St. Bernard, to designate what is now commonly called 'the mystical experience' ".

The mystical experience is nothing else than Union with God, and the Great Mystics all teach that this experience is literally, although momentarily, or at least temporarily, the enjoyment upon earth, whilst in the body, of the Bliss of Heaven.

St. Augustine, whom it may be observed, Professor Allison Peers [67], following Abbot Butler, considers the "Prince of Mystics", "for in his own field he can have no rival", in his *Confessions* has the extraordinary phrase quoted below, a phrase astounding in its simplicity, overwhelming in its profundity.

Abbot Butler and Professor Peers in their praise of St. Augustine follow the train of a long line of writers. "Eximius pater," Erasmus hails the saint, "most excellent and admirable Father," and "chiefest among the most lustrous Lights of Holy Church." Dr. Conel in his *Answer to John Burges* (p. 3), writes that the Bishop of Hippo was "a man far beyond all that ever were before him, or shall in likelihood follow after him, both for divine and human learning, those only being excepted that were inspired", that is those of the canon of Sacred Scripture. Dr. Field, *Of The Church*, calls him "the greatest of all the Fathers, and the worthiest divine the Church of God ever had since the Apostles' time". The learned Forester (*Monas. Thessagraph, in proem, p.* 3.), writes that St. Augustine is "The Monarch of the Fathers".

Incidentally the Proper Collect [68] of St. Augustine commences thus: "Deus, qui abditiora sapientiae tuae arcana beato Patri Augustino (revelasti), O Lord God, Who has revealed to our Blessed Father Augustine the most close and hidden secrets of Thy Heavenly Wisdom . . .", words of much significance. St. Augustine, then, in one of his sublimest apostrophes cries: "(Mens mea) pervenit ad id, quod est, in ictu trepidantis aspectus, tunc vero invisibilia tua per ea quae facta sunt intellecta conspexi, sed aciem figere non evalui. My mind in the swift flash of a motitation, attained to the Absolute Being, the Ultimate and Only Reality, All that Is. Then, of a truth, I saw and understood What is Invisible comprehended by Things Created. Yet I could not sustain the sight of Infinity and Eternal Reality. It was a glimpse, transient, a second's space" [69].

Contemplation (i.e. Mysticism), again, according to St. Augustine is "the conscious and direct striving to grasp and understand those things which truly and in absolute reality ARE", and, when apprehended, the mind reaches "an entire enjoyment of the Highest and Real Good", and man eventually attains to "the Ultimate Cause, the First Principle,

26

the Highest Motivity, the Divine Kinetic Energy, whereby all things were made and exist" [70].

It must be emphasized that this is not merely a possible, but an actual experience. Not unseldom mystics have attained this state, although (as the Saint remarks) commonly it does not endure. Yet it can hardly be called rare, and in the higher grades of mysticism it is, perhaps, not unusual.

This transcendent experience, beyond spirit, beyond self, was by one school of mystics termed "Unknowing", since knowledge implies a perception which is able to differentiate one thing from other things, and fundamentally postulates the ability to separate this thing from that. But in the Unitive Life all is one. There is no desire for, and hence no faculty of differentiation. As it was said: Abide in me, and I in you. "Manete in me, et ego in vobis" (St. John, xv, 4). And again: I am in my Father, and ye in me, and I in you. And the consummation of mysticism is: That they all may be one: as thou, Father, art in me, and I in thee, that they also may be one in us. "Ut omnes unum sint, sicut tu Pater in me, et ego in te, ut et ipsi in vobis unum sint." It should be remarked that the Latin *unum* conveys a union which can hardly be conveyed, or at least not so emphatically and completely conveyed, in English (St. John, xvii, 21).

In the second half of the fourteenth century we have the English treatise *The Cloud of Unknowing*, the author of which has not been identified. It is the work of a contemplative of the highest order, and one who was saturated with the spirit of the Areopagite. It is almost certain that the same mystic made the first translation of the *Theologia Mystica, Dionise His Divinite*, a work which in the ages of faith "ran across England like deere".

We may recall Maritain's remark that "to believe, humanly speaking, is much less than to know; but to believe by supernatural faith is much more, incomparably more, than to know in a natural way".

It is hardly an exaggeration to say that the teaching of St. Augustine was authoritatively passed on—the word "popularized" has not unfittingly been used—by St. Gregory the Great (reigned A.D. 590–604), who was steeped in and, perhaps sometimes unconsciously, reproduced the doctrine of the Bishop of Hippo [71]. We shall find much in St. Gregory, it is true, which, if not entirely new, at any rate opens up new ideas and fresh suggestions. A monk, yet, as called to be first a Papal Nuncio, and then Supreme Head of the Church, actively engaged in many businesses, St. Gregory looks upon Contemplation as one of the most desirable and pleasant of all things, yet not such a repose and a reward as God allots to all, since many are called to the active life, to battle in the world in the Divine service, and inasmuch they are so called for them this is the highest vocation.

St. Gregory's celebrated *Homilies on Ezechiel* [72] contain his most noteworthy and detailed observations upon Contemplation, and it is here that occurs the famous passage contrasting and relatively balancing the question of the Two Lives, that is to say the Contemplative Life and the Active Life. He utilizes and expounds in detail the illustration of Mary of Bethany and her sister Martha (St. Luke, x, 38–42). "Maria, sedens secus pedes Domini, audiebat verbum illius. Martha autem satagebat circa frequens ministerium." Mary, sitting at the feet of the Lord, hearkened intently to His words. Martha, however, was busily engaged in serving. St. Gregory emphasizes that Martha's occupation is not blamed. But Mary is praised as having chosen the best part. The Active Life, as typified by Martha, ceases with this world. The Contemplative Life, as typified by Mary, does not so cease but is continued eternally, more fully unto completest perfection. St. Gregory does not, I think, remark that it is not the service of Martha which is referred to in Christ's reply, but the remonstrance is addressed to her on account of her rebuke of her sister. Service is praiseworthy and good. To be critical of others, whose service differs from our own, is blamed. Parenthetically, I may observe that the word "cumbered" which is used in the Authorized Version —"Martha was cumbered about much serving"—has led to much mis-interpretation and a good deal of popular and long-seated misunderstanding. The word is very expressive, and its employment in this passage is all the more unfortunate because it is so expressive.

In the same Homily, to which reference has just been made (*On Ezechiel*, II, ii), St. Gregory formally defines "the two lives of which we learn from the written word of Almighty God, namely, the active life and the contemplative". The active life consists, for the greater part, in what are known as "corporal works of mercy", to wit, feeding the hungry, instructing the ignorant, nursing and caring for the sick, doing good to all men so far as lies in us. Our Lord Himself by His own example taught us all these things. He fed the hungry with loaves and fishes, as is recorded in all four gospels; He "taught as one having authority"; He healed the sick; He went about doing good. We have then the Highest example and divine precept in the active life.

But when we remember the three years of active ministry we must not forget the thirty years of contemplative life. As William Blake writes in *The Everlasting Gospel*:

> *What was He doing all that time,*
> *From twelve years old to manly prime?*
> *Was He then idle, or the less*
> *About His Father's business?*

St. Gregory says that the contemplative life consists in "having ever a lively love of God and one's neighbour, yet to rest from exterior activities and not concern oneself in businesses, but to cleave closely and solely to the desire for God, whence the mind has no pleasure in aught else, and is unconcerned with the world outside, so that, all cares being cast away, the mystic burns to see the Face of his Creator".

The mystic may be called from his retirement, and he obeys. At the word of his sometime pupil, Blessed Urban II, who became Pope in 1088, St. Bruno, the Father of the Carthusians, without a murmur left his solitude among the mountains, and in 1089 betook himself to Rome to assist with his aid and advice the new Pontiff in the ruling of a tumultuous and brawling court, distracted with political quarrels and clamouring. St. Bruno was one of the greatest of anchorites, whose sole happiness was uninterrupted contemplation. Beckford [73] says that "Saint Bruno was certainly a mighty genius; I admire the motives which drew him to this desert", the Grande Chartreuse, a "wonderfully wild" spot. But "the request of Christ's vicegerent was not to be refused; and Bruno quitted his beloved solitude". "The pomp of the Roman court soon disgusted the rigid Bruno, who always poetical, singular and visionary, had weaned himself entirely from worldly affections. Being wholly intent on futurity, the bustle and tumults of a busy metropolis became so irksome that he supplicated Urban for leave to retire; and, having obtained it, left Rome, and immediately seeking the wilds of Calabria, there sequestered himself in a lonely hermitage." Beckford who, during his stay at the Grande Chartreuse, took occasion to read St. Bruno's works, remarks that they dwell on "the delights of solitude" and are "full of enthusiasm".

The point is that the most ascetical and eremitical anchorite, St. Bruno, one of the profoundest contemplatives in all history, did not hesitate at the bidding of authority and the call of duty to repair to the world's metropolis, to take up a burden of political activities and share in the crowded life of a court.

Of St. John of the Cross, a nun wrote: "It always seemed that his soul was at prayer." Yet it was said of him "he had a great gift for government." He was the bulwark and stay of St. Teresa, the Foundress of no less than seventeen convents of the Discalced. St. John, then, certainly had to exercise very actively his genius for organization; he wrote a great many letters, letters which must have cost him much time and thought, in training the nuns under his direction. He was sub-prior and novice-master at Duruelo. He was sent to undertake the supervision of a newly-established Carmelite College at the Cathedral City of Baeza, which meant "not unseldom presiding at the students' exercises, and sometimes taking part in the disputations" [74], which ran high, and in which, moreover, Doctors and Dons of Baeza University joined with a good deal of brio and zest. But all the while he was putting into practice perfected detachment.

In a letter dated 6th July, 1591, only five months before his death, when already he had been "thrown into a corner like an old rag"—to use his own phrase—St. John says to a nun, who bewailed the seeming triumph of his persecutors and enemies, "As to my affairs, daughter, let them not trouble you, for none of them trouble me. . . . These things are not done by men, but by God, Who knows what is meet for us and ordains things for our good. Think only that God ordains all. And where there is no love, stablish love there, and you will find love."

These instances of St. Bruno and St. John of the Cross—and many more might be cited—show how right was St. Gregory the Great when he wrote that in the order of things the mystic may often find himself called to pass from his real life, the Contemplative, to the Active Life, and he even says that it is useful for the mind to turn from the Contemplative to the Active. We conclude that those mystics to whom it is given to lead uninterruptedly the Contemplative life are indeed highly favoured, but at the call of duty (that is, the voice of God) the Active Life, in which they are bidden take part, by no means deranges, impedes, or even intrudes and impinges upon the Contemplative Life. The mystic may well shrink from the Active Life. In fact, St. Gregory says that a mystic should avoid, and, if possible, refuse secular business. At best, he submits to it. In his *Regula Pastoralis* the Saint instances the prophet Jeremiah [75] who longed for the Contemplative life, and who was sent, most unwillingly to "go and cry in the ears of Jerusalem" and proclaim the message of God.

St. Gregory, following St. Augustine, is quite clear that the Contemplative Life is better than the Active. He emphatically lays down that "the Contemplative Life is greater in merit and higher than the active", and again he urges that the Contemplative Life, although "second in time, is in merit far exceeding the active" [76].

There are few figures in history which stand out more prominently than St. Gregory. He is generally acknowledged to have been one of the greatest of all the successors of St. Peter. Dom Aegidius Ranbeck [77] gives a long list of his labours—"the relief of the famine which succeeded the plague at Rome; the exhaustion of the treasury in procuring corn supplies; the feeding of multitudes of the poor; the providing for the necessities of the Church throughout the world", the mission to England; the reform of church music; and numberless other businesses. Indeed, owing to the negligence of the Emperors and their exarchs, St. Gregory was obliged to take upon himself the burden of the civil government of Rome. None the less St. Gregory was a mystic of a very high order, and more than once in his works he speaks of experiences, which must have occurred to himself, such as rapts and ecstasies, psycho-physical phenomena, in fact. Although he does not dwell upon these "passings beyond the barriers of the flesh", his mention of such trances and the like is very important. Moreover his *Dialogues* are full of occultism, and strange as it may appear in reading this fine work one is constantly reminded of such authors as the Capuchin Taillepied (*Psichologie ou traité de l'Apparition des Esprits);* Joseph Glanvil (*Saducismus Triumphatus*), and Richard Baxter (*The Certainty of the Worlds of Spirits*).

Abbot Butler, however, reminds us that "what is now called a purely contemplative life, in which the works of the active life are sought to be reduced almost to a vanishing point, lay quite outside St. Gregory's mental horizon; he seems to take for granted that such a life is not liveable in this world" [78]. It remained for St. Romuald with the Camaldolese and St. Bruno, Father of the Carthusians, to show that actually such a life was liveable in the world. Although perhaps in his works he does not explicitly and in detail counsel in set phrase and precisely pattern the purely contemplative life, there can be no doubt (I think) that St. Augustine envisaged and approved it as the best. When he was dwelling in community near Tagaste, he utterly withdrew from the world, "living for God alone, wholly occupied in fasting, prayer, and similar good works, meditating day and night upon the things of God, and closely following the manner of life of the solitaries of the Egyptian desert" [*79*].

In his *Benedictine Monachism* Abbot Butler points out that among the monks of Egypt, "we find the conception of the contemplative life pushed to the extreme limit". He draws attention to the fact that St. Benedict and other famous Founders wished agricultural work to have an integral place in their monastic institutions. The Trappists are a contemplative Order, and are great agriculturists. Hence, adds the Abbot, "judged by the Egyptian standard, Trappist life is not contemplative, nor any form of Western monastic life for men [*80*], except, perhaps, the Camaldolese and Carthusian, who are half-hermits." The abbé Nicholas Lenglet-Dufresnoy (1674–1755) in his *Traité Historique et Dogmatique sur les Apparitions*, 2 Vols., Avignon and Paris, 1751, has almost precisely the same observation, I, p. 245. He says; "Les Chartreux and les Camaldules, qui sont nos seuls Solitaires, s'occupent de l'Office Divin, de la prière, de l'étude."

It may, however, be remarked the Order of Vallis Umbrosa founded by St. John Gualbert in 1015—or, according to Ascanio Tamburini in 1012—is entirely contemplating. Hélyot, *Histoire des Ordres*, V. pp. 300–01, distinctly says that the holy Founder built his Vallombrosans on "l'amour de la solitude et le désir d'une plus grande perfection". He speaks of "la vie Eremetique" of the Monks, and details their exact observance of the most rigid rule, their almost perpetual silence, their enclosure and meditations. The contemplative ideals of the Vallombrosans are also insisted upon by such authorities as Eudosio Locatelli in his *Vita del glorioso Padre san Giovanni Gualberto*, Florence, 4to, 1633; and Diego Franchi in his *Historia di san Giovanni Gualberto*, Florence, 4to., 1640. Almost precisely the same may be said of the original rule of the Sylvestrians, founded by St. Sylvester Gozzolini, the hermit of Osimo, in 1230, for whom see Sebastiano Fabrini's *Chronica della Congregatione de' Monachi Silvestrini*, Camerino, 8vo., 1618; and the *Constitutioni di Monachi Silvestrini*, Camerino, 4to., 1610. The Olivetans founded by Blessed Bernardo Tolomei of Siena in 1319 are, strictly speaking, contemplatives, for whom see Lancelotto's *Historiae Olivetanae*, 4to., Venice, 1623. The contemplative monks and cloistered nuns of the Olivetan Order must be distinguished from the Olivetan Oblates founded by St. Francesca Romana, a surpassing mystic, in 1437. The Oblates, or *nobili dame* of Tor dé' Specchi still have their house at Rome in the street so-called, at the foot of the Capitol.

The Vallombrosans, Sylvestrians, and Olivetans follow the Rule of St. Benedict.

There are also Hermits of St. Jerome, Hieronymites, an Order to which an ascetic Rule was given by Blessed Pietro Gambacorta of Pisa, as related in Pietro Bonacciosi's voluminous chronicle of the hermits, *Pisana Eremus, sive vitae et gesta Eremitarum D. Hyeronimi qui in Religione B. Petri de Pisis floruerunt*, 12mo, Venice, 1692.

It should be observed that the Order of the Most Holy Saviour, founded by St. Birgitta of Sweden in accordance with the Rule and Statutes divinely revealed to her, is purely contemplative. "The life of both monks and nuns was to be wholly contemplative and the enclosure was of the strictest kind, such as is now called papal enclosure," writes Sister Mary Dominic, O. SS. S., in her admirable study of St. Birgitta, *God's Ambassadress* (by Helen M. D. Redpath), The Bruce Publishing Company, Milwaukee. Sister Mary Dominic is a Bridgettine of Syon Abbey. To-day there are no Bridgettine monks, but happily Syon Abbey, founded by King Henry V in 1415, remains, and can claim unbroken continuity.

St. Augustine held in highest esteem hermits and recluses, and there can be little doubt that he designed his Order of Augustinians, founded in 388, to be purely contemplative [*81*]. The very name Eremites, the Hermits of St. Augustine, proves as much. The Rule of St. Augustine is, however, elastic, and it could be interpreted and followed in several ways. Additions were made in various places; local customs were introduced; and as the centuries went on there were great divergences, until in the year 1256 Alexander IV united all the houses, and even the anchorites and recluses, into one Order by a special Bull, which constituted four Provinces. Three hundred years later, in 1567, Pope St. Pius V, ranked the Augustinians with Mendicant Friars (the Franciscans, Dominicans, Servites, etc.), but for all that, as Tuker and Malleson remark [*82*], "The Augustinians, or Austin friars, although now classed among Mendicants, are really an Order of hermits", that is to say they should be purely contemplatives. To-day the Augustinian Eremites are often engaged in parish work and other activities, excellent in themselves, but none the less businesses which (strictly speaking) ought to lie outside their Rule, since the ideal is that the Eremites should be purely contemplative, "judged by the Egyptian standard". From time to time there have been Congregations of Augustinian Solitaries, as for example that of Centorbi, so-called from a mountain of that name in Sicily, where a hermitage was founded by Andrea del Guasto, and approved by Pius V, Sixtus V, and Paul V. The Augustinian Congregation, Coloriti, named from their monastery on Monte Colorito, near Morano in Calabria, founded by Bernardo de Rogliano, were anchorites. Their Rule was approved by Pius IV in 1560.

I have emphasized the fact that the Eremites of St. Augustine were intended by their Founder to lead a strictly contemplative Life, because St. Augustine, as a mystic, should be placed with St. Bruno and St. John of the Cross, and the fact that whilst the sons of St. Bruno remain the sons of solitude and silence, that houses of the sons of St. Augustine are to be found, not so often in remote places, but in populous cities might seem to require some explanation.

So the truth of Abbot Butler's words is borne out. To-day, of men only the Camaldolese and Carthusian are in the integral sense Contemplatives. This applies, of course, to the general and formal Rule and Regimen of Religious Orders. Many members of other Orders, glorious and saintly names, have been mystics who walked the heights, and dwelt in heavenly contemplation whilst on earth. St. John of the Cross was a Carmelite, although it is very significant that, as he informed St. Teresa, "for many days the Lord had been calling him to a stricter observance, that he had already resolved to go to the Carthusians and that they had assured him that they would receive him" [*83*]. St. Peter of Alcántara and St. Joseph of Copertino (one of the most amazing mystics in all hagiology) were Franciscans; St. Albertus Magnus, Blessed Henry Suso, and John Tauler, were Dominicans; Benet Canfield, Père Yves de Paris, Zacharie de Lisieux, authors of the profoundest mystical treatises, were Capuchins; St. Miguel de los Santos, subject of astounding and perhaps unique mystical phenomena, was a Discalced Trinitarian; the stigmatized Fra Bernardino de Reggio was a Capuchin; Blessed Dodo of Hascha [*84*], who was marked with the Five Wounds, was a lay-brother of the Order of Prémontré. Such a list might be almost indefinitely prolonged.

"The Carthusian is essentially a solitary," says Dom Lawrence Hendriks [*85*]. "To begin here on earth in the least imperfect manner possible, the life of mystic contemplation we are destined to lead in Heaven, such is the object of the Carthusians" [*86*]. "Contemplation is for all, but the contemplative life is only for a few," writes Father Bede Jarrett [*87*], the famous Dominican. We may all be mystics to some degree, however little, but we cannot all lead the Mystical Life.

Parenthetically, the Persian philosopher Al-Ghazzali, a Moslem theologian of the eleventh century says: "The Science of the Sufis aims at detaching the heart from all that is not God, and at giving to it for sole occupation the meditation of the Divine Being." This Oriental parallel is, at least, interesting.

St. Augustine [*88*] very plainly enlarges upon the three kinds of life, all in their kind excellent. There is the contemplative life (*vita otiosa*) [*89*]; the active life (*vita negotiosa*); and the mixed life, which latter combines the former two. He instructs us that if activities are imposed upon us, we must undertake and fulfil them for the love of our neighbour, as the Gospel enjoins, yet we should not abstain all the while from drinking deep of the well of contemplation. He himself was called to the See of Hippo, with its responsibilities and multifold charges, and he did not refuse the burden. None the less it was a burden. St. Thomas Aquinas is often quoted as laying down that the "mixed life" is the best—the Saint does not use the actual phrase "mixed life"—but he only allows this under certain very important conditions, which qualifications are not unseldom overlooked and ignored to the misapprehension of St. Thomas's teaching. Active works must be added to the Contemplative Life, and must be derived from contemplation, in no way subtracting from it. Any businesses which hinder or impede contemplation are not to be pursued but rather abandoned, since, if such prove the case, they cannot be good or desirable. In view of St. Dominic's foundation of strictly cloistered nuns, and his insistence upon enclosure, it would not have been possible that the teaching of St. Thomas should bear the complexion too generally put upon it; Some extremists, utterly mistaken,

C   33 have gone so far as to represent St. Thomas as being somewhat critical of the purely Contemplative Life.

In 1680 Padre Paolo Segneri, who was the most popular preacher throughout Italy and high in favour at the Papal Court published a rather argumentative little volume, *Concordia tra la fatica e la quiete nell'orazione* in which he contended that the highest form of life possible on earth is the "Mixed Life", activity tempered with contemplation. This aroused some criticism, and Segneri followed up his *Concordia* with a *Lettera*, emphasizing rather too rashly his previous argument. The *Lettera* was placed on the Index, and although the *Concordia* escaped any official censure it was quietly discountenanced, and Segneri was privately instructed to revise and modify it. For us the whole matter is finally settled by an Apostolic Constitution, 10 August, 1924, of Pope Pius XI, who on the occasion of his "Considered Approval of the Statutes of the Carthusian Order" wrote: "They lead a life by these constitutions so shielded and protected from the din and folly of the world that not only are all their contemplative faculties focused upon the divine mysteries and the eternal truths, while with fervent and continual prayers to God, they seek the prosperity of His Kingdom and its daily extension, but in addition by mortification, both prescribed and voluntary, of mind and body, they cleanse and expiate the faults not so much of themselves as of others. In fact, it must be said of them that, as did Mary of Bethany, they have chosen the better part. For no more perfect adjustment and regulation of life could be proposed to men than that which at the call of God they take up and embrace." The Pope praises St. Bruno as "A man of remarkable sanctity who restored the contemplative life to its youthful integrity," and, he continues, "if ever it was of importance that there should be such anchorites (as the Carthusian monks) in the Church of God, surely this is the time when they should flourish most." "There are some perhaps," the Pontiff remarks with deep emphasis, "who still think that the virtues which are mis-named passive, have long grown obsolete, and that for the ancient disciple of the cloister a wider and more liberal exercise of active virtues should be substituted. This opinion met with refutation and condemnation at the hands of our Predecessor, Leo XIII, of immortal memory, in his letter *Testem Benevolentiae*, which was given on the 22nd day of the month of January in the year 1899; and no one can fail to recognize how this woefully mistaken idea is harmful and destructive to theory and practice of Christian Perfection."

When Pope Honorius III (1216–27) wished to impose enclosure upon a number of religious women and *beatas* (to use a Spanish word which has no exact equivalent in English), who were living under no rule, St. Dominic warmly exerted himself to carry out the Pontiff's will, and it was due to him that the Sisters of Santa Maria in Trastevere cloistered and confined themselves in the convent of St. Sixtus, where Blessed Diana d'Andaló was professed, and of which house Blessed Cecilia dei Cesarini, a daughter of one of the noblest Roman families, was elected prioress [*90*]. St. Dominic himself fastened the grille.

34

St. Augustine, whilst freely allowing that Contemplation, which is to say the Mystical Life, is open for all to follow, and, it may be, achieve if they persevere, emphasizes that hermits, such as those of the Thebaid, enjoy exceptional advantages in this respect, and are most blessed and holpen in their way to the highest things [91]. He does not fail, moreover, to point out that the way is no mere intellectual path. It can be trod by quite simple souls, who are single and tireless in their desire for the Eternal [92]. We must not fall, however, into the opposite error and suppose that natural genius and learning are in any sense impediments to the approach. Denys the Carthusian, whose De Contemptu Mundi and Scala religiosorum are handbooks of mysticism, was a most profound and prolific author. He himself says: "O my God, devoutly I give thee thanks for having called me, whilst I was still young, to the Order, wherein by Thy good grace, ever aiding me, I have passed six-and-forty years; and during all this while—blessed be Thy Holy Name—I have ever been a most diligent and unwearying student." The "Ecstatic Doctor", as he is called, continues: "This work, although wholly and entirely intellectual, has often proved to me the occasion of much suffering. And it is precisely this which has made it so profitable to my soul. For it has greatly helped to mortify my senses; it has held in check and subdued unruly passions and desires; it has increased my love for my own home, my cell" [93]. The complete works, Opera omnia, of holy Denys the Carthusian, of Roermond, who lived 1402–71, are comprised in no less than forty-five folio volumes [94].

If the question is asked—and it certainly suggests itself—why the Works of Denys the Carthusian are not so well known as those of St. Teresa, for example, or St. John of the Cross, or Blosius, the answer is not far to seek. Even scholars have been intimidated by the immensity of his writings; his profundity of thought, and he was deeply read in St. Dionysius the Areopagite and Blessed John Ruysbroeck, whom he had assimilated into himself, so to speak; moreover, from a practical point of view, the Carthusian's Works are not easy to be obtained [95].

Nor was the Ecstatic Doctor at any pains to make the way he taught easy. His hours were spent in raptures and the fruition of heavenly apparitions. A Spanish Dominican, Fr. Juan G. Arintero, has written a treatise The Heights of Contemplation Accessible to all [96]. In one sense this is true. All may contemplate, but few can reach the Heights. It is necessary to distinguish very carefully here. The learned Alban Butler, discoursing of the two works of St. Catharine Fiesca Adorna of Genoa, On Purgatory and A Dialogue, whilst speaking with unstinted praise and admiration of these writings, adds in a foot-note, "These treatises are not writ for the common class of readers" [97]. Denys the Carthusian is very emphatic that "without special grace given no one can be raised to the heights of contemplation"; he affirms (what is amply evident, but too often forgotten) "that temperaments differ widely", that "all men are not suited nor called to be contemplatives", and ordinary folk "must be restrained from climbing too far up the holy mountain" [98], where, in fact, the air is over rarified for them to breathe. He says, moreover, in another place, that "God endows those whom He will with the faculty of mystic contemplation", and "who shall dare to dispute the will of God in this?" [*99*].

Deep writers are doubtless correct when they magnify the Contemplative State as superior to all others, yet, it must be borne in mind, very few (comparatively) are capable of it, and none ought to pretend to it but those who are called by God to so sublime a State, which is not to be proposed in its fullness to all persons indiscriminately.

Denys Ecstaticus, then, regards it as a question of vocation. In some sense it may prove to be a question of terms. But a delusive vocation, the result of fleeting enthusiasm, a mirage, if obstinately persisted in is bound to end in unhappiness and disaster and spiritual discontent. On the other hand, it is impossible to disregard a true vocation, to attempt to fly from it, to smother it, because of temporalities and the wiles of the world. The result in this case will be equally fatal, and spell misery.

It has been asked, and the query is very pertinent, "For Whom is St. John of the Cross writing?" [*100*]. In *the Ascent of Mount Carmel* St. John makes it quite clear that his teaching is not for all. Indeed he reiterates this, and is so emphatic upon the point that Professor Peers observes [*101*]: "Such counsels are not given to all. On this St. John of the Cross insists so often that it seems impossible that those of his critics who write as if his rules were intended for all can have read him, except possibly in extracts." Nothing could be more strongly worded. Professor Peers is an acknowledged authority upon and a deep student of St. John.

For whom, then, is the Saint writing? In the first place, as he himself avers, he is addressing "certain persons of our Holy Order of Mount Carmel of the primitive observance, both friars and nuns". But, secondly, he is writing for all contemplatives, even for such as are constrained to live in the world. And, thirdly, his teaching may in its degree and so far as they are able to receive it (but no more) be profitable to all Christians, even to those who are the merest novices in mysticism, who have hardly taken a preliminary step on the way, and who, humanly speaking, cannot be conceived of as ever attaining the heights of the Mystic Mount, but who will continue humbly doing their duty in the estate to which they are called, where God has placed them, and who accordingly in their measure are leading the perfect life as their lights allow.

To read with thoughtful care, to meditate upon the writings of St. John, even to follow (as far as in us lies) the precepts of St. John—all this is excellent. Were such not the case St. John would not have been proclaimed on 24 August, 1926, a Doctor of the Church by that most sagacious and unerring of Pontiffs, Pope Pius XI. But St. John himself says in his teaching of the Dark Night, that amazing psychological experience he typifies under this name, that although the Night of Sense, which it is essential to pass through on the journey to the Ultimate Conception, comes to many mystics, the Darker Night, the Night of the Spirit, is traversed by very few. These Nights are terrible to endure, but the

Night of the Spirit is incomparably more agonizing than the Night of Sense.

Dean Inge, analysing St. John's teaching, speaks of "the night of sense"; "the night of faith". "Faith is midnight; it is the deepest darkness"; and the third night, "the night of memory and will," when the dawn is about to break.

It may be well, here, to correct a popular and mischievous misapprehension of St. John's teaching with regard to pilgrimages, oratories, images, and rituals. It has been said that he considered these as nugatory and of no worth. Nothing could be farther from the truth, and, indeed, nothing could be more impious. St. John plainly writes that images are "most important for Divine worship and most necessary". What he does say is that when the soul is overwhelmed with God, and filled with God, there will be no room for aught beside. But this essence of spirituality is hardly conceivable in this world.

For example, most elaborate and detailed instructions were given with reference to the making of the Ark (Exodus, xxv), even the two craftsmen to be employed were particularly named, Bezaleel and Aholiab (Exodus, xxxi), whilst the Shekinah, the visible glory of the Lord, descended and rested on the mercy-seat. There was a Mystic Ark in Heaven (Apocalypse, xi, 19).

St. Alphonsus Liguori tells us that a tepidity with regard to Shrines, Relics, Pilgrimages, the wearing of the Scapular, and the like is a sure sign of dry rot in the soul. It would be most blameable and evince a complete lack of spirituality if the votary were not inspired to a more fervid devotion by Loreto, Campocavallo, Genzano, Fatima, Limpias, Caravaggio, Hal, Asserbroeck. There is no mysticism without Mary. So St. Alphonsus teaches, and so taught St. Bernard of Clairvaux, St. Bonaventura, and numberless other Saints and doctors.

St. John of the Cross, then, could not and did not minimize the value of these holy things. Perhaps we shall best understand his thought if we consider Relics. St. Alphonsus considers a devotion to Relics a sure mark of true spirituality. But there will be no Relics in Heaven.

Incidentally, I may mention that the sublimest contemplatives, the Carthusians, at their house of St. Hugh's, Parkminster, Sussex, for example, have a most glorious and magnificent Relic Chapel, where are religiously venerated a large number of important and Sacred Relics. The Carthusian nuns of Var preserve the Relics of St. Rossolina of Villeneuve (1263–1329), a Carthusian [102]; and the Relics of Blessed Beatrice d'Ornacieu [103], who died in 1303, a stigmatized Carthusian nun, are preserved by the Carthusian nuns of Beauregard, near Voiron (Department de l'Isère). Moreover, the eighth of November, the Feast of Holy Relics, is observed as a high Solemnity throughout the whole Order. This devotion to Holy Relics, which prevails so strongly among the Carthusians, who alone, with the exception of the Camaldolese, according to Abbot Butler (as we may remind ourselves) strictly fulfil the ideal of the highest form of the Contemplative Life in Orders of men, is most striking and significant. The Camaldolese have the same devotion.

37

To suppose that St. John of the Cross in any sense rejected the veneration of Relics, then, is a most grievous error and an entire misunderstanding of the precepts of the Saint. No one would have been more horrified and pained than he at so impious a suggestion. The famous sentences in the *Ascent of Mount Carmel* do not mean this.

> *In order to arrive at having pleasure in everything,*
> *Desire to have pleasure in nothing.*

Thus he writes, but he is speaking to souls who are very far on the way to the Ultimate Union. If we are going to follow those who have so misrepresented the Saint it is but a short step to saying that prayer itself is a useless and vain thing. A point may be reached when prayer itself is emptied into adoration, which after all is essentially prayer. Thus in *The Excursion* Wordsworth wrote of the mystic:

> *In such access of mind, in such high hour*
> *Of visitation from the living God,*
> *Thought was not; in enjoyment it expired.*
> *No thanks he breathed, he proferred no request;*
> *Rapt into still communion that transcends*
> *The imperfect offices of prayer and praise,*
> *His mind was a thanksgiving to the power*
> *That made him; it was blessedness and love!*

The English poet is in these lines exactly describing the supra-sensual state to which the Spanish mystic guides us. Again, Wordsworth in *The Prelude* speaks of looking towards the Uncreated with a countenance

> *Of adoration, with an eye of love.*

It seemed to him that earth and heaven and every creature, of whom he was one, gazed upon God:

> *One song they sang, and it was audible,*
> *Most audible, then, when the fleshly ear,*
> *O'ercome by humblest prelude of that strain,*
> *Forgot her functions, and slept undisturbed.*

The ear was deaf to human sounds because it heard the music of the spheres. The lips were mute and dumb, but they moved in fervent prayer.

A contemporary (if prejudiced) record [*104*] tells us that the first indication of the Quietist heresy was the laying aside "the use of the *Rosary*, the daily repeating the *Breviary*, together with the common *Devotions* to the *Saints*", and it was found that certain communities "instead of their *Beads*, and their *Hours*, and the other Devotions to *Saints*, or *Images*, were much alone, and oft in the Exercise of *Mental Prayer*: and when they were asked, why they had laid aside the use of their *Beads*, and their ancient *forms*; their Answer was, that their *Directors* had advised them, to wean themselves from these things, as being but Rude Beginnings, and hindrances to their further progress." The poison was fearfully insidious, and those who had thus strayed were at once required "to return again to the use of their *Beads*, and their other abandoned *Forms*". Pope Innocent XI (1676–89) forthwith explicitly condemned nineteen Quietistic doctrines which were being secretly taught, the first being a complete misunderstanding of what is meant by Contemplation. The Third Error was that *"All Study and Learning, even in Sacred Matters and in Divinity, is a Hindrance to Contemplation"*. The thirteenth Error to be condemned was that *"the Images of Christ and of His Saints, are hurtful to contemplative Persons, and they ought to be avoided and removed, that so they may not hinder Contemplation"*. The very fact that many gave up the use of their beads is enough to indicate that something extremely subtle and extremely evil was at work; for, as we know, Our Lady Herself revealed the Rosary to St. Dominic, who may truly be said to be the Author of this Devotion, and a possessed person (however unwillingly) was compelled on one occasion to confess that all who are constant in their love of the Rosary will receive the reward of Eternal life [*105*]. If we disarm ourselves how can we fight the foe?

The great and stalwart Pontiff, Alexander VIII (Pietro Ottoboni), who succeeded the Venerable Innocent XI on 6 October, 1689, Alexander VIII "an Angel to look upon and an Apostle when he spoke" [*106*], very actively prosecuted the Quietistic heresy. He amply recognized how dangerous is the contamination of truth by a substruction of errors, the infective masquerade of corruption as seeming good. His successors, Innocent XII (1691–1700), and Clement XI (1700–21), were no less diligent in their zeal for the right. These Pontiffs—although there were eruptions of evil, now and again, as was inevitable—may be said to have stamped out the plague.

Pseudo-mysticism there has always been, and always will be. Cockle is oversowed among the wheat. In the garden of the mystics alongside the lilies and roses of Paradise grow Deadly Nightshade, and the scarlet poisonous berry, so fair to the eyes, and the fascinating exotery of brightly-blooming venomous flowers. Needs must we be careful which buds we pluck.

It is undeniable that in England for the past fifty years, and more, the interest in and a desire for the understanding of "mystical literature" has been steadily increasing. When the Rev. Robert Alfred Vaughan published in 1856 his singularly unsympathetic and boorish study *Hours with the Mystics, A Contribution to the History of Religious Opinion*, he felt it necessary to preface his arid chapters with explanations and apologies. The book is in execrable taste. On the evening of a November day three friends who "sat about their after-dinner table, chatting over their wine and walnuts" lightly embark upon a discussion of the profoundest problems of the spiritual life. When their talk is not leaden dull it is facile and flippant to a degree, nay more, it is not unseldom (although I am willing to believe unwittingly) profane. There is something that disgusts and revolts in the gross-daubed caricature of the beauty of Blessed Angela di Foligno, which finishes on a sneering note with "Catharine of Siena is a specimen somewhat less wretched, of this delirious mysticism".

"A *history* of Mysticism," Vaughan writes, "old visions and old obscurities—who is bold enough to expect a hearing for that? . . . While we are rejoicing in escape from superstitious twilight, is it well to recall from Limbo the phantasms of forgotten dreamers? . . . Mysticism is confessedly more or less a mistake." His defence for touching these "bygone speculations" is that "Mysticism, though an error" has from time to time been associated with a measure of truth, that *on the whole* good may be said to have outweighed the evil, that historically the Neo-Platonists and Bernard of Clairvaux are important. Although R. A. Vaughan quite plainly regards mysticism as a dream, one may learn valuable lessons even from the history of delusions. It is useful to erect a guide-post, since, even in the mid-nineteenth century, some were "not free from liability to mistakes in the direction" of the mystics.

In fact the Preface to the First Edition (1856) and the Preface by Wycliffe Vaughan to the Third Edition (1879) are both very dryly significant.

It is true that contemporaneously Thomas Richardson and Son of Derby were issuing a number of small (but extremely useful) mystical treatises, for example Blessed Henry Suso's *Little Book of Eternal Wisdom*, translated by Richard Raby, which ran into at least two editions, second edition, 1866; a few fragmentary excerpts from *The Revelations of St. Bridget, Princess of Sweden*, London, 1873; *The Stigmata*, a chapter or two translated and drastically abridged from the *Mystik* of Görres, and edited by the Rev. H. Austin, Derby, 1883; but all these had a limited circulation, and were practically unknown save to the few.

In 1846–7 Father Faber was enthusiastically planning and published the Series generally known as the "Oratorian Lives of the Saints", a series which included *St. Rose of Lima*, 1847; *St. Benedict Joseph Labre*, 1850; *St. Paul of the Cross*, 3 Vols., 1853, and many more. But these, although heartily approved of by Cardinal Wiseman, were not generally liked. Faber took every precaution to guard against misunderstanding and forestall adverse criticism. He protected himself, so to speak, by including a work of the last authority, *Heroic Virtue: A Portion [107] of the Treatise of Benedict XIV on the Beatification and Canonization of the Servants of God*, 3 Vols. In his Preface to *St. Rose of Lima*, Faber is at considerable pains to warn readers that in the book they will find "several stiff and unenglish expressions", which, however, "belong to the proper and recognized terminology of Mystical Theology" [108], and he observes that "English readers . . . may be a little startled with the Life of S. Rose. The visible intermingling of the natural and supernatural worlds . . . may even offend", but he earnestly bids his readers to whom these chapters may at first flush seem something extraordinary, "grotesque" even, reflect deeply and reflect again before they venture to carp or criticize.

None the less, the Mysticism of the Saints was looked askance at, and "it seemed to many a departure from Christian prudence" to continue the publication of the Series. Faber consulted the Oratorians, who were never formally responsible for the Series, and Dr. (afterwards Cardinal) Newman writing from Maryvale on 30 October, 1848, whilst he explicitly tells Faber, "For myself, you know well without my saying it, how absolutely I identify myself with you in this matter," is obliged to convey the general opinion of the Fathers of the Congregation "in advising you to suspend the series at present". "It appears," says Newman, "that there is a strong feeling against it on the part of a portion of the Catholic community in England, on the ground, as we are given to understand, that the lifes of foreign Saints, however edifying in their respective countries, are unsuited to England."

The fact is that one hundred years ago Catholicism in England was sadly tainted with Jansenism, inert and easily enervated. A mere spark of the Faith remained. Mysticism was taboo.

Faber submitted. At no small sacrifice to himself, after an interval, he continued the Series with certain modifications. Even this did not please, and eventually the publication of the *Lives of the Saints* was brought to an end. It must be borne in mind that those years 1840 to 1860, and even later, were extremely critical, and doubtless in the circumstances all acted for the best, as they saw it.

Mysticism, then, was regarded with distrust and suspicion, and (it is no exaggeration to write) with a certain hostility.

To-day it may fairly be said that the Mystics have come to their own. Occasionally a shrill scolding voice may be heard, but the tiny pipe at once dies away in nothingness and is forgotten. Meanwhile studies of the subject of mysticism are eagerly read, and with a very real sympathy. Many who do not understand show themselves respectful, at least, and sincerely seek an explanation, an exposition of the *areana coelestia*.

The fact is "that personal religious experience has its root and centre in mystical states of consciousness" [*109*]. Fundamentally, there can be no religion which is not personal and institutional. And where there is religion there must be mysticism, however inchoate and unformed (perhaps even unrecognized) it may be. Mystical states of consciousness are in the highest degree *Knowledge*. It has been well said, that whether we relish it or not the mystic is *invulnerable* [*110*]. Actually, although in many cases all appearance may seem to be against it, a non-mystic cannot and does not exist. He may have almost quenched and muddied his mysticism with materialism; he may have fouled and sullied it with coatings and coverings of animalism and lubricity; he may hotly and scientifically deny its presence, and repudiate the whole idea; but willy nilly the divine spark—and immortal because divine—has been once lit in every man's heart, although only too often it is eclipsed and dim and ineffectual, and (humanly speaking) it might seem impossible that it should be blown even to the faintest flicker of a rush-light flame.

Startling as it may sound, it is in the very strictest sense true to say that we are all mystics. It will therefore seem contradictory, or at least paradoxical when certain persons or their writings are declared to be utterly destitute of any mystic quality. But it will be understood that this latter use of the words "Mystic", "Mysticism" is the generally received, current, and accepted phraseology. The little mystic seed is dormant, stifled, hardly alive, in many instances quashed, in so far as it is possible to kill it, but dead, stark dead, it cannot be. Accordingly it must be emphasized and clearly borne in mind that in these chapters the words "Mystic", "Mysticism" are not used in this the narrowest, and perhaps the nicest sense. A more particular definition of "Mysticism" and the meaning attached to the word in this book will be given later. It seemed fitting, if not entirely necessary, to draw attention to the widest sense the word may bear.

It were good if in English we had other terms to connote Mysticism. But we have not, and hence this explanation must and will reasonably suffice. We might certes use the word "spirituality", for every man being created a spiritual being must possess spirituality. This alternative would not, in fine, clear the ground any more successfully.

It is understandable from what has been said that Mysticism may be and has been taken to denote many things of most varied kinds, and accordingly serious writers on the subject at the very beginnings of their studies are careful to explain and insist upon precisely how they intend to employ the term in their chapters, and what they mean by it, no more and no less.

Dean Inge [111] says that "no word in our language has been employed more loosely than 'Mysticism'". Abbot Butler [112] remarks, "there is probably no more misused word in these our days than 'mysticism'".

The word "Mysticism" has been used to mean metaphor and moonshine; literary symbolism; poetical rhapsody and dithyrambs; primitive music and surrealist paintings of a fantastic not easily comprehensible kind; a dreamy amorousness or nonchalance; a sweet sickly sentimentalism, "the worse for being warm"; vague and irresponsible theories about God, heaven, the stars, the supernatural; curious and unexplained phenomena; abstractly verbose Emersonianism; pantheistic and even atheistic reveries [114]; a vapid emotionalism; hauntings; pseudo-psychical investigations; illusions and hallucination; abnormalities; vaudeville telepathy; autosuggestion; judicial astrology; faith-healing, so-called; theosophy; spiritualism (spiritism) and necromancies; with kindred dark experiments and many a charlatanism it were unprofitable and bootless to rehearse. At the outset all these phantasmagoria and pathologies we sweep aside once and for all.

In view of what has been just said it is little to be wondered at that there have been put forward scores of definitions of "Mysticism", that a large number of them are flatly contradictory, and that many do not define at all. R. A. Vaughan in his *Hours with the Mystics*, a work so uncouthly written in dialogue [115], has: "*Willoughby*. Here's another definition for you: Mysticism is *the romance of religion*. What do you say? *Gower*. True to the spirit—not scientific, I fear", and (I would add) not a definition, although a pretty enough phrase. Dean Inge cites in Appendix A to his *Christian Mysticism* no less than twenty-six definitions and attempted definitions. As he indicates, this list might be almost endlessly prolonged, but quite profitlessly. Of set purpose he does not separate the chaff from the wheat, and a few, at any rate, of the specimens he presents are deliberately chosen to show what ignorances and bathos certain authors have not been ashamed to posit and present.

Since an explication of Mysticism is admittedly so different and so profound it were worse than waste of thought and time to do other than go at once to the great authorities and hear what they have to say.

Perhaps the greatest historian of Mysticism is Johann Joseph von Görres (25th January, 1776–29th January, 1848) "um die Erneuerung des Katholischen Deutschlands hoch verdienter Mann". His influence in his own day was enormous, and his encyclopædic knowledge has set him in the very front rank of writers on the subject. His chief work is *Die Christliche Mystik*, Regensburg, 5 Vols., 1836–42. "No man was better equipped to treat so intricate a subject than he, and none have dealt with it more lucidly yet more learnedly along the lines he planned." The French translation of *Die Christliche Mystik* by Charles Sainte-Foi, *La Mystique Divine, Naturelle et Diabolique*, 5 Vols., Paris, 1854, has taken its place as a classic, and the translator's own commentary and epilogue, although brief, are of the first importance. (I use the Second Edition, 5 Vols., Paris, 1861–2.) Görres says that Mysticism may be considered under two aspects. It is implanted in the very nature of man, but it also is supernatural, above and beyond the nature of man. Mysticism is pre-eminently Christian, and therefore the ineffable truths of Christianity must have the deepest influence in moulding and developing it. That there was precursory mysticism of the patriarchs and prophets and other holy persons is true, but Görres holds that Mysticism had its birth on the day of Pentecost, that it increased and grew, and attained perfection amongst the solitaries and monks of the desert, whence it has flowed like a river of many waters irrigating the whole world.

There is a Divine Mysticism; there is what may be loosely termed a Natural Mysticism; and necessarily there is the counterpart of Divine Mysticism, a Diabolic Mysticism. Natural Mysticism, according to Görres, may be held to include clairvoyance, second-sight, dowsing, somnambulism, hypnotism, and the like. He speaks of the malign power of the Evil eye [116], which has been recognized from dateless antiquity, since Pliny in his *Natural History* tells us of the *Fascinatores* among the Triballi and Illyrii, histories which have been handed down from remotest records. Apollonides speaks of females among the Scythians who can use this fearful gift. They were known as Bythiael. Under Natural Mysticism Görres mentions those who have secret and occult relations with the earth, instancing the Spanish *Zahories*, who claimed to be able to see through the crust of the earth, provided it were not covered with blue silk or cloth, and who were often resorted unto to discover springs of water, veins of ore, buried treasures, concealed corpses, as also to cure various diseases. The *Dorset Daily Echo*, 22nd July, 1947, reports how when engineers and water diviners had during many years failed to find more drinking water for a town near Simla, a sadhu from the Himalayas came to the place, and after standing silent for a while with eyes closed, seemingly absorbed in communion with some exterior force, pointed to a particular spot, and said: "Dig here, and you will find much cool pure water." This was done, and water gushed forth with great force in large quantities. The *Zahories* repudiated any magic, even so-called "white magic". It was, they declared, a natural gift with which they were indued. The Holy Office, however, thought fit to draw up elaborate and detailed forms of interrogation when questioning a Zahori, who is particularly to be examined whether anything was done over and beyond his exercise of "natural power", whether masses had been said, if holy water were used, or if there were fumigations, the invoking of Saints or the use of unknown formulas with strange names, and anything more of this kind. In a later chapter it will be particularly discussed whether the classification "Natural Mysticism" is admissible, and if so, to what category are we to assign these curious businesses.

Diabolic Mysticism is the dark realm of black magic, possession, demoniality, evil evocations, goety, witchcraft with its hideous pacts and sabbat assemblies. Satanism must necessarily, as it occurs, be dealt with in these chapters, as illustrative of the shadowed side of Mysticism, which it is impossible should entirely be ignored in hagiography and other mystical studies.

NOTES TO CHAPTER ONE

1. In case this sentence is liable to be misunderstood, it may be advisable to emphasize that, of course, no sort of reflection is intended upon the business life or the crowded career of a public man. Such admirable activities obviously have their important and indeed essential place in the divine scheme. Many, in the world but not of the world, have attained, and (I doubt not) are attaining a very high degree of perfection. For example, St. Yves was a lawyer; St. Thomas More practised at the Bar, was Speaker of the House of Commons and later Lord High Chancellor of England; St. Ferdinand, King of Castile and Leon, was a monarch whose reign proved one of the most stirring events; St. Wenceslas, Duke of Bohemia, "glorious for holiness and miracles", who was martyred in A.D. 938 under great difficulties held the reins of government with a firm hand. St. Zita of Lucca was a poor serving-maid, whose one aim was "to give God glorious service in her daily work". Blessed Anna Maria Taigi, a married woman and the mother of several children, valued by her husband as an "excellent housewife and manager", was a mystic of the highest order. St. Teresa of Ávila, the great contemplative, travelled about Spain, and founded seventeen nunneries of her reformed Carmelites, which entailed a world of business.

Our Lord and Our Lady sanctified all social functions by their presence at the wedding-feast at Cana of Galilee. Our Lord supped with Simon the Pharisee. Nevertheless, it was said, "Maria optimam partem elegit" ("Mary hath chosen the best part"). The late Holy Father, Pope Pius XI, in an Apostolic Constitution, 10th August, 1924, addressed to the Carthusians, distinctly states that there can be no more perfect way of life than that which is found in the solitude and silence of the cloister. "Avarus non implebitur pecunia: et qui amat divitias, fructum non capiet ex eis: et hoc ergo vanitas." ("He that loveth silver shall not be satisfied with silver: nor he that loveth abundance with increase. This is also vanity." *A.V.*) *Ecclesiastes*, v. 9. I have thought it well to put a note on these points, here, at the very outset, although actually and necessarily they will be dealt with and discussed in ample detail in the body of Chapter I.

2. The phrase is that of Professor William James, *The Varieties of Religious Experience*, Ed., 1916, p. 7. But his application of the phrase is erroneous.

3. *The Acts of the Apostles*, xvii, 28 (*A.V.*).

4. Our Lord said: "Nisi conversi fueritis et efficiamini sicut parvuli non intrabitis in regnum coelorum." Sec. Matthaeum, xviii, 3. ("Except ye be converted, and become as little children, ye shall not enter into the kingdom of heaven, *A.V.*) Little children implicitly trust, believe in, and obey their father and mother. They are, then, to be followed in this, and we are bidden to trust, believe in, and obey divinely constituted authority. The actual conversion takes place when a man bends his will to do this. He is, as Our Lord said elsewhere, "born again". "Nisi quis renatus fuerit denuo, non potest videre regnum Dei." Sec. Joannem, iii, 3. To endeavour to see, and hence to attain (to enter into) the kingdom of heaven is the true religious impulse. The mere conversion *per se*—although it is impossible to separate genuine conversion from its consequences—is the opening of the "heavenly door", as Richard Rolle calls it, but it is not necessarily the entering in. A man may turn aside to pantheism or some other specious allurement, not without a mirage of spiritual joy. True conversion is known by its development, its growth; false conversion by its standstill, its sterility. "Ex fructu arbor agnoscitur." Sec. Matthaeum, xii, 33. ("For the tree is known by his fruits", *A.V.*)

It were superfluous to do more than mention the abuses of thought, verbiage, and practice, the term "New Birth", grossly misunderstood, has lead to among disordered enthusiasts. When an unbridled hysteria accompanies so-called "conversion"—and this symptom only too often occurs—it is a very morbid sign. The sense of newness and the shouting for joy so piously expressed by Billy Bray, an illiterate "evangelist", when he described his "conversion" in November, 1823, are just exuberant emotionalism. See W. F. Bourne, *The King's Son, a memoir of Billy Bray*, London, Hamilton, Adams & Co., 1887, p. 9. How different, how dignified, how lasting and sincere, the conversion of Matt Talbot, the Dublin labourer, 1857-1925. This "poor, ignorant, labouring man, lived and prayed in a Dublin tenement room". As a young man he was addicted to strong liquor and spent all his wages in the public house. He would often sell the boots off his feet for drink, and walk home in his stockings. One Saturday night—he was twenty-five years old—he quietly announced his intention of giving up drink. There were no histrionics, no vehemence and impetuosities. But there can be no doubt that this poor man led an intensely mortified life, and attained a very high degree of interior spirituality. See Sir Joseph A. Glynn, *The Life of Matt Talbot*, 7 and 8, Lower Abbey Street, Dublin, 1926. A decree of the Sacred Congregation of Rites signed by the Holy Father, announcing the introduction of the cause of the beatification of Matt Taylor, has just been publicly proclaimed (June, 1947).

The Latin word *conversio* signifies a revolving, revolution, of the sky and heavenly bodies, in which sense Cicero uses the term. In general, it came to mean any alteration or change. The younger Pliny in his *Letters* uses the word of a change of view, or the modifying an opinion. St. Augustine has "conversio ad verum deum," *De Civitate Dei*, vii, 37, which is obviously "a striving towards righteousness".

5. *Psychology of Religion*, p. 64.

6. *Ascent of Mount Carmel*, I, xiii. *Works of St. John of the Cross*, 3 Vols., translated and edited by E. Allison Peers. Vol. I, p. 63.

7. Hesychius Lexicographus (5th century, A.D.?) accepts this derivation and emphasizes that the mystics shut their eyes and mouths to all worldly things, so

that they may interiorly concentrate their thought, and thus be divinely illuminated. *Hesychius*, edited M. Schmidt, Jena, 1858–68.

8. Actually the epoptes (ἐπόπτης) was fully and finally initiated in the Greek mysteries, but *mystes* (μύστης) by an extended use also came to imply the complete and ultimate initiation. Lidell and Scott, ἐπόπτης an overseer. One who has been admitted to the highest grade of the mysteries.

9. I surmise that A. Lasson in his *Meister Eckhard der Mystiker*, Berlin, 1868, is the only writer who holds the extraordinary view that the relation of the word Mysticism to the Greek mysteries has no bearing on the subject.

10. In the *Lysistrata* of Aristophanes the Chorus of Women says: "I was little bear to Artemis at the Brauronia."

11. Among the Red Indian Apaches to-day the Bear is spoken of with the greatest respect, and given the title *Ostin*, Old One, equivalent to "Sir".

12. See, for example, the *Iphigeneia in Tauris* of Euripides, in which drama it is ordained that the priestess Iphigeneia should sacrifice her own brother, Orestes, to the goddess, against whose savagery she cries out. The conscience of a humanized Greece was stirred and shocked by these primitive barbarisms.

13. One may compare the secret rites of the Bona Dea at Rome. Juvenal describes the degradation to which fell "The secrets of the Goddess nam'd the Good", "At whose feasts no men were to be present". Dryden's translation of the Sixth Satire, and his note.

14. *II*. 1. Scholiast edited by E. Rohde, *Rhein. Mus.* xxv. p. 549.

15. Photius Lexicographus, the ninth century, A.D. Migne, *Patrologia Graeca*, Vol. CIII.

16. Eustathius ad *Il.* ix, 530, 772. Eustathius of Constantinople, Bishop of Thessalonica, died A.D. 1198. He was one of the most learned scholars of his day. *Commentarii ad Homeri Iliadem*, ed. G. Stalbäum, 3 Vols., Leipzig, 1827–29.

17. As St. Thomas Aquinas says, "umbram fugit veritas, noctem lux eliminat".

> Panem, vinum in salutis.
> Consecramus hostiam.

18. *Revue des études grecques*, xxxii, p. 462.

19. Scholars generally are agreed upon this. Miss Jane Harrison *Prolegomena to the Greek Religion*, Cambridge, 1903, p. 150 dissents, but is singular in her views which are, to say the least, extremely hypothetical and hardly borne out.

20. "*Ego vitis vera.*" Sec. Joannem, xv. 1. ("I am the true vine").

21. *The Religion of Ancient Greece*, p. 22.

22. *Euripides*, Translated into English Rhyming Verse by Gilbert Murray, ed. 1924, introductory essay, pp. lviii–ix, and passim. First edition, 1902.

23. *Life's a Dream*: From the Spanish of Calderon by Richard Chevenix Trench, 1856, pp. 97–8.

24. Herodotus, VII, 110. A great many authors, historians and poets, bear witness to the Thracian origin of Dionysos. The Roman poet Ovid has "Threcia Bacche," *Amores*, I, xiv, 21. But in Statius, *Silvae*, III, iii, 193. Thracius is Orpheus.

25. Mount Edon, a spur of the Pangaeus range, in south-eastern Thrace, was a famous shrine of Dionysos, whence in Roman poets, Propertius I, iii, 5; Silius Italicus, I, 1, Lucan, I. 1: *Edonis* is a votary of Dionysos, a Bacchante.

26. The *Bacchae* opens with the speech of Dionysos:

> *Behold, God's son is come unto this land*
> *Of Thebes, even I, Dionysos, whom the brand*
> *Of heaven's hot splendour lit to life, when she*
> *Who bore me, Cadmus daughter Semelé,*
> *Died here.*

I quote the translation by Dr. Gilbert Murray. When Semelé's lover, Zeus, at her urgent entreaty, appeared to her in his full glory, the mortal maiden died in the blaze of the coruscating levin. Her child, Dionysos, prematurely born, was fostered until the full time had come by his divine father, and miraculously born again. Hence Semelê is Keraunia, she of the thunder, or, the thunder-smitten. Any place struck by lightning was regarded as sacrosanct. Primitively this would have been a taboo. There was in historical times a tomb of Semelê on a blasted spot at Thebes. Pausanias, IX, xvi, 7, saw "Semelê's Monument".

27. Strabo X iii, 470. Strabo the Geographer, born *c.* 66 B.C. d. *c.* A D. 24.

28. Herodotus, II, 81.

29. Dr. Gilbert Murray's fine translation here unfortunately obscures the point.

30. Apollodorus, I, iii, 2, 3. Apollodorus Mythographus A.D.I. (?). Edited by R. Wagner, *Mythographi Graeci*, I, Leipzig, 1894.

31. Reference to Calderon's *El Divino Orfeo* has just been made in the text.

32. The *Orfeo* was composed in two days at Mantua, on the occasion of the visit to his native town of Cardinal Francesco Gonzaga. The rôle of Orfeo was taken by Messer Baccio Ugolini, singing to the viol. I quote from the exquisite translation of John Addington Symonds. The queer drug-twisted mind of Edgar Allan Poe utterly misunderstood the *Orfeo* of Poliziano.

33. See Ovid *Metamorphoses*, V, 79–85. Phanocles, apud Stobaeum, *serm* LXIV, says that Orpheus was killed by the frenzied women owing to his introduction of paiderastia. But there is the legend of Laius, son of Labdacus. See also Aristotle, *Politics*, II, 10. For Dionysos and Polymnos see Arnobius, *Adversus Gentes*, V, p.177, ed. 1651; also Clement of Alexandria; *Protrepticus (Hortatory Address)*, ed. O. Stählin, Leipzig, 1905–09; Julius Firmicus, *De errore profanarum Religionum*; Theodoret, *Sermo 8 de Martyribus*; Nicetas on St. Gregory Nazianzen, *Oratio* XXXIX.

34. *Orphica Lithika*. Edited by E. Abel, Leipzig and Prague, 1885.

35. *The Athenian Drama*, III, Euripides. First ed., 1902. Ed. 1924, p. 1 viii, and p. 165.

36. Professor Lewis Campbell, *Religion in Greek Literature* 898, p 253.

37. *Iliad*, xxiii, 103.

38. *Odyssey*, xi, 466.

39. *Aeneid*, ii, 790–4; and vi, 700–02.

40. Porphyry, De *Abstinentia (On Abstinence from Animal Food)*, iv, 16. Libanius the sophist, 4th century A.D., speaks of the Mystics as "pure of soul", as well as ritually uncontaminated.

41. Theon of Smyrna, p. 22, preserves the precise formulary. The latter phrase is ambiguous, and instead of meaning "any who spoke an uncouth savage tongue" may apply to any having some natural impediment of speech. I am inclined to think this is the truer interpretation, as balbuties or stuttering would prevent the utterance of the sacred words with the necessary clarity and correct intonation.

42. Clement of Alexandria, *Stromateis*, V., 689.

43. Vincent Barclay Head, *Historia Nummorum, A Manual of Greek Numismatics*. Oxford, 1887, p. 328.

44. As by Dean Inge, *Christian Mysticism*, p. 353.

45. *Fasti, II.*

46. Published, 1640, at Cambridge, by Roger Daniel, the University Printer.

47. Euripides has: Θαλάσσα κλύξει πάντά τάνθρώπαυ κάκα. *Iphigenia in Tauris*, L. 1193.

48. Strabo, X, iii, II.

49. Clement of Alexandria, *Protrepticus, II*, 18.

50. The suggestion has even been made that in the Mysteries silence was imposed not so much because there were any secrets to reveal, but rather because the Holy Things should not be profaned by being brought into contact with common life. Inge, *Christian Mysticism*, p. 351. Whilst it is true that the *Sacra* must be carefully guarded from any vulgarization, there was an Ultimate Mystery, a very real and sacrosanct thing.

51. *Against the Valentinians*. The Valentinians were the most numerous and most powerful of all the Gnostic sects. Their theosophy was exceedingly complicated and esoteric, and it is hardly surprising that so arcane a doctrine should have split up into two schools, W. Bousset and some other scholars link up their gospels with the licentious Syrian worship and black magic. Valentine himself was at

47

Rome from A.D. 136 to 165. St. Irenaeus wrote against him, and from this work Tertullian (circa A.D. 145–220) has taken over much.

52. For the worship of Sabazios there are many references. See Strabo. X, iii, 471, Aristophanes, *Birds*, 875; Clement of Alexandria, *Protrepticus*, *II* Arnobius, *Contra gentes*, *V*.

53. Father Cyril Martindale, S. J., article *Paganism*.

54. Juvenal, *II*, 92, and see the Sixth Satire.

55. Father Martindale, *The Religion of Ancient Greece*, p. 24.

56. *Christian Mysticism*, p. 350. See further an excellent little popular pamphlet *Catholic Rites and Pagan Customs* by Sir Bertram Windle, Sc.D., Ph.D., F.R.S., who utterly refutes the so-called "historical" attack upon the church.

57. So Dean Inge, of course, intended it, and his comments upon some of the wordy statements he cites are both pungent and pointed. The late Miss Evelyn Underhill exhausted a volume of 539 pages (Seventh Edition, 1918), in "tracing the Mystic Way", and was no nearer nor more knowledgeable at the end than when she began.

58. Quidam vero viri adhaerentes ei (Paulo) crediderunt: in quibus et Dionysius Areopagita, et mulier nomine Damaris et alii cum eis. *Actus Apostolorum*, XVII, 34. "Howbeit certain men clave unto him, and believed: among the which was Dionysius the Areopagite, and a woman named Damaris, and others with them," *Acts, xvii*, 34 (*A.V.*).

59. *Natilitia*, birthday, technically signifies "Heavenly Birthday", that is the day of the martyrdom. Pope St. Clement I is dated A.D. 92–101, or by some authorities A.D. 88–97. For St. Dionysius "commonly called St. Denis," see Butler, *Lives of the Saints* under 9th October. Four treatises of the Areopagite are preserved: *Concerning the Heavenly Hierarchy; Of the Ecclesiastical Hierarchy; Of the Divine Names;* and the *Mystic Theology*. It is generally accepted that these works are not actually from the pen of the convert of St. Paul, and as we now have them it is believed that they are revisions belonging to the fifth century. The author of the tractates in their present form is unknown. But they contain and reproduce the teaching of St. Dionysius the Areopagite, and they have exercised so immense an influence upon and so essentially informed religious history that a vast literature surrounds the whole subject. Erudite commentaries were written very early, and the excursuses of the monk Maximus, who died in A.D. 662, are printed with most editions of the Areopagite. Dionysius (as we have him) is an extremely difficult author, his language is often obscure, and the singularly acute annotations of Maximus prove of considerable value. As early as the Lateran Council of October, 649, Pope St. Martin I had occasion to complain that many passages of Dionysius were being (perhaps wilfully) misunderstood and misinterpreted. It has been said, and not without some truth, that John Scotus Erigena "popularized Dionysius for Latin Christendom". St. John Damascene, again, in *De Fide Orthodoxa* appeals to the authority of Dionysius, St. Thomas Aquinas was well acquainted with and often uses the wisdom of Dionysius, whom, however, he does not hesitate to say is liable in some passages to be taken in a wrong sense. This is due to the fact that the Areopagite employs out-of-the-way phrases, and expressions which may seem startling but are in reality, when examined, perfectly orthodox and consonant with solid dogma. The fact is that Dionysius is a writer for theologians, and not for the many.

The *Opera Omnia* of Dionysius are in Migne, *Patrologia Graeca*, 3–4. This is a reprint (not without some errors) of the Venice edition of 1755–6. The *Works* were translated into Latin: *Opera S. Dionysii Areopagitae . . . a Balthazar Corderio Latine interpretata; folio*, 1634. The Abbé Darboy published a French translation, *Oeuvres*, with an introduction, Paris, 1845. There are English versions. *The Works of Dionysius the Areopagite* translated by the Rev. J. Parker, 2 Vols, Oxford, 1897, and in one Vol. *The Divine Names* and *The Mystical Theology*, with an introduction, by C. E. Rolt, S.P.C.K. 1920.

60. See *St. John's Gospel*, I, 43–51. The identity of Bartholomew and Nathanael is proved by Rupertus, Gayanti, Fr. Stilting the Bollandist, and many other authors of weight.

48

61. St. John of the Cross, a supreme mystic, has realized and expressed so intensely the mystic doctrine, that he has been called the *Doctor de la Nada* (Professor Allison Peers *Spirit of Flame*, Student Christian Movement Press, Ltd., 1943 pp. 96–7), but this is equivalent to *Doctor del Todo*. Doctor of the All. For he who discards everything, gains everything. "The Super-Essential Ray of Divine Darkness"; says Dionysius, Rolt, p. 192.

62. *Spirit of Flame*, Student Christian Movement Press, Ltd., 1943, pp. 120–1.

63. *Western Mysticism*, 1922, p. 5. To Abbot Butler's works the student of mysticism is more deeply indebted than any single acknowledgement in a note can convey. Yet not to overload page after page with references to these studies, which are among the very horn-books and gazeteers, so to speak, of the subject, one only recognition of and grateful expression for the Abbot's profound and inspiring Studies must (however inadequately) suffice.

64. This is the heresy of Quietism, a dangerous shadow-land; doubly dangerous, indeed, because of its half-truths and the mirage of its beauty. So much is profoundly true, so much is beautiful, but the quicksands of Quietism are treacherous. Many precepts of the Quietists might be paralleled with sayings of the Saints and orthodox mystics. Perhaps the best printed account—there are many MSS. sources—is to be found in Bernino, *Historia di tutte L'Heresie*, IV, 726, etc., Venezia, 1717. Quietism was condemned by Pope Venerable Innocent XI (1676–89), in his bull *Coelestis Pastor*, published 19 February, 1688; by Pope Alexander VIII (1689–91), and by other Pontiffs. Heppe has written *Geschichte der quietistischen Mystik*, Berlin, 1875.

65. *Adornment of the Spiritual Marriage*, Book II, c. 54. Blessed John Ruysbroeck (1293–1381). Canon Regular of St. Augustine, was beatified in 1908. In his writings can be traced the influences of Aristotle, Plotinus, St. Dionysius, St. Augustine, Richard of St. Victor, and others, whilst amongst his followers are such great mystics as the Benedictine Blosius (1506–65); Denys the Carthusian (1402–71); the Carthusian Laurence Surius, who translated into Latin the Works of Ruysbroeck, *Opera Omnia*, Cologne, 1652. The original *Werken*, written in the Flemish of Brabant, have been edited by J. David, 6 Vols. Ghent, 1858–68. There are French and English translations, some paraphrases of various treatises, and general studies. The English life is by Dom, V. Scully, London, 1910; and there is a brief monograph by Dom Hubert Van Zeller.

66. Abbot Butler, *Western Mysticism*, p. 3.

67. *Spirit of Flame, A study of St. John of the Cross*, p. 94. The only mystics Professor Peers parallels with St. John are St. Augustine and Blessed John Ruysbroeck.

68. This collect is Proper to the Augustinians, and is also used by the Dominicans and some few other orders following the Augustinian Rule, e.g. the Servites.

69. *Confessions*, Book VII, c. 17. The Latin text is Knoll's (Teubner, 1909). I have paraphrased, as giving the fuller sense, rather than literally translated, the original. In the Loeb series, col. 1922, the passage will be found, Vol. I, p. 386.

70. *De Quantitate Animae*, 75, 76.

71. F. H. Dudden, *Gregory the Great: his place in History and Thought*. 2 Vols., 1903. See Vol. II, p. 293 and p. 468.

72. *II*, ii, 8–11.

73. *The Travel-Diaries of William Beckford of Fonthill*, edited by Guy Chapman, 2 Vols., 1928. Vol. I., pp. 277–310. "An excursion to the Grande Chartreuse in the year 1778."

74. Jean Baruzzi, *Saint Jean de la Croix*, Paris, 1924, p. 208. n.1.

75. "Dixi, A.a,a, Domine Deus: ecce nescio loqui, quia puer ego sum. Et dixit Dominus ad me: Noli dicere; puer sum: quoniam ad omnia, quae mittam te, ibis. . . . Et factum est verbum Domini ad me, dicens: Vade, Et clama in auribus Jerusalem." Then said I, Ah, Lord God! Behold, I cannot speak: for I am a child. But the Lord said unto me, Say not, I am a child: for thou shalt go to all that I shall send thee. . . . Moreover the word of the Lord came to me, saying, Go and cry in the ears of Jerusalem. *Jeremiah*, i, 6, 7, and ii, 1, 2.

76. *Homily on Ezechiel*, I, iii, 9, and *Moralia*, vi, 61.

D   49

77. *Saints of the Order of S. Benedict.* Vol. I, 1896, pp. 345–9. Translation ed. by the Very Rev. J. Alphonsus Morrall, O.S.B.

78. *Western Mysticism*, p. 269.

79. Père Hélyot, *Histoire des Ordres Monastiques*, Paris, 1715, Tome III, p. 2.

80. The strictly enclosed Orders for women are purely contemplative. Thus, to name but a few, we have certain cloisters of Augustinian nuns: Similarly, Benedictine nuns; Bridgettines; Carmelites; Poor Clares; the *Sepolte Vive* or *Farnesiane* nuns who have three grates, curtained; Capuchin nuns; Servite nuns of the Second Order; Discalced Trinitarian nuns; Redemptoristines—their convent (Dames Rouges) at Bruges will be known to many—Dominicanesses. For the latter see *Dominican Contemplatives* by a Dominican of Carisbrooke. It is much to be regretted that the stricter observance for Dominicans, men, instituted by the Venerable Antoine le Quieu (1601–76), commonly known as the Congregation of the Blessed Sacrament, was not continued and developed, for this would have been an order of purely contemplative Dominicans. *The Life of the Venerable Antoine*, written by a member of his Reform, Father Archangel Gabriel of the Annunciation, was published at Avignon in 1682.

81. Hélyot, *ut cit.* pp. 3. sq. q. The discussion as to the origins of the Eremites (Hermits) and the Austin Canons belongs to monastic history, and accordingly I feel it impertinent to enter into it here.

82. *Christian and Ecclesiastical Rome*, 1900, Part III, p. 214. There are, it is true, Recollect Augustinian Fathers, and in England they have a house at Ivybridge, Devon. But, as the Prior, Fr. Arostegui, writes to me the Recollects to-day lead "a mixed life, contemplative and active".

83. St. Teresa. *Foundations*, Chapter 3, St. John agreed, at St. Teresa's suggestion, to remain a Carmelite in order that he might aid her to restore the Primitive Carmelite Rule.

84. He died in 1231. See the *Acta Sanctorum*, 30th March, *De Beato Dodone, ordinis Praemonstratensis in Frisia.* Marchese, *Diario Dominicano*, Naples, 6 Vols, folio, 1668–81, by an error lists Bl. Dodo as a Dominican.

85. *The London Charterhouse*, 1889, p. 33.

86. *La Grande Chartreuse* par un Chartreux, 3me édition, p. 367. The Lay brothers of a Charterhouse, under the supervision of Dom Procurator, "perform Martha's part". The Procurator is the Officer who attends to the essential business of a monastery.

87. *Dominican Contemplatives*, Preface p. v.

88. *De Civitate Dei*, XIX, 19.

89. *Otiosa* is sometimes taken to mean "lazy", "idle", and although in classical and later authors the word has this sense, it is far from implying anything of the kind here. "Idle" is, in fact, a late meaning. *Otiositas*—idleness is late Latin. The Vulgate has "multam malitiam docuit otiositas", Ecclesiasticus, xxxiii, 29. ("Idleness hath taught much evil," Douay). Cicero uses *otiosus* as signifying "calm", "free from passion", "tranquil".

90. *Vita delle Beate Diana d'Andalò, Cecilia, ed Amata.* Tradotta dal Francese (di P. Fr. Giacinto Maria Cormier dei Predicatori) per cura del Revmo Mons. Egido Mauri, O. P., Vescovo di Osimo e Cingoli, Roma, 1922, pp. 64–70, and *passim*.

91. *De Moribus Eccl, Cath.* 66.

92. *Epistolarum Liber*, CXX, 4.

93. *Opiscula aliquot*, Cologne, 1534, folio. 386.

94. Edited by the Carthusian Fathers of Montreuil-sur-Mer. It is recorded that 150 volumes of the works of Denys are preserved in the Charterhouse at Ruremonde.

95. There are very few monographs on Denys Cartusiensis. D. A. Mougel, *Denys le Chartreux*, Montreuil-sur-Mer, 1896; and K. Krogh-Tonning *Der Letzte Scholastiker*, 1904, will be found useful.

96. *Cuestiones misticas, o sea Las alturas de la Contemplacion acesibiles a todos*, Salamanca, 1920.

97. *The lives of the Fathers, Martyrs, and other Principal Saints.* Four Vols.; Dublin, Coyne; London, Booker, 1833. Under date 14 September, p. 443, col. 2.

THE PHYSICAL PHENOMENA OF MYSTICISM

98. *De contemplatione*, Book I, art., 15; Tornaci, 1912, Vol. 41, p. 151. Denys constantly appeals to the authority of St. Gregory, "dicit Gregorius"; "ut docet Gregorius".

99. *De fonte lucis*, *ibid*, p. 115.

100. *St. John of the Cross*, E. Allison Peers, Faber and Faber, 1946, p. 45.

101. *Ibid*, p. 28, n.5.

102. Feast of St. Rossolina, 16 October, *Sainte Roseline des Arcs, de L'Illustre Famille des De Villeneuve, Religieuse Chartreuse*, par le Chanoine A. Arnaud. Aux Arcs (Var), et Avignon, 1913.

103. Feast of Bl. Beatrice, 13 February. Some of her Relics are also at Parménie (de L'Isère).

104. *Three Letters Concerning the Present State of Italy, written in the year 1687, sine loco.* Printed in the year 1688, pp. 17, 42.

105. *Vita S. P. Dominici Ordinis Praedicatorum Fundatoris*, Auctore R.P.E Nicholas Ganssenio . . . Antverpiae M.D.C. XXII. Liber I. Cap. V. *De auctore Sanctissimi Rosarii, ejusque efficacia*, pp. 31–40.

106. Bernino. *Historia di tutte L'Heresie*, *IV*, 727–8.

107. Chapters XXI–XXX, inclusive, of the third book of the great work of Benedict XIV.

108. This particular reference is to passages in the Life of Blessed Colomba of Rieti, translated from the Italian, 4to, Perugia, 1777, and included in the same volume as St. Rose.

109. William James. *The Varieties of Religious Experience*, ed. 1916. p. 379.

110. *Ibid*, p. 424.

111. *Christian Mysticism*, 1899, Lecture I, commencement. The apogee of muddledom in attempting to define mysticism has been attained by a recent author Mr. Lewis Spence, *The Magic Arts in Celtic Britain*, 1945, Preface, p. iii, who employs the term "Magic" as usefully describing . . . Mysticism itself. which, he adds "has, I believe, intimate associations with it, in the historic sense at least!"

112. *Western Mysticism*, 1922, Prologue, p. 2.

113. For example, the address to the graduating class at Divinity College in 1838. *Miscellanies*, 1868, p. 120.

114. *The story of my Heart*, by Richard Jefferies, who (it is true) is said to have made a good death, breathing the Holy Name.

115. The Rev. R. A. Vaughan appears to have read fairly widely among the mystics, but, it must be confessed, with little or no grasp of what he was reading. His book, despite some interesting features, is a thoroughly bad one. The flippant dialogue is often awkward and silly. Ignorance and gross prejudice slime every page. Even so cautious a writer as Dean Inge observes: "There is something almost offensive in telling the story of men like Tauler, Suso, and John of the Cross, in the form of smart conversation, at a house-party, and the jokes cracked at the expense of the benighted 'mystics' are not always in the best taste."

116. The authoritative work on the evil eye is *Tractatus de Fascinatione*, auctore J. Christiano Fromanno, Norimbergae, M.D.C. LXXV. There is a study, a very uncommon book, by Nicolo Valletta, *Circulata sul Fascino Volgaramente detto Jettatura*, Napoli, 1787; and 1819. The *jettatore* is a person reputed to have an evil eye. *The Evil Eye*, published by Murray, London, 1895, by Frederick Thomas Elworthy, is a valuable and comprehensive volume.

CHAPTER TWO

Mysticism Defined—The Goal of Mysticism—Deification—The Three Ways—The Nineteen Phenomena of Mysticism Catalogued and Classified.

OUR theme is the Physical Phenomena of Christian Mysticism.

We are now ready to consider some half-a-dozen authoritative "dictionary definitions" of Mysticism.

Corderius says that "Mystical theology, which is to say the science of mysticism, is a certain experimental knowledge, deliberately sought and followed up but without effort of our own, centring and wholly concentrating upon God, who is all in all. This knowledge is a divine inspiration, an infused contemplation, which by supernatural acts of Faith, Hope, and Charity, so purifies the intellect to join it as closely as possible with God. Mystical theology, in truth, as the celestial name of this science implies, signifies a particular, hallowed and sacredly occult knowledge of God and the things of God."

Thus St. Teresa in a letter of February, 1576, to her Jesuit confessor, P. Rodrigo Álvarez, writes: "I term a mystical state that which no skill nor effort of our own, however much we labour, can attain to, notwithstanding we should prepare ourselves for that state, and this preparation on our part will inevitably prove to be of immense service and a very help." In the *Way of Perfection*, Chapter XXI, she advises those who are embarking on this divine voyage to give themselves much to prayer, but not to many prayers, "the Paternoster and Ave Maria suffice". The Prayer of Quiet is the first step to pure contemplation, and the Prayer of Quiet is a supernatural state to which no industry of our own or reliance on ourselves can raise us [1]. It may also be remarked that St. Teresa emphasizes how arduously and with what perseverance the Dark Powers assault and endeavour to turn aside and mislead any soul essaying to commence upon the mystic way.

The Seraphic Doctor, St. Bonaventura, says that Mysticism is "an act of the intelligence, which, set free from all that can let or hinder and purified by the grace of God, concentrates its gaze upon the supernatural vision of things eternal; and having seen intellectually, and seeing, known and being certain, remains rapt in blissful admiration" [2].

The Venerable John of St. Samson [3], a French Carmelite of the Reform, 1571–1636, an extraordinary mystic who almost normally, so to speak, worked miracles of the highest order both during his life and after his death, a profound master of the spiritual heights, of whom it was said "he welded the mysticism of St. Teresa and of St. Ignatius Loyola together in one", writes that "Mystical theology in its very essence is nothing else than God, ineffably perceived" [4]. It has been said by a great authority that the Works of the Venerable John of St. Samson are not for all to read, but are the pasturage of the "sovereign mystics" alone.

Another Carmelite, Philip of the Trinity, states: "In the mystical union God is perceived by an interior close embrace; he is very really felt by the soul which rests in His arms, beloved and secure. The soul knows that it is indeed God, because God thus gives it the absolute certitude of the Divine presence and enfolding" [5]. This is what Gerson calls "the embrace of an intuitive immortal Love" [6].

In his treatise *La Mystique et la Perfection Chrétienne* [7] Mgr. Waffelaert, Bishop of Bruges, sets forth that a thing may be deemed perfect when it fully attains its fit and proper end, and that the perfecting of a mystic consists in the complete accomplishment of Love. It is love which unites us to God, our ultimate and only end. Mystical union or contemplation (in its right sense), says Sandaeus [8] is "a mutual embrace between God, who is the spouse, and the soul, which is the bride". Whence St. Alphonsus Liguori tells us that "passive union is not altogether necessary for a soul to become perfect; it suffices to achieve active union. Now active union is the perfect conformity of our will with the Divine Will, and in this of a verity consists all the perfection of Divine Love" [9].

Bossuet in his condemnation of Quietism very pertinently comments that to teach flatly "leave God to act" is "to pretend to a love which is no love" [10]. *Merely* to leave God to act would be to forego all co-operation and be unfaithful to grace. We must shun this spiritual sloth, and the commandment was given "Thou shalt love the Lord thy God with all thy heart, and with all thy soul, and with all thy mind" [11]. Love then is active, but activity reaches a repose of pure union, which is the true passivity. Passivity not laziness. The Quietists taught indolence, which is the death of love.

The traveller, as St. Teresa says, rests when he has come to his journey's end. It is true, that on the way he may halt and stop awhile, but only for refreshment's sake so that he is enabled to continue his path with renewed courage and strength [12].

Gianbattista Scaramelli, S. J. (1687–1752) in his great work upon Mysticism, *Il Direttorio Mistico* (ed. Roma, 1900), writes that "Experimental mystical theology, according to its proper aim and end is a certain knowledge of God which the soul (ordinarily speaking) receives in the state of darkness which is infinite light, that is to say the ineffable glory of the highest contemplation, essentially accompanied by so assumed and intimate an experience of love that the soul discards and forgets all else—to be united with and (in a sense) transformed into God, so close is the Union."

The Abbé Ribet in his *Mystique Divine* (1878; new edition, 3 Vols., Paris, 1895) writes that "Mysticism is the science which treats of supernatural phenomena, be they interior or exterior, which duly prepare, essentially accompany, and closely follow upon the *passive* attraction of souls to God and by God, which is Divine Contemplation; and this science classifies these phenomena and attests them genuine and good, by the authority of Scripture, by the authority of the Doctors of the Church, and by reason. Moreover, this science distinguishes these phenomena from seemingly similar (but illusive) phenomena which are due to satanic and diabolical agencies, as it also distinguishes them from happenings which, however strange and unusual, are purely natural. Finally, this sublime science lays down practical rules for the guidance of souls in these ascents to heavenly things, ascents which unless regulated and rightly understood are not without danger."

There are then mysterious influences which operate in the soul of man, there are psychological and physical phenomena, which are from without, from God, from natural causes, or, it may be, wrought by the devil. Hence the absolute necessity for caution and direction, in fine that "discerning of spirits" of which the Apostle speaks, I Corinthians, xii, 10.

The Abbé Migne [14] in his *Dictionnaire de Mystique* (the third *Encyclopédie théologique*, 1885) writes thus: "Mysticism is the completer knowledge of that supernatural state of the soul which is manifested and visible in the body of the mystic, as well as in the order of exterior and physical phenomena, by its effects which are (as itself is) wholly supernatural." This is to say, the interior and spiritual mysticism finds expression in exterior and corporeal phenomena.

Parenthetically, we would emphasize that as Benedict XIV, quoting many approved theologians, in the twenty-first chapter of the Third Book of his great work on *The Beatification and Canonization of the Saints* instructs us for any sort of cultus of a holy person heroic "virtues are indispensable, and they must have been exercised in the highest, that is to say, in a heroic degree". Without this essential preliminary all else is regarded as valueless, and impertinent to the cause. Wherefore Scacchus [15] and Castellinus [16] agree and assert that "not all the just are to be canonized by Holy Church, but those who have shone forth brightly with Heroic Virtue".

The Mysticism, as exhibited with Exterior Physical Phenomena, is the *Mystique Divine*, the attraction of souls by God to God, whence it is necessary in the very first instance only to study those souls who, just and holy, have practised virtue in an exemplary (perhaps a heroic) degree.

It does not at all follow that such—although doubtless worthy of Canonization—are, or will be, even Beatified by Holy Church. If we take the Calendar, for example, of the Carthusian Order, we find only some thirteen or fourteen Carthusian Saints and Beati. And yet these Holy Souls, entirely worthy of formal Canonization, who are Sons and Daughters of the Patriarch St. Bruno, outnumber and outshine the stars.

Mysticism, although ultimately so profound a knowledge of, and a magnetic attraction to, God, is not (as some might mistakenly suppose) an erudite and esoteric science, only for the chosen few. The Abbé Henri Bremond makes this abundantly clear when he says that the study of mysticism is for all. A man may be deeply interested in the biographies of mystics, and learn much from long quotations derived from recondite

54

writings of the Mystics, without thoroughly understanding (and far less personally experiencing) what Mysticism is. "It is enough to appreciate that a Mystic is a person as human as any one of us, but he is moreover a privileged person, one to whom God communicates Himself in an especial manner beyond all ordinary understanding. Those who seek enlightenment, and yet who have not the time to study first hand" [17], the works of the Mystics, may profit much by reaking studies of Mysticism, the more so as such works necessarily cite important passages from the writings of the Mystics themselves.

There are few, if any, studies of the Physical Phenomena of Mysticism in English. Our authors have dealt rather with the history of Mysticism; with Mysticism as a psychological experience; with the religious philosophy, that is to say, the theology of Mysticism. Or else, there has been selected and separatedly treated one supremely pre-eminent mystic, whose writings are examined carefully and paralleled with the teaching and utterances of other great mystics; whose influence, contemporary and through the centuries, is treated in detail.

The Physical Phenomena of Mysticism, however, have been touched upon but incidentally [18], and one might almost say imprecisely. Nevertheless, these phenomena are of the first importance and in many languages most erudite and profound studies are devoted to this one aspect of the Mystical Life. We may instance the encyclopædic *Die Christliche Mystik* of the learned Görres; Doctor A. Imbert Gourbeyre's two works, each in a couple of volumes, *Les Stigmatisées* and *La Stigmatization*; the *Institutiones Theologiae Mysticae* (also in two volumes) of the Benedictine Dom Dominic Sehram; Abbé Ribet's standard *La Mystique Divine, distinguée des Contrefaçons diaboliques*; and very many more.

During the last fifty years there has been steadily growing an interest in and, one may happily say, a better understanding of Mysticism. Not a few serious and scholarly writers have notably helped this. At the risk of seeming invidious by mentioning only three or four names out of many, I would instance Dean Inge's Bampton Lectures *Christian Mysticism*, first published in November, 1899, together with several other of his works, *Studies of English Mystics*, 1906, his introduction to *Light, Life and Love* (selections from German Mystics) 1905, for example. Baron Friedrich von Hügel's *The Mystical Element of Religion as Studied in Saint Catherine of Genoa and her Friends*, 1908, is enrolled among the books of reference of its kind. Dr. Rufus M. Jones, an American Quaker, published in 1909 a volume, *Studies in Mystical Religion*, which has exerted considerable influence. Abbot Butler's *Western Mysticism*, 1922 (but commenced in 1904), is of ultimate authority. The work of Professor Allison Peers in the rich field of Spanish Mysticism, his studies and translations of St. Teresa, St. John of the Cross, Blessed Ramon Lull, and many others, may be regarded as indispensable handbooks on the subject. I do not say that we shall all of us agree in every point with these scholars. In fact on occasion we may differ pretty widely, and prefer an entirely contrary view. But all that they have written is stimulating, worthy of deep consideration, not lightly to be dispatched, and of permanent value.

Translations, too, from the French, such as Monsignor Farges' *Mystical Phenomena*, 1926, and the English version of Lejeune, *Introduction to the Mystical Life*, have borne the test of years and proved immensely helpful, thorough, staunch and sound.

Experience shows that *The Oxford Book of English Mystical Verse*, issued in 1921 when "the fortunes of Mysticism were mending", has given a very real pleasure, and something far more valuable, far more lasting, stirring deeper spiritual depths than pleasure. We are so grateful for this anthology that we do not hesitate to draw attention to one sad blemish, the admission—especially towards the end of the collection —of more than one writer who was no poet, and more than one copy of verses which are not in the least degree mystical.

It is significant, too, that within the last fifty years a very wide popularity has been achieved by books, purporting to deal with mysticism, but which in fact ladle out a soppy sticky sentimentalism, not to mention those silly little feminine manuals which profess to teach Mysticism for the million.

Far more undesirable than even this persiflage are the works emanating from certain schools of theosophy, which after all is merely an unintellectual Gnosticism, newly furbished and revived, together with the grimoires—for they are nothing else—of spiritism and mediumship, which masquerade as Mysticism, and delude their thousands.

Truly, as Professor Allison Peers says in the Foreword to his *Spirit of Flame* (1943), a Study of St. John of the Cross, the word Mystic "for some time past has been getting into the wrong company". It is, indeed, no easy task for the student of Mysticism to avoid these misadventures and dangers. It is equally difficult, wellnigh impossible, to frame any general advice. The safest and best way is to be guided by an expert director, and upon this the Mystics have always insisted. Yet there are many circumstances in which such help is not to be had.

Mysticism, the great quest of Mysticism, even for the student, the man who is—as it were—merely interested from the outside, has its very real dangers. How much more difficult is it for one who essays to tread the mystic path, to practise as well as learn.

There is no Bibliography of Mysticism. Whether such an encyclopædia could be compiled, I am tempted to doubt. Several authors have appended "select bibliographies", but these ate necessarily very meagre, although useful enough so far as they go. For example, the works of Pierre Poiret (1646–1710) give a longish list of titles, which prove very useful, and other writers [19] have essayed something of the same kind [20]. The *Enchiridium mysticum*, Veronae, 1766, of Gaetano Marcecalea is a very rare book. Perhaps the most comprehensive Bibliography is Albert Caillet's *Manuel Bibliographique des Sciences Psychiques ou Occultes*, 3 Vols., 1912, Dorbon, Paris. This great work, however, is to-day five and thirty years old, and even for its date there are not a few omissions. Moreover, there will be found included very many titles which are nothing to the purpose. None the less, granted these reservations which I do not minify, Caillet is (I believe) the most recent reliable bibliography of a general kind.

Much, then, remains to be done. So much that a beginner may well feel a trifle daunted. A reasonably comprehensive bird's-eye view of Italian Mysticism [21], following it may be the lines Professor Peers has sketched out in his *Studies of Spanish Mysticism*, is an urgent desideratum. More important still would be an ampler work modelled, perhaps on the Abbé Bremond's *Histoire Littéraire du Sentiment Religieux en France*. The Revelations of St. Maria Maddalena de' Pazzi with her Life should be rendered accessible in English. It is true that we have *The Life of Mary Magdalene of Pazzi, a Carmelite Nun*, "newly translated out of Italian by Vincent Puccini by the Reverend Father Lezin de Sainte Scholastique, Provincial of the Reformed Carmelites of Touraine, Paris, 1670. And now done out of French, London, 1687. With an appendix, pp. 85–134, *A brief discourse about discerning and trying the Spirits whether they be of God*." But such works are of the last rarity. The *Diario* of the stigmatized Capuchiness, St. Veronica Giuliani, is a treasury of mystic experience of the first importance. There are literally a score of such treatises which seem the very rudiments of the subject. There is, so far as I am aware, no adequate translation of the *Opere* of St. Catharine of Siena. Not even a selection from Denys the Carthusian is to be found. The *Revelations* of St. Gertrude, the *Works* of St. Hildegarde, the *Revelations* of St. Mechthild of Hackborn have not been competently englished and edited. Above all, perhaps, we lack a translation of the *Revelations* of St. Birgitta of Sweden, than which there is no more important work, a very fount of mysticism. The *Mystica ciudad de Dios (The Mystical City of God)* of the Ven. Sor Maria Coronel de Ágreda is not available. Only a very little of the *Visions* of and the vast literature which has concentrated around Anne Catherine Emmerich is accessible [22].

It were easy, but it were tedious to prolong the list. I have cited enough to show what huge gaps there exist in mystical works to be read in English, gaps which are grievously frustrating to any student.

But the goal is great enough to compensate for all obstacles, all disappointment on the way.

The end of Mysticism and the aim of the Mystic is to achieve the soul's conscious union in this life with Ultimate and Absolute Reality. We may use such metaphysical terms as "Cosmic Consciousness", or speak of "Transcendental Reality", or "the Absolute", or "Ultimate Reality", or "Absolute Being"—St. Augustine [24] has "Id quod est", "That Which Is"—but after all it is far simpler and more explicit to say GOD. The Mystic's claim then is that even in this life it is possible to achieve a complete union with God. This does not merely imply a sense or even a sensible interior conviction of the Presence of God, but the union of "spirit with Spirit". Which experience is quite literally Heaven upon Earth since Heaven is nothing other than the conscious enjoyment of the Presence of God.

Professor Seth says that "God ceases to be an object, and becomes

57

an experience. . . . Mysticism bids the individual aim at nothing less than an interpenetration of essence".

Thus St. Catharine of Genoa writes [25]: "The soul, when purified, abides entirely in God; its being is God."

St. Francis de Sales speaks of the soul being united to God, fastened, firmly fixed, and, as it were, glued to God in "unions déifiques", so that it cannot in any wise be separated from God, being inextricably mingled with, absorbed and engulfed in God. This union is not to be attained without the long exercise of great (heroic) virtue [26].

Professor William James [27] emphasizes that "as a matter of psychological fact, mystical states *"are"* authoritative over those who have them. They have been "there", and know. It is vain for rationalism to grumble about this. The mystic is *invulnerable*, and must be left in undisturbed enjoyment of his creed."

The Mystic does not, of course, become God by any actual deification or identification with God, but he can only rise to the supreme union through the humanity (derived from Mary) of Christ, of Whom St. Athanasius says: "He became man that we might be deified." Blessed Henry Suso, the Dominican, in a passage, which is admittedly difficult and profound, at least implies that there is a certain spark of the Divine Essence in man's immortal soul, and it is this which can be most closely and inseparably united to God. Blessed Henry further says that the Mystic's "Essential Reward consists in the contemplative union of the soul with the pure Divinity, for rest she never can till she be borne above all her powers and capacities and introduced to the natural entity of the Persons, and to the clear vision of their real essence. And in the emanation of the splendour of Their essence she will find full and perfect satisfaction and everlasting happiness; and the more disengaged and abstracted the self-egression of such souls is, the more free will be their soaring exaltation; and the more free their exaltation, the deeper will be their penetration into the vast wilderness and unfathomable abyss of the unknown Godhead, wherein they are immersed, overflowed, and blended up, so that they desire to have no other will than God's will, and that they become the very same that God is: in other words, that they are made blessed by grace, as He is by nature" [28].

Blessed Henry tells us how some persons are unconsciously attracted by God, and he explains the intimate and essential part which Our Blessed Lady takes in the divine operation of Mysticism, since without Her there is nothing.

Blessed John Ruysbroeck, also, in the conclusion of the *Spiritual Nuptials* says that mystics "see that they are the same simple ground as to their uncreated nature, and are one with the same light by which they see, and which they see". The soul is a divine spark, ever seeking union with the Divine Fire whence it has been struck. It is, writes St. Bonaventure "apex mentis seu *scintilla*". This Union, then, is the goal. What of the way or ways by which that goal happily may be reached?

Suarez [30] says that "Mystics classify three stages or ways, the purgative way, the illuminative way, and the unitive way", which latter actually is hardly to be distinguished from the goal.

This is confirmed by Pope Benedict XIV, who speaks of "those who are in the state of beginners, of others who are in the state of making progress, and of others who are in the state of perfection. We also find mention of a threefold way, the purgative way (as they call it), the illuminative way, and the unitive way" [31]. These ways or states—they may be called by other names—are axiomatic in Mystical Theology, and Pope Innocent XI, expressly condemned a proposition, number twenty-six, of Michael de Molinos, who denied that there were three ways or states in Mysticism.

Molinos insisted upon an "interior" state. He held that there was but one way "unica via, scilicet interna", an internal and passing experience, which actually either resolves itself into aridity, so that the soul is—so o speak—frozen, and makes no progress at all—or else this state resolves itself into complacency, pride, and self-satisfaction, wherein lies the deadly danger that the soul being puffed up imagines the goal (in reality far off) has already been attained, and hence it becomes lazy, effortless, and inert, it slumbers and sleeps perilously, as did the foolish virgins.

It has been observed "Molinos believed that he had found a royal road to God, without any intermediaries at all. Provided that the believer treated both Church and Jesus as a means to an end beyond themselves, Molinos was willing to make use of both. Beginners might begin with the Church. Through the Church they found their way to devotion to Jesus. At the third and highest stage both were left behind, and God remained alone" [32]. Thus concisely and clearly phrased the horrid blasphemy of Molinos is very apparent. His teaching led to blank atheism, but he so very cleverly disguised it that for a while he deceived many.

Internal and Mystical silence is good, but we must not stop here. It has pleased the Divine Power to exhibit Physical Phenomena of Mysticism, to stamp His servants, as it were, with His own supernatural sealing, visible, and cognizable to all. These sealings of God are what we term the Physical Phenomena of Mysticism.

There are, of course, many, very many Mystics of the highest order who have not been thus favoured by God, for, as it was said, "the wind bloweth where it listeth" (St. John III, 8), and the Apostle tells us that "there are diversities of gifts" and "diversities of operations" but the manifestation of the Spirit is given to every man to profit withal, I Corinthians, xii.

Be the reasons what they may, English writers upon Mysticism have not dealt with—or at any rate very incidentally touched upon—these Manifestations, and the time is over-ripe for a Study of the Physical Phenomena of Mysticism.

These phenomena are so many and so varied that it is almost impossible to give a full list of such mysterious happenings and to classify them, but it will be useful to essay some kind of conspectus, however inadequate.

In the first place, and almost parenthetically, we may take examples of mystical experiences and knowledge connected with the Blessed Sacrament. There have been mystics who could distinguish by a kind of spiritual perception the sacramental presence, and who recognized an unconsecrated host from one which was consecrated. Such was Jane the Meatless, a Norfolk maiden. A holy Carmelite, Casset; St. Francis Borgia, and others enjoyed this extraordinary gift, as also does Theresa Neumann, of Konnersreuth, to-day.

The appearances in the Host to certain mystics are in many shapes [33], but it should be noted that mystics seem in some supernatural mode to attract the Sacrament, as approved theologians have said there is "a double magnetism". The Augustinian, Blessed Veronica of Binasco [34], drew the Blessed Sacrament from the Altar through the air to herself. The same marvel is related of Elizabeth of Jesus. When the priest was about to give communion a Host detached itself from the ciborium and leapt into her mouth. Similar instances are recorded of St. Catharine of Siena, of St. Teresa the Great, of the Venerable Domenica dal Paradiso, whose miraculous communions were by no means infrequent, and of St. Gemma Galgani. This even happens at a considerable distance as is told of St. Veronica Giuliani the Capuchiness, and of Ida of Louvain. Rader in his *Bavaria Sacra* relates the same of the daughter of King Bela, the cloistered Dominican nun, St. Margaret, canonized by Pius XII in November, 1943.

A very exceptional phenomenon occurred when at Mass after the Consecration the chalice momentarily disappeared from the altar and was swiftly returned. It had been put to the lips of Saint Maria Francesca of the Five Wounds, a stigmatized Alcantarine of Naples [35].

There have been Saints and holy persons who could *feel* the Blessed Sacrament. Such was St. Rose of Lima, and the Venerable Maria d'Ágreda. Some could *taste* it, for example the Franciscan Blessed Angela of Foligno, Ida of Louvain, Lucy of Aldehausen. Others could *smell* a heavenly fragrance, the Premonstratensian St. Herman Joseph, St. Catharine of Siena, St. Philip Neri, Giles of Rheggio. Others could *hear* it, St. Pascal Baylon, St. Joseph of Copertino, Blessed Henry Suso, the Spanish mystic Jerome Gratian of the Mother of God. Very many could *see* It miraculously, as St. Catharine of Siena, St. Joseph of Copertino, Blessed Mary of Oignies, Blessed Veronica of Binasco, Peter of Toulouse, Ven. Domenica dal Paradiso, Teresa Higginson, and a great number beside.

The more usual higher Physical Phenomena of Mysticism may be conveniently (but by no means exhaustively) listed as follows:

Ecstasies, rapts, and trances, which must be carefully distinguished from any morbid, cataleptic, or hypnotic state; from any form of hysteria, or pithiatism (to use Babinski's [36] nomenclature) or temporary amnesia, or somnabulism; or again from a "natural ecstasy", which is an alienation of the senses due to intensive concentration or emotion. These ecstasies, rapts, and trances must in the case of a mystic be shown to be supernatural or divine ecstasy.

Stigmatization. That is to say the supernatural imprinting upon .the body of the mystic of the Five Sacred Wounds. Sometimes the punctures of the Crown of Thorns, or the stripes and weals of the scourging, are superadded. The divine stigmata must be distinguished from false stigmata, or consciously counterfeited stigmata, or what are known (incorrectly) as "natural stigmata". Stigmatization will be the subject of the following chapter. All true stigmatics have received the wounds in a rapture of ecstasy.

Levitation. Mystics are not only raised from the ground by some divine psychic force, however exercised, for a few inches but for many feet, and are even wafted hither and thither. This phenomenon has been parodied at spiritistic séances. The case of the medium Home is well-known, and the medium Colin Evans is said to have been raised several feet from the ground, at a public séance. A photograph was taken of this happening by infra-red light. Benedict XIV instructs us that "No natural power can cause levitation of the body, but this is not beyond the power and subtle craft of the devil to effect" [*37*].

Bilocation. The appearance of the same person in two entirely separate places, often far away from each other, at the very same time. The theological implications of bilocation are to be carefully distinguished. Philosophers hold that there is no absolute impossibility (and indeed such a phenomenon has been known) in the same body being at once circumscriptively in one place and definitively elsewhere, since local extension is consequent on a naturally universal, but still not essentially necessary, property of material substance. God in His omnipotence may delocalize the material substance, which then by Divine Agency would be rendered capable of receiving definitive, and consequently multiple location. St. Antony of Padua, preaching on Holy Thursday, 1227, in the church of St. Pierre du Queriox at Limoges, remembered how at that very time he was due to chant a lesson of Tenebrae in his own community. He broke off his sermon, and drew his hood over his head. At the same moment he appeared among the friars, went to the lectern, chanted the lesson, and when he had finished withdrew from choir. Simultaneously, in the pulpit, he put back his hood and resumed his discourse. Another example of bilocation is that episode in the life of St. Alphonsus Liguori, who whilst seated in his chair at the Episcopal Palace of St. Agata dei Goti, of that small diocese lying between Naples and Capua, passed into a deep trance, and was seen by those present to enter the bedchamber at the Quirinal, Rome, of Pope Clement XIV, and for several hours to assist with his prayers and consolations the dying Pontiff, who expired on 22nd September, 1774. A few minutes later St. Alphonsus awoke from his trance. In two letters, written in obedience to her Director, on the First and Second of January, 1881, Teresa Higginson with the great simplicity of truth, says how whilst not neglecting her duties at home, she found herself mysteriously transported to some country, which she supposed to be Africa, among aborigines whose peculiar habits and dispositions she describes very fully. She was enabled to instruct them and help them in many ways [*38*]. Bilocation must not be confused with apparitions and spectral appearances at the

61

moment of death, very many examples of which are recorded, as, for example, by St. Gregory in his *Dialogues*, by Mrs. Catharine Crowe in *The Night Side of Nature* (1848), by Dr. F. G. Lee in his *More Glimpses of the World Unseen* (1878), and by many other writers. These apparitions are technically known as "wraiths".

A luminous irradiance, not rapid like a flash of light, but steadily shining, bright and clear, and (says Benedict XIV) "of some sensible duration of time" often surrounds the heads and faces, sometimes the whole bodies of mystics. It is, as it were, an aureole of glory. This irradiance, so the same Pontiff lays down, must be seen in the full light of day. (It is, therefore, quite another thing from the phosphorescence which has been known to glow in the darkness or owl-light of the séance room.) It must be observed by several persons, not a few; so there shall be no question of hallucination. It must be prolonged and steady, no flash or electric spark. The person who emits this supernatural splendour must be known to be an individual of great virtue and very holy, and the irradiance shines forth beautifully when they are engaged in some religious act, such as a deep meditation, preaching, or, it may be, rapt in ecstasy. Benedict XIV emphasizes the fact that a natural phenomenon of seeming fire has been known to burst out and illumine all the head and even the human frame under certain conditions. This is a very different thing from the supernatural glory which environed Jean Calaguritanus whilst he was lost in profound prayer. Those present saw the Carthusian Dom Matthias Torner bathed in light at the moment he began his first mass, and this irradiance continued until he descended from the altar. The Venerable Orsola Benincasa, the Theatine nun, was often seen as though in the midst of a lambent flame, but she herself was quite unconscious of the prodigy. Upon one Lady Day, as he was preaching to a crowded congregation, the face of St. François de Sales glowed with unearthly light. All present marvelled at it, and since it was immediately recorded and attested there can be no question of its truth. Precisely the same prodigy occurred to St. Alphonsus Liguori, when he was preaching at Foggia, and was witnessed by a crowded church. In the diocese of Foggia (Capitanata) and by the Redemptorists a Commemoration of this marvellous happening is solemnly observed on 22 March each year.

Supernatural fragrances and perfume. The phenomenon of sweet-smelling effluvia scattered from the person and clothes of the mystic is so common that cases are numberless and indisputable. Dr. Imbert-Gourbeyre reckons them by hundreds, and there are hundreds more which have not been recorded. Where St. Catherine of Ricci had walked through the cloister was known to the nuns by the delicious scent that clung even to the flags whereon she had trod. Father Beyonne says that objects she touched were often impregnanted for days with perfume. St. Thomas Aquinas often irradiated male frankincense from his habit and cowl. "The odour of sanctity" is more than a mere phrase. St. Herman Joseph could be traced through the corridors of Steinfeld by the rare fragrances he scattered as he went to and fro. St. Francis of Paola and

Venturini of Bergamo diffused heavenly aromas when they offered the Holy Sacrifice.

Inedia, or supernatural abstinence. This abstinence from food which occurs so frequently in the case of Saints and Mystics is quite another thing from the Ecclesiastical Lenten Fast, or any other Fasts prescribed throughout the year. These are cases of complete abstinence from food or drink, especially among ecstatics who are marked with the Stigmata. Parenthetically, there have been, of course, impostures such as Ann Moore, known as the Fasting Woman of Tutbury, and Mary Thomas of Tanyralt in Merionethshire, who was feigned to have lived many years without taking food. Paullus Lentulus wrote *The Wonderful History of the Remarkable Fast of the Maiden Appolonia Schreiber, of the Canton of Berne*, Berne, 1604, to which he appended accounts of other remarkable fasts. There are, also, the public and very reprehensible exhibitions of "fasting men". It may be well here to quote briefly from Dr. Imbert-Gourbeyre, *La Stigmatisation* (II, p. 183): "Blessed Angela of Foligno remained twelve years without taking any nourishment; St. Catharine of Siena about eight years; Blessed Catharine of Racconigi ten years; the Venerable Domenica dal Paradiso (or Il Paradisino, a tiny hamlet near Florence) twenty years; and in our own day Maria-Rosa Andriani (d. 1848) twenty-eight years; Maria Domenica Lazzari (d. 1848) and Louise Lateau (d. 1883), fourteen years." Since the 30th September, 1927, Theresa Neumann has lived solely on the Eucharist.

A supernatural lack of sleep. Or rather perhaps one ought to say no need for sleep has been observed in many Mystics and Saints. This is not insomnia, which brings about a low state of health, depression and even a settled melancholy. Nor is it the natural faculty, which is recorded, that desires very little rest or sleep. Thus Nicholas Ferrar of Little Gidding slept only two or three hours each night, but this had not the slightest effect upon his physical fitness and energy. His constitution did not require any further repose. This is entirely different, being natural, from the supernatural vigils of the Saints and Mystics. St. Catharine of Siena, for example, hardly slept for half-an-hour every two days. Yet she was never weary, or harassed, or fatigued. The Franciscan St. Colette, spent a whole year without sleeping, whilst Agatha of the Cross (1547–1621), a Spanish Dominicaness, for the last eight years of her life did not sleep at all. This is an extraordinary phenomenon and infrequent. For it to be supernatural it is necessary that the Mystic should be proved to remain well and energetic, with no injury to health nor exhaustion, no morbid hypochondriasis.

Supernatural dreams. These phenomena are among the most difficult, although not among the most important, in the study of Mysticism. "Dreams! What age, or what country of the world, has not felt and acknowledged the mystery of their origin and end?" Le Fanu exclaims. That a dream may have a spiritual origin is a question no Christian could for a moment debate, since there are so many instances, and those of profoundest importance and meaning, recorded both in the Old and New Testaments, and in the Lives of the Saints. The observing and interpretation of dreams, oneirology and oneiromancy, are known in all ages to all peoples and connected with much that is superstitious and profane. The heavenly command was given [*39*]: "You shall not divine nor obscure dreams", Leviticus xix, 26, and again, Deuteronomy xviii, 10, "Neither let there be found among you any one that . . . observeth dreams and omens". Among the impieties and sorceries of King Manasseh of Judah are reckoned that "he observed dreams, followed divinations, gave himself up to magic arts". II Chronicles xxxiii, 6. But we also have the dreams of St. Joseph, St. Matthew i, 20, and ii, 19; also the dream in which the Magi were bidden not to return to Herod, but to journey back to their own country by another way. Warning dreams have been dreamed by many who were not even mystics, far less Saints. There are very informative and striking chapters upon this in Mrs. Crowe's *The Night Side of Nature*, and Dr. F. G. Lee's *More Glimpses of the World Unseen*.

The question how to distinguish supernatural dreams from the ordinary (and often meaningless or confused) dream is dealt with by many authors, notably by Benedict XIV, and even more fully by Gaspar à Rejes (*Jucund. Quaest. Elys. Campo, qu.* 37) who treats the whole subject of dreams at great length. Preternatural visions and admonitions are some from God, some from the devil; some occur in sleep, and some whilst men are waking. Very briefly the signs by which the supernatural origin of a dream may be recognized are, firstly, a dream divinely sent is always extremely reasonable and directive, without any diversion of romantic imaginings; *secondly*, the dream affords intelligible and wise guidance, or may foretell in plain fashion some future event; *thirdly*, a divine dream leaves a complete and ineffable impression, and is remembered in detail as one simple whole, whereas natural dreams are often complicated and confused in detail, not easy to recall; *fourthly*, a divine dream is often sent to two or more persons simultaneously without any previous discussion or mutual conversation concerning the subject of the dream. Such a dream was that when Our Lady appeared in their sleep to St. Peter Nolasco, St. Ramon de Peñafort, and King James of Arragon, severally, directing that the Mercedarian Order be founded in Her honour. Jean Gerson adds that an increase of humility after a dream betokens a divine origin, and this agrees with what St. Hildegarde tells us that the devil fell through pride, and humility is the touchstone, the measure whereby to measure divine promptings. (*Responsum Hildegardis ad Epistolam Monachorum Sigebergensium*, CXXXVII, Migne, *Patrologia Latina*, 197, pp. 366–67.)

There is an old sentence, current in mediæval England, which is really derived and condensed from the *Revelations* of St. Birgitta, "Thus may thou know the unclean spirit: for he stirreth thee to seek thy own worship and praising; to be proud of the gifts that God hath given thee; he stirreth thee to intemperance in all thy members; to these he inflameth thy heart."

Gerson, *De distinctione verarum Revelationum a falsis*, is very emphatic that in the matter of all supernatural and supernormal phenomena humility is the proof whether their origin be divine. "Monitiones intrinsecae, omnis Revelatio, omne Miraculum, omnis amor extaticus, omnis raptus, si humilitas praecedit et comitetur et sequatur; si nihil eam perimens misceatur (crede mihi) signum habet quod a Deo sunt aut bono ejus Angelo, nec fallens."

Of dreams Sir Thomas Brown in his *Religio Medici* profoundly says: "I thank God for my happy dreams, as I do for my good rest . . . and surely it is not a melancholy conceit to think we are all asleep in this world, and that the conceits of this life are as mere dreams to those of the next; as the phantasms to the conceit of the day. There is an equal delusion in both, and the one doth seem to be but the emblem or picture of the other; we are somewhat more than ourselves in our sleep, and the slumber of the body seems to be but the waking of the soul. It is the ligation of the sense, but the liberty of reason . . . we must therefore say that there is something in us that is not in the jurisdiction of Morpheus."

Visions and Apparitions. These phenomena, again, are amongst the most difficult, yet also amongst the most important in the study of Mysticism.

Revelations, Locutions, and Prophecy. These are equally difficult, and equally important phenomena. Fortunately we have a very safe guide in Pope Benedict XIV, whose immense learning treats of such matters in great detail. The Revelations of the Saints are among the Classics of Mysticism. No student of the subject can advance very far without some knowledge, at least, of the *Revelations* of St. Gertrude; the *Works* of St. Hildegarde; the *Life and Revelations* of Blessed Angela of Foligno; the *Revelations* of St. Birgitta of Sweden; the *Works* of St. Catharine of Siena; of St. Teresa, the Great Carmelite; of St. Maria Maddalena de' Pazzi; and I will add that incomparably beautiful book, *The Mystical City of God,* by the Venerable Sor Maria de 'Ágreda, together with the *Revelations* and *Visions* of the Augustinian, Anne Catharine Emmerich of Dülmen. Benedict XIV is cautiously emphatic that even the Revelations, approved by the Apostolic See, of great Saints, such as St. Birgitta of Sweden and St. Catharine of Siena, although undoubtedly true and Divinely inspired are to be accepted as of human faith, and in the words of Cardinal Torquemada "piously and modestly understood". A greater weight is given to the *Revelations* of St. Birgitta on account of their liturgical use by her Daughters. St. Birgitta teaches the Immaculate Conception. It has been said that St. Catharine taught that Our Lady was conceived in original sin [40], but scholars and theologians are agreed that the passage in question is an interpolation. Contelorius [41] goes so far as to say that sanctity is not to be inferred from Revelations, Scacchus [42], however, and the authoritative Delrio [43] agreeably modify this opinion.

Telekenesis. That is to say the knowledge of things which are happening or have just happened at a considerable, sometimes a very great, distance. Saints and Mystics have had an extraordinary knowledge of what is going on elsewhere, although it may be far away, and there could be no normal channel through which the information could be so immediately transmitted. Telekenesis, of course, is entirely different from and far

E

beyond telepathy, which is merely thought-transference. Again, it must be distinguished from clairvoyance. According to the *Oxford English Dictionary* [44] Clairvoyance is "The faculty of mentally perceiving objects at a distance or concealed from sight, attributed to certain persons, or to persons under mesmeric conditions" [45]. There is no question here of any mesmeric condition, and, of course, we entirely exclude from consideration the humbug and frauds of the "professional" clairvoyant, whether at some private gathering or at a public séance. No mystical gift can be bartered for money, and it is much to be feared that this "clairvoyance" is very largely of diabolical origin, for the Church has always recognized that evil spirits may obtain a knowledge of things passing in distant places. One of the most striking instances of divinely supernatural telekenesis is when Pope St. Pius V on 7 October, 1571, was informed of the result of the Battle of Lepanto and the Victory of Don John. The Holy Father at the very decisive moment was discussing some business of the first importance with a Congregation of Cardinals. Suddenly he rose, left them abruptly, and went to the window which he opened. For a moment his eyes were fixed on the heavens, and then returning to the table he said: "It is not now a time to talk any more about affairs, however pressing; it is the time to give thanks to Almighty God for the signal victory which He has vouchsafed to the Christians." This fact was carefully attested at the very moment and authentically recorded so as to admit of no shadow of doubt. There is (apparently) a natural telekenesis, outside the midnight and murk of the séance-rooms, of which an example was displayed by Mr. Stephan Ossowiecki, a Polish gentleman, whose supra-normal gifts are described in Dr. Gustave Geley's work, Paris, 1924, *L'Ectoplasmie et la Clairvoyance* [46].

Vision through opaque bodies. This phenomenon of Mysticism has been known to occur in cases of normal subjects, that is to say persons who were decidedly not mystics and had neither read nor were interested in mystical works. Science has carefully investigated and is still making experiments in regard to this subject. Much that is valuable has been discovered, but nothing has been arrived at in regard to the super-natural gift of the mystic. One of the most extraordinary examples of a person upon which this gift was conferred is the Trinitarian, Blessed Anna Maria Taigi. She saw the bottom of seas and lakes, and of the fathomless ocean; she penetrated the heights of heaven, and saw into the abyss of the earth, as clearly as she discerned the four walls of the room [47].

Infused knowledge. This is a supernatural aptitude for learning and a truly divine wisdom which in almost infinite variety and measures have been miraculously bestowed upon Saints and Mystics of all ages, so that they were able to understand and explain the most difficult and intricate problems of psychology and theology. Many mystics, of course, St. Augustine, St. Albertus Magnun, St. Thomas Aquinas and St. Bonaventure, for example, were erudite scholars and masters. On the other hand, St. Joseph of Copertino (1603-63), who was born of poor parents in a tiny village on the gulf of Tarento, received no education (humanly speaking) and yet he was easily able to resolve the most complex problems in mystical theology, which professors of the science were at a loss to interpret and understand. Blessed Osanna Andreasi of Mantua (1449–1505), a Dominicaness, was miraculously instructed by our Lady in an instant how to read and write, so that the humble nun became a great mistress of the spiritual life, and we possess forty-two letters, replete with the highest mysticism, which she addressed to priests and religious [48]. Perhaps the most remarkable example of infused knowledge is St. Catharine of Siena, whose works explore the highest and untrodden realms of the spirit and soar profoundly to the very throne of God, who is recognized by all as a Supreme Mistress of the Mystical Life—*doctrina ejus infusa, non acquisita fuit*— [49], and yet she was a tremendous force in the politics of the day, she was concerned with many domesticities, and had not been tutored by scholars or learned men. The daughter of a respectable bourgeois family, her education—such as it was—must have been of the very simplest.

Discernment of spirits. "Believe not every spirit, but try the spirits whether they are of God; because many false prophets are gone out into the world," says St. John [50], who proceeds to give the rule how we may know a good spirit from an evil spirit. And never was this precept more needed than to-day [51]. It is essential that the mystic should be able to recognize, however cunningly devised and clever the masquerade, the evil, which imitates and impersonates the good. As will be noted later, doctors give many signs whereby we may distinguish the divine from the diabolical. St. Catharine of Siena, Cardinal Bona, Gerson, Tanner, the Capuchin Taillepeid, and many more have written most convincingly upon this difficult subject.

The Franciscan Cardinal Brancati de Laurea [52] points out that the true mystical gift of discernment of spirits is "a special instinct whereby man without human industry, discerns spirit from spirit". No doubt the rules and tests "which are to be learned by human industry and toil", which are taught by theologians and writers on occultism, are scientifically very valuable and in practice of infinite use, but the mystic's gift of discernment of spirits is a grace *gratis data*, that is to say not derived from ascetical love and the like, but a supernatural faculty divinely and freely bestowed. And yet so subtle prove the devices of the demon that many are not only deceived, but persist in their deceit and become ardent propagandists of necromancy and every kind of dark diabolism.

The gift of healing should be mentioned as granted to many mystics, not of their own seeking, and sometimes almost without their knowledge, or at least with their having only a very indirect apprehension of their power. Here we distinguish the gift as enjoyed by mystics who are not formally acclaimed as Saints, who possibly will not ever be distinguished by the honours of Beatification.

A supernatural and extraordinary empery over nature and creatures is a phenomenon which has characterized many mystical souls. Thus, on one occasion, when St. Hugh of Grenoble, the Bishop who allotted to

St. Bruno the first (the Grande) Chartreuse, was residing among the Carthusians with whom he loved to sojourn, on entering the refectory upon a high festival found the monks sitting motionless before their repast. By some accident, no other food being obtainable, fowls had been served at table, and the Rule forbade them to eat this flesh. Taking his place, the aged prelate making the sign of the cross on the birds changed them into small tortoises, which are edible and are classed as fish. So the fathers partook and were satisfied. Zurburan has painted this incident. A similar miracle over nature is related of St. Ulrich, first bishop of Augsburg, who on a fast day converted a joint of meat into fish by the sacred sign. In pictorial art he is often represented with a fish as his symbol. There is a fine drawing of St. Ulrich and his fish by Albert Dürer. The same thing is told of the great St. Alphonsus Liguori, who although bidden by the Major General of the Redemptorists to eat a plate of veal converted it by the holy sign into a cod cutlet.

The Augustinian mystic, St. Nicolas of Tolentino, as he lay wasted and weak on his death-bed, exhausted by the broiling August heat, so excited the pity of his sorrowing brethren that they brought him a dish of doves, most delicately dressed, to tempt his appetite. The Saint, however, reproved them, firmly, but in gentle terms. He had never tasted animal food in his life. Painfully raising himself on his poor pallet, he stretched his hands over the dish, and lo! the birds rejoicing were in a flash covered with plumage, and flew out of the window of his little white-washed cell towards the blue sky beyond. But they hovered around until in a few days the Saint breathed his last [53], when they were seen mounting into the air, accompanying (as it is piously believed) his soul to Paradise. For as he breathed his last the room was filled with a heavenly fragrance, as of lilies, and gleamed with a radiant light.

A cup of wine blessed by St. Dominic from which he drank first, was partaken of in the refectory by twenty-five brethren at their meal, and when the thirst of all was quenched, was yet found to be brimming full as though nobody had so much as touched it with his lips, St. Dominic, moreover, when on board a galley which was like to be over-whelmed in a fierce tempest by his prayers immediately calmed the storm [54]. The Francisan mystic St. Peter of Alcántara [55], the director of St. Teresa, an ascetic of surprising holiness, walked upon the waves of the sea as though it were dry land, as also did St. Peter Nolasco, Father of the Mercedarians, and St. Maria de Cervellione of the same Order, and the Dominican St. Peter Gonzalez.

It were superfluous to detail the power over animals, wild and gentle, exercised by St. Francis of Assisi; how St. Giles the hermit was companioned by a hind which he loved; how a lion dwelt, like a dog, with St. Jerome and protected him; how a wolf guided the blind St. Hervé; and St. Sylvester Gozzolini, the founder of the Silvestrine monks, was served by a fierce wolf which dwelt near the Saint's retreat at Monte Fano and obeyed in most docile fashion his least word [56]. Amazing as it may appear, the mystics had reached such heights that animals and nature itself devotedly submitted to them and were lovingly subject.

This is even shown in those small domestic matters, which may appear trifling, but which are so essential to our well-being and health. From 1873 to 1876 Teresa Helena Higginson was an elementary school-teacher at St. Mary's, Wigan. She shared her humble little room with another teacher, Miss Susan Ryland, who is now a religious. One bitterly cold morning they found that by some accident their little stock of fire-wood was exhausted. Teresa Higginson told Miss Ryland to look in a certain cupboard. "I have, and it is quite empty," was the reply. "Just ask St. Joseph to help, and look again," said Teresa. "You had better ask him. He won't do it for me. I'm not good enough," answered Miss Ryland. "Well, look again, dear," suggested Teresa. Miss Ryland did so, and found a neatly stacked pile of wood, of quite a different and a better kind than the bundles they usually bought. A child was suffering from some ailment of the chest. By rubbing on some ointment Teresa Higginson cured the little boy at once. The delighted mother cried out: "Oh, how wonderful! Where can I get a supply? Tell me the chemist's name." In distress Teresa turned to Miss Ryland and whispered: "Whatever shall I do? It was just ordinary lard." On one occasion a fire was wanted immediately for some poor woman who had been taken ill. Teresa made the sign of the cross over the cold dead embers in the grate, and at once they sprang into a bright blaze. Such is the power of mystics over inanimate nature, even in the simplest domestic details, the lowly paths of life [57].

The King of Mystics, our Lord Himself, was tempted of the devil. Naturally Satan and his legions will assault and molest all those who, however, inadequately and with many a fall, are trying to attain to the supernatural light. Mystics, as is to be expected, will be the especial objects of his enmity; against mystics he will (so to speak) concentrate his malice and exercise the fullness of his power. Mysticism is essentially rooted in faith, and Canon Ribet warns us "It is rare that faith, which is the foundation of the spiritual life, is not subject to the most terrible diabolical assaults" [58]. To this extraordinary temptation are often superadded those of hideous blasphemy and hatred of God. Instances of such awful trials might be cited from the lives of Blessed Angela of Foligno, Saint Margaret of Cortona, St. Teresa of Ávila, St. Maria Maddalena de' Pazzi, St. Francis de Sales, and many more. These phenomena teach us that there must be no false security. The Mystic must ever watch and pray.

There are also actual demoniac molestations, most terrifying and weird experiences. St. Christina of Stommeln was constantly harassed, beaten, battered, and bruised by a fiend. On one occasion when two Dominican friars came to visit her, and she rose to greet them an invisible force hurled her backwards and struck her head repeatedly against the wall with horrid violence. She was cut and stabbed until blood came. These manifestations occurred before most trustworthy witnesses, and there cannot be a shadow of doubt that such outrages are reported with scrupulous accuracy. Again and again she was bespattered and polluted with deluges of indescribable filth [59]. St. Gemma Galgani was also tortured and assaulted by demons. Once, she says, "I got such a strong blow of a cudgel on my left shoulder that I fell. Even to-day I feel sick and ill from the pain." Again, the devil seized her and dashed her to the floor, where she lay senseless. Such phenomena were frequent [60], and greatly alarmed all in the house.

The Curé d'Ars, St. Jean Vianney, was sensibly persecuted by devils. At night the infernal enemy would rouse him from his few hours' sleep by thundering blows upon the doors and walls of the presbytery. It was at first thought that a gang of armed thieves had broken into the house, there were creaks as if all the furniture had been shattered in a thousand pieces. An awful silence followed for a few moments, and there were heard yells of maddened laughter which froze the very blood of the listeners. It was soon evident that the hubbub was preternatural. This persecution of the demon—the *grappin* as St. Jean Vianney called him —continued for a period of no less than 30 years, and the phenomena are attested by dozens of impeccable witnesses. Thus the infernal enemy would drum incessantly upon the table or chimney-piece, would imitate the clearing of wood, planing boards, hammering nails, just as if a carpenter were noisily at work in the house; would overthrow platters and smash a water-jug to smithereens. M. Monnin, who was actually present, relates how one night the evil one set fire to the heavy serge curtains of the Saint's bed. "Ah, this is a good sign," mildly observed the Curé, "the demon is very angry with us."

In the Lent of 1875 when Teresa Higginson and Miss Susan Ryland were living at Wigan, the latter was terribly alarmed as the house rang again and again with hoarse yells and shrieks of piercing agony, whilst a crash of thunder seemed to shake the very walls, and pale ghostly lights flickered about, dancing round the room. Miss Ryland cried out in terror, but Teresa said: "Don't be alarmed, dear. It's only the devil. He wants to be noticed, but he cannot really harm us. Let us say our prayers." One night, or rather early one winter morning, there came a low insistent rapping at Miss Higginson's bedroom door. Thinking that someone had suddenly been taken ill she got up quickly and opened the door, only to receive a violent blow on the face so that her cheek was bruised and swollen, whilst a soft laugh of bitter malicious glee was plainly heard.

Such phenomena are well known. They have, indeed, been described and classified by the learned Peter Thyraeus, S. J., of Nuys (Cologne) in his great work *De Locis Infestis* and the *Libellus De Terrificationibus Nocturnisque Tumultibus* (*On Haunted Places*, and also a *Treatise on The Terrors of Darkness and Midnight Noises*).

The physical phenomenon known as *Incendium Amoris*, the Burning Fire of Love, is far from uncommon in the annals of sanctity and is often recorded in the biographies of exalted mystics. It is the merest truism to observe that even in the most ordinary individual a great emotion has a corresponding corporeal effect, that there will be an actual rise of bodily temperature, an expressive flushing of the face; and when the ardour of love is experienced (a love far other than gross sensuality and carnal desire) a flood of happiness will pulsate and permeate both mind and body, resulting in a kind of ardour and joy that lighten the meanest trivial round, whilst all nature, things animate and inanimate, wears a smile. The keener the emotion the more intensive the result. In the case of mystics this result is raised to the highest possible degree, and becomes even violent in its vehemence and excess. Father Cepari, a Jesuit of very holy life and great discretion, who after Father Fabbrini was the confessor and later the biographer of the Saint, tells us how St. Maria Maddalena de' Pazzi was transformed by sudden overwhelmings of love, "for her face, losing in a moment the extreme pallor which had been produced by her severe penances and her austere cloistral life, became glowing, beaming with delight, and full; her eyes shone like twin stars, and she exclaimed aloud, crying out 'O love! O Divine Love! O God of Love!' " Moreover, such was the excess and abundance of this celestial flame which consumed her, that "in the midst of winter she could not bear woollen garments, because of that fire of love which burned in her bosom, but perforce she cut through and loosened her habit". She was even compelled to run to a well and not only to drink a quantity of icy cold water, but to bathe her hands and her breast, if haply she might assuage the flame [62]. Very much the same is related of St. Peter of Alcántara, who was often obliged to unfasten his habit even in winter, and to go out into the chilly air, so torrid were the fires that burned and broiled in his breast. He even burst into jubilant song, and withdrew into the recesses of a lonely wood that he might the more freely hymn the divine goodness. Not infrequently peasants who passed by would hear the liquid music of his voice [63].

It is recorded of St. Philip Neri that often as he said Mass his face was illumined, and it seemed that sparks of fire darted from his eyes. He sometimes swooned away, overcome by divine love, and on one occasion the flame of interior supernatural love so scorched and blistered his throat that he was ill for several days [64].

When in the Church of the Madonna della Pietà (SS. Bartolomeo ed Alessandro, piazza Colonna) at Rome, the venerable Cardinal Pedicini gave Holy Communion to the Trinitarian, Blessed Anna Maria Taigi, streams of perspiration poured down her face, she wept abundantly and uttered deep sighs. Her cheeks became rose-red, and often surprised by a spasm of divine ecstasy she fell swooning to the ground. "Often," the Cardinal said, "have I seen her fall, after receiving Communion, as if struck by lightning, and thus remain a long time burned in the sweet flames of divine love" [65].

Of the Venerable Serafina di Dio, a Carmelite nun of the Capri convent, who died in 1699, it is recorded that after Communion, and sometimes when she was rapt in prayer, the community saw her with her face glowing like a red flame and her eyes sparkling fire. "It burned them if they but touched her", and she declared that she was consumed and shrivelled with heat, that her blood was as molten lead in her veins [66].

Suor Maria Villani of Naples (1584–1670), a Dominicaness, who with pardonable exaggeration her daughters considered almost to rival the Seraphic Mother, St. Catharine herself in her profound knowledge of mystical theology, is described as "a furnace of love, a furnace thrice-heated". When she drank cold water a sizzling sound was heard as if the liquid was being poured upon red-hot iron [67].

The extraordinary heat phenomena manifested in the cases of that noble figure St. Catharine of Genoa, of the Capuchin Fra Girolamo da Narni, of St. Stanislaus Kostka, of the Venerable Orsola Benineasa [68], from whose throat there not unseldom came a perceptible white smoke as if ascending from a brazier lighted within, and other extraordinary but amply attested cases are recorded on unimpeachable evidence.

The most perfect degree of mystical union with God, the mystics' goal, which rises through and above ecstasy, the height of earthly contemplation, and a sure foretaste of heavenly bliss is the state known as the *Mystical Marriage*. That great master of mystical theology, Gianbattista Scaramelli, S. J. (1687–1752), in his *Il Direttorio Mistico* says that the Flame of Love is conceded only to those on the very highest peak of the Mystical Marriage, which is an ineffable Spiritual Union with Deity. "The essentials of the Spiritual Marriage are," Scaramelli considers, "in the first place, the intellectual vision of the Holy Trinity; and, secondly, an intellectual vision of the Divine Word, that is of Jesus Christ, together with some intellectual locution in which a mutual consent is given, and vows of fidelity exchanged." I would add that a Vision or the Presence of Our Lady is necessary to the fulfilment of the Mystical Marriage, since the Son will not give Himself in wedlock without the consent and approval of His Mother, and the Mother must be present at the marriage of Her Son. Thus in the Mystical Marriage of St. Gemma Galgani, "Gemma gave herself to Mary, and Mary to Gemma". She was then able to exclaim "The Heart of Jesus and my heart are one and the same thing" [69]. "Rich presents were not wanting to these espousals of Jesus and His beloved. Jesus appeared to her in the form of a lovely child in His Mother's Arms, and the Holy Mother, taking a ring from His finger, put it on that of his fortunate servant."

True Mysticism has well been called "The Mystical Love-Story". "Quia amore langueo" is the refrain of the exquisitely beautiful Middle English Poem, which is usually cited under this title [71]. In the case of the Premonstratensian, St. Herman Joseph of Steinfeld, the Religious gave him the name "Joseph" because of his tender devotion to Our Lady. The Saint's humility was deeply wounded, but under obedience he took that name, and he was regarded as the Spiritual Spouse of Mary. His joy was full when Our Lady Herself greeted him as Joseph, and acclaimed him as Her spouse indeed. In Mystic Marriage the Queen of Heaven Herself placed the nuptial gold ring upon his finger. There are few love-songs sweeter than that commencing, "Gaude, plaude, clara ROSA", with which St. Herman salutes Her [72]. Canon Augustine Wichmanns puts the following lines in St. Herman's mouth—who thus salutes "Deiparam suam sponsam":

72

Cor mihi cor excors, mens amens, nescia vitae.
Vita est; quod reliquum, funeris urna mei est.
Quid? mirum-ne? rosa et spina es mihi suavis et acris,
Quae modo delectas, quae modo pungis amans.
Delectas quoties mihi te considero sponsam:
Pungis in amplexus dum nequeo ire tuos.
Ergo MARIA veni, nostrosque incurre lacertos;
Quae modo me pungis spina, futura rosa es.

The passionate song is that of Catullus. "This monk can give lessons to lovers!" Arthur Symons once wrote, wondering at the ecstasy of St. John of the Cross [74]. May we not echo the words of one who was himself a poet of the finest and first quality? When we read St. Herman's poem to Our Lady we cry "This Nobertine can give lessons to lovers!"

Father Auriemma [75] relates that the brother of a King of Hungary used daily to say the Office of Mary, to whom he vowed himself body and soul, and thus he advanced far along the mystic path. However, for grave political reasons he was persuaded that he must marry. The day before the celebration of these very splendid nuptials he was kneeling in his room, reciting as was his wont the Office of Our Lady with great fervour and devotion. When he came to these words *Quam pulchra es, et quam decora!* [76] (How beautiful art thou and how fair!) there entered the chamber a lady of surpassing loveliness, who said to him, "If indeed I am as beautiful and fair as thou sayest, why dost thou abandon me for another bride? Know, then, that if thou wilt break off this marriage I will be thy Spouse, and thou shalt inherit the Kingdom of Heaven, where I am Queen, instead of an earthly empire." The prince fell prostrate before Her, and that very night privily leaving the palace he went far away into a lonely spot where he dwelt as an anchorite, and lived a most holy life, dying amid the songs of angelic choirs.

In his "Examples Appertaining to the Blessed Virgin Mary", Number 65, of that sublime work *The Glories of Mary* [77], St. Alphonsus Liguori tells us how a young man, who intended to become a cleric, in the ardour of his love one day placed a valuable ring, an heirloom, upon the finger of a statue of Our Lady, vowing he would renounce the world and choose Her only for his spouse. After some time he relaxed in his devotion, and decided to live in the world, since he had fallen in love with a lady of high rank, who accepted his hand. Mary appeared to him and rebuked him gently for his infidelity. Thereupon he gave up all idea of the intended match, and became a monk of a strictly eremetical and contemplative Order.

The Mystical Marriage, the consummation of the spiritual life, is a state not easily to be attained, but once it has been reached the most watchful fidelity and caution are needed. It is a supreme privilege, but also a supreme responsibility. This, "the most intimate of all human experiences" [78]—the phrase is that of Professor Peers—has been most amply described, as far as language can reach, for it is literally an ineffable experience, by St. Teresa of Ávila. It should be emphasized

73

that Christ impressed upon the Saint "Ut vera sponsa meum zelabis honorem". ("As My Bride and Spouse in very deed thou must with all care most zealously guard Mine Honour") [79]. These words have an especial significance when it is borne in mind how scrupulous and how nice the honour of a Spaniard was, the honour of a Grandee, nay more than a Grandee, the honour of His Majesty, the King. The proper preface of the Mass of St. Teresa speaks of the Saint "Sibi (Christo) spiritali connubio sociatam, data dextera", that is to say "joined in spiritual wedlock to Christ, Who gave her His own Right Hand" [80].

As St. Teresa insists the Mystical Marriage is indissoluble. It is *para siempre*, for ever and ever, an eternal Union.

The Mystical Marriage of the Holy and Seraphic Mother, Catharine of Siena, was accompanied by celestial phenomena of the most extraordinary and exalted kind. There is in the Saint's house in Fontebranda a very beautiful painting by Professor A. Franchi, 1896, depicting "Il mistico sposalizio di S. Caterina" as the Saint herself described it [81]. In the year 1364, about Carnival time, when the world without was indulging in all lusts and follies, St. Catharine was praying in her own little room, and there appeared to her Our Lord and Our Lady, accompanied by a vision of Saints, St. John the Evangelist, St. Paul, St. Dominic, her spiritual father, with the holy King David, who played sweetly upon a harp of gold. Our Lady presented the humble virgin to Christ. Whereupon Our Lord taking her hand in His placed upon her finger the wedding ring of four orient pearls and a diamond which shone like the sun. "Thou art my spiritual Spouse in faith, and one day thou shalt be wedded to me for ever in Paradise", came the Divine words, and slowly the heavenly vision faded from the sight of the enraptured Saint. Formerly the Feast of the Espousals of St. Catharine was observed in the Dominican Order, but since 1855 the title of the Solemnity has been changed to the Translation of the Relics of the Saint.

Mystical Marriage, this sublime experience of the Saints, is described by one of the most remarkable of English mystics, Margery Kempe of King's Lynn [82]. The wife of John Kempe, a prosperous middle-class citizen, Margery, who lived at the turn of the fourteenth century, could neither read nor write, but she dictated the story of her life; her pilgrimages, near and far, to the Holy Land, to Rome and Assisi, to St. James at Compostella, to Aachen; and above all she told of her marvellous spiritual experiences. When she was praying in St. Peter's at Rome, on the 9th November, 1414, she heard the Father of Heaven say that He would have her wedded to the Godhead, and that anon she should live with Him in bliss everlastingly. In utter abasement she wept bitterly, but "the Father took her by the hand, in her soul, before the Son and the Holy Ghost, and the Mother of Jesus, and all the twelve Apostles, and St. Catharine, St. Margaret, and many other Saints and Holy Angels, yea, a great quire of the Angelic hosts", and thus the Mystic Marriage was made. Whereupon "the Mother of God, and all the Saints that were present in her soul, prayed that they might have much joy together.

And there was a sound of harps and other instruments of music, for 'it is full merry in Paradise'."

It is interesting and not without significance that Margery Kempe learned much of St. Birgitta of Sweden, and was much influenced by the teaching and example of that Saint, who was canonized during Margery's visit to Rome.

Mystical Love, as Bastide observes, is a very rich and very complex sentiment, which overflows on all sides [83]. Indeed it is no exaggeration to say that consciously or subconsciously it focuses into itself every fine emotion and energizes them all to an unexampled degree. It is the completest Union and the Highest Experience possible in this life.

A posthumous phenomenon of Mysticism is *Incorruption*, that is to say the complete absence after many years (it may be centuries), of the normal cadaveric putrefaction. Through some extraordinary and supernormal cause the bodies of many Saints and Mystics have been entirely preserved and are immune from decomposition or decay.

In the first place it is necessary to say that there is no question of embalming or of exceptional conditions of sepulture. As is well known there exist bodies, like the natural mummies of Peru, which although intensely desiccated are yet whole and not fallen to dust. There are, again, the shrivelled corpses—a gruesome sight—in the Capuchin cemeteries of Palermo and Malta. Human decay can be naturally retarded, or even wholly arrested, by the process known as saponification. At Kiev there is (or was) a "laura", known as that of the Pescery, which exhibited twenty-three bodies of Saints, all entire, if mummified, robed in richest vestments and lying in open sarcophagi. At Cettinje, the village capital of Montenegro is venerated in the Greek Monastery the incorrupted body [84] of the Bishop King, St. Peter I, the Vladika, who died in 1830. The Saint lies vested in his Pontificalia of scarlet and gleaming gold, the face when the shrine-tomb, which is lined with blue velvet and silver, is opened for veneration, being reverently covered with the thinnest veil of white china-silk, through which the features are clearly discernible. Upon his great Feast-day, Petrov-dan, in July, the little chapel, and in fact the whole town, is thronged with pilgrims, many sick and suffering, who have come from near and far, to touch the holy remains with their lips, and haply the infirm, the halt, the lame, and the blind are healed there. A Montenegrin will tell you the histories of cures innumerable, which personally I do not question.

The preservative property of the crypts under St. Michan's Church, Dublin, are most remarkable. Any decay in the bodies committed to them is strangely arrested. These antiseptic qualities are believed to be largely attributed to the extreme dryness of the vaults, and to the great freedom of their atmosphere from dust particles [85].

Now and again history or antiquarian research records isolated examples of the same extraordinary preservation, for which it has been extremely difficult to supply any explanation that seems adequately to cover the separate cases.

It may be remarked that in the calendar of the Orthodox Russian

Communion there are a number of holy persons, whose bodies, after the lapse of many years, were discovered to be entire, and indeed this phenomenon appears to have been regarded as a sufficient testimony for official canonization or at least as a very strong and convincing argument [*86*].

This is assuredly not the case in the Catholic Church. It were a great error to suppose that all cases of immunity from corruption after death, many of which might be either accidental or due to certain conditions of entombment capable of scientific explanation, would result in the person concerned, however pious and holy, being raised to the altars of the Church. St. Bernadette Soubirous died, humble and hidden, in the Convent of St. Gildas at Nevers in 1879. She was 34 years old. In 1909 her body was exhumed, and a careful eye-witness records: "Not the least trace of corruption nor any bad odour could be perceived in the corpse. Even the habit in which she was buried was intact. The face was somewhat brown, the eyes slightly sunken, and she seemed to be sleeping" [*87*]. St. Thérèse of Lisieux, the Little Flower, died on 30th September, 1897. She was 24 years old. From the hour of her death her cultus commenced, and has spread the whole world over. She was originally buried in the Grand Cimetière on the hillside at Lisieux. When the coffin was disinterred it was found that the body had crumbled to dust, the bones only remaining. These were, as is customary, enclosed in a beautifully modelled figure of the Saint, venerated in the Carmel at Lisieux. St. Thérèse was canonized on 17th May, 1925.

The phenomenon of mystical Incorruption then, has no bearing upon canonization. It is true that Baron Freidrich von Hügel regards (to a very great extent at least) the popular cultus of St. Catharine Fiesea Adorna of Genoa, a veneration which may be said to have begun with the week-long honour paid to her holy body immediately after death and the discovery in May or June, 1512, of the incorruption of her remains, as in some degree a determining factor in the canonization of the Saint, which solemnity was performed by Clement XII, on 18th May, Trinity Sunday, 1737 [*88*]. But the heroic virtues and genius of St. Catharine of Genoa, without due examination and official approval of which she would not have been raised to the altar, are one thing; and the phenomenon of her incorrupted body, a very great and especial grace of God, another. Possibly Baron von Hügel is right in his interpretation of these events, but as he himself very candidly allows many other weighty circumstances enter into the matter. I will merely observe that when at Genoa forty years ago, and upon subsequent visits, I was privileged to venerate at a very close distance the Incorrupted Body of St. Catharine, and it remains an unforgettable experience. Ineffable sanctity pervaded the whole of that little chapel where she sleeps.

The ecstatica, Anne Catharine Emmerich, died on 9th February, 1821. She was buried at Dülmen, on the 13th February. Rather more than six weeks afterwards, in consequence of a rumour that the holy body had been stolen, the grave was opened. There was no corruption, and the face, sweetly smiling, was unflecked and pure. So Luisa Hensel and others who were present bore witness. The grave was opened a third time on 6th October, 1856. The body was intact as before, after four-and-thirty years. Yet Anne Catharine Emmerich has not as yet received the honour of beatification.

This extraordinary phenomenon, this great and signal grace of supernatural Incorruption does not pave the way to canonization. It is regarded as in some sense accidental, although certainly a divine prodigy. The reason for this lies in the fact that whilst the privilege has been bestowed upon a number of Saints and Mystics in whom have been verified (in their secondary application) the words of the Psalmist-Prophet: "Neither wilt thou suffer Thine Holy One to see corruption", Psalm xvi, 10, yet at the same time many Saints and Mystics of exceptional innocence of life have in their death shared the common lot of man, dust to dust, and their bodies have suffered natural decay. Such has been the case, for example, with St. Aloysius Gonzaga, S. J., St. Stanislaus Kotska, S. J., St. John Berchmans, S. J., and the Passionist St. Gabriel of Our Lady of Sorrows.

We can only say that the Divine Plan as regards the Phenomenon of Supernatural Incorruption has not been made clear to human intelligence. Wherefore Holy Church, whilst glorifying Heaven for these instances of Saints to whom this marvellous privilege has been granted, does not pronounce in this particular.

Yet at Siena—most blessed sight!—upon the Feast of the Seraphic Mother, St. Catharine Beniscasa "in the blaze of sunlight and of tapers, far away behind the glass and gilding of a tawdry shrine, is seen the pale white face which spoke and suffered so much years ago. The contrast of its rigid stillness and incorruption with the noise and life and light outside is very touching" [89].

At Bologna, in the convent adjoining the Church of Corpus Domini, Via Tagliapietre may be seen the miraculously incorrupt body of another St. Catharine, St. Catharine Vegri, a Poor Clare who died in 1463. In a small sanctuary, hung with crimson damask, the Saint is seated, richly robed, in a gilt chair. The flesh is desiccated but there is no putrefaction. On the contrary a heavenly perfume and a heavenly peace fill that little room. No one can enter it and venerate those sacred remains without reverence and awe.

At Florence the Carmelite nuns honour in its superb crystal shrine upheld by great rococo cherubim, the holy body of their Mother, St. Maria Maddalena de' Pazzi, that supreme mystic, whose life (it has been said) was one long ecstasy. She died in 1607, and the flesh is still supple, the body absolutely entire [90]. Moreover a fragrant oily liquid which has miraculous properties exudes from these hallowed remains. To kneel there in veneration and love is an experience which transforms, an experience never to be forgotten. The same good nuns possess the incorrupt body of the Dominicaness, Blessed Maria Bartolommea Dei Bagnesi [91]. There she lies, robed, crowned with a silver crown, in the superb *châsse* presented by Maria Luisa, Queen of Tuscany. Two angels guard her, holding triple girandoles. The Beata died in 1577.

When St. Rita of Cascia, O.S.A., the "Saint of the Impossible", died in 1457 a marvellously fragrant perfume exhaled from the body. In 1627 and again in 1682 when her coffin was opened the remains were found without the least spot of corruption, and the chapel was filled with the sweet scent of newly-gathered roses [*92*]. The Dominicaness Blessed Osanna of Mantua [*93*] died in 1505. Three years later her body was shown to be incorrupt, and this proved the case upon re-examinations in 1602, 1686, and 1871. Blessed Lucia of Narni, a stigmatized daughter of St. Dominic, maintained the same supernatural incorruption, and 175 years after her death (1544) the wound in the side was yet open and bathed in fresh blood [*94*].

The psychology, then, of Mysticism is corporeally plastic, and evidences itself in certain phenomena some of which impress themselves materially upon the living body of the Mystic, for example, the Stigmata, Levitation, Bilocation, whilst other phenomena are mental, for example, Visions, Telekenesis, Infused Knowledge. But all these may be widely classed as the Physical Phenomena of Mysticism and extraordinary graces.

I would emphasize that we are none of us bound to more than "the observance of precepts", and comparatively few fulfil even their obligations, or at least they fulfil them with tepidity. We are not, however, bound to more than correspondence with these graces bestowed on us. Some generous souls aim higher, and strive to obey the counsels of perfection.

Supernatural phenomena, wonderful though they may be beyond all words, count for nothing in reference to sanctity, I mean *that Sanctity* the Church insists should be primarily and manifestly proven before any person is raised to the altars. Benedict XIV expressly says [*95*]: "Manifold excellence of life is required both for Beatification and Canonization." Francesco Maria, Cardinal à Monte, Bishop of Porto, in the year 1622, in the case of St. Teresa, lays down that "canonization requires virtues of a heroic and prominent Degree", and he proceeded, to show that the virtues of St. Teresa had fully attained to this degree. It were superfluous to multiply authorities. So much having been said; the Physical Phenomena of Mysticism are of the utmost significance and importance. There is unhappily in a material age a tendency, which is at root very evil, and indeed an inspiration of the demon, to under-rate or minimize these. There are few studies of Mysticism in English which do not relegate these phenomena to the background, so to speak, or treat of them gingerly and even shamefacedly. This is very deplorable, and it seems highly advisable, nay necessary, that there should be a treatise concentrating upon and emphasizing the Physical Phenomena of Mysticism.

I am very well aware that each chapter of the present work could be extended to a separate volume. To instance one phenomenon alone, Stigmatization, which has been exhaustively studied by a great authority, Dr. Antoine Imbert-Gourbeyre, Professor at the School of Medicine at Clermont-Ferrand. Dr. Imbert-Gourbeyre has written *Les Stigmatisées*, 2 Vols. (630 pp.), Paris, Palmé, 1873; *La Stigmatisation*, 2 Vols. (xlix

576 pp. and 576 pp.), Clermont-Ferrand, Bellet, 1894, and second edition, 2 Vols., Clermont-Ferrand, Bellet, and Paris, Ch. Amat, 1898; *L'Hypnotisme et la Stigmatisation*, Paris, Bloud et Barrat, 1899; to mention no other of the Professor's treatises. Madame Jeanne Danemarie's *Le Mystère des Stigmatisés*, Paris, 1933, giving some account of Anna Catharine Emmerich and Theresa Neumann and a visit to Dülmen and Konnersreuth, is of much interest. In fact, a whole literature concerns these two stigmatics alone.

Accordingly this one single volume, although I have tried to make the purview as wide as possible, can (in some sense) only be regarded as a preliminary and of necessity a curtailed study.

At the risk of some repetition it may be useful to give here a list under nineteen heads of the principal Physical Phenomena of Mysticism.

Ecstasies, rapts, and trances.
Stigmatization.
Levitation.
Bilocation.
The Luminous Irradiance.
Supernatural Inedia.
The Supernatural Lack of Sleep.
Supernatural Dreams.
Visions and Apparitions.
Telekenesis.
Vision through opaque bodies.
Infused knowledge.
Discernment of spirits.
The Gift of Healing.
Supernatural Empery over nature.
Demoniacal Molestations.
Incendium Amoris.
The Mystical Marriage.
Supernatural Incorruption.

It is the tritest truism to insist upon and emphasize the extraordinary influence of the Mind upon the Body. Mysticism must so far as possible be entirely divorced from moods, which are in fact various forms of mental enslavement. They are that "alloy of self", of which St. Catharine of Genoa so profoundly discourses, and with what depth of wisdom does she pronounce that "selfishness is the root of all the evils to which we are exposed either in this life or in the future". No question the Mystic whose feet are set upon the path will, nay, necessarily must, at the beginnings of the pilgrimage towards Ultimate Reality encounter and have to fight with and overcome these dissatisfactions and distractions, these human tendencies to halt, even, for a moment or two, maybe, to stray. The Mystic, to use a phrase of Cowley, "must never stop nor ever turn aside in the race of glory—no, not like Atlanta, for golden apples", and the Mystic's glory—the Mystic's goal—is a Perfect Union with God.

The Mystic is not the commonplace conventional man. As Jonson has it of the ordinary individual, "What a deal of cold business doth a man misspend the better part of life in—in scattering compliments, gathering and venting news, following feasts and plays, making a little winter love in a dark corner." And then, Bishop Earle tersely writes his epitaph, "When he is gone, there wants one, and there's an end."

St. Teresa of Ávila was once, she says, "a prisoner to things of the world". The distinguishing feature of Isabel de Flores, whom we know better as St. Rose of Lima, "The Rose of Mary", was "a great tranquillity". In one of her treatises St. Catharine of Siena tells us how "God had taught her to build in her soul a private closet, strongly vaulted with Divine providence, and to keep herself always close and retired there. He had assured her that by this means she should find peace and perpetual repose in her soul which no storm or trouble would disturb."

St. John of the Cross, only a few months before his death, when he had been deprived of all official standing in the Order, when his health was utterly broken, and his enemies banished him with contumely to the lonely little house at La Peñuela, when malice was assaulting him on every side and ugly whispers were being deliberately circulated up and down the country, wrote to a nun at Segovia, a holy Carmelite, who had longed for him to return as Provincial, "As to my affairs, daughter, let them not trouble you, for none of them trouble me. What I greatly regret is that blame is attributed to him who has none; for these things are not done by men but by God, Who knows what is meet for us and ordains things for our good. Think only that God ordains all." So intense was the hostility against him that it appears an attempt would be made to expel him from the Order. A disciple in sore distress privily warned him of the bitter conspiracy—for it was nothing else—and, in the last in date of his letters the Saint replied: "Son, let not this grieve you, for they cannot take the habit from me save for incorrigibility or disobedience, and I am quite prepared to amend my ways in all where I have strayed, and to be obedient, whatever penance they give me."

"As to my affairs, daughter, let them not trouble you, for none of them trouble me." "Son, let not this grieve you." To what sublime heights of perfection had not the Mystic attained who could under such conditions write with this unearthly serenity and calmness. Truly John of the Cross had reached the summit of the mystical Carmel, and was far above the clouds and storm-wracks. He looked down with clear unwinking eyes upon this wretched weary world so full of jars and strife and rankling hate that lay far far beneath his feet.

Comfort is not the Beatific Vision. Thomas à Kempis sagely says:

Sint Temporalia in usu, aeterna in desiderio.

PLATE II: Bl. Marianna de Jesús
From a painting by Mercedarian

NOTES TO CHAPTER II

1. *Les Oeuvres de la Sainte Mère Térèse de Jésus* . . . nouvellement traduites . . . par le R. Père Cyprien de la Nativité de la Vierge, Carme Dechaussé Paris: 1650. *Le Chemin de Perfection*, p. 387, and Chapter XXXI, pp. 416–22.
2. *Tertio itin.*, Dist. 2.
3. Jean du Moulin. He was blind from the age of three years old. He was a great Latin scholar and a most accomplished musician. His mystical works which are many have been compared to those of Ruysbroeck, since he is among the profoundest of mystical writers. *Vie du vénérable frère Jean de Saint-Samson*, par le R.P. Sernin-Marie de Saint-André, Carme dechaussé, Paris, 1881.
4. *Maximes*, Ch. XXI.
5. *Disc. prelim*, Art 8.
6. *Theologia mystica*, No. 28.
7. Bruges, 1911.
8. Fr. Sandaeus, S.F. (1578–1650) *Theologia Mystica*, Ed. Mainz.
9. *Homo apostolicus*, app. i, 16.
10. *Oeuvres*, edit, Lachat, Vol. XIX, p. 310.
11. St. Matthew xxii, 37.
12. *Le Chemin de Perfection*, Chapter XXXI, *ut supra*.
13. Vol. I, p. 15.
14. Jacques Paul Migne, 1800–75.
15. *De notis et signis Sancitatis*, II, c, iv.
16. *De Certitudine Gloriae Sanctorum;* in app. ad. c. iv.
17. *Histoire Littéraire du Sentiment Religieux en France, II. L'Invasion Mystique*, Paris, 1925.
18. Dean Inge in the Preface to his *Christian Mysticism*, emphasizes that he concentrates upon "the philosophical side of the subject", and takes a full page to inform his readers that he ignores the Physical Phenomena of Mysticism.
19. Fr. Scheuer in the *Revue d'ascétique et de mystique*, July, 1923, and January, 1924.
20. Zero has been plumb reached in a "short-title catalogue" which lists rather superficial studies of Ann Catharine Emmerich, St. Bernadette, Levitation, alongside of a reprint of Pierce Egan's *The Life of an Actor*, and rubbish such as *The Little Book o' Tricks*, George Bernard Shaw's *My Spoof at a Seance*, Louisa Lawford's *Fortune-Telling by Cards*, together with a romance such as Dumas, *Memoirs of a Physician*, and Henry Cockton's farcical novel *Valentine Vox, the Ventriloquist*.
21. Emile Gebhart has written *L'Italie mystique*, Paris, 1890, 5th ed. 1906, which is useful but very tentative and restricted in its survey. The Italian Mystics of the seventeenth and eighteenth centuries are hardly known in England.
22. To-day (1947) as I write, any book concerning Anne Catharine Emmerich is of the last rarity, and is not to be found outside a very few libraries. But such books should be generally obtainable, and I fear that it is by being constantly baffled in his search for works on Mysticism that the inquirer loses heart and eventually abandons a quest which seems hopeless.
23. Dr. R. M. Bucke, a Canadian psychiatrist, names his work *Cosmic Consciousness: a study in the Evolution of the Human Mind*. Philadelphia, 1901.
24. *Confessions*, vii, 23.
25. *Vita e Dottrina*, Genoa, 1551, p. 178b. (Reprint.)
26. *Traité de L'Amour de Dieu*, vii, 3; and vi, 12. This treatise was immensely popular, and (it is said) the precepts of St. Francis were studied and followed in every convent. When Pius IX declared St. Francis a Doctor of the Church the Pontiff in his decree uses the following most striking and significant words: "in mystica theologia mirabilis Salesii doctrina refulget."
27. *Varieties of Religious Experience*, pp. 423–4. I do not quote the whole section which is of some length.
28. Blessed Henry Suso's *Little Book of Eternal Wisdom*, translated from the German by Richard Raby; Richardson, Dublin and Derby, 1866. Second Edition, p. 74.

F

THE PHYSICAL PHENOMENA OF MYSTICISM

29. *Itinerare*, c. i.

30. Tom *II* de relig. lib. 2. *De Oratione*, c. xi, n. 3.

31. *Heroic Virtue: A Portion of the Treatise of Benedict XIV on the Beatification and Canonization of the Servants of God.* English translation; Richardson and Son, 1850. Vol. I, p. 262 *sqq.*

32. *The Spiritual Guide*, reprint of the translation of 1688. Foreword by Dugald Macfadyn, pp. 21–2.

33. Our Lord often appeared in the Blessed Sacrament to St. Catharine of Siena, and under different forms. Sometimes she saw Him as an Infant, sometimes He was older and radiant with light. At Christmas Blessed Mary of Oignies saw Our Lord in the host as an Infant on His Mother's lap; in Passiontide she saw Him on the Cross, and swooned away with grief.

34. See the Bollandists under 13th January.

35. The incident is related in *The Life of the Saint*, by Father D. Bernardo Laviosa, C.R.S., a work of authority not to be gainsaid since it received the imprimatur of the Dominican Magister Sacri Palatii.

36. J. Babinski, *Hypnotisme et Hystérie du Rôle de L'Hypnotisme en Thérapeutique.* Paris, 1891.

37. *De canonizatione Sanctorum*, III, c. XLIX, n. 3.

38. *Teresa Higginson Servant of God 1845–1905*, by the Rev. A. M. O'Sullivan, O.S.B. (1924.)

39. In these passages I quote Douay. *A.V.* has "times". The Vulgate has "somnia".

40. Nicolas Lancizzi deals with this point. Tom. 2. *Opuse*, p. 49.

41. *De Canonizatione Sanctorum*, C.V., n. 17.

42. *De notis et signis Sanctorum*, VIII, c. 4., p. 922.

43. *Disquisitiones magicae*, Lib. IV, c.i. qu. 2, sect. 2, *Objiciat forte aliquis.*

44. A poor and inadequate definition. The word "clairvoyance" or at any rate "clairvoyant" is far earlier in use than the *O.E.D.* notes.

45. It is significant that a Leaflet issued by a Spiritualistic Society about 1870 says: "A powerful physical medium is usually a person of an impulsive, affectionate, and genial nature, and very sensitive to mesmeric influences", and, I would add, the more likely to be possessed.

46. English translation by Stanley de Brath *Clairvoyance and Materialization.* T. Fisher Unwin, 1927.

47. *Life of the Venerable (Blessed) Anna Maria Taigi.* Third Edition. Burns and Oates, 1879. Chapter XVII, p. 281.

48. *Vita della B. Osanna Andreasi*—Sescritta de Mons. Corradino Cavriani, Monza, 1888. Parte seconda. Capo I. *La beata Osanna, coll' ajuto della SS. Vergine, e mediante una scienza supernalmente infusa impara ottimamente a leggere ed a scrivere.* pp. 103–08.

49. Lectio VI (ex Romans Breviario) ad Matutinum, die XXX Aprilis. *Breviarium juxta Ritum Sacri Ordinis Praedicatorum.* Mechliniae. H. Dessain, 1893.

50. Epistle I, iv, 1–3.

51. See the very important book by J. Godfrey Raupert, K.S.G., *Christ and the Powers of Darkness.* First published in 1914, the warning is as cogent and as necessary, perhaps more necessary, to-day as when this very serious volume was originally issued. Also see, by the same author, *The Dangers of Spiritualism*, which had reached a fifth edition in 1920.

52. 3 *Sent.* tom. 4, dist. 19, art. 10, ii, n. 361.

53. St. Nicholas died at the convent of Tolentino, 10th September, 1306. The incident of the doves, restored to life, has been painted by the assistant of Raphael, the "capo-scuola of the Ferranese school", Benvenuto Tisio, often known as Garofalo.

54. *Vita S. P. Dominici*, auctore R. P. E. Nicalao Tanssenio. Antuerpiae. M.D.C. XXII. Lib. II. XIV. 188–9.

55; See his life written by Fr. John of St. Mary in 1619; and also another biography written in 1644 by Fr. Martin of St. Joseph.

THE PHYSICAL PHENOMENA OF MYSTICISM

56. Sebastiano Fabrini, *Chronica della Congregazione dei Monachi Silvestrini.* Camerino, 1618.

57. *Teresa Helena Higginson, School Teacher and Mystic,* by Cecil Kerr, 1928, p. 21.

58. *La Mystique,* Vol. I, p. 396.

59. *Acta Sanctorum.* June. Vol. IV. Antwerp. 1707.

60. *Life of Gemma Galgani,* by Father Germanus, C.P. Translated by the Rev. A. M. O'Sullivan, O.S.B., 1914. Chapter XIX.

61. Cologne, *ex officina Mater cholini* 1598, and several subsequent editions.

62. *La Santa di Firenze.* Firenze, Libreria Luigi Manuelli, 1906. See also the *Life of St. Maria Maddalena de Pazzi* in the Oratorian Series, pp. 235–37.

63. *Historia de las vidas y milagros de S. Francisco, Petro de Alcantara y de los Religiosos insignes en la Reforma de Descalzos,* por F. Martin de S. Joseph, 2 Vols. folio, Arevalo, 1644. Also *Vie de Saint Pierre d'Alcantara,* écrite en Italien par le P. Marchese de L'Oratoire, et traduite en François. 4to. Lyons. 1670.

64. Bacci's *Life of St. Philip Neri,* edited by Fr. Antrobus, 1902. Vol. I, pp. 26, 141.

65. *Life of the Venerable (Blessed) Anna Maria Taigi, the Roman Matron,* 1769–1837. London, 1879. Chapter XI, pp. 178–183.

66. *Vita della Venerabile Serafina di Dio.* Rome, 1748, p. 260. Written by two Oratorians, Sguillante and Pagani.

67. *Vita Della Serva di Dio, Suor Maria Villani.* Naples, 1674. By the Dominican, Fra Francesco Marchese, O.P.

68. *Vita della Madre Orsola. Benincasa, Fondatrice delle Monache Theatine* per il Padre Francesco Maria Maggio. Folio, Rome, 1655.

69. *Life of Gemma Galgani,* by Father Germanus, C.P., 1914, p. 275. pp. 251–2.

70. The mystics of Islam, the Sufis, develop on their own lines this aspect of mysticism. In the twelfth century we have such writers as Al Ghazzali, and in the thirteenth such poets as 'Attar (c. 1140–1234); Sâdi (1184–1263); and Jalâlu-Ddin Rumî (1207–1273). The *Divan* of Hafiz has been translated (in selections) by John Nott; by H. W. Clarke, 2 Vols., London, 1891, and also by John Payne. The poet Jâmi still conserved the tradition in the fifteenth century. He lived 1414–1492.

71. This poem may conveniently be found in *The Oxford Book of English Mystical Verse.* 1921, p. 6. Here it is dated fifteenth century. Such a stanza as the following is very significant:

> What shall I do now with my spouse?
> abyde I will hyre iantilnesse;
> wold she loke onys owt of hyr howse
> of flesshley affeccions and vnclennesse;
> hyr bed is made. hyr bolstar is in blysse,
> hyr chambre is chosen, suche ar no moo;
> Loke owt at the wyndows of kyndnesse,
> *Quia amore langueo.*

72. *Beati Hermanni Joseph Canonici Steinfeldensis Ordinis Praemonstratensis Opusula* . . . olim vulgata a R. D. Joanne Chrys. Vander Sterre Abbate S. Michaelis Antverpiai typis denuo edi curavit Ignatius Van Spilbeeck, Cam. Tong. Namurci, 1899, pp. 29–43.

73. Augustini Wichmans Canonici Tongerloensis *Epigrammata* Taminiae, 1895, p. 12. "Apostrophe Divi Hermanni ad Deiparam suam sponsam dum nimio Ejusdem amore languescebat."

74. *Contemporary Review,* April, 1899.

75. Tom. I.C., VIII.

76. Canticles, VII, 6.

77. *The Glories of Mary,* Part II, p. 215. St. Peter's Press, 1948.

78. *Mother of Carmel,* by E. Allison Peers. S.C.M. Press, 1945, p. 119.

79. The Carmelite Breviary. First Antiphon of First Vespers, 15th October,

Feast of St. Teresa, "Zelo zelata sum pro honore sponsi mei Jesu Christi, qui dixit mihi, ut vera sponsa meun zelabis honorem".

80. The proper Mass (with Preface) of St. Teresa; the Carmelites, Spain, *et alibi.*

81. The Mystical Marriage of St. Catharine is the subject of a painting by the great Dominican master, Fra Bartolommeo (1475–1517). In this Our Lady is enthroned holding her son, and St. Catharine receives the mystic ring from the Infant Christ. On one side of the throne stand St. Peter, St. Bartholomew, and St. Vincent Ferrer; on the other St. Dominic and St. Francis of Assisi. Originally designed for the convent of San Marco, this picture excited the intense admiration of Raphael when he visited the artist at Florence between 1505 and 1507. Lectio VI of the Office "In Translatione S. Catharinae Virg. O.P.", authorized by the Sacred Congregation of Rites on 5 May, 1891, describing the Solemn Translation of the Relics of St. Catharine to the High Altar, which Pius IX himself consecrated, of Santa Maria sopra Minerva, concludes: Cujus solemnions Translationis, idem Pontifex ex sacrae Rituum Congregationis decreto in ulsit, ut in Ordine Praedicatorum quotannis sub ritu Toto Duplici memoria celebrasetur, assignata Feria quinta post Dominicam Sexagesimae, qua die antea fieri solebat sub ritu Duplici Commemoratio sanctae Catharinae Senesis, seu Desponsationis ejus, quoniam ea die Christo Virginum Sponso seraphicam Virginem mystics desponsatam fuisse tradebatur, quemadmodum venerabilis Raymundus, sanctus Antoninus altique gravissimi testantur scriptoses."

The Solemn Translation of the Relics took place on 5 August, 1855. The Feast is annually celebrated on the Thursday following Sexagesima Sunday.

82. *The Book of Margery Kempe, a Modern Version*, by W. Butler-Bowdor, 1936. See also Katharine Cholmeley, *Margery Kempe Genius and Mystic.* London, 1947.

83. *The Mystical Life*, by Roger Bastide. Translated from the French G. H. F. Kynaston-Snell and David Waring. London, 1934, p. 213.

84. "Dieser dürre, steinharte, Kadaver," says Schwarz, *Montenegro*, Leipzig, 1883, pp. 81–2.

85. I quote from D. A. Chart, *Story of Dublin.* Fuller details are to be found in *The Registers of the Church of St. Michan*, edited by H. F. Berry, M.R.I.A., Dublin, 1907. Preface, p. vi.

86. J. Bois, *Dictionnaire de Théologie Catholique*, Vol. II, 1665–1669; and see also P. Peeters, *Analecta Bollandiana, XXXIII* (1914), pp. 415 *sqq.*

87. Kempf. *Holiness of the church in the nineteenth century*, English translation, p. 212.

88. F. von Hügel, *The Mystical Element of Religion*, 2nd ed., 1923, Vol. I, pp. 300–306.

89. J. A. Symonds, *Siena*, reprinted in *Sketches and Studies in Italy and Greece.* Third Series, New Edition, 1898, p. 65. In quoting I have ventured to amend a couple of words. The body of St. Catharine lies under the High Altar of Santa Maria Sopra Minerva, Rome.

90. *La Santa di Firenze*, Firenze, 1906. At p. 129 there is a photograph of the shrine.

91. *La Santa di Firenze*, Firenze, 1906. At p. 39 there is a photograph of the shrine.

92. Cardi, *Vita della B. Rita de Cascia*, Foligno, 1805. St. Rita was canonized in 1900 by Leo *XIII.*

93. Mgr. Corradino Cavriani, *Vita della B. Osanna Andreasi di Mantova*, Monza, 1888.

94. Padre Domenico Ponsi, *Vita della B. Lucia virgine di Narni*, 1711.

95. *De servorum Dei Beatificatione et Canonisatione*, III, XXI. The Oratorian translation of a part of this great work, *Heroic Virtue*, 3 Vols., London, Dublin, and Derby, 1850, is admirably done.

CHAPTER THREE

Ecstasy—The Ecstasy of the Neo-Platonists—The Demoniacal Ecstasy of Witch Folk—Natural Ecstasy—Divine Ecstasy—Rapture—The Intermingling of the Natural and Supernatural Worlds.

THE word Ecstasy, derived through the late Latin *exstasis* [*1*] from the Greek ἔκτασις "displacement", and in late Greek "a trance", is etymologically defined as that state of transport in which the soul, liberated from the body is absorbed in the contemplation of divine things. Dr. Henry More, the Cambridge Platonist, speaks of "the Emigration of humane Souls from the bodie by Ecstasis". Mystic theologians poise the question whether the soul does actually cease to animate the body, but St. Thomas, who amply discusses this point, decides that a complete alienation of the senses, so that the soul is incapable of producing any conscious or sensible corporal operation, is sufficient. Thus when St. Paul was "caught up into paradise and heard unspeakable words" II Corinthians, xii, 3, he says "whether in the body, or out of the body, I know not: God knoweth"; St. Thomas tells us that the Apostle "rapt to the third heaven by the power of God contemplated the Divine Essence (that is Ultimate Reality). But it is impossible that a man in his normal bodily state should contemplate the Divine Essence, unless such a one were wholly estranged from the senses" [*2*].

But if the senses are ravished away and (so to speak) annihilated, the human intelligence and understanding by the operation of divine grace are upheld, and the spiritual sight and hearing and reason remain, so that the Mystic after the ecstasy can remember, even if he cannot, in human phrase, express the height and depth of this supernatural experience. Moreover, the functions of the vegetative life persist, that is to say breathing and the circulation of the blood, notwithstanding they persist insensibly. St. Augustine, although quite familiar with the phenomenon of ecstasy and all its conditional effects, never relates it as a psycho-physical experience of his own enduring, but this may well be on account of the humility of the great doctor who would not so much as speak of so supreme a favour. He says, however, that "when the mind is wholly concentrated on higher things, and thus completely abstracted and entirely withdrawn from the bodily senses it is called an Ecstasy. The soul is caught away so as to be rapt from the body and feeling more than in sleep, but less than in death" [*3*].

In a supernatural or divine Ecstasy the soul is withdrawn from the body and updrawn unto God Himself: but afterward the soul is restored to the body, to the members of the human frame [*4*]. When commenting upon St. Paul's words "whether in the body, or out of the body, I know not", St. Augustine very profoundly says that the Apostle, when rapt to Paradise, did not know "whether he was in the body, as the soul is in a body and sustains the life of the body, whether it be awake or asleep, however deeply slumbering and comatose, or whether his soul had actually parted from his body, which must then have lain dead, until the revelation being ended, it was restored to his dead members which came to life again. And since it was so uncertain whether his soul was for a while entirely separated from his body which thus was left stark and dead, or whether in some ineffable way the soul although caught up to the third heaven yet vivified his body, hence it appears that St. Paul said: Whether in the body or out of the body, I know not; God knoweth" [5]. St. Augustine from this and other passages concludes that probably the soul (*anima*) remains in the human body during ecstasy, but the mind (*mens*); or *animus*, the vivifying sensible principle leaves the body. Yet in some cases he seems to imply that the soul itself (*anima*) is parted from the body, which accordingly must be sustained in some miraculous manner. St. Augustine in fact distinguishes at least two kinds of ecstasy, and we feel convinced that he experienced ecstasies, although (as noted above) he would not describe them. Plotinus and the Neo-Platonists were acquainted with Ecstasy. In fact Plotinus, who is echoed even as late as Amiel, considered that as the visible world of sense is only a shadow of the real world of intelligence, so action is only a shadow of higher things, of mystical contemplation. The things we see with human eyes, the things we do are glamour. In his *Journal* the God-tortured morbidly introspective Amiel cries out that "action is coagulated and clotted thought".

It is hardly to be surprised at that the doctrine of ecstasy in Plotinus can be paralleled in the writings of Christian Mystics, but with that subtle difference which is basically as wide as a gulf between. "The soul," says Plotinus, "when wholly and entirely occupied by fervent love of Him eagerly strips herself of all form which she has, yea, even of that which is derived from Intelligence itself, for whilst in conscious enjoyment of any other attribute or accident it is impossible that she should either behold, and in far less degree that she should be assimilated with, Him" [6].

"In the reduction of your soul to its simplest self (ἁπλωσις), its divine essence," says Plotinus, "you realize this Union, this Identity (ἕνωσιν). Like only can comprehend like" [7]. Ecstasy is the liberation of the mind from its finite consciousness, in which state it may attain to the Infinite.

It is recorded that Plotinus experienced this ecstasy of the Neo-Platonists four times; Porphyrius his disciple, five times; Iamblichus thrice. The Neo-Platonism of Plotinus and Proclus had, it must be frankly admitted, considerable influence in the West. St. Augustine in his *Confessions*, vii, ix, relates how certain books of the Platonists, translated out of Greek into Latin fell into his hands, and how an intensive study of these proved to be the beginning of his Conversion. Little question these were the works of Plotinus which he came to know in

A.D., 385, and the following year he was baptized by St. Ambrose. In these volumes, he found many things agreeable to the Christian doctrine, and to a certain degree his whole intellectual outlook was permanently coloured by what is good in Neo-Platonism. This is not to say that he had anything but contempt for the aberrations and debasement of this school, the abracadabra of the theosophists [8], which find so much favour to-day, and seem to flourish with lush luxuriant corruption, as indeed was the case in the fourth century.

Neo-Platonism unless most strictly safeguarded is full of danger. It will only too soon be sensed in most subtile manner to deviate from Christianity, this mysticism of human invention. In the first place it proves to be pantheistic at the core, and has as its goal not Union with God, as rightly understood, but fusion (one might say confusion) with Deity.

Aristotle himself would have eschewed this. And he makes the Vision of God τὸν Θεὸν Θεωρεῖν the ultimate end of man [9].

So kaleidoscopic is it, so mutable in terms and teaching, and often so charlatanical in its conjurors' ecstasy, that it is far from easy to discern what Modern Theosophy may or may not mean. Professing itself to be the ancient wisdom allegedly underlying all philosophies and religion, a secret known only to the initiates, it resolves itself into a mass of contradiction inextricably mixed up with Buddhism, and further gives a strong Brahmin colour. Such vagaries as Mrs. Besant's *Esoteric Christianity* (1901) a "theosophical classic", and the earlier *Key to Theosophy* and *Isis Unveiled*, in point of scholarship are valueless, whilst their philosophy has run riot in berserker frenzy. Theosophy, so called to-day, is the heir of all the ages of Gnosticism, as full of tricks as a monkey, as full of holes as a sieve [10].

It has just been observed that Theosophy has borrowed largely from, and "conveyed" as the wise call it, many details and characteristics of certain Oriental religions. In these we find, however ill-directed and askew, such an innate yearning for Mysticism that there have actually been evolved methods and means by which to attain to Ecstasy. That these are largely practised and performed, openly advocated even, in the West to-day there can be no question. The following four recipes by which ecstasy may be attained are quite frankly recommended by Hindu Yogi. (*Yoga* is defined as "in Hindu philosophy, union with the Supreme Spirit; a system of ascetic practice, abstract meditation, and mental concentration, pursued as a method of obtaining this.") *Mantra-Yoga*, to repeat monotonously for an indefinite period the same word, above all some word signifying the name of God. *Laya-Yoga*, to concentrate for a very long while upon some one object, which is especially effective if the object be shining or brilliant. *Raja-Yoga*, gradually to suspend the breath in respiration. *Hatha-Yoga*, to fix the gaze intently, and to support bodily postures (generally with extreme discomfort) for a very long space of time. Of Oriental practices and beliefs I have nothing to say, but it is a saddening thought that it ever should be supposed in the Western world that God could be attained by this sort

87

of purely mechanical and unhealthy process. Such artifices are truly reprehensible in the highest degree, and, I fear, are dangerously akin to a dark and evil occultism. The Christian suspects and abhors the impiety of contrivances which are so essentially artificial, materialized, and unnatural.

It is not without significance that Mr. Arthur Lillie in his *Modern Mystics and Modern Magic* relates how Mr. Stainton Moses, a well-known devotee of Spiritism, at one period of his mediumship passed through a terrible crisis. Evil spirits assailed him. He saw their forms; he heard their hideous voices. Foul stenches defiled his rooms. "He tried the Indian Yoga. This only made matters worse."

A great deal more might be said. This much was necessary, and it is painful to dwell further upon these mystical aberrations and spiritual deceptions, which can only have as their least injurious result a morbid self-hypnotism.

At this point before seeking a definition of true Ecstasy, it may be well to emphasize that Ecstasies, Rapts, and Trances, must be distinguished from any cataleptic state, from any alienation of the senses through intense concentration, or from that experience which is known as natural ecstasy.

Incidentally Doctor Paolo Mantegazza, a declared materialist and free-thinker, most of whose suppositions and hypotheses have been refuted and disproved by the later school of Professors of Science— many of whom frankly confess their groundwork is just shifting sand —is the author of a study *Le Estasi umane*, utterly demolishing his confrère Dr. Henri Legrand du Saulle, a physician of the Hospital of Bicêtre, who attempted to make a clean sweep of Ecstasies and the concomitant circumstances of Ecstasy with the two words "hysterical phenomena".

Mantegazza was, at any rate, too honest and clear-minded to tolerate such shallow ineptitudes, but some theory had to be evolved to meet the facts. Accordingly in his *Human Ecstasies* he elaborated the suggestion that man, in virtue of his own natural powers, can so profoundly concentrate his mind on the contemplation of Heavenly things as to lose himself, rapt in God. To this state he gave the name "Human Ecstasy". A contradiction is at once apparent. If the mind is enraptured by Heavenly things, how can 'Human' be applicable or appropriate? Again, what could Mantegazza, who did not even believe in God, know of Heavenly things?

In a manuscript treatise Father Baldelli, whose opinion is quoted with approval and confirmed by Benedict XIV, writes "As to the causes of Ecstasies and Raptures, these are assigned by St. Thomas, namely, Almighty God; the power of the devil, as permitted by God; and a certain natural temperament. Now, although an intense concentration upon divine things and a complete abstraction from the senses, the natural conditions and functions of the body, can be only from God, because it is from Him that every good thought and every holy inspiration which avail to the right estate of our salvation must proceed, nevertheless on occasion the total suspension of the senses, whether such alienation result because the mind is wholly occupied with and absorbed by some object, or whether because, without it being intent upon any especial thing, it is simply deprived of the use of its senses, may proceed also from the working of the devil, and likewise from physical causes of one sort or another. There can be no question that the ecstasies and raptures of would-be contemplatives who are without humility and utterly corrupt with hateful pride come from the devil, as that great theologian Cardinal Tomaso de Vio Gaetani [11] very plainly proves. From the demon also proceed the trances of men and women witches, when they remain utterly inert in one spot like dead persons, and are verily deceived by phantasy and fictitious appearances which the devil, their master, conjures up and produces in their imagination, and then they are persuaded that they have been in various places, and have satiated themselves with wickedness according to their abominable desires."

The authors of the *Malleus Maleficarum* [12] an authority not to be gainsaid, expressly lay down that although the transvection of witches to the Sabbat or nocturnal gathering may "often happen by illusion and merely in the imagination", yet to decry the actual and bodily transvection of witches to and fro their hellish rendezvous, where they are present in person, savours of heresy. It is found then that some witches are transported only in imagination, but it is also found in the writings of learned Doctors that many have been bodily transported. Thomas of Brabant [13], a Dominican and suffragan bishop, 1201–70, in his famous work *Bonum universale de Apibus* has much to say both of these real and imaginary transvections. During these fantastical journeys the witch lies as if dead, and is utterly without sensation. In fact the witch has fallen into a diabolic ecstasy. St. John Grahame Dalyell in his *Darker Superstitions of Scotland* [14] gives an account of the trial for witchcraft on 2nd October, 1616, of Jonka Dyneis who was "discovered and seen standing at her own house wall, in a trance, and being questioned she gave no answer but stood as if bereft of her senses". Johann Scheffer (1621–79), Professor of Law and Librarian of the University of Upsala in his *History of Lapland* [15], English translation, Oxford, 1674, studied very closely the sorceries of the Laplanders, and describes how when a warlock is consulted, he dances an extraordinary dance, presently falling to the ground as if dead, and when he rises from his diabolic ecstasy he answers the questions which have been put to him. Meanwhile his fellow wizards carefully guard the inert body, and no living thing is suffered to touch it.

Henry Boguet, a great authority, in his *An Examen of Witches* [16] (1590), Chapter XVII, discussed "Whether Witches go in spirit to the Sabbat", and decides: "There can be no doubt that there are times when witches go to the Sabbat both in body and spirit", so there is no question at all that most frequently, perhaps, witches are actually and corporeally present at the Sabbat, but he also cites cases, when witches attend the Sabbat whilst they are demoniacally entranced. "Certain witches, who after having remained in their houses and dead for the space of two or three hours, have confessed that they were at that time at the Sabbat in spirit, and have given an exact account of all that took place there." Such were the warlock Groz-Jacques, and Clauda Coirieres, "a most pestilent hag". One Holy Thursday night George Gandillon of Aranthon lay in his bed for three hours as if he were dead, and then suddenly came to himself. He had been rapt in a diabolical ecstasy. Innumerable sorceries and murders were proved against him and he was duly executed. So Boguet concludes that with regard to these witches "who remain unconscious and as it were dead (*i.e.* in a diabolical ecstasy) it is probable that Satan sends them to sleep, and in their sleep reveals to them what happens at the Sabbat so vividly that they are fully assured they have been actually present". But, he adds, "this never happens except to such as have previously attended in person the witches' assembly, and have already enlisted beneath Satan's standard" [*17*].

Pedro Ciruelo, Canon of Salamanca, who for thirty years acted as Inquisitor at Saragossa, and was a theologian of profound knowledge and long practical experience, in his *Opus de magica superstitione* [*18*] (*A Study of the Evil Craft of Black Magic*), Alcalà, 1521, which at once took its place as supremely authoritative, describes how witches, male and female, after smearing themselves with horrible unguents (the witches' salve) and pronouncing certain cantrips are carried through the air to the sorcerers' rendezvous. This transvection may be actual and real, or illusory. In the latter case the fiend enters their bodies and they lie stark and stiff, utterly without feeling, dead and cold. The demon then presents to their imagination the horrors and filth of the Sabbat, which upon recovering their senses they remember, and are very clearly aware of all that has passed. Whilst they are rapt in this devil's ecstasy they have no feeling whatsoever, and may be beaten or burned without any effect. Ciruelo holds that whether the transvection be actual or in a trance the guilt is the same, since it initially arises from the pact with the devil. Francisco Torreblanca Villalpando [*19*], and the sagacious Arnaldo Albertino [*20*], with many other authorities maintain precisely the same view. Villalpando definitely speaks of "the power of the demon to produce these ecstasies, in which the subject becomes as it were, a corpse, utterly insensible to all feeling".

It is proven, then, that there is an ecstasy of sorcerers, as well as an Ecstasy of Saints.

The famous psychic investigator, the late J. Godfrey Raupert, K.S.G. in his work *The Dangers of Spiritualism* [*21*] gives in detail the case of a gentleman, M., who after dabbling in spiritism developed certain mysterious powers which first fascinated and then obsessed him. Among these phenomena was that of passing into trance. "Throwing himself back into an easy-chair, and closing his eyes, M. gave one or two gasps and twists, and then passed into a quiet trance-like state. The next moment, however, his eyes partially re-opened, a violent contortion shook his frame, and his features, undergoing a strange and startling metamorphosis, assumed those of an old man of a most crafty and cunning type. A rasping voice and a defective enunciation suggesting a toothless mouth, poured forth a stream of the most horrible and unheard-of blasphemies." Here we have a case of diabolic ecstasy immediately succeeded by possession. Father Stanislaus M. Hogan, O.P., who has deeply investigated the subject says [22]: "The methods used by Spiritists are pretty well known to most persons. There is a darkened room, and a medium . . . the medium goes *into a trance or hypnotic sleep*."

There exists, indeed, a particular class of mediums known as "trance-mediums". The records of Spiritism give dozens, one may without exaggeration write hundreds of typical and uncontested instances. J. Godfrey Raupert in his *Christ and the Powers of Darkness* [23] very clearly explains that there is a certain receptivity of mind which is intimately connected with the spiritual life, and which (in a sense) co-operates with God so that the Christian is uplifted and led to the consideration and contemplation of divine things. This is an active and definite operation of the will, the co-operation of the human will with God's will, and this in its higher stages leads to Ecstasy, and ultimately, if persevered in along the right lines, to Sanctity itself.

But there is an *Unlawful Mental Passivity*, the abandonment of reason and self-control. This is a complete and ignorant surrender of the will to unknown forces and intelligences, and this terminates in that loss of consciousness, which travesties and in every particular imitates (or endeavours to imitate) the Ecstasy of the Saints.

How are we to differentiate in the first place? The answer has been divinely given. "Ye shall know them by their fruits. Every good tree bringeth forth good fruit; but a corrupt tree bringeth forth evil fruit," St. Matthew, vii, 16, 17.

Yet there are difficulties and complexities, and great caution must be exercised, since, we are warned, "false Christs and false prophets shall rise, and shall show signs and wonders to seduce, if it were possible, even the elect", St. Mark, xiii, 22. Among the manifest evidences of diabolical ecstasy the following may be named. Should the person who is rapt be of notoriously evil life, holding false and impious opinions, or should the subject falling into ecstasy be engaged upon some wickedness, such as foul necromancy, then it is a diabolic trance. Again, should the individual whilst in ecstasy, make any obscene exhibition or lewd movements, that state is clearly diabolical. Under the same heading come those distortions of the limbs, the hideous grimacing and writhing features, with foaming and frothing at the mouth, which are so frequently observed in spiritistic mediums. Gravina, Cardinal Tomaso de Vio Gaetani, the Carmelite Thomas of Jesus, and indeed all mystical theologians maintain this opinion. Moreover if the person "under control" in the trance talks very rapidly and incoherently, babbling and stuttering, and if blasphemies or if ribald and filthy words are spewed forth, then unquestionably it is a satanical ecstasy.

In his study *The Dangers of Spiritualism* (pp. 157–8) J. Godfrey Raupert relates the pitiful case of a Noncomformist minister who began quite innocently and unknowingly to dabble with occultism, automatic writing and the rest. For a few weeks the communications were very pure and beautiful. Then they became mixed with unclean language. He at once tried to break away from the influence which was overcoming him, but too late. In trance he was haunted with the foulest language and suggestions. The ecstasies so exhausted and wore him down that the end was death in the saddest circumstances. Benedict XIV observed that if these ecstasies are trafficked for money, or exhibited before a number of people convened for that purpose, in modern parlance "a circle", they are undoubtedly of infernal origin. St. John of the Cross so keenly appreciated the danger of ecstasy, unless it be certainly from God, that he refrained from desiring it. In the Life of *Mother Frances of the Mother of God* we read that at her urgent prayer Our Lord, strengthened her so that she was able to bear these divine operations without any phenomena appearing visibly.

The true receptive attitude towards God brings joy, tranquillity, peace of mind, interior happiness and calm. There is a burning desire to draw nearer to Christ, a growing devotion to His Mother, a submission to God's will, and all these show themselves in the daily round. There is a distaste for, an abhorrence of, any feverish excitement. The relations with those persons who have to be dealt with in the way of friendship, acquaintanceship, business, are characterized by a new kindliness, which incidentally need not be divorced from firmness, as justice may require. The moral fibre is strengthened.

The effects of unregulated and unlawful psychic passivity are soon apparent. There begins a curious inexplicable restlessness of mind; an inability to concentrate shows itself; a seemingly unfounded apprehension supervenes; the psychic sickness manifests itself in irregular motions of the limbs. There is a morbid craving for continual excitement. There are frequently pains in the head which can only be eased by giving way to an intermittent inertia, abandoning oneself to the seizures, for such and nothing else are these ecstasies and trances of spiritism. Religion in any true sense of the word becomes detestable, Prayer, the Sacraments, the view (much more the touch) of Holy Relics, cause actual repugnance and are shunned. Nay, further they are mocked, often with obscene blasphemy. Health and happiness are destroyed. In many cases, not traceable to the pitiable effects of heredity, dipsomania develops. It is not necessary to dwell upon the complete moral deterioration of many of these unfortunates [24].

It is a sad and sickening subject, but so much—and I have understated rather than emphasized the fact—it is essential to record. The conclusion is inevitable, and humanly speaking, proven [25]. Except when there are impostures and fraud [26], and the frequency of such charlatancy, trickery often carried through with the most consummate cunning, is notorious, spiritistic trances cannot but be held to be diabolical. The Ecstasies of sanctity they certainly are not; neither can they be supposed to be natural rapture. One category alone is left.

It is a relief to turn from these fearfully dark and sordid businesses to the consideration of those states which are known as "natural ecstasy", perhaps not entirely a happy nomenclature, but one in traditional use and generally accepted, and sanctioned by the great authority of Benedict XIV.

St. Thomas says that ecstasy is an abstraction which arises from one of three causes, from a physical cause, which is natural ecstasy; from the working of Satan, which is diabolic ecstasy; from the supreme power of God, which is Divine Ecstasy, and, as I understand it, true Ecstasy in the real sense of the word.

The learned Pope tells us that a natural ecstasy results from natural causes, whereas Catalepsy (or Catochus, Catoche, as the disease was called) is in some sense a natural ecstasy, since persons seized thereby are deprived of all movement, and there is a total suspension of any sensation or consciousness.

Paolo Zacchia, who was physician to Innocent X, makes a very important point in reference to natural ecstasy. He tells us that it is never accompanied by levitation, "for it is altogether contrary to nature for a body to be raised up of its own strength, and be supported in the air" [27]. Benedict XIV observes that a natural ecstasy is followed by a certain weariness and fatigue. Zacchia writes of this in detail, and says that if heaviness of the limbs, torpor, a mental sluggishness, a paleness of the face, which may be drawn and sad, and depression generally, are the after effects of the ecstasy, it is certainly natural. Consalvo Durante confirms this opinion when he writes [28] that the body of a holy person, who is rapt away to the contemplation of divine mysteries, is not (as might be surmised) on his coming to himself left weak and languid, but that on the contrary the ecstatic is refreshed and invigorated.

Girolamo Cardano, the celebrated philosopher and physician [29], who was born at Pavia, 1501, and died at Rome in 1576, in his great folio *De rerum varietate libri xvii*, published at Basle, 1557, relates that he was of his own volition able to induce a natural ecstasy, and in that state was insensible to any pain, even the agony of an intense attack of gout, nor did he in the slightest feel blows and stripes, with whatever force and how roughly he might be cudgelled and batooned. Benedict XIV ascribes this to a particularly unusual organization of his nervous system and the membranes.

Cardano discusses *natural ecstasy* in his *Somniorum Synesiorum . . . libri quatuor*, Basle, 1562, Book ii, cap. 8, a passage which may haply be given in the old-world paraphrase of John Aubrey's *Miscellanies* [30]. "Men fall into an Ecstasy many ways, either by a syncope, by a vanishing and absence of the spirits, or else by the withdrawing of every external sense without any other cause. It most commonly happens to those who are over solicitous or fix their whole minds upon doing any one particular thing. An Ecstasy is a kind of medium between sleeping and waking, as sleep is a kind of middle state between life and death. Things seen in an Ecstasy are more certain than those we behold in dreams; they are much more clear, and far more evident. Those seized with a (natural) Ecstasy can hear, those who sleep cannot." Aubrey then gives three instances, of which one (at least) supposed to have befallen the Archbishop of Armagh, Dr. Usher (1586–1656) is not admissible, as Aubrey himself allows. Another of his examples runs as follows: "'Tis certain, there was one in the Strand, who lay in a trance a few hours before he departed. And in his trance he had a vision of the death of King Charles II. It was at the very day of his apoplectick fit," 3rd February, 1685. The King died on the following 6th February.

It must be borne in mind that, however interesting, these are only rough notes made by Aubrey, and except in the case of the Saints, when the evidence has been sifted, re-sifted, and sifted again, any death-bed phenomena require the most scrupulously careful investigation. They are, for our purpose, alien to the point at issue.

A certain school, rather audaciously, denies the existence of natural ecstasy, but all authority is against them. Contemporary psychology, also, accepts the ruling of St. Thomas, which is in itself of ample weight and hardly open to discussion: *Intensa meditatio unius abstrahit ab aliis* [*31*]. When we further find that scientific inquirers such as were Cardano and Zacchia, who have the approval of Benedict XIV, and mystical theologians such as Dom Dominic Schram, O.S.B. (1658–1720), that great authority, Cardinal Brancati di Lauraea, and Fr. Rolli *La magie moderne*; to mention no more, are agreed that there is a state which is commonly called "natural ecstasy" the denial of this condition by Père Poulain, S.J., and the Olivetan Dom Maréchaux, is more than a little startling, not to say temerarious. It may be true that the instances cited are few, but some at least are of themselves amply convincing. Nobody would venture to assert that because a certain state is but seldom recorded, it does not exist.

Moreover there have no doubt been many examples which were not noticed. "If human nature truly possessed this power, we should not be reduced to a mere three or four anecdotes during centuries. . . . In the course of the last two or three hundred years Europe has been filled with scholars of the first order who have plunged into deepest meditation and concentration of thought over metaphysical and mathematical problems. Not once have they been observed in an attitude of ecstasy with the eyes fixed, the arms extended towards the theorem upon which they were so completely engaged. No ecstasy is cited in the cases of Newton, Leibnitz, or Euler, or Lagrange, Laplace, and so on" [*32*]. These statements of Père Poulain are hardly correct, and his argument—if argument it can be called—is nugatory.

There is no writer who treats more clearly and more concisely of natural ecstasy than Dom Schram [*33*], who says that (as we have already seen) it certainly must proceed from natural causes, it may be from sickness, or from an unusually intensive concentration of the imaginative and mental faculties. He cites many examples, for instance that personally known to St. Augustine [*34*] of the priest Restitutus, who when he pleased could entirely abstract himself from and (as it were) divest himself of his senses, falling prone, as if dead, in which state he did not flinch or move if he were knocked about and buffeted soundly, nor yet if he were pinched and pricked even to blood, no, not even if his flesh were scorched with fire. Whilst rapt in his self-induced trance he was conscious of nothing—save that sometimes (he said) if those present bawled and shouted in his ear he heard a faint far-off whisper—but when he returned to himself he at once felt the ache and pain of the contusion or injury. St. François de Sales in his *Traicté de l'Amour de Dieu*, Paris, 1647, vii, 6, expressly states: "Certain philosophers and profound scholars by intensive mental concentration have been rapt in ecstasy, which is a natural ecstasy."

Dom Schram lists eight signs which denote that this preternormal state is a natural ecstasy. It may, then (1), be the consequence of some disease of debility. (2) If the natural ecstasy recurs at fixed and regular intervals. (3) If after the ecstasy, the subject (as Zacchia remarks) is found to be weak and suffering pain. (4) If the mind appears confused, and the subject is bewildered and perplexed. (6) If the ecstasy originates from concentration upon some thing not of the divine order, but of the earth, earthly. (7) Natural ecstasy may be induced by an extremity of fear. (8) In certain cases music will produce a form of rapture, which is natural ecstasy. So Cassiodorus (*c.* 480–575) in his *Variarum* (*Miscellanies*), II, 5, and the learned Dom Augustin Calomet (1672–1757) in his treatise upon Ancient Music, are agreed. To these signs we may add that the ecstasy is natural if it can be self-induced, as auto-hypnotism; and if there is no levitation during the trance.

As has just been remarked, St. François de Sales makes mention of philosophers and profound scholars who have been rapt in natural ecstasy. Benedict XIV cites the case of Plato who was sometimes so immersed in metaphysical speculations as to lose the use of his senses. Socrates, also, as is related in the famous passage of the *Symposium*, whilst in the besieged camp at Potidaea, remained standing and entirely without external sense or movement, forgetting either to eat or drink for the space of twenty-four hours, absorbed in deepest meditation.

With regard to Archimedes of Syracuse, the greatest mathematician and engineer of antiquity, who when he had solved the true principle of the equilibrium between the weight of a floating body, and the hydro-static pressure of the liquid wherein it swims, in a transport leaped from the bath and, oblivious of all else, rushed naked through the streets of the city, crying aloud *Eureka* (*I have found the answer to the problem*), this might indeed be a natural ecstasy, and so some authorities account it, but Mgr. Farges favours the view that it was an extraordinary distraction. Again, when Syracuse was captured by Marcellus in 212 B.C., the Roman soldiers bursting into his library found him seated in meditation upon some profound problem and when the sword passed through his body his only cry was: "Do not disturb the circles traced upon the ground." The aged scholar may well have been in a natural ecstasy, but the truth is we lack the precise data to pronounce upon the phenomenon. It would be necessary to inquire into such concomitants of natural ecstasy as anæsthesia, muscular rigidity, analgesia, and the like.

William Tocco, prior of Benevento, who had been personally acquainted with the Saint, tells us of the natural ecstasies of the Angelic Doctor. One instance is very widely known. Upon a certain occasion when, as obedience compelled him, he was seated at a royal banquet where King Louis IX of France and the Queen entertained a number of their highest nobles and eminent men, it was observed that he was lost to all around. The Dominican Prior, his neighbour, plucked him sharply by the sleeve to recall him to himself. All was in vain, until suddenly with a mighty blow of his fist on the board which made the golden goblets and the trenchers jump and ring again, he cried out in his sonorous voice that echoed through the hall, "Yes; that is a conclusive argument utterly refuting the Manichees." The Saint had been rapt away, seeing and hearing nothing round him, threading the logical intricacies of some clinching redargution to confound the foul sophistries of the Vaudois and Cathari. Good Father Prior rebuked him, bidding him remember the presence, and St. Thomas in his humility seemed abashed. Not so King Louis, who with a kindly smile, bade one of his secretaries at once write down what was in the Saint's mind lest by any chance so brilliant and convincing a train of thought with its conclusion be lost. Further, Baltellus relates, how once when St. Thomas was absorbed in reflection on the mystery of the Holy Trinity, the lighted candle which he held in his hand burned down and was consumed, scorching his fingers without his perceiving it.

Again, in the year 1272, when he had come back to the convent at Naples, St. Thomas was one day bidden to betake himself to the cloister, where two great prelates, the Cardinal Legate of Sicily and the Archbishop of Capua, had arrived to consult with him on urgent business. The holy Doctor at once descended the stairs, but to the surprise of the Cardinal and Archbishop he passed them by, his gaze fixed and intent, his face aglow with joy. They caught, however, the murmur: "That, and none other must be the solution." The Archbishop followed, and pulled him by the sleeve, upon which the Saint came to himself, and returned with many apologies to the distinguished visitors, for he was the soul of courtesy. "I have just hit upon the solution of a very nice and much-debated theological point," he said.

These then were natural ecstasies, but St. Thomas was more often caught away and rapt in divine Ecstasy.

What is Divine Ecstasy? Álvarez furnishes us with a dictionary definition: "Divine Ecstasy is the complete and entire Uplift of the mind and spirit to God, which is necessarily accompanied by a total abstraction from consciousness and the bodily senses, an inevitable and essential concomitant circumstance of the overwhelming force and power of this very Uplifting" [35].

Schram draws attention to several sublime accidents which are frequently, but not always experienced by ecstatics. Such, for example, are levitation, inedia, radiating light, and in some cases the impression of the stigmata, with other celestial phenomena. He also gives various signs whereby the Ecstasy may be recognized to be Divine. Only persons of a very holy life and advanced in mysticism are the subjects of such Ecstasies during which they contemplate the things of heaven and, it may be, that there are made to them from God Revelations, which they

PLATE IV: SOR PATRGINIO
From a contemporary print, 1868

remember and oftentimes divulge. Not unseldom the ecstatic, whilst caught up to the third Heaven, will speak of paradisial mysteries, inflaming the hearts of all present, if bystanders there be, with the love of God, and, as it were, drawing them sweetly towards Him. A Divine Ecstasy very often enraptures the ecstatic during prayer, and especially after receiving Holy Communion. The effect of a Divine Ecstasy results in an increase of holiness and a greater desire for God.

Cardinal Bona [36] and the Venerable Thomas of Jesus [37] hold that (for the most part) Divine Ecstasy is of no long endurance. The Carmelite, Philip of the Trinity [38], goes so far as to say that it lasts seldom, if ever, above an hour. But, in seeming disagreement with the ruling of these great masters of the mystical life, there are recorded many instances of prolonged Divine Ecstasies, as we shall see below in their place.

This circumstance is not so contradictory as it may appear. These mystical theologians were speaking only of the height or culm of the "Great Ecstasy", and so Benedict XIV clearly understands them. Indeed it can be interpreted in no other way.

St. Teresa [39] says that the soul seeking God experiences an infinitely sweet but almost over-powering joy so that it falls into a kind of heavenly swoon, which is of such profundity that the living frame is deprived of breath, and all bodily forces fail. It is true that at the beginning this state only lasts a very little time. "If it lasts for a full half-hour, it is ample. At any rate so it seems to me. Myself, I have never experienced it for so long a while as that." And yet the Saint who wrote these words, "St Teresa herself died after fourteen hours of ecstasy" [40].

Benedict XIV very clearly and concisely sums up thus: "The signs of a Divine Ecstasy are principally to be derived from his conduct who is subject to them. A Divine Ecstasy takes place with the greatest tranquillity of the whole man, who is placid and calm, both exteriorly and interiorly. He who is rapt in a divine ecstasy speaks only of heavenly things, which mightily move the bystanders to the love of God; on returning to himself he appears humble, and even, as it were, daunted and abashed. Overflowing with heavenly delights and consolations, his face is cheerful and glad, whilst in his heart there is ineffable peace and security. He is far from relishing the presence of bystanders, since he fears he may haply acquire the reputation of sanctity. Most generally, whilst he is praying fervently, or assisting at Mass, or after he has received Holy Communion he falls into an ecstasy or sublime trance." Martin Delrio [41] speaks of a certain servant of God, who in the year 1585 dwelt at Burgos, a town of Castile, and who after receiving the Blessed Sacrament was straightway rapt into an ecstasy. Upon returning to herself, overcome with shame and confusion, she would hurry quickly away from the church, and when she had returned home, she was wont to retire for a good while to her chamber. The learned Scacchus relates the same thing of St. Catharine of Siena.

In his Life of St. Peter of Alcàntara, the Franciscan ascetic of the Discalced Reform [42], Father Francesco Marchese, an Oratorian, who incorporated in his work [43] much material from the processes of canonization, after speaking of the Divine Ecstasies and Raptures which the Saint was wont to experience whilst saying Mass, continues: "When, after he had finished his Mass, he unvested, the Saint at once left the sacristy and without any delay returned to his cell. It was noticed, too, that although usually he walked in a very quiet and grave manner, nevertheless, at these times, he hastened along in a remarkable way, not unseldom breaking into a run, swift as the wind, in order that he might reach his cell as quickly as possible, and close the door. His profound humility would not suffer him to divulge what extraordinary favours and graces Heaven was pleased to bestow upon him in this retirement. None the less the friars heard deep sighs and, as it were, a sweet plaint with sharp cries he was unable to suppress. So the religious were very certain that at these moments he was visited by Our Lord in some extraordinary manner." This, as we shall note later, was Rapture.

To learn something of the more pregnant details of Divine Ecstasy we must turn to the pages written by that great Mistress of the Spiritual Life, St. Teresa of Ávila, whose descriptive powers and psychological insight are of the very highest order, and whose autobiography, the *Vida* "covers her outward and inward life . . . (so) that no one can be said to know her who is not familiar with it" [44]. And not to know St. Teresa is to be ignorant of mysticism.

The latest Spanish editor of St. Teresa's *Works*, P. Silverio de Santa Teresa, frankly considered the *Vida* her masterpiece. Ribot writes [45]: "The autobiography of St. Teresa may inspire us with full confidence. It is a confession made by order of her spiritual director, it is the work of an acutely sensitive and receptive mind very gifted in observation, knowing precisely the use of languages to express the finest shades of her meaning."

Divine Ecstasy consists of two states [46], which are to be entirely differentiated, and yet which are essentially united and confixed. The one state is psychological and interior, but wholly of the supernatural order. This is the uplift of the soul to God, a most powerful, active, and transcendent emotion, when the soul (so far as is possible) sees God, holds converse with Him, and learns from Him the arcana of heavenly mysteries. This, the essential element cannot in itself be ocularly perceived, but it is none the less invariably manifested, and exhibits itself in the phenomena of the second state, the physical state [47], which produces a complete alienation of the senses, muscular rigidity, and is very often the occasion of other extraordinary mirables and prodigia.

It is an error to suppose that mystical writers have given the name Ecstasy exclusively to this second state, which is indeed an inseparable concomitant of the spiritual rapture, wherein the soul has found God. In speaking of Divine Ecstasy we always postulate and presuppose the first state.

In the *Vida* St. Teresa describes the Fourth Degree of prayer, Divine Ecstasy. The soul is "fainting almost completely away, in a kind of swoon, with an exceedingly great and sweet delight". "The soul feels close to God and . . . there abides within it such a certainty that it cannot do other than believe." "I could not cease believing that He was there, for it seemed almost certain that I had been conscious of His very presence. Unlearned persons would tell me that he was there only by grace; but I could not believe that, for, as I say, He seemed to me to be really present; and so I continued to be greatly distressed. From this doubt I was freed by a very learned man [*48*] of the Order of the glorious Saint Dominic: he told me that He was indeed present and described how He communicated Himself to us, which brought me very great comfort" [*49*].

In *The Interior Castle*, a later work, St. Teresa treats of Ecstasy in even ampler detail. First we must recall St. Teresa's love of water, limpid crystal streams, "unpathed waters, undreamed shores", "waters at their priest-like task" [*50*], that "river of God which is full of water"; above all, draughts from that "well of water springing up into everlasting life", and says the Saint "I cannot find anything more apt for the explanation of certain spiritual things than this element of water". Expanding this metaphor of water, she writes: "But now the great God, who controls the sources of the waters and forbids the sea to move beyond its bounds, has loosed the sources whence water has been coming into this basin; and with tremendous force there rises up so powerful a wave that this little ship—our soul—is lifted up on high. And if a ship can do nothing, and neither the pilot nor any one of the crew has any power over it, when the waves make a furious assault upon it and toss it about at their will, even less able is the interior part of the soul to stop and stay still where it likes, while its senses and faculties can do no more than has been commanded them" [*51*].

God, the Divine Being, the Ultimate Reality, is the supreme object of interior Divine Ecstasy. But the matter is complex. It does not end here. It is true that some mystics, such, for example, as the marvellous St. Maria Maddalena de' Pazzi, had a direct perception of the Ancient of Days. Yet the supreme object of Divine Ecstasy is also Christ our Lord, and it is an abominable heresy, a most black and damnable error to attempt to separate the Divinity and the Sacred Humanity of Jesus Christ [*52*]. The Beghars and Michael Molinos essayed to do this with very subtile snake-like casuistry. So perfidious a fallacy was expressly condemned by the Venerable Innocent XI in his bull *Coelestis Pater*, which was signed 20th November, 1687; and again by that holiest of popes, his successor, Alexander VIII (1689–91), who is aptly described by Bernino [*53*] as "an Angel in looks, in speech an Apostle".

The contemplation of Our Divine Lord, of His Sacred Heart as so wonderfully revealed to St. Margaret Mary Alacoque, the Precious Blood, His holy Wounds, His adorable Face, all these have enraptured mystics of the highest order.

The Seraphic Mother, St. Catharine of Siena, had a particular devotion to the Precious Blood. In fact she has been termed the Prophetess of the Precious Blood, and she singled out this devotion with a more than ordinary predilection. The mere thought of blood, as she remembered the

Blood which stained the Cross on Calvary, would throw her into a Divine Ecstasy. In all hagiography, in all the Lives of all the Saints there are few episodes more striking and none more profoundly moving than that when she comforted and was present at the execution of the young gallant of Perugia, Niccolò Tuldo—the lad was only about eighteen—who was cruelly and so unjustly condemned to death [*54*]. All the world lay fair and smiling before him; there promised a high and noble career. St. Catharine accompanied him to the scaffold. "Stay with me, and leave me not," he had pleaded, "Then all will be well with me, and I shall die content" [*55*]. Whereupon, says the Saint, "I felt the sweet fragrance of his blood, and it was a fragrance blended with the odour of my own blood, which I have so often longed to shed for the sake of Jesus, my loved one, my spouse." They prayed to the Madonna, and to the Virgin Martyr, St. Catharine of Alexandria. "Remember, dear brother mine, the Blood of the Lamb," she murmured. The axe fell. Catharine at the moment saw his soul in the realms of heavenly bliss. In ecstasy she saw Christ her Spouse radiant as the golden sun. In her hands she held the youth's severed head. Her dress was saturated and soaked with his hot streaming blood. And so she passed on her way, still in Ecstasy. "My soul," she says, "was so filled with gentle peace and a calm not of this world, so fragrant was the odour of blood, that I could not bear to wash off the blood which incarnadined my habit and crimsoned my hands." In her own Oratory, to which she had retired, she fell into Ecstasy after Ecstasy. In some mystic way she was bathed in the Blood of Christ, whose love so exhausted and refreshed her that she could only sigh: "O Blood! O burning fire! O Love ineffable! O blood!"

There is no profounder mistress of the depths of the spiritual life than the Seraphic Mother, Catharine of Siena, who stands with Teresa of Ávila, and some few more, higher than the very heights of heaven.

Another Dominicaness, Blessed Osanna of Mantua, fell into an Ecstasy at the sight of blood, so intense was her devotion to the Mystery of the Precious Blood, since anything which reminded her of the Blood of Christ threw the Beata into a trance of love, wherein her soul was utterly submerged and immersed, and she vaguely describes herself as bathed in a great light and elevated to union with God. Human language failed when she attempted to relate these supernatural experiences. Moreover she was extremely anxious to keep these phenomena secret, and when, in spite of her efforts, the rapture descended upon her whilst others were present she was, on returning to herself covered with confusion and shame. In her Spiritual Letters she addresses the monk Girolamo da Monte Oliveto as "my dear son born to me in the Blood of Our Lord" and she tells him how in a celestial radiance far outshining Sol at hottest noon she saw and mystically perceived the Father, the Son, and the Holy Ghost, and how also a celestial voice spoke to her saying: "My daughter, leave the father who begat and the mother who bore thee. Come unto Me, beloved child. I am thy Heavenly Father, Eternal God, and thy mother is the most Blessed Virgin Mary." She also beheld a vision of Christ, covered with wounds and carrying His Cross under the weight of which He tottered, about to fall prone, so faint and weary was He. The sight of His Blood, as it were, intoxicated her, and pressing her lips to the Wound in His Side, where the lance had pierced, she drank and was inebriated with the Precious Blood [56].

I have as an example selected this one aspect of Our Lord's Humanity, the Precious Blood, to show that the contemplation of such subjects may be the culm of Divine Ecstasy. It would be easy, but superfluous, to enlarge upon this, to show that the Blessed Sacrament; the Holy Infancy; the hidden mystery of the Thirty-Three Years, so honoured by Blessed Michael of Florence, the Camaldolese; by the Carmelite lay-sister of Dôle, Anne of the Cross; by Mother Louisa of Jesus; and other saintly souls; and many more Mysteries can uplift to the highest Ecstasy.

One of the most extraordinary of mystics St. Joseph of Copertino [57], fell into Ecstasy upon hearing the Holy Name of Mary, to which Name the Trinitarian Blessed Simon de Roxas [58] also had a burning devotion, which often threw him into a Divine Ecstasy. Similarly, the Passionist [59], St. Gabriel of the Sorrowful Virgin, was enraptured when he meditated upon the Dolours and Joys of Mary.

In the *Life of St. Benedict Joseph Labre* (beatified by Pius IX, 20th May, 1860; canonized by Leo XIII, 8th December, 1881) by Don Antonio Maria Coltrano, a priest of Rome, which was published by Galomini, Rome, 1807, there is a striking passage, Part III, Chapter 9, in reference to the Ecstasies of this great Saint. "If his sublime and rapturous contemplations show clearly the interior fire of love, which consumed the burning heart of Benedict Joseph, the Ecstasies wherewith he was from time to time favoured by Almighty God, yet more clearly make it manifest, for St. Thomas says that nothing can cause Divine Ecstasy in man, save only Love: "Divine Love is the direct cause of Divine Ecstasy." Now, Ecstasy, as this state is commonly defined by mystical theologians, is a total and entire suspension of the senses, caused by a very lively apprehension of the greatness of God and of the overwhelming force of His Love, and this with so much sweetness and calm that there is nothing in it of that violence which is the peculiar property of Rapture. Such Divine Ecstasies were very common with St. Benedict Joseph, and they were mistaken by the ignorant and ordinary folk for bodily diseases, fainting fits and physical seizures, arising from nothing other than his extraordinary abstinence, the weakness of the stomach from which he suffered, and the like. This need not surprise us in the least, for not unseldom many persons striving to lead spiritual lives and devoted to God have fallen into this error.

The Ecstasies with which God favoured His beloved servant, the Venerable Sister Gertrude Salandri, were taken to be sickness and fits of epilepsy. Thus, when, before the foundation of the monastery of Valentano, she was staying at the Convent of St. Catharine in Viterbo, she suddenly passed into Ecstasy and seemed like a dead person. The good nuns, confused and amazed, hastily called in a skilful physician, who on examining her proved to be just as mistaken. It was thought proper, however, to resort to drastic remedies, blisters and cautery.

Sister Gertrude remained insensible to everything. After several hours she came out of her Ecstasy, and when the nuns asked how she felt, she tenderly replied: "I have no pain whatsoever save what you caused me whilst I was entranced. You have hurt me very sorely, but let that pass, let it be for the love of God."

St. Benedict Joseph had sometimes scarcely begun to pray before Heaven overwhelmed him with a most sweet Ecstasy. He was absorbed in God, and, as in Ecstasy the senses are lost and have no power to perform their natural functions, the ecstatic is insensible to the effects of fire or iron when employed to arouse him. Thus St. Benedict Joseph was utterly unconscious of all, and some, quite misunderstanding, shook and struck him very roughly, but all to no purpose. At Loreto, as Father Temple judged, he was overwhelmed by Rapture. A priest also saw him carried away in Rapture in Santa Maria sopra Minerva, when the Saint uttered sobs and sighs and tore open his ragged coat at the breast to assuage the fiery flame within. A Professor of Dogma at the Roman College, when meditating in the Church of San Ignazio, piazza San Ignazio, Rome, saw St. Benedict Joseph pass into a Rapture with extraordinary concomitant phenomena.

St. Benedict Joseph Labre was a Frenchman, being born at Amettes, near Boulogne, on 26th March, 1748, and died at Rome on 16th April, 1783.

It should, incidentally, be said here that, as the learned Matthaeucci [60] observes, Divine Ecstasy with concomitant phenomena, is one of God's gifts *gratia datae* (as the theologians have it), that is to say it is granted by God to whom He will, when He wills, and as He pleases. There are many holy persons, and canonized Saints even, who do not experience the rapture of Ecstasy, and who are none the less holy because of that. Yet we must always bear in mind that Ecstasy is a surpassing great Gift. Divine Ecstasy although not regarded as a proof, is assuredly a sign of remarkable sanctity.

Benedict XIV lays down that "The character of the ecstasy being ascertained, yet of itself, although divine and proceeding from God, it does not avail to prove sanctity, implicitly, for it neither sanctifies, nor is it a necessary effect of sanctifying grace, being a grace *gratis data* wherefore, in order that it may be taken into account in the official process of Beatification and Canonization, it is necessary to prove that the ecstatic was endowed with heroic virtues; for then it will be a Sign of sanctity and of the ecstatic's love of God, and on the other hand of God' love to him. . . . These Divine Ecstasies are for the most part not granted to every one of the faithful, nor to those of ordinary spiritual attainments, but only to the perfect and established in the spiritual life, and so to those who are remarkable for virtues and especially for their charity. . . . Divine Ecstasies, therefore, accompanied with heroic virtues, in causes of Beatification and Canonization, though not directly (as the Schoolmen's phrase runs), yet indirectly furnish some very weighty evidence of sanctity" [61].

As the same learned Pope says, not only many Martyrs but a large number of other Saints have been raised to the Altar without their having been endowed with any mystical gifts from God or having trod the extraordinary and phenomenal paths of holiness. "Numberless souls," writes Sandreau, "do arrive at perfection, and consequently the unitive way, without receiving such sublime favours. Hence it is necessary to conclude that there is a unitive or perfect way without contemplation (Divine Ecstasy). Wherefore some bifurcation at a certain point must be admitted. This is strictly logical, but it hardly accords with traditional doctrine" [*62*]. We may conclude, then, relying upon the authority of Benedict XIV that it is in some circumstances possible, but in fact excessively rare and altogether unusual.

Does a Divine Ecstasy differ from a Divine Rapture, and, if so, in what particulars? St. Thomas teaches us that Rapture is accidentally more than Ecstasy, since Rapture is accompanied by a certain degree of violence, the onrush of the Divine. The Saint writes [*63*]: "Rapture involves something more than Ecstasy, for Ecstasy precisely speaking implies a transport out of and beyond oneself, so that a man is removed from his normal well-ordered condition, but Rapture entails something of violence" [*64*].

The Cistercian Cardinal Bona (1609–74) in his great work *De Discretione Spirituum* (*On the Discerning of Spirits*), c. xiv; n.2; very amply discusses the matter. "This, then," he says, "is the essential difference between Ecstasy and Rapture. The former estate withdraws the mind from the senses more gently and (as it were) persuasively. The latter more powerfully and not without violence of a kind, so that Rapture adds this to Ecstasy, namely it catches up the resistless soul with power and might, most rapidly and by divine compulsion sweeping upwards and onwards away from the senses and all things appertaining, so that it is swiftly carried and borne aloft to the enjoyment of the intellectual vision and aflame with the ardent love of heavenly things."

Many mystical theologians conceive that there cannot be rapture without the manifestation of extraordinary phenomena. Cardinal Brancati holds this opinion.

None the less the learned Cardinal allows that Ecstasy and Rapture are terms used indiscriminately, and Consalvi Durante quite plainly writes: "We may take it as very certain that mystical theologians sometimes apply the words Ecstasy, Transport, and Rapture to the same state, and that even in the Holy Scriptures they are similarly employed." I find that in the French translation (1650) of the Works of St. Teresa the words *Evanoüissement* and *Ravissement* are regarded as identical.

Bearing in mind what St. Thomas says, it is yet allowable, then, yet not very precisely accordingly to the Mystical Doctors, to use Ecstasy, Transport, Trance, Rapture, without the nice (yet actual) distinction being made. A Rapture cannot be resisted, no, not for a moment, even if the ecstatic be in company with others, or in a public place. It overwhelms and overpowers. Thus in the case of Teresa Helena Higginson (1844–1905), this Spouse of the Crucified, whilst living at 15 Ariel Street, Bottle, that insignificant little two-storeyed house in an absolutely commonplace rather drab row, where she had lodgings with the Misses Catterall, her fellow-teachers at St. Alexander's School, the rapture would descend upon and overwhelm her. At first the Misses Catterall were, not unnaturally, alarmed, and tried to rouse her by bumping her pretty forcibly in her chair all round the room, but it was absolutely useless. After a while they recognized the supernatural, and ceased to notice her condition, merely remarking to one another: "Teresa has popped off again."

Of St. Miguel de Santos, the glory of the Discalcead Trinitarians, we are told in his Proper Office *crebis et mirificis rapiebatur extasibus*, "he was very frequently caught up in Raptures and altogether phenomenal Ecstasies" (Matins, Lectis vi). When he fell into rapture, often during prayer, he ran through the cloisters at wonderful speed uttering loud cries of joy, and darting hither and thither with such celerity that nobody could stay him.

In the Bull of Canonization of St. Maria Maddalena de' Pazzi it is related how when the rapture overwhelmed her she rushed to and fro, up and down the stairs and along the corridors, through the nuns' garth, with inconceivable rapidity, often tearing her habit in her haste, and throwing to one side anything which came in her way.

These Saints, sublimest mystics both, were literally inebriated with God.

"A Divine Ecstasy," says Benedict XIV, "takes place with the greatest tranquillity of the whole ecstatic, both outwardly and inwardly." The same circumstances accompany a Divine Trance.

Gianbattista Scaramelli in his great work *Il Direttorio Mistico* says that there is Ecstasy properly so called, and Rapture. Ecstasy is truly the Mystical Union of Love in so far as the soul is transported without any violence but even with a certain tranquillity. The distinguishing feature of Rapture is that there is always some element of suddenness, of surprise and violence. He further divides Rapture into three classes: those Raptures in which the exterior senses are suspended, whilst the interior senses are retained, which is not strictly speaking a Rapture at all, yet is (as it were) a promise of Rapture to come. There are, secondly, the Raptures in which both exterior and interior senses are suspended, which Scaramelli terms "Perfect Raptures", and of these, the third degree (or class) of Rapture is the highest point of Rapture when both exterior and interior senses are suspended in the contemplation of the Beatific Vision. Scaramelli judges that this third Rapture, which is, so to speak, an extension of Perfect Rapture is rarely experienced during life. But, since we know that in Heaven, Christ still bears the marks of his Wounds, we must not separate the Humanity of Christ from the Divinity of Christ, or we shall fall into peril, nay, into the pit. Nor must we separate the Humanity of Christ from the source whence He derived it, Mary. These are very deep matters, and scrupulous care is needed.

Scaramelli gives his opinion that a state of Rapture may last for several hours or even for days, but that there will be fluctuations in its intensity. Which is to say that Rapture must and will ebb back to Ecstasy. At its highest point Rapture (he says) will scarcely exceed half-an-hour, which seems to be consonant with what St. Teresa writes.

It were best, it appears to me, to be more exact and stricter and differentiate in our use of the terms "Ecstasy" and "Rapture", and in so doing we shall be adhering more closely to what St. Thomas says, and more scrupulously following the mind of Benedict XIV. For, the Pontiff writes, "Divine Raptures are not long, but frequently brief, as Cardinal Bona [65] and Thomas a Jesu [66] quite plainly prove". The fact is that the human soul and body are unable (unless, indeed, miraculously sustained) to stand the sweetly violent influx and onrush of the Divine.

So we find that Mgr. Farges—or his English translator—says "Ecstasy lasts but for a few moments, as St. Teresa declares many times" [67]. This is very misleading, and in the next paragraph the statement is at once qualified (not to say contradicted) by more than half-a-dozen examples of Saints whose Ecstasies endured for hours, days and weeks. I have already pointed out that the culm or height of the Great Ecstasy is here spoken of by St. Teresa, as quoted, but even so the learned author of *Mystical Phenomena* does not, so it appears to me, differentiate between Divine Ecstasy and Divine Rapture, the latter of which is inevitably accompanied by extraordinary phenomena, which can be and are remarked by witnesses and bystanders. Such, as we have just observed, occurred, in the cases of St. Miguel de los Santos and St. Maria Maddalena de' Pazzi. With regard to St. Joseph of Copertino Rapture was accompanied by Levitation.

On one occasion, 18th October, 1501, the Venerable Domenica dal Paradiso [68] fell into an Ecstasy, which increased with a violent spasm to Rapture, when she saw the Mother of God attended by St. Gabriel and an Angel, who was (Domenica understood) her own Guardian Angel. At the command of the Madonna the two celestial Spirits conducted Domenica to Heaven, and here by a special privilege of the Mother of Wisdom she was permitted a clear understanding of the Humanity of Our Lord and the Divine Essence. Extraordinary phenomena accompanied this Rapture, which lasted for three hours according to her confessor, Canon Benivieni, who was a witness of these marvels which he communicated to Domenica's later director Fra Francesco de Onesti [69].

Blessed Osanna of Mantua during one Lent fell into an Ecstasy which lasted three days; and, once, after having received Holy Communion on Ascension Thursday she was rapt into Ecstasy for forty-eight hours. In his mystical Prologue to the Life of Saint Mary of Oignies [70], Cardinal Jacques de Vitriaco [71], speaks of the great sanctity of many religious women in the diocese of Liège, for the most part, as I take it, Béguines. He says that many "were so carried out of, and beyond, themselves, by their sweetly plentiful draughts of the Holy Ghost, that they passed practically the whole day in an ecstatic silence. So long as His Majesty, the King of Heaven, deigned to repose within them, they had not the least perception of anything that was going on around. So deeply in its profundity did that Peace of God, which passeth all understanding, absorb and encloister their exterior senses, that they could not be aroused by any noise, no, however loud and clanging it might be, nor could they be hurt by any buffet or knock upon their bodies. Even pricking them sharply, again and again, had no effect whatsoever." "I have myself seen," continues the Cardinal, "a religious who frequently fell into Ecstasy, yea, very oft as many as five-and-twenty times in the space of one short day. I have seen her in Rapture more than seven times, and that for a long while together. Whenever the Rapture fell upon her she remained stationary, motionless, and immobile, until she returned to herself. Yet, however unusual a position she was in, however ill-balanced and precarious for the moment, she never tottered nor fell, but was supported most wonderfully by her Guardian Angel. Sometimes if the Rapture overwhelmed her as she was stretching out her hand far, it would remain steadily in that awkward and difficult gesture. And when she came to herself the limb was not stiff and benumbed, but lithe and lissom, nor was she in the least weary, rather she was active and nimble, and her heart was full of great joy."

The Servant of God, Elisabetta Canori Mora, a Tertiary of the Discalced Trinitarians, on 23rd October, 1816, passed into a Rapture, during which she saw the Madonna Who held in Her arms the Infant Jesus. There also appeared St. Joseph; the three Holy Magi; the two Patriarchs of the Trinitarians, St. John de Matha and the royal hermit St. Felix of Valois; together with an infinite host of Angels. The Divine Child placed upon the finger of the ecstatica, whose hand He took in His, a ring brilliant with heavenly jewels. Such were the effects of this Rapture that Elisabetta remained in ecstasy for a full fortnight. In 1823 upon the Feast of the Visitation, 2nd July, Elisabetta fell into a Rapture during which she endured the Mystery of the Transverberation of her Heart, and from that day until her death on 5th February, 1825, her life, whether she was in church, in her little private Oratory, at home, at table, and even in the street, was one long almost uninterrupted series of Ecstasies and Raptures [72].

The Ecstasies of the Venerable Orsola Benincasa, Foundress of the Theatine Nuns (1547–1618), were so frequent as to be almost uninterrupted. Directly the trance came on she at once became entirely insensible to any exterior happenings. When she was a child these Ecstasies were not understood, and rough methods were employed to arouse her. She was pricked with needles and even cut with sharp lancets; her hair was pulled; bystanders nipped and pinched her black and blue; they bruised her with their blows; they even went so far as to burn her with a naked flame, but all these injuries affected her not in the slightest, although when she returned to herself she keenly felt the result of such ill-judged, and indeed cruel, maltreatment. Later, ignorance and misunderstanding turned to admiration and awe. Those who dwelt with her, or had the opportunities of observing her almost daily realized that she was indeed a saint. Thus the Superior, Suor Angela Raparo, who lived with Orsola for twenty-eight years, deposed on oath that the holy ecstatica was rapt many times each day, and that not a day passed without her being entranced in heavenly wise. The priest, Don Vincenzo Nero, solemnly averred: "With my own eyes I have beheld her very many times rapt in ecstasy . . . absolutely immobile, absolutely insensible." In very deed the life of this holy nun is described as one long Ecstasy of Divine Love. Moreover in Rapture she was levitated [73].

Blessed Maria Ana de Jesús, in the world Doña Mariana Ladran de Guévara, a Discalced Mercedarian nun (1565–1624) of Madrid, was subject to the most extraordinary and prolonged Ecstasies, and overwhelming Raptures during which she was frequently levitated. In her *Revelations* she acknowledges (under obedience) that her soul received extraordinary illuminations from God, to Whom she was closely united in mystic vision [74].

In the New World Mystical Phenomena glorified the supernatural life of *la azucena de Quito*, the Lily of Quito, Blessed Marianna di Gesù de Paredes y Flores, who was frequently entranced in Divine Ecstasy, so that as her director P. Camaccio attested she was overwhelmed in Heavenly Love to so intense a degree that she was ineffably united to God. Moreover, on one occasion when a priest Don Sebastiano Delgado came to speak with her, she was discovered to be so entranced in Ecstasy that it was impossible to arouse her, and the good father gazed with awe and wonderment upon such holiness and purity.

When San Franciso de Borja, S.J., was in contemplation he remained motionless, as if carved in stone, and once when a wooden column fell upon him, inflicting a severe wound, he knew nothing of it, until he came out of his ecstasy and to his surprise found he was in bed, whither the bystanders had carried him, with a physician in attendance [76].

In her little hermitage, which she had built with great palm leaves and other branches of trees in the most sequestered and remote corner of her father's garden, St. Rose of Lima, who may truly be called Wonderful even among the Saints, passed entire days in Divine Ecstasy. Herself the "Flower of the New World", "the Passion-Flower of Christ", her virginal seclusion, her austerities, her fasts and penances, were such that men read of them with a kind of wonderment, and feeding only on the Bread of Angels she appeared truly in some sense to share the angelic nature and to become a Sister of the Seraphim. "It is in a garden we always seem to find her", says a mystic writer, and we are told that the very flowers smelled more sweetly as she plucked them with her fair and lovely hands, hands which had been clasped in those of her Secret Bridegroom to Whom His Mother had given her, and Who had whispered so tenderly, "Rose of My Heart, My Rose be thou My Spouse, Mine own". And one day, in the cool of the evening, when she was walking in a parterre planted with fragrant flowers in which she took great delight, she saw that they had been gathered. Upon which she sorrowed not a little, until presently she heard her Lover's voice: "Rose, My Rose, thou art a flower. Give Me all thy love, for know that it was I Who gathered these flowers, for I will have no rival, no, not any creature even be it a flower shall share with Me in thy heart." It was her custom to retire to her mysterious hermitage on Thursday very early and to remain there, encloistered and unseen until Saturday night. And there, as the poet says [77], she would

take possession of that sacred store
Of hidden secrets and holy joys.
Words which are not heard with Ears
(Those tumultuous shops of noise)
Effectual whispers, whose still voice
The soul itself more feels than hears;
Amorous languishments; luminous trances;
Sights which are not seen with eyes;
Spiritual and soul-piercing glances
Whose pure and subtil lightning flies
Home to the heart, and sets the house on fire
And melts it down in sweet desire
Yet does not stay
To ask the windows leave to pass that way;
Delicious Deaths; soft exaltations
Of soul; dear and divine annihilations;
A thousand and unknown rites
Of joys and rarefy'd delights . . .

Isabel de Flores y Oliva, whom the world knows as St. Rose of Lima. "It is in a garden we always seem to find her." When with the early dawn, in the cool of morning ere the sun had yet risen in his might, she passed through the garden—herself the fairest flower of all—she bade Nature awake and praise with her their common Creator, Who had made both trees and shrubs and fragrant herbs and flowers, the dawning and the evening, the golden disc of the sun, the silver orb of the moon. Then the boughs rustled gently as she went on her way to her anchorhold, and the breeze that softly stirred them seemed to make music to God. The flowers also swayed and bowed to greet her, opening their petals and rousing from sleep, to send forth their rich perfume from nature's thuribles, an incense to the Most High. The birds sang in sweet chorus, and loved to nestle on her arms and shoulders. The insects, too, welcomed her footsteps with their joyous hum, a low bourdon note of praise, and together with her all living things gave matin thanks to the Lord.

At eventide before they sought their nests the feathered choristers would wing their way to sing their vesper hymn with Rose. So when she gave the sign one little voice would pipe in harmony with her own canticle of love. "Do thou begin, my dear little bird," said she, "do thou, sweetling, begin thy glad song. Let thy tiny throat, so full of melody, pour forth thy song. I then in concert will join with thee. Together we will praise Him Who made us both." And so they sang, as it were in choir antiphonally, and when the bird uttered his notes Rose would sit silent and watch him with her lovely eyes; but as his voice died away she took up the song, and he in his turn perched near would listen with marvellous attention, until when the hour came, at the end, their voices would blend in heavenly harmony. And so she blessed him and thanked him for his melody, and he would take leave, flying to his nest, while veiling her face she would in silence withdraw to the house, there to seek her chamber, very privily, not to sleep but to pray and macerate her innocent body with those disciplines and penances, which seem to us so terrible, that we can hardly understand, can scarce bear to hear of them. Even her director, a holy man of the strictest austerity, felt bound to bid her moderate her mortifications [78].

It is true we cannot understand the visible intermingling of the natural and supernatural worlds. We cannot understand the joy of pain, the foolishness of the Cross. It has been admirably said by a profound spiritual writer that "so completely child-like was St. Rose herself, and so child-like the wonders with which her Divine Spouse encircled her, that in reading her Life it seems hardly ever to strike us that she was anything but a little girl . . . yet he will find a thorn who shall dare to handle roughly this sweet mysterious Rose which St. Dominic planted in the garden of his Master".

A little girl. Yes, in her twelfth year St. Rose had attained the Unitive Life, by means of which "the soul becomes one spirit with Him". Why speak of her Raptures and Ecstasies? Her whole life was one long Ecstasy. Little wonder that all God's creatures loved her, that the birds sang softly round her Hermitage, that when she was ill one little bird perched near the window and began to sing so sweetly that she fell into a Rapture which lasted from dawn until dusk. Little wonder that when on one occasion she passed swiftly through the streets of Lima to Santo Domingo that holy woman Louisa de Melgarcyo knelt down, and with deepest veneration kissed the places where the feet of Rose had trod [79].

The Raptures and Ecstatic experiences of St. Rose were described by her, under obedience, to her Director, to several learned Dominican and Jesuit divines, and especially to the famous mystical theologian, Juan de Castile, the author of a very profound treatise on Mysticism, but so far as possible she lived retired from the world. On the other hand, the Raptures and Ecstasies of the Béguine Blessed Christina of Stommeln (1242-1312), who was under Dominican direction, were carefully recorded by the parish priest Dan John, and collected by Father Peter of Dacia [80], who knew her intimately and who put together much material for a projected work (not fully completed) *Liber de Vertutibus Sponsae Christi Christinae* (*A study of that Holy Woman and true Spouse of Christ, Christina*). Peter of Dacia was a man of great talents and learning, we might almost say of genius. At Cologne he had studied under St. Albertus Magnus himself. It was upon 24th February, 1268, that he first beheld Christina in ecstasy. Someone had been singing the hymn "Jesu dulcis memoria" and upon hearing she was rapt in Ecstasy, unconscious, immobile. This state continued four hours. Again and again in the presence of a little group of friends, pious women and good religious who visited her, Christina passed into Divine Ecstasies. On Whit-Sunday, 1268, after she had made her communion she remained motionless for many hours, her face covered by her veil, wrapped in her cloak, caught up in Ecstasy. Extraordinary phenomena accompanied these trances, and her Raptures were frequent. As will be dealt with in a later chapter she was further subject to diabolical attacks of the most furious kind. Here we have the case of a Mystic whose Ecstasies were carefully observed by a trained theologian, a Dominican friar of whose good faith and clear balanced apperception there can be no doubt. There were, of course, many other witnesses, and all describe without deviating or exaggeration precisely identical happenings. Such evidence it is impossible to gainsay.

The Passionist, Father Germano of St. Stanislaus, a trained, cautious and most careful investigator, for a long while remarked and recorded the Ecstasies and Raptures of St. Gemma Galgani of Lucca [81]. Gemma Galgani was born 12th March, 1878, and died 11th April, 1903. She was canonized by Pius XII on Ascension Thursday, 2nd May, 1940. The Divine Ecstasies and Raptures of St. Gemma overwhelmed her when she least expected the Heavenly afflatus, whilst she was seated at table, working in the kitchen, quietly conversing with others, walking in the streets, anywhere. There was generally a forewarning, a burning flame of love towards God and Our Lady seemed to blaze more fiercely in her heart and consume her. If there happened to be the time and opportunity she would quickly retire, and this sometimes was the case. But often she was unable to do so through the circumstances in which she was, and not unseldom the Rapture was instantaneous, sweeping her away to Heaven. There was no ghastly pallor, no agitated and convulsive movements, no muscular contortions and grimacing, such as (Fr. Germano aptly comments) almost invariably occur in the trances of mediums. Simply, her exterior senses ceased to act. "One might puncture her hands, her head or arms with a pin; apply fire to her tender skin; make deafening noises; all without effect." "If you had seen Gemma yesterday," wrote one of the family, "My God! one could not look upon her without awe. She did not seem to be a mortal, her countenance was that of a seraph. We were moved to tears and deepest devotion. That hour, whilst Gemma was in ecstasy, that hour 'twas but a minute to us." This phenomenon proved to be very frequent in the home circle. Naturally they did not talk of it abroad. It was too sacred and too reverend for that. Father Germano himself says: "How often have I not melted into tears, while praying at her side or saying the Divine Office with her, and she, all the while, was rapt in Divine Ecstasy."

The Rapture, or Extraordinary Ecstasy, frequently accompanied by mystical phenomena, used (as it was observed) to entrance her every Thursday evening about eight o'clock (the hour of the Last Supper) and on Friday afternoon about three (the hour of Calvary). As soon as she knew what was going to happen she hastened away to seclude herself in her own little room, where very often she was found, if any one followed her, stretched immobile, overwhelmed by the Divine Assault, upon her humble pallet-bed. Fr. Germano tells us much of the celestial locutions, certain vibrated words from Heaven, which she uttered during Rapture. These are St. Paul's "hidden words". *Audivi arcana verba*, said the Apostle.

There were also apparitions of our Blessed Lady which at once threw Gemma into an Extraordinary Ecstasy. "Gemma gave herself all

to Mary, and Mary to Gemma." The Passionist, St. Gabriel, appeared
to Gemma many times. Just before her death Gemma fell into an Ecstasy
which lasted a very long while, and Fr. Germano tells us that when he
administered the Holy Viaticum she was in Ecstasy. In a sublime Ecstasy
on Holy Saturday, 11th April, 1903, she passed to Heaven.

It was in Ecstasy that the wonderful visionary, holy Anne Catharine
Emmerich, on 9th February, 1824, after indescribable sufferings, passed
to her exceeding great reward. It was remarked that at this supreme
moment her stigmata shone, radiant with light.

Johann Joseph von Görres in his *Die Christliche Mystik* [*82*] gives
many examples of Ecstasies which lasted many hours, and even for days.
Thus the Ecstasies of the Franciscan friar, Blessed Nicolas Factor of
Valencia [*83*] usually lasted twenty-four hours. Blessed Oringa of Lucca,
an Augustinian nun, frequently remained in Ecstasy for several days
together [*84*], Blessed Angela of Foligno [*85*] was often three days at
a time in Ecstasy; on occasion St. Ignatius of Loyola was rapt for a
whole week. St. Maria Maddalena, St. François di Paola, and other
mystics, especially the Béguine, Venerable Gertrude de Oosten [*86*], who
died in 1358, endured even longer transports. The great Augustinian
Archbishop of Valentia, St. Thomas of Villanova (1488–1555) fell in a
rapture lasting twelve hours, during which time he was levitated [*87*].
Once when preaching on Maundy Thursday before the Emperor Charles V
in the Cathedral at Valladolid he was ravished in Ecstasy in the pulpit
to the great admiration of a crowded congregation.

An ecstatic of the highest order was the Trinitarian Fra Bernardino
dell' Incarnazione. Born at Terracina on 1st May, 1819, Filippo Vicario
entered the Order of the Most Holy Trinity in 1835, and was ordained
priest in 1842. The ancient church of San Crisogono in Trastevere having
been given by Pope Pius IX in 1856 to the Trinitarians is the headquarters of the Order. From 1856 until his death on 12th September,
1893, Padre Bernardino lived as one of the community of San Crisogono.
His holiness and humility was known by all. He was famous for his
ecstasies which he in vain endeavoured to conceal, since he was rapt at
Mass, which he usually said at Our Lady's Altar in San Crisogono; he
was gifted with the power of miracles and of healing. When in old age
he tottered, feeble and infirm, through the cloisters, the ecstasy like a
divine breath, came upon him; his strength and energy returned, he
walked with a firm step; his eye lit with an eagle fire. On his death, his
confessional was literally broken to pieces by the thousands who rushed
into the church to secure relics. The beatification of Fra Bernardino is
(it is confidently awaited) merely a matter of the official process.

Examples could be multiplied. It should be noted that neither the
frequency, nor the prolonged duration of these Divine Ecstasies ever
injured the health of the mystics, nay rather these sublime experiences
seemed to invigorate them and renew all their forces. As St. Teresa of
Ávila writes: "This Prayer (Ecstasy) last as long as it may, never does
the least harm, at any rate my experience is that I have never suffered
the slightest hurt or injury from it. Nor do I remember, however

physically sick and weary I may have been, that when Our Lord has granted me the favour of this surpassing grace, I have ever felt the worse therefor. Nay, rather, I was always very much better afterwards, and obtained notable relief, and was strengthened, body and soul. In sober truth, what harm can so signal a Divine Blessing do? The exterior signs and effects are most plainly to be seen, and amply suffice to show that one is invigorated and braced up to a remarkable degree, and there must have been some especial cause and active power for good inasmuch as it ravishes away our bodily forces and perceptions with such a heaven of delight that they are restored to us reinvigorated, rejuvenated and most sweetly refreshed" [88].

Divine Ecstasy may not untruly be said to be the Gateway to the Mystical Life. Of course God can lead His chosen souls to the Supreme Union, to Himself, by many paths and guide them in channels we know not. But so far as mere human knowledge ventures (with all due reservation and in all humility) to pronounce, Divine Ecstasy is that great gift, freely given, when and as He will, whereby we are drawn to the Ultimate Reality. Perhaps only a few comparatively are found worthy of such a gift, only a few could correspond with such a grace. Nevertheless it is the lot of the Mystics.

It is during Divine Ecstasy that the highest phenomena of the Mystical Life occur, for the most part. It is during Divine Ecstasy that the choicest gifts are bestowed, that the Bridegroom adorns the Bride with the most radiant argentry of light.

We follow the sure guidance of Benedict XIV, who in his great work, treats at considerable length "Ecstasy, Transport and Rapture", as being in some sense preliminary to other remarkable phenomena of the higher states of Contemplation. This is our groundwork, our preface to the Physical Phenomena of Mysticism.

In Trance Divine ecstatics and ecstaticas have received and yet receive that wondrous charism, the stigmata; in Trance Divine they are dowered by the Heavenly Bridegroom with those rich red rubies, the crimsoned jewels of Christ.

NOTES TO CHAPTER III

1. *Extra stare*. In the Vulgate, *Acts* iii, 10, we have *exstasis* used as meaning "amazement". At the miracle of the healing of the lame man all the people "impleti sunt stupore et extasi", which both Douay and A.V. render "they were filled with wonder (*stupore*) and amazement (*extasi*)". But in later Latin *exstasis* signifies "ecstasy" in the true technical sense.

2. St. Thomas, II–II, q. clxxv, aa. 3 and 4. I insert "Ultimate Reality" since as St. Thomas writes *Summa Con. Gent.* XV, "God is *being* by His essence, because He is being itself; whereas everything else is being by participation".

3. *De Genesi ad litteram*, xii, 12, 25, and xii, 26, 53.

4. *Sermones*, lii, 16.

5. *De Genesi ad litteram*, xii, 5, 14. I have paraphrased a long passage of the holy doctor.

6. *Enneades*, vi, 7, 34. *Plotini Enneades*, Edidit R. Volkmann, 2 Vols., Leipzig, 1883–4.

7. Quoted by R. A. Vaughan, *Hours with the Mystics*, 3rd col., 1879, Vol. I, p. 81.

8. For Modern Theosophy see a history of contemporary Societies in the *Nouvelles religieuses*, 1st September, 1919. This informative essay was written on the occasion of the solemn and supreme condemnation of Theosophy by the Holy Office, *Acta Apostolicae Sedis*, 1st August, 1919, p. 317.

9. Aristotle *Mor. Eud.*, VII, xv, 16; *Mor. Nicom.*, i and x; *Metaph.* xiii.

10. The best brief, and probably the most accessible, account of this extraordinary movement is *Theosophy*, by the Rev. C. C. Martindale, S.J., London, Catholic Truth Society.

11. Dominican Cardinal, philosopher, theologian, and exegete. Born at Gaeta, 20th February, 1469; died, Rome, 9th August, 1534. His Commentaries on the *Summa Theologia* of St. Thomas are recognized as a classic in Scholastic literature. This great Thomas was called by Clement VII "the Lamp of the Church".

12. *Malleus Maleficarum* translated by the Rev. Montague Summers, London, John Rodker, 1928, Part I, Question 1, p. 3; and Part II, Q. i, Ch. 3, pp. 104–109.

13. Thomas of Brabant is often referred to as Thomas Cantimpratensis, Thomas of Cantimpré.

14. Edinburgh, 1834, p. 481.

15. *Lapponia*, 1674. There is also a French translation, *Histoire de la Laponie*, 4to, Paris, 1678.

16. *Discours des Sorciers*. English translation, John Rodker, 1929, pp. 46–51.

17. Bartolommeo Spina, O.P. (c. 1480–1546), Magister Sacri Palatii, *Quaestio de Strigibus*, 1523, c. XIV; Peter Binsfeld, Suffragan Bishop of Trier, *Tractatus de Confessionibus Maleficorum et Sagarum*, Trier, 1589, conclus. vii, dub. 5.

18. The work was translated into Spanish, Salamanca, 1530, and 1556. In 1628 Miguel Santos, Bishop of Solsona, entrusted Doctor Pedro Antonio Jofreu to supervise the issue of a new edition. This appeared, Barcelona, 1628. Glosses were furnished, as also a quantity of additional matter.

19. *Epitome Delictorum, sive de Magia*, Seville, 1618. There are several reprints.

20. Inquisitor of Sicily. The *De Agnoscendis Assertionibus Catholicis* is a posthumous publication, Palermo, 1553; and Rome 1572.

21. Fifth Ed., London, Kegan Paul, 1920, p. 90.

22. *The Catholic Church and Spiritism*. Dublin, 1931, p. 11.

23. Heath Cranton, and Ouseley, London, 1914, pp. 185–193.

24. Sir William Barrett says: "As a rule, I have observed the steady downward course of the mediums who sit regularly." Horace Greeley, in his *Recollections of a Busy Life*, writes: "I judge that laxer notions respecting marriage, divorce, chastity, and stern morality generally have advanced in the wake of Spiritualism." Dr. B. F. Hatch, the husband of a famous medium, Cora V. Hatch, does not mince his words in his *Spiritualism Unveiled:* "I have heard much of the improvement of individuals from a belief in Spiritualism. With such I have had no acquaintance. But I have known many whose integrity of character and uprightness of purpose rendered them worthy examples all round, but who, on becoming mediums, and giving up their individuality, also gave up every sense of honour and decency." Such testimony from men of so high a standing, and men who had exceptional opportunities to observe the points at issue, requires no further attestation, although, as a matter of fact, their witness could be supported by unimpeachable and multiplied evidence.

25. The Holy Father has not as yet infallibly pronounced upon the essential nature of Spiritistic phenomena, and has not directed the Sacred Congregation of the Inquisition to promulgate a definite and authoritative judgement, although we are at liberty to say that there has been an indicative judgement, giving reason to believe that the Church strongly suspects that in these Spiritistic manifestations diabolic agencies may and do *per accidens* intervene. The Church absolutely forbids

H   113 the faithful to take any part whatsoever in Spiritistic practices. In 1898 the Holy Office explicitly forbade automatic writing, and this applies to the use of planchette, the ouija board, and any similar contrivances. In 1917 any participation in Spiritistic séances, although such participation might be strictly limited to the rôle of an onlooker, was banned. But Catholic authority does not prohibit the investigation of Phenomena commonly classed as psychic research. Naturally such investigation must be undertaken by the properly qualified, not employed as a means for self-advertisement or allowed to be indulged in by vulgar curiosity. See further *La Religion Spirite*, Paris, 1921, by the learned Dominican Professor, Père Mainage.

26. F. W. FitzSimons in his *Opening the Psychic Door*, 1931, deplores that Spiritism "is so mixed up with fraud, vulgarity, contradiction, and humbug". There can be no doubt that on many occasions the medium Eusapia Palladino obtained so-called "supernatural effects" by trickery. The medium Monck was caught red-handed. Archdeacon Colley discovered the frauds of William Eglinton. "It unfortunately fell to me," he wrote in a letter to *The Medium and Daybreak*, 15th November, 1878, "to take muslin and a false beard from Eglinton's portmanteau." These properties had been employed in a fake materialization. Henry Slade, the Holmeses, and dozens of other notorious mediums were caught in covert mummeries. At one time Mr. H. Dennis Bradley remained a firm believer in the preternatural powers of the American medium, George Valiantine. Yet it was Mr. Bradley himself who detected Valiantine in a most flagrant forgery of a thumb-mark. See—*and After*, 1931, by Herbert Dennis Bradley.

In fairness it should be added that not unseldom Eusapia Palladino (and others) did exhibit the most extraordinary and inexplicable powers. It does not follow that because a medium is discovered once or twice (or several times) to be fraudulent the phenomena surrounding this medium are always imposture. But this does not in the least help the matter. The history of witchcraft affords many striking parallels.

27. *Quaestiones Medico-legales.* Liber iv; Lit. 1. *De Miraculis*, q. 6, n. 10. This pronouncement has a very pertinent bearing on the trances of spiritistic mediums, which are certainly not divine, and cannot (Zacchia tells us) be natural, since levitation at séances is not unknown. It is said that the medium, Colin Evans, whilst in deep trance, was levitated at a public meeting.

28. *De Visionibus*, c. iii, p. 69.

29. He professed medicine and mathematics at the Universities of Milan, Pavia, and Bologna, ultimately residing at Rome where he practised under St. Pius V and Gregory XIII.

30. John Aubrey, F.R.S. 1626–1697. *Miscellanies upon Various Subjects*, 1696.

31. *Summa*, I–II, q. xxviii, a. 3.

32. Père Poulain, *Des extases naturelles*, p. 7.

33. *Institutiones Theologiae Mysticae*, Leodii, 1848, II, pp. 328–36.

34. *De Civitate Dei*, Lib. XIV, c. 24.

35. *De vita spirituali*, lib. v; 3, c. 8.

36. 1609–74. General of the Cistercians. *De Discr. Spir.*, c. xiv.

37. Carmelite, 1564–1627. *Opera*, I, II, disp. iii, c. 8.

38. Carmelite, 1603–71. *Summa theologiae mysticae*.

39. *Les Œuvres de la Sainte Mère Térèse de Jesus.* Paris, 1650. "La Vie de la Saincte Mère Térèse de Jesus," chapitre XVIII, p. 103.

40. Mgr. Farges, *Mystical Phenomena*, "Translated from the Second Edition by S. P. Jacques," Burns Oates and Washbourne, 1926, p. 171.

41. Martin Antony Delrio, S.J., born at Antwerp, 1551; died at Louvain, 1608. He did not enter the Society of Jesus until he was thirty, after he had served as Counsellor of the Supreme Council of Brabant. He also acted as Auditor General, and in many other offices of great responsibility. He was familiar with at least nine languages, and is justly regarded as a prodigy of learning. This famous scholar was a Doctor of several Universities. He professed Philosophy and Theology at Salamanca, Douai, Liège, and Louvain.

42. St. Peter of Álcantara, 1499–1562. Founder of the Barefooted Reform of

THE PHYSICAL PHENOMENA OF MYSTICISM

the Franciscans, known as Alcantarines, or the Friars of the strictest and eremetical observance.

43. I have used the French version, the original not being accessible. *Vie de Saint Pierre d'Alcantara, écrite en Italien par le P. Marchese de l'Oratoire & traduit en François.* 4to, Lyon, 1670.

44. Professor E. Allinson Peers, *Mother of Carmel*, S.C.M. Press, 1945, p. 39.

45. *Psychologie de l'Attention*, Paris, 1889, p. 143.

46. J. J. von Górres, *Die Christliche Mystik*. 5 Bände, Regensburg, 1836–42. French translation by Charles Sainte-Foi, 5 Vols, Paris, 1861 (deuxième édition), II, ch. ii, pp. 10–11.

47. It is impertinent to argue that the second state is not inevitable in the absolute sense, since God could (if such were His will) immunize ecstasies from it. Further, it is pointless to quote the only two examples, Our Lord and Our Lady, Who enjoyed the Beatific Vision always and uninterruptedly, without any alienation of the senses.

48. Fray Domingo Bañez, O.P.

49. I quote the translation of Professor Allison Peers, as also in the following passage from *The Interior Castle*.

50. Θάλασσα κλύζει πάντα τἀνθρώπων κακά. Euripides.

51. *Interior Castle*, VI, v.

52. Unhappily, certain frenectic theosophists have endeavoured to revive these pernicious and pitiful follies, for example Mrs. Annie Besant in her *Esoteric Christianity* (1901); Charles Webster Leadbeater in his *The Hidden Side of Things* (1913); Mr. Kingsland in his *Esoteric Basis of Christianity;* and others.

53. *Historia di tutte l'Heresie;* Venezia, 1717; IV, 711, seq.

54. St. Catharine's letter to Blessed Raymond of Capua gives the details.

55. *Storis di Santa Caterina da Siena* (from the French of P. Chavin de Malan), versione Italiana a Prefazione di Pietro Vigo, Siena, 1906, pp. 105–109, gives a useful and concise summary, and reproduces Sodoma's exquisitely beautiful picture of the Execution of Tuldo.

56. Blessed Osanna Andreasi, 1449–1505. The *Vita*, Monza, 1888, by Monsignor Cavriani, Bishop of Ceneda, reprints certain *Laudi* and seven of the 42 extant *Lettere Spirituali* of the Beata. A number of unedited MSS., poems and letters, were in 1888 still preserved in the Casa degli Andreasi, then the property of the Conte Magnaguti.

57. *Vita di Ven Giuseppe*, by Conte Domenico Bernini, 1722. St. Joseph was canonized in 1767.

58. *Officia Propria Festivitatum et SS. Ord. Discalceatorum SS. Triinitatis.* . . . Romae, Typis Salviucci, 1840, Die Septembris xxviii, In Festo B. Simonis de Roxas . . . Fundatoris Congregat. Ave Maria.

59. *Vita del Beato Gabriele del l'Addolorata, Studente Passionista.* Scritta dal P. Germano di S. Stanislao. Roma, 1908, St. Gabriel (1838–1862) was canonized by Benedict XV on 13 May, 1920.

60. *Pract. Theologo. Canon.* tit. vi; c. 6, n. 10.

61. Benedict XIV quotes several authorities who support this view, Cardinal Brancati; Scacchus, Matta *De Canonizatione Sanctorum*, pars III, c. iv, n. 31; and Matthaeucci.

62. *The Mystical State*, by Auguste Sandreau, Canon of Angers. English translation, London, 1924, p. 141; n. 158.

63. *Summa*, II, 2dae; qu. 175, art. 2.

64. Benedict XIV cites a number of authorities who follow St. Thomas and add further explanations, for example, Arauxo, Scacchus, Consalvi Durante, Castellini, and Antony of the Annunciation. Silvius in his glosses upon St. Thomas says that violence is not essential to rapture, but it suffices if the rapture exhibit something like a sweet violence.

65. *De Discretione Spirituum*, c. XIV; n. 6.

66. *Opera*, tom. II, disp. iii, c. 8.

67. *Mystical Phenomena*, by Mgr. Albert Farges, translated from the Second French Edition by S. P. Jacques, London, 1926.

115

68. A hamlet near Florence.

69. *Intera Narrazione della Vita, Costumi e Intelligenze Spirituali della Venerabile Sposa di Gesù Suor Domenica dal Paradiso*, by B. M. Borghigiani, a large quarto, partially printed, Firenze, 1719, and completed 1802. In the seventeenth century the author was able to make use of the copious material preserved in the convent "La Crocetta" at Florence. Here are (or were) preserved six or eight folio MSS. volumes written by Domenica's director for thirty-seven years, Fra Francesco Onesti de Castiglione.

70. Butler calls her "Saint", but Papebroke styles her "Blessed". In the Flemish Calendars, however, she is St. Mary of Oignies. There is, moreover, a church dedicated to her.

71. Canon Regular of Vitry, afterwards Bishop of Acon, in Palestine, and thence translated to the See of Jerusalem. He died at Rome in 1244.

72. *Compendio della Vita della Serva di Dio Elisabetta Canori Mora, Romana, Terziaria dell'Ordine de'Trinitari Scalzi*. Roma: Tipografia degli Artigianelli, 1896. This *Compendio* is based upon the letters of the servant of God, written under obedience at the desire of Padre Ferdinando di San Luigi, a Discalced Trinitarian, who was her director, and also upon the writings of Elisabetta's daughter, Maria Giuseppa, who was requested by Padre Giovanni, the General of the Trinitarian Order, to put on paper everything she remembered of her mother's life. All this material, after having been closely examined by a number of skilled theologians, was embodied in the Process of the Cause for Beatification, the Ponente being Cardinal Raphael Monaco La Valletta, Bishop of Ostia and Velletri.

73. *Historia Clericorum Regularium*, by Joseph de Silos, 3 Vols., folio Rome, 1658. *Histoire della Religione dei Padri Chierici Regolari*, raccolta del P. Gio, Battista del Tuffo, 2 Vols., folio, Rome, 1609. Father Placidus a Sancta Theresia, *Compendium vitae Matris Ursulae Benincasae; et Regulae Virginum Romanarum Teatinarum*. Francesco Maria Maggio has written *Vita della Madre Orsola Benincasa, Fondatrice della Monache Theatine*, folio, Rome, 1655, and a *Compendium (ejusdem vitae)*, 8vo, Brussels, 1658. I have seen it stated that in 1514 and 1679 Maggio's two works were censured, but either upon some slight correction the note of censure was withdrawn, or else an error has been made, as Maggio is quoted with approval by orthodox and correct authors.

74. Feast, 17th April. The Mercedarian Breviary, Matins, Second Nocturn, *Lectio* V, says: "Tanto divini amoris aestu conflagravit, ut saepe tota supernis ardoribus colliquesceret, et frequenter a sensibus abstracta admirabiles raptus, et suavissimas extases pateretur."

75. *Vita della Beata Marianna di Gesù da Pasedes e Flores Vergine Secolare Americana, detta Il Giglio di Quito*, descritta da D. Giovanni del Castillo, Canonico della Cattedrale di S. Giacomo del Chile. Roma, Tipografia Bernardo Morini, 1854. B. Marianna was born 1618; died 1645. *Vita*, Lib. II, c. iv.

76. Sgambata, *Compendium Vitae S. Francisci Borgiae*, cap. XXI. Père Verjus, a French Jesuit, in his life of San Francisco de Borja, drawing upon original and some MSS. sources with which he was furnished by the Borja family, gives an account of the Ecstasies and Raptures of the Saint.

77. Crashaw: *Prayer. An Ode which was praefixed to a little Prayer-book given to a young Gentle-woman*.

78. *Le Pérou et Ste Rose de Lima*. By M. T. de Renouard de Bussière, Paris, 1863.

79. Of the older Lives of St. Rose these may be cited as amply authoritative the Dominican Leonard Hansen's *Rosa Peruana. Vita Mirabilis et Mors pretiosa S. Rosae a Sancta Maria*. Ulyssiponte Occidentale, 1725; and also *La Vie de Ste. Rose* by Père Jean-Baptiste Feuillet, O.P., Missionary Apostolic in the Antilles. The third edition (which I have used) of Père Feuillet's work was published in Paris, 1671, the year of the Canonization of the Saint by Clement X.

80. Peter of Dacia was born in the island of Gothland. The Dominican province, Dacia, included Sweden, Norway, and Denmark.

81. *The Life of the Servant of God Gemma Galgani an Italian Maiden of Lucca.* By her Spiritual Director Father Germanus of St. Stanislaus, Passionist. Trans-

116

lated by The Reverend A. M. O'Sullivan, O.S.B., with an introduction by Cardinal Gasquet, London and Edinburgh, Sands and Co.; St. Louis, Mo., B. Herder, 1914. The Appendices, pp. 377–433, in which Father Germanus examines various mystical phenomena or any kind of spiritism and spiritistic manifestations, and shows that such cannot be attributed to hysteria, or hypnotism, are especially valuable.

82. *La Mystique Divine*, tra. M. Charles Sainte-Foi. Deuxième Edition. Vol. II, pp. 45, *sqq.*

83. 1520–1583, Feast, 23rd December. "Quoties . . . amarissimae Passionis Dominicae, sive inter concionandum, sive inter aliquid faciendum, meminisse contingit, raptus atque in extasim factus est." *Martyrologium Franciscanum* authore Arturio a Monasterio, folio, Paris, 1653. See also Luke Wadding *Annales Minorum*, 8 Vols., folio, Lugdumi, 1647, etc., and Fortunatus Hueber, *Menologium . . . Beatorum, etc. Ab initio Minoritici instituti usque ad moderna tempora*, 2 Vols., folio, Monachii, 1698.

84. 10th January (or 18th February), 1310. Acta Sanctorum, January, tom. 1, p. 651.

85. Franciscan. Died 4th January, 1309. *Acta Sanctorum*, 4th January *De Beata Angela de Fulginio*. The works of Blessed Angela were conveniently published in Part V of the *Bibliotheca Mystica et ascetica; Beatae Angelae de Fulginio Visionum et Instructionum Liber*, Cologne, 1849.

86. *Acta Sanctorum*, 6th January, *De venerabili virgine Gertrude ab Oosten beghina delphensi in Belgio.*

87. The *Vida* of St. Thomas, O.S.A., was written by Miguel Salon of Valentia; and also by two Augustinians, Jerome Canton and Nicasius Baxius.

88. *La Vie de la Saincte Mère Térèse de Jésus*, chapitre XVIII. *Les Oeuvres de la Sainte Mère Térèse de Jésus . . . nouvellement traduites . . .* Paris. MDCXXXXX, p. 103.

CHAPTER FOUR

The Mystery of Stigmatization—The Ferita, or Heart Wound—Stigmatization, True and False—Hypnotism—Autosuggestion—Pathological Phenomena—Clara of Monte-falco—Passitea of Siena—The Seraphic Tradition—Carthusian Ideals.

THE mystery of stigmatization, that is to say the reproduction upon a living subject of the Wounds and bodily suffering of Christ, as inflicted by the nails and lance, the Crown of Thorns, and other instruments and circumstances of the Passion from Gethsemane to Golgotha, is perhaps the most widely known, one might even venture to say (using the word in its first sense) the most notorious, of all the extraordinary physical phenomena of the supernatural life.

This mystery, its repercussion, accomplishes itself in various ways, and under widely differing conditions. Generally speaking, the hands and feet are pierced clean through, and the side is gashed, more or less deeply, as if by the nails and the soldier's spear of Calvary. These wounds are, in the majority of cases, distinctly visible; in some instances they are hardly to be seen. There are also stigmata known as "concealed stigmata". These are none the less real and very true. The wounds have been inflicted supernormally and ecstatically; they have been endured and with pain throughout life, but are only manifested upon death. Occasionally, when the wounds have been clearly apparent for a certain period of time, it may be many months or years, they disappear from sight, but later recur and become as distinctly expressed as hitherto, but so far as can be ascertained without any predetermining cause or interior impulse or exterior foreaction.

The marking with the Five Wounds, accompanied or unaccompanied by the Crown of Thorns, has been designated by some writers "Complete Stigmatization", and the term may be allowed to stand for convenience' sake. Yet other stigmatic imprints are recorded. Such are the weals of the scourging; the wound in the shoulder; on the wrists, the livid bruising of the cords; and on the mouth the hyssop mark of the sponge sopped with vinegar which was set upon a reed.

The *Ferita*, as it is technically known, the heart-wound, or trans-verberation of the heart, under which condition normally the subject would die, since the wound (humanly speaking) ought to be mortal, is a phenomenon which may be considered separately. In some rare instances autopsy has revealed in the heart characters and symbols, or flesh formations of the Instruments of the Passion.

The state of rapture known as the "Plastic Stations of the Passion" with its mysterious concomitants, so nearly akin to stigmatization, and often as it were colleagued, is more understandable after inquiry into and discussion of the main subject-matter.

118

Stigmatization is to be divided into two kinds, each one of which varies in degree and is disuniform. There is sacred or divine, true stigmatization, sometimes called mystical or religious or hagiological stigmatization; and also diabolic or satanical stigmatization, which is simulated stigmatization. Sacred stigmatization is that divinely imprinted, and a true pattern of the Wounds of Christ. It has in very many cases been authoritatively approved as such by the solemn judgement of the Church.

Thus Howard C. Warren, Princeton University, in *A Dictionary of Psychology*, 1934, under "Stigmatization" gives the definition of divine (true) stigmatization and no other. It may be noted that, wisely perhaps, no explanation is discussed. The fact of true stigmatization is denied by none. For example, the fact is honestly and candidly admitted by such eminent specialists, both of the free-thinking school, as Dr. Pierre Janet in the *Bulletin de l'Institut psychologique international*, Paris, July, 1901; and the then Professor of Religious Psychology at the Sorbonne, Dr. Dubois, writing in the *Revue des Deux Mondes*, 1st May, 1907. Dr. Janet and Dr. Dubois suggest, it may be remarked, some sort of explanation, but very tentatively, and what they have to say is frankly hypothetical.

A very voluble and dogmatically assertive school has announced its theory that stigmatization may be produced by unconscious autosuggestion, which in psychoanalytical cant is defined as "the subconscious realization of an idea in more or less complete independence of heterosuggestion", which latter is "the subconscious realization of an idea suggested by another, or, the act of suggesting an idea to another". Self-hypnosis is a term also flung about with considerable effect and little meaning. The stigmatization produced by autosuggestion or self-hypnosis is regarded as, although in no way fraudulent, due to the dominant working of an *exalté* imagination. This is classed as "natural stigmatization".

We also find the term "false stigmatization" used with a certain meaning, which is intended to denote a "stigmatization" resultant upon any deep-seated nervous disease. It is purported to have occurred in the case of sufferers from hystero-epilepsy, and then is accompanied by writhing, by horrid convulsions, and uncouth distortions of the facial muscles and the limbs. (We are reminded of the foul fanaticism of the Camisards, whom Pope Clement XI styles "that execrable race of ancient Albigenses", a fanaticism which expressed itself in unholy raptures and demoniac extravagances. One of their leaders penetrated to England, and caused a great stir in London, a wave of madness which was agreeably exposed by the dramatist D'Urfey in his satirical comedy *The Modern Prophets*, produced at Drury Lane, 3rd May, 1709. "The abominable Impostures of those craz'd Enthusiasts" reached such a height that their leader was expelled the country as a common nuisance, and many of his followers flocked after him. Further, we should not forget the *convulsionnaires* of St. Médard, concerning whom there will be something to say later.)

"False stigmatization", it has been advanced, may also be induced by the exterior suggestion of a hypnotist, heterosuggestion, in fact, and it will be the more marked and more complete the more fully the patient is controlled by the directing will. Dr. Albert Moll in his work *Hypnotism*, English translation, 1890, p. 229, quoting the Berlin psychologist, Max Dessoir, writes: "I say to some one who is quite awake, 'A rat is running behind you'. The man can assure himself at once by turning round that there is no rat, but according to experience he has a mental image of a rat for a moment, because I spoke of it; *i.e.*, there is already a trace of hallucination." This is just specious nonsense. The phrase "according to experience" is very artfully introduced, but actually is an obvious smoke-screen, whilst to write "there is already a trace of hallucination" is deliberate sophistication, employed in hopes that the word *hallucination* may deceive and mislead the reader. We deny such a vague generality as "Modern Psychology, following such men as Dugald Stewart and Taine, for the most part supposes every idea includes an image, *e.g.*, the idea of a knife includes the image of a knife". Half a dozen lines lower down, intercalated as a decoy, we have "in the case of the rat there is a transitory hallucination". The "trace of" has now been stretched to "a transitory", and will be emphasized a little more and more. In Vergil's words "Viresque acquirit eundo". The whole proposition is just a flam.

Although any opinion emanating from the same source (Moll) must be regarded as more than dubious, and carries scant weight, as a matter of interest it may be well to observe what he has to say concerning stigmatization. "Everybody" he writes, "will here remember the stigmatics of the Roman Catholic Church. Bleeding of the skin is said to appear in them, generally in spots (!) which correspond to the wounds of Christ. The best known is Louise Lateau, of Bois d' Haine, near Mons, who was much talked of in 1868." Louise Lateau, 1850–1883, will be dealt with in some detail later. "I will not," continues Moll, "enter into the question of stimulation which a Belgian doctor Warlomont, decided was impossible, after personal investigation." With Dr. Warlomont, Moll, who is very insufficiently informed, might have associated Dr. Crocq, an anti-clerical Professor of Brussels, who attested the same as his *confrère*. Professor Rudolph Virchow of Berlin "thought that fraud or miracle were the only alternatives". Fraud was proved to be impossible. Moll goes on to assert that "the ecstasy of Louise Lateau has a great likeness to the hypnotic state". This is an absolutely unauthenticated statement to make, and his chicanery is not helped by citing the long-exploded dictum of Professor Mantegazza that "Ecstasy and hypnosis have many points in common, and are, perhaps, identical conditions".

Professor Elie Méric of the Sorbonne very justly emphasizes that stigmatics are certainly not in an abnormal condition, but quite awake.

Can hypnotism produce the stigmata upon a subject under control? The answer is, No: it is not possible. But it certainly can produce by suggestion upon an abnormal subject, who is morbidly predisposed, a number of pathological phenomena, some of which are not very pleasant to describe.

It should be mentioned that experiments have been essayed upon hypnotic subjects, who whilst under the influence are told that a blister, or mustard poultice or some sort of cataplasm or even vesicatory liniment was being applied to the skin, whilst actually simple linen or a piece of plain paper or pure water was thus being used. Carl du Prel notes how in 1819 a subject thrown into a somnabulistic sleep by a magnetizer was informed that a strong plaister must be clapped upon him, and although nothing but a clean square of fine lawn was employed, there resulted a sloughing and cutaneous scurfing in that very part. In 1840, an Italian doctor, Prejalmini, made trial of this experiment, and sometimes was partially successful, sometimes not. A chemist of Nancy, M. Focachon, in 1885, under the close inspection of Drs. Beaunis, Bernheim, and Liégeois, applied pieces of tissue paper to a subject under control, who was hypnotically made to believe these were astringept plaisters. In some cases the skin appeared slightly discoloured, and in some cases small serous pustules arose, but the experiments were by no means certain, in fact, the result proved very unequal and evanescent. This is very far from stigmatization, which is permanent and entire.

J. Milne Bramwell in his *Hypnotism, its History, Practice, and Theory*, refers to several cases recorded by Forel, who claims to have produced "red patches" by suggestion. "In one instance this appeared at the end of five minutes; the subject being carefully watched at the time by Ford and other medical men. . . . Schrenck-Notzing cites an interesting experiment which he and Dr. Rybalkin of St. Petersburg made upon Camille, Lièbault's celebrated somnambule. They suggested to her in the waking state that the skin below her ear was red and inflamed and that she had evidently been bitten by an insect. In about three minutes there appeared a patch of erythema with a distinct rim." If this has any evidential value it merely points to diabolism, and is entirely alien to the true stigmata.

These "red patches", produced by suggestion, are as much out of date and as valueless as Charcot's *oedeme bleu des hystériques* "the blue mottling of hysteriacs"; and Dr. Krafft-Ebing's obsolete thermometrical experiments with the highly suggestive Ilma S——, who was either an excellent actress or a clever impostor; Dr. R. von Krafft-Ebing, *An Experimental Study in the domain of Hypnotism*, English translation.

Of no account and not worth detailing are the experiments of Dr. Biggs of Lima as reported in the S.P.R. *Journal*, May, 1887. Dr. Jendrássik further investigated the case of Ilma S——, but the whole business is absolutely foreign to, and has no bearing upon, the phenomena of stigmatization.

Since the experiments of Dr. Rybalkin at the Hôpital Marie, St. Petersburg, were much talked of in their day it is, perhaps, well to mention them here; *Revue de l'Hypnotisme*, June, 1890. The subject was Macar K——, aged sixteen, who is described as "hysterical and almost anæsthetic". A pathological case, at once. "He was hypnotized at 8.30 a.m. and told:—'When you wake you will be cold. You will go and warm yourself at the stove, and you will burn your forearm on the line which I have traced out. This will hurt you, a redness will appear on your arm; it will swell and blisters will form.' On being awakened the patient obeyed the suggestion. He even uttered a cry of pain at the moment when he touched the door of the stove—which had not been lighted. Some minutes later, a redness, without swelling, could be seen at the place indicated.'' The next day it was found that the arm had blistered, and by three o'clock one large blister had formed. Such experiments and such happenings can be paralleled in the pages of Remy and Delrio.

This horrible fact is proved when we reach a case of actual hæmorrhage by suggestion. The subject was Louis Vivé, a hystero-epileptic who suffered from a complication of disorders, hemiplegia, anæsthesia and schizofrenia. On 5th August, 1885, Vivé was hypnotized, and it was suggested that he should go to bed and fall asleep at 8 p.m., awaking at five o'clock the next morning. At precisely eight o'clock the patient fell into a profound sleep. The "Stigmatization" was then suggested. "V. a quarter of an hour after you wake there will appear on your arm a 'V' at the place which I am now marking. . . . You hear? I wish it to bleed." A quarter of an hour later Vivé has the attack to which we are accustomed when stigmata are suggested to him. When the attack is over we examine his arm and find on it a "V" covered with blood. . . . The same phenomena have been produced twice in one night in the same region and by the same mechanism." Dr. M. Mabille, "Pathologie Mentale. Note sur les hemorrhagies cutanées par auto-suggestion", *Le Progrès Medical*, 29th August, 1885.

The underlying power which causes the results of such experiments as these essayed by Dr. Rybalkin and Dr. H. Mabille is not difficult to discover. It is simply demonianism. The "mechanism" is the fiend.

Among these pathological phenomena is ecchymosis, which is a blotch caused by extravasation of blood below the skin. The subcutaneous cellular tissue is torn and there is hæmorrhage, which however does not escape, being confined by the texture of the skin, and it is only indicated by the crimsoned or livid appearance of the injured place. Dr. Van der Elst, *Les stigmatisations, Revue pratique d'Apologétique*, 15th December, 1911, p. 428, maintains that there can be a spontaneous dripping of blood through the normal orifices of a perfectly healthy skin, although he hastens to insist upon the extreme rarity and unlikelihood of such an occurrence, yet he avers it is possible. We can admit this, but it is very far removed from the stigmata which flowed from blood, and which were imprinted in certain fixed members, the hands, feet and side. Moreover Dr. J. Parrot in the *Gazette hebdomadaire de médicine et de chirurgie*, 1859, having apparently met with one of the cases, noted that after the blood had been washed away it was not possible to distinguish from which pores it had exuded, there was no swelling nor discolourment. All this is a vastly different matter from stigmatization, when the wounds remained fresh and open, and as in the case of Joanna de Jesús-Maria, the Poor Clare of Santa Clara at Burgos, when they bled every Friday at the hour of the Passion, a definite and specified time. Musgrave mentions a young man who was under his care on account of a regular monthly haemorrhage from the thumb of his left hand. There were no headaches, or feeling of sickness, or any other symptoms of illness. In fact the young man in question enjoyed robust health until he was about thirty years old. Irked by and impatient of this curious loss of blood he was foolish enough to cauterize the place whence it issued with a red-hot goffering-iron. The flow of blood ceased, but the results proved most unhappy, since he fell into a rapid consumption. Latour in his *Histoire des hémorrhagies* refers to a very similar instance given by Doctor Carrière. A young man, by name Jacques Sola, was affected when about fifteen years old with a flow of blood from the little finger of his right hand. This took place every four weeks, with extraordinary regularity almost on the very same days, and lasted for forty-eight hours. The blood exuded in great drops, but when these were wiped away no puncture nor mark could be seen. There was no pain. One cold winter Jacques Sola had occasion to cross a brook or a little stream of icy water. He felt a shock, and the bleeding ceased, but a light attack of pneumonia followed. No sooner was he up and about than he fell ill with dysentery, which gave the doctors a good deal of trouble to treat successfully. He was eventually restored to complete health, and the hæmorrhage never returned.

Paul Radestock (died 1879) in his *Schlaf und Traum* relates an odd happening vouched for by the physiologist Carl Friedrich Burdach (1776–1847). A friend of Burdach's was informed that one night his wife had been seen by the neighbours walking in her sleep upon a roof. Naturally he was considerably disquieted, and called in Burdach who hypnotized the lady. Then she gave him a full account of her nocturnal ramble, and added that she had hurt her left foot, an injury she had not previously mentioned. Upon waking she was questioned whether she felt any pain in the place of which she had spoken. With some surprise she answered "Yes", and upon the foot being examined it was found to be pierced or at any rate deeply marked by a wound for which she was unable to account.

These, and similar other very rare cases, have from time to time been cited by writers of the materialistic school, who thence try to "explain" and parallel the stigmatization of mystics. Nothing could be more fruitless and more ridiculous. Yet they endeavour somehow to confuse the issue, and hence it seems necessary to expose their tactics.

To give some idea of the extent to which hypnotic power can be carried a couple of examples may be cited, and it must be remembered that there are hundreds of cases of the same nature. Dr. Alphonse Teste, a famous hypnotizer and homœopathist of his day—he was born at Gray in 1814—and a voluminous author tells us in his *Le Magnétisme animal expliqué* how he ordered one of his "subjects" to have a big fire blazing in her room next day exactly at noon—it was mid-July—to light a couple of candles and to wait for him there for an hour, occupied with certain needlework. When he arrived he found that everything had been done as he directed. She was busy with her embroidery by the candlelight, a winter fire had heated the room almost to suffocation, although she was not in the least incommoded. The hour struck. She jumped up, threw aside her work, blew out the candles, and flung aside the window to admit fresh air. "We shall be stifled!" she exclaimed. But she had not the least idea why she should have kindled a fire, why candles should be burning, why she was so intent upon her crewel. The whole thing to her was a mystery.

Professor Wilhelm Preyer of Berlin in his *Der Hypnotismus* (1882) gives in detail an account of an evening party at Norderney, during the course of which social gathering a magnetizer compelled a lady to fetch a wet sponge from the bathroom and to wash the face of one of the gentlemen present with it. She was extremely abashed and ashamed, but in spite of her visible reluctance she felt obliged to obey and perform this ridiculous act.

Ridiculous indeed! Although in execrable taste there does not seem to be much harm in the fact that a lady at a soirée should wipe a gentleman's face with a damp sponge; and that a lady should light a fire and burn candles to see by at midday in July looks like a practical joke. None the less

> *Oftentimes, to win us to our harm,*
> *The Instruments of darkness tell us Truths,*
> *Win us with honest Trifles, to betray us*
> *In deepest Consequence.*

and setting aside these fooleries, how would it be if an individual were compelled by this mysterious power to do some wrong, to commit an offence, even a criminal act? Who is to limit this unknown empery, these despot commands? Matters would assume a very different complexion. In 1888, a case of hypnotic suggestion to the committal of a crime in a convent occurred in Hungary. The object was to rifle the treasury of the house, which was unusually rich in golden chalices, jewelled reliquaries, and other sacred vessels, the heirlooms of the ages, of unique value. A girl obtained admittance, feigning to make a retreat, and under the influence of the mesmerizer nearly succeeded in carrying out the robbery which had been so deeply planned. Details may be read in a pamphlet *Eine experimentale Studie auf dem Gebiet des Hypnotismus*, Second Edition, Stuttgart, Ferdinand Enke, 1889, by Professor R. von Krafft-Ebing of Vienna. Another case is recorded where a hypnotizer, a diabolist, influenced some wretched creature over whom he had obtained control secretly to attempt to break open the tabernacle in the chapel belonging to a religious house. The object was to steal the hosts for the foul rites of a gang of Satanists. Happily, this was frustrated. There have, indeed, been not a few similar cases.

But, it will be argued, hypnotism has been successfully employed to relieve and indeed cure nervous (and, it is claimed, physical) disorders and diseases. I answer with Tertullian: "When demons cure diseases, it it because they themselves caused the malady. They suggest effectual remedies, and thus it is believed that thereby the sickness is healed, whereas it is in fact because the cacodemons have ceased to cause it" (*De prescriptionibus haereticorum*, xxxv).

I subscribe then to the solid opinion of that great and learned Professor Dr. Antoine Imbert-Gourbeyre of the School of Medicine at Clermont-Ferrand, who in an important monograph *L'Hypnotisme et la Stigmatization*, 1899, as well as in various articles in *L'Univers* and *Le Monde* proves that all these phenomena obtained by hypnotists, phenomena the reality of which there is no thought of denying, are manifestly diabolical. An eminent theologian, Sancha y Hervas, Cardinal Archbishop of Toledo (1838–1909), condemned hypnotism on precisely the same grounds.

An extreme rationalist, Dr. Charles Baudouin of the Jean Jacques Rousseau Institute, Geneva, in his *Suggestion and Autosuggestion* (English translation, 1920, p. 100) speaks of *dermographism*, that is to say "an image existing in the subject's mind becomes outlined on the skin". The next sentence may be quoted as a monument of ineptitude. "The authors make a passing reference to the witches of the middle ages upon whose backs, it is asserted, the word 'Satan' was inscribed." One may ask who are "the authors"? In my reading of demonologists I can only say that I have never met with this statement nor indeed with anything in the least like it, and until further references are forthcoming I am constrained to think that Dr. Baudouin has drawn upon his rather fertile imagination. I do not, for my part, remember such a detail in any witch trial, and it would be too striking and too rare easily to be forgotten.

Dr. Baudouin proceeds to cite from Dr. Charles Richet of Paris a well-known instance of dermographism. A child, playing about the room idly loosens the catch which fastens a chimney draw-plate, and narrowly escapes being guillotined by the quick fall of the heavy steel-edged mechanism. The mother receives such a shock on seeing the danger that a flushing erythematous circle forms round her neck—the corresponding part was threatened in the case of the child—and this remains swollen for several hours. Similarly, as recorded by Père Coconnier O.P. in his *L'Hypnotisme franc*, a child's foot is on the point of being crushed by the swing-to of a heavy iron gate. Happily the accident is averted, but the mother, who saw it with horror, was seized with a pain in her ankle. The foot then became inflamed, and through lameness she was forced to keep her bed for nearly a week. A servant, devoted to her mistress, was present when a doctor lanced the lady's arm. The abigail, who seemed a little nervous, felt something like a prick with a sharp knife in her own arm, and ecchymosis temporarily supervened. A man in a very vivid dream imagines that a spectre clutched one of his feet and twisted his toe. He awoke with a sharp cry, and perceived that there was in the foot redness, and swelling with considerable pain. This was questionless gout, and I do not think that this example will hold. It was the attack of gout that gave rise to the dream of the malicious goblin, not the visionary goblin who was responsible for the pain.

Dr. Baudouin proceeds: "From dermographism we pass to stigmatization, the latter being merely a variety of the former." It is unnecessary to examine this irresponsible statement, which is absolutely*without a shadow of foundation, and which shows us how much reliance is to be placed upon the speculations and conjectures of *Suggestion and Autosuggestion*. We are the less surprised, then, to find that Dr. Baudouin rapturously follows the vagaries of Couéism—if it be permissible to coin such a word—and is learned in the *patois* of the psychoanalyst, proclaiming with infinite satisfaction that even Shakespeare has been psychoanalysed!

It is as well to remark these eccentricities and vagaries since they throw considerable light upon the point of view adopted by too many writers who attempt to deal with and profess to explain stigmatization, without, indeed, having any idea of the meaning and implications of this phenomenon.

Unfortunately many of the general books of reference and technical dictionaries are also apt to mislead. Stedman in his *Medical Dictionary* (13th edition, 1936), says that in pathology a stigma is (*a*) any spot or blemish on the skin; (*b*) a bleeding spot on the skin of an hysterical person. He defines "major hysteria" as a condition in which there is anæsthesia, or contractures with well-marked stigmata, and in which convulsions or violent emotional attacks may occur. "Major hysteria" has rather an ugly sound, and accordingly the well-known Parisian neurologist, Dr. J. Babinski (1857–1932) to get rid of the unfortunate associations drew a red-herring across the trail by introducing the word "pithiatism", which is explained as "a morbid condition curable by suggestion". Pithiatism is altogether more suave and elegant.

F. T. Roberts in his *Theory and Practice of Medicine* (3rd edition, 1877, I, p. 37), writes that "cutaneous hæmorrhages assume the form of *stigmata*, or minute points; *petechiae*, or rounded spots; and *vibices*, or lines".

It may very justly be emphasized that these are all pathological definitions of stigmata, and do not concern us here. It is necessary, however, to insist upon and underscore this point, as the word Stigmatization has been wrested from its hagiological and mystic meaning, and so to speak, secularized. Writers, then, who try to explain Divine Stigmata, the only true Stigmata, by autosuggestion, or by pithiatism, or by any other save a supernatural cause, are either employing the term in a distorted and debased sense, or else deliberately attempting to inspissate and materialize spiritual things. In the former case a writer should at the outset define his terms. From the latter category we cannot excuse Dr. Baudouin—I cite him merely as a typical example of the school—when he writes (*op. cit.* p. 100): "In the case of Catharine Emmerich, the circulation was directly controlled by autosuggestion, the blood being distributed as it would have been distributed in an actual crucifixion." It is difficult to think that this erroneous statement was other than designedly enunciated and given this prominence to fit the author's preconceptions which he does not depart from, and in the face of such overwhelming proof to the contrary I do not find it easy to suppose that he was morally and philosophically concerned by what he posits. The bigotry of science is obstinate and blind.

126

"Autosuggestion" is some sixty years old now. I believe the word in English is not found before 1890, whilst its equivalent "self-suggestion" would appear to be hardly earlier than 1899.

Pietro Pompanazzi, who was born at Mantua in 1462, and who died at Bologna about 1525, having professed Philosophy at Padua, Ferrara, and Bologna, drunk with his own intellectual insolence and high-flying conceits, did not hesitate to spawn in his copious *Works* such horrible errors as the proposition that the curative power of Holy Relics consists in the faith of the pilgrim who comes to venerate them. That very learned and impartial doctor, Thomas Fyens, who occupied the Chair of Medicine at Louvain and was body-physician to the Archduke Albert of Brussels in his *Tractatus de Viribus Imaginationis*, the earliest work scientifically to examine and discuss autosuggestion and the extensive influence of the mind, snubs the presumptuous old philosopher pretty sharply for this, and sends him sprawling. For Pompanazzi a miracle is the effect of some natural cause which may in future be discovered, although as yet we do not know the material reason. Nor, I will add, are we likely to know it, until God in His own good time reveals it. Which will not be here. Pompanazzi is very eloquent, not to say verbose in expatiating upon the Power of the Will, and maintains that man within himself is a perfect battery of marvellous force, which he can (if he knew how) energize with amazing results.

No one will be at all surprised to hear that the sorcerer Cornelius Agrippa exactly follows the sceptic scoffing philosopher, and the atheist Giordano Bruno, who was executed for his crimes at Rome in 1600, companions them well in his subversive ideas. I have mentioned these three men, who proclaimed that the psycho-physical parallelism of such a sublime phenomenon as the stigmata was but the intensified effect of a too vivid and fructuous imagination, in order to show how respectable an ancestry have the misnomered rationalists of to-day, who with their wearisome reiteration of such sibylline tags as "psychosensorial hallucinations" and "abnormal motivation" but echo the long since exploded fantasies of the sixteenth century.

That the Divine Stigmata could be produced through the force of the emotions acting upon a lively subject is altogether impossible. The utmost that physiological science can urge is that it has not advanced far enough to explain the Stigmata, to which we add—and never will it advance far enough.

Hæmophilia, a tendency to bleeding, either spontaneously or from any slight injuries, has no connexion whatsoever with the Stigmata, but must be mentioned here since the more ignorant have been known to speak very much at random of "hæmophilic tendencies".

Certain stigmaticas, for example St. Lutgarde of Tongres, the Cistercian nun who died in 1246; the Capuchiness St. Veronica Giuliani, 1660–1727; Blessed Catherine of Racconigi, a Dominican of the Third Order, 1486–1547; and many others suffered the sweat of blood in Gethsemane. There is a pathological condition, hæmatidrosis, in which occurs what is seemingly a blood-sweat. But as Dr. Imbert-Gourbeyre and Dr. Lefebvre have shown, this blood-sweat, arising from a specific malady is not an exudation of blood. The red humour which oozes out when microscopically examined, is shown not to be blood, since it does not contain red globules, and its coloration is derived from certain bacilli. Since this extravasation is always coincident with some lesion of the sudoriparous glands, hæmatidrosis, in spite of its name, must be classed among the many varieties of sweats, which are of several shades of hue.

It is only of comparatively recent years that hæmatidrosis has been medically inquired into and understood.

The immensely learned Abbot of Senones, Dom Augustin Calmet O. S. B., who was born at Ménil-la-Horgue, 26th February, 1672, and died at his Abbey of Senones, 25th October, 1757, at the request of Benedict XIV collected from the observations registered by the doctor-regent of the Faculty of Paris, Allicot de Mussey, a number of cases of hæmatidrosis, and these he described in a memorial which the Sovereign Pontiff found intensely interesting, conveying his warmest congratulations to the author. This particular malady had not then been so thoroughly diagnosed from a medical point of view as in more recent years, but none the less Pope Benedict was not in any sense misled. He weighed the evidence, and his enlightened perception led him to the authoritative pronouncement that there is no case of actual action upon the tissues, far less of any permanent action, *De Canonisatione*, III, xxxiii, n. 31.

Incidentally it may be remarked that we shall not of course classify under stigmatization, counterfeit stigmatization which is simply an imposture, wounds or cicatrices deliberately and craftily produced by cutting, piercing, or stabbing with some weapon, by blistering with a caustic or in some other subtle way, in order to deceive, generally for the sake of bolstering up a spurious revelation or pretended visions, some-times feigning for propaganda and politically directed, sometimes for mere publicity—*monstrari digito*, as the poet has it—for bastard honour and personal gain.

To sum up then, there are (it may be repeated) only two kinds of stigmatization, sacred or divine Stigmatization; satanical or diabolic stigmatization.

Satanical or diabolic stigmatization is that imprinted and produced through the medium or by the aid of the demon, whether it is actually recognized and known that the agent is a dark power, or whether it be that he is masquerading and disguised as a celestial messenger. Such simulation is easy for an evil entity. St. Paul writes that "Satan himself is transformed into an angel of light", and Tertullian shrewdly enough remarks that it is no hard matter for Satan to blind the eyes of the body once he has sealed the eyes of the soul.

It will be useful here to enumerate the characteristics of true or Sacred Stigmatization.

In True Stigmatization the wounds are spontaneous, that is to say not caused by any external or physical injury or accident, and, as imprinted upon the bodily members of the stigmatic, they are very definitely restricted to the Wounds of the Passion of which they are the replica. From these wounds, flows, more or less freely, new pure blood in contradistinction to the hæmorrhage normally extravasating from ordinary wounds, such as are lacerations and stabbings humanly inflicted. Thus the blood of true stigmatization is entirely clean and uncontaminated by any peccant humour or by that sero-purulence, which accompanies exulceration and obstinate unhealing hurts. The flow of blood from true stigmatization is not due to any defect in the coagulating power of the blood. There is, then, non-suppuration.

Moreover, it is known that in not a few instances where the blood flowing from the wounds of a stigmatic has been collected and carefully preserved in a glass phial or ampulla or some similar suitable vessel, hermetically stoppered and sealed, although as consonant with the ordinary natural law it coagulates to a crassament, and solidifies to a darkish hue, dull and opaque, yet this blood from time to time has been observed to liquefy and assume a ruby red colour as though full of life and vital [2].

This phenomenon, the ebullition of stigmatical blood, has been freely submitted to the most searching scientific examination, and it is demonstrated beyond question or shadow of doubt that the blood has acted in a manner impossible to any ordinary blood as known to physiology. Every delicate test under the most rigid conditions has been applied, the result being it is proven that the liquefaction does not in any way depend upon and is not in the least influenced by light, air, heat or changes of temperature, position, or any other conceivable circumstances.

The most famous, and perhaps in some ways the most remarkable, of all such recorded stigmatical phenomena is the case of St. Clare of Montefalco [3], whose incorrupt and exquisitely beautiful body sleeps at Montefalco, a little old hillside town from whose lofty walls one may overlook the outspread panorama of the luxuriant Umbrian plain so sweetly sung in Vergil's inspired line.

Born in 1268, Clara di Damiani from her very infancy was called at home "the little nun". Her life seemed scarcely stained with the shadow of sin. As a child, at her earnest desire, she was received as a member of the strictly contemplative community living under the rule of St. Augustine whose Superior was her own sister, Giovanna, *"la beata Giovanna"*. To her dismay upon the death of Giovanna in 1291, Clara was elected Abbess of Holy Rood. Her virtues, her charity, her raptures, her revelations, her miracles, are told at length by her biographers, and it is noteworthy that the first to write her life was a contemporary, Berengario di Donandei, who commenced the Process necessary for her official canonization in the very year of her decease, 1308. The cult of the Lady Clara may be said in some sense almost to have begun whilst she was yet alive, so venerated and loved was she for her goodness by her fellow townsfolk. Very early is she authoritatively spoken of as the Blessed Clara, but so diverse and so extraordinary were all the circumstances to be investigated, that Pontiff after Pontiff, from John XXII, who reigned 1316–34, to Pius IX, 1846–78, ordered more and more searching and scrupulously careful examination into these phenomena, which through

I

five centuries were again and again accurately observed, medically tested, proven, confirmed and re-confirmed, and it was not until 8th December, 1881, that, after a final investigation formally initiated on 27th August, 1846, and covering the whole ground in every detail, Leo XIII canonized St. Clara of the Cross, professed nun of the Order of the Hermits of St. Augustine, of their house at Montefalco.

The record drawn up by Berengario, who acting as Commissioner of Pietro Paolo Trinci, Bishop of Spoleto—a city some twenty miles from Montefalco—visited the Holy Rood Monastery with the express object of inspecting all documents, hearing witnesses, and collecting first-hand information, and who was writing in 1308–9, is of primary importance. There are numberless other processes, chronicles, and attestations. Of great value is the Work, composed in the pontificate of Innocent X, by Gianbattista Piergigli; who, as historian and critic enjoys a considerable reputation for the most minutely industrious scholarship, impartiality, and solid judgement. Bevagna, of which town he was *Vicario*, that is to say Rural Dean, something more than Vicar or Rector, is only three miles from Montefalco, and this gave him every opportunity for the most exhaustive research into the Life of the Saint whose History he wrote in the year 1645. When we add that he was also Confessor to the nuns of St. Clara's own monastery, it is hardly too much to say that he had unique facilities for the freest access to the manuscript archives.

So learned and careful a writer, for example, as the Most Reverend Mgr. Lorenzo Tardy, O.S.A. [4], who published the standard *Life of St. Clare of Montefalco*, Rome, 1881, largely relies upon Berengario and Piergigli.

In the *Cornhill Magazine*, October, 1881, John Addington Symonds describes a visit to Montefalco [5]. His account is so beautifully written and phrases in such exquisite taste that at least a partial quotation therefrom cannot come amiss.

The reason why he, in company with his friend and fellow traveller, Christian Buol, had climbed the long gradual road which leads to this little hillside town was, he says, a wish to inspect the many fine frescoes, especially the legends of St. Francis and St. Jerome, from the brush of Benozzo Gozzoli. "Full justice had been done to these, when a little boy, seeing us lingering outside the church of S. Chiara, asked whether we would not like to view the body of the saint. This privilege could be purchased at the price of a small fee. It was only necessary to call the guardian of her shrine at the high altar. Indolent, and in compliant mood, with languid curiosity and half-an-hour to spare, we assented. A handsome young man appeared, who conducted us with decent gravity into a little darkened chamber behind the altar. Then he lighted wax tapers, opened sliding doors in what looked like a long coffin, and drew curtains. Before us in the dim light lay a woman covered with a black nun's dress. Only her hands, and the exquisitely beautiful pale contour of her face (forehead, nose, mouth, and chin, modelled in purest outline, as though the injury of death had never touched her) were visible. Her closed eyes seemed to sleep. She had the perfect peace of Luini's S.

Catherine borne by the angels to her grave on Sinai. I have rarely seen anything which surprised and touched me more. The religious earnestness of the young custode, the hushed adoration of the country-folk who had silently assembled round us, intensified the sympathy-inspiring beauty of the slumbering girl. S. Chiara's shrine was hung round with her relics; and among these the heart extracted from her body was suspended. The guardian's faith in this miraculous witness to her sainthood, the gentle piety of the men and women who knelt before it, checked all expressions of incredulity. We abandoned ourselves to the genius of the place; forgot even to ask what Santa Chiara was sleeping here; and withdrew, toned to a not unpleasing melancholy. I have often asked myself, who, then, was this nun? What history had she? And I think now of this girl as of a damsel of romance, a Sleeping Beauty in the wood of time, secluded from intrusive elements of fact, and folded in the love and faith of her own simple worshippers."

This impression put on paper by so cultured a scholar and so fine a poet as John Addington Symonds, who frankly confesses that he knew nothing of St. Clara of Montefalco, is very remarkable. It was not until twenty years after that I myself was privileged to visit the shrine of St. Clara, but as I knelt there his sweet English words were sounding in my ears, and I thought then, as I think now, that for loveliness and delicacy and the beauty of natural reverence the music of his sentences could hardly be improved.

Her own order, the Augustinians, observe the feast of St. Clara upon the 18th August, and upon the 30th October is kept a second feast, the Impression of the Crucified and the Marks of His Passion in the heart of St. Clara of the Cross, Virgin, of our Order. The two masses, and the two offices, August and October, of St. Clara are proper.

During her last illness, on the evening of the 9th August, whilst good Sister Joanna of St. Giles was watching by the bedside of her much loved mother, moved by some sudden impulse, this nun raised her hand and made a great sign of the Cross over the dying Saint. "Why do you bless me thus, dear Sister?" murmured Clara, "why do you bless and sacre me thus? Know then that in my very heart I have and hold Christ crucified. All is well with me, exceeding well." These last words she repeated many times, and for pure glee and joy she sang blithely in a soft voice.

Although at the moment what she said was not fully understood, upon the evening after her death, whilst the body was being composed —now the members still remained flexible, for there was no rigor mortis —it was decided to extract and open the heart, and herein, in a concavity was bisected by the razor of the operator, all wrought out of the flesh, filaments, muscles, and nerves, were indeed discovered the Crucifix and other Instruments of the divine Passion. All these were modelled and ensculptured, clearly represented, by means of hard nerves of flesh, each in its own cellule. Thus in the moiety of the heart were contained the Crucifix, the three nails, the spear, and the reed with the sponge; in the other ventricle were the pillar of scourging, the scourge itself with five thongs, and the crown of thorns, all most plainly to be seen. Such minute details—for naturally each separate object is figured in little—as the five knotted cords of the scourge; the Figure on the Cross, and a gaping wound in the right side of that Figure; can each be unmistakably distinguished.

It should be remarked that the Crucifix and the Scourge, the only two Emblems which are still venerated at Montefalco, are entirely separate from and not in any way connected with the heart, which was—so to speak—the casket of these objects.

Even though a miniature, the scourge most accurately depicts the Roman "flagellum". Of that there can be no question. The Crucifix is tiny, about two inches in length, but in detail perfect. Of course, after the passage of more than six hundred years, after the various medical and scientific examinations and handlings, the uncoverings and replacements and continual exposure to atmospheric action, it cannot be expected that these Emblems should to-day appear quite as freshly coloured and vitally vivid as they were when Berengario saw them, and as he describes them. Not that there is the slightest taint or tinge indicating the approach of putrefaction or decay. The heart, rather irregular in contour, but entire, is reddish, one might almost say a murrey. The Crucifix and the scourge appear somewhat faded in hue, and, as it were, anæmial. It is more than possible that this is solely a result of the infinitesimal particles of finest dust which have spread a grey film or coating over them, an accident impossible to prevent when one considers how delicately these sacred relics must be touched and how infrequently it is advisable that they should be moved about.

Parenthetically there may be mentioned here another extraordinary phenomenon. Berengario relates that there were found in the gall-bladder of the Saint three hard pellets, like stones, exactly of the same dimension, weight, colour, and appearance, each one being of the size of a very small hazel-nut, and the three were set in a triangular form. The physicians attested that these were no ordinary calculous formations, and the Commission appointed to inquire into this prodigy had no hesitation in acknowledging that the three spherical globes were emblematical of the Most Holy Trinity. This Commission sat in the autumn of 1308, less than four months after the death of the Saint.

At the bisection of the heart that Sunday evening there were present four senior members of the community, Francesca, Lucia, Catharine and Margaret. To collect the considerable rush of blood they had carefully prepared a glass vessel or large phial, that had been most scrupulously washed and purified. When the flow was a little staunched, the Crucifix with the other Emblems lay revealed. Recognizing that there was something here beyond the ordinary, the sisters with that practical common sense which distinguishes nuns, at once locked up in a chest the heart and the phial. Early the next morning they requested the attendance of the leading citizens of Montefalco, before whom they opened the chest, exhibited the phenomena, and swore a solemn affidavit as to what had precisely occurred. There were present the Podestà or Chief Magistrate, Gentile di Giliberti, with his deputy; the leading physician in the town, Messer Simone da Spello; and a public notary, Angelo di Montefalco; all four men of note, influence, and the highest integrity. To these was added a very important visitor, the Father Guardian of the Franciscan house at Foligno, who happened to be staying in Montefalco for a few days. It was decided that the Bishop of Spoleto must be at once informed, and the officials withdrew to indite, sign, and seal the necessary documents for transmission to his Lordship.

But, as Mgr. Tardy says, the devil will have his finger in every pie, and by some breath of gossip—nobody quite knew how—rumour began to fly about with amazing stories and busy whispers of mysterious happenings at the Convent of Holy Rood. The visit of several important personages at so unusual an hour to the nuns could hardly have escaped remark. The fruit-women on their way to the market square had sharp inquisitive eyes and long tongues; the burghers wives as they came from mass lingered in the porch to drink in with greedy ears the tale of Holy Mother Clara. Speculation was rife; a word or two dropped here and there was soon buzzed in every corner of the town. Early that afternoon, before the report, which had to be drawn up with meticulous exactitude, could be completed, much less dispatched to the Palace, off sped to Spoleto an idle and indiscreet busy-body, not merely a Paul Pry but a clerical Paul Pry, and a fellow of scant fame beside, who waking the porter from his siesta demanded an instant audience of Mgr. Donadei. It was imperative—but imperative! His frock gained him admittance, and in a very few minutes with greasy unction he was pouring out before the astonished prelate a disquisition on supposed miracles, blatant imposture, cozening nuns, and matter for gravest scandal. With such cunning and address did the mischief-maker play his part that the good Vicar General became extremely uneasy and disturbed. In such a case it was his plain duty to act, and to act at once. There is nothing of which ecclesiastical authority is more suspicious than the report of a miracle or some extraordinary phenomenon. In recent times the histories of Lourdes and Fatima, for example, have displayed a policy of procrastination, of actual discouragement, long chilling silences, rebuffs, retardment, deterrence. Such discipline is hard, no doubt, but it is the vital testing, and it is essential to the truth. Donadei dismissed his visitor, merely cautioning him to be prudent and to avoid all tittle-tattle concerning such deep and difficult mysteries.

The next morning the Sisters of Holy Rood were not a little startled when the portress shaken out of her usual calm, came hurrying to announce that a very important company had halted at the gate. The street outside was full of unwonted bustle and noise; stalwart grooms and slim pages in those brilliant parti-coloured jerkins and hose with which the Trecentisti have made us so familiar, were jostling and running to hold the stirrups of their grave and reverend masters as they alighted from their horses and caparisoned mules; whilst the whole mobile of Montefalco crowded behind, agape, with goggling eyes. In order that there should be no possible grounds for a rumour that things had been

133

clandestinely managed or that there had been a private and partial inquiry, the Vicar General of Spoleto without giving any previous notice or warning of his intention, had come not merely openly, but with some state and formality of pomp, to make a strict visitation of the convent. Since the community lived under the rule of St. Augustine, and since (as he had learned) the Guardian of the Friars Minor at Foligno had already entered the testimony on the nuns' behalf, Mgr. Donedei brought with him the Prior of the Augustinians at Spoleto and the Guardian of the Franciscan convent there. They were attended by religious of the two orders. A canon theologian, two doctors of divinity, an eminent physician, a master surgeon, Monsignor Tignosi from Rome, and a secular dignitary, Messer Teodorico of Orvieto, were of the company. Not the least imposing figure was the representative of civil law, Messer Bartolo, a justiciar of Perugia.

In his quality of Vicar General and Episcopal Delegate, Donadei with his assessors entered the enclosure. They seated themselves in the chapter house, whither was summoned the whole sisterhood. Without any word of greeting or preliminary Mgr. Donadei began to rebuke and reprimand the frightened women in the sternest and most menacing tones. Here was grave matter toward, a scandal already gossiped in the common market-place. He was himself willing to believe that perhaps they had acted from a giddy enthusiasm rather than from any ill design prepense, but none the less their rashness, nay, their flaunting folly was like to cast a slur upon the honour of the Lord Bishop, and were it noised abroad in so sad and unbelieving Days 'twere odds it might besmirch on blasphemers' tongues the holy Catholic Faith itself. Punishment must follow, and no light penalties would suffice. The nuns pleaded that they had but spoken truth. Would not his Excellency deign to see the Relics and assure himself? Certes, yes, to that end was His Excellency come with the Reverend Fathers and Doctors at no small cost and inconveniency, and attended by his theologians, his physicians, his lawyers, and his friars, Donadei proceeded to view the body of the late Abbess, and to examine with most scrupulous care the Relics.

The result was, that, falling on his knees before the whole company, he there and then gave thanks to God in a loud voice that he had lived to see this day, and he vowed to devote himself to the task of declaring and making known the eminent sanctity of Lady Clara of blessed memory, swearing upon the crucifix that none other than himself with his own hand should draw up all those documents and attestations which were necessary to initiate the process of canonization.

This solemn oath was to take him more than once a long and toilsome journey, to Avignon, to the court of Pope John XXII [5] and it is to this oath that we are indebted for the contemporary record of St. Clara's life, the witness to these phenomena, Codex A, as palæographers would call it, to which reference has already been made.

When the four senior nuns so reverently and lovingly bisected the heart of their much venerated Abbess, the blood (as has been stated) was collected in a large glass phial, and this was most carefully preserved.

In the year 1608, Cardinal Visconti, Bishop of Spoleto, gave orders that a portrait of St. Clara, then generally known as the Beata Clara, should be painted, and he commissioned an artist of great local celebrity, Ascensione Spracchi, whom he especially patronized, to undertake the work.

Upon the 21st July, whilst preparations were being made for this, and the holy body was being lifted from its shrine, a nun observing that the vessel containing the Saint's blood had in the course of years become very dusty took it up and wiped it round with a fine linen towel, when by some mischance the fragile object slipped from between her fingers and broke all to pieces on the marble pavement. Sobbing bitterly, she at once gathered up every tiniest particle of the blood, and every splinter of glass, all of which was deposited in a larger glass vase. The accident is noted by Piergigli, who ascertained the precise details, and he adds, "So this is just as we see it to-day", about the middle of the seventeenth century.

The blood, says Piergigli, appears red in colour, like a rich ruby. That also is as we see it to-day, only the second beaker has been at some time cracked—it would seem to be the result of a sudden sharp knock—and for safety sake it has been placed in a larger glass vessel, which is thus actually the third vitrine. It should be remarked here that the three containers are crystal clear on all sides and perfectly transparent, without the least opacity which might prevent the closest inspection of the blood. This lies in mass coagulated at the bottom of the second beaker. A little however has oozed through the cracks.

What is very remarkable is that this blood of St. Clara of Monte-falco, normally concreted and coagulated, has been known during the years not only to liquefy, but even to boil up and bubble—*disciogliersi e bollire*, is Mgr. Tardy's striking phrase. Instances of these ebullitions are historically recorded and attested.

Unfortunately no exact and consecutive chronicle has been kept, a negligence in the past Piergigli very justly blames, since obviously it would have been of great value had the archivists of the convent noted in order the various dates when this phenomenon occurred. One Saturday in October 1495, the blood was observed to have become fluid, and presently it began to spume and froth in so marked a manner as seriously to alarm the watchers, who knew that traditionally this movement of the blood prognosticated some very untoward and serious events. In less than forty-eight hours the combined forces of the Baglioni and of the Orsini had swooped down, and for two months continued to pillage and harass the whole countryside, whilst the departure of Charles VIII of France from Turin on 22nd October and his return to his own realm, was the direct cause, says Guicciardini, "of changes in states, downfalls of kingdoms, desolation of many a fair province, destructions of noble cities, the most barbarous butcheries".

Five years later, in 1500, the Duke Valentino, better known as Cesare Borgia, established himself in Montefalco and the environs with a host of eleven thousand soldiers. He had determined that, when on the point of departure, he would issue orders the town should be sacked and despoiled. However, be the reason what it may, he suddenly changed his plans, gave his captains and commanders strictest injunctions that there should be no looting or plunder, and, hastening his departure, as it seemed, the Duke left Montefalco in peace. During the time that he was stationed in the town the Saint's blood remained in a state of liquefaction, and bubbled in its glass.

Ebullitions of the blood are recorded in 1508, and again upon the 20th March, 1560. In both cases these proved the presage of warfare and other misfortunes. In the year 1570, yet again the blood was observed to boil up, which signified the loss of Cyprus to the Turks in the following year.

Several remarkable ebullitions are recorded during the seventeenth century. In 1601 the blood boiled before a crowded congregation, upon which Monsignor Castrucci, a noble canon of Lucca, who was present, taking the vessel into his hands, exhibited it to the people, and delivered a solemn address. The same phenomenon was repeated in July, and October, 1608; and once more in October, 1618, during the exorcism in the church of a man who was demoniacally possessed.

All these liquefactions are attested and proven by persons of the highest quality and unquestioned integrity, by prelates and professors and doctors, men of scientific mind, trained to observe and discriminate, to weigh and pronounce. In the mid-seventies of the last century, that is to say about seventy years ago, three experts, each of whom investigated independently of the others, and no one of whom was aware that any other opinion had been called in, were deputed to conduct a thorough examination into the phenomena that occurred in connexion with the body and blood of St. Clara of Holy Cross.

In 1880, two of the leading medical men of the day, specialists at the very head of their profession, were commissioned jointly to draw up a full and detailed report, every facility being offered for the strictest inspection and inquiry. Their finding, as well as the three previous testamurs, all agree in stating quite unequivocally that here is something unexplainable by, and to all appearance outside and beyond, the ordinary course of natural law. Monsignor Tardy draws a striking analogy between these happenings and the phenomenon of the flow of blood from the Relic of the arm of St. Nicolas at Tolentino. St. Nicolas who was born about 1245, died at Tolentino (Marche) in 1309. An ecstatic of a very high and extraordinary kind, he was so distinguished by his burning devotion and amazing austerities that it has been said of him "he did not *live*, but languished through life". Whilst yet a young student he joined the Order of Augustinian Eremites, of which he is regarded as one of the chief glories. Upon his death crowds thronged the church if only to touch his body or his garments.

In accordance with the feeling of the fourteenth century, a custom which perhaps to the English way of thinking has something of a barbaric complexion, relics of the venerated friar, already canonized in the hearts of the townsfolk, were distributed by his brethren to certain other houses of the Order. The right arm of the Saint was detached from the trunk and is to-day preserved separately at Tolentino with great honour. The limb, although incorrupt is desiccated, but upon occasion it is known to gush with fresh blood, a portent which is taken to foreshow some impending calamity. More than five and twenty effusions of liquid blood from the arm of St. Nicolas are recorded, and some of these are recent in date.

It may be objected here that these blood marvels are not, strictly speaking, the liquefaction of stigmatic cruor, that is of blood which has flowed from mystical body wounds during the lifetime of a stigmatist, which has carefully been gathered there and then by attendants and bystanders into some vessel, and having in due course coagulated in perfectly normal fashion, becomes fluid even to the extent (at times) of ebullition. The blood prodigy of the arm of St. Nicolas may be more conveniently considered in reference to the famous miracles of St. Januarius of Naples and others, but the phenomena in the case of St. Clara of Montefalco are justly to be classified as stigmatical.

Another instance of blood flowing from the stigmata and after congelation becoming liquid on occasion is that of the Venerable Passitea Crogi, a Capuchin nun of Siena [7]. Passitea, who was born on the 13th September, 1564, from the very first exhibited such unusual sanctity that her father declared to a friend: "My little daughter is indeed a child of God. She leads us all in the paths of holiness." When she was five-and-twenty, Passittea felt a particular inspiration to observe the Lent of that year, 1589, as a season of more than ordinary rigour and fasting. Upon the morning of Palm Sunday, she received Holy Communion according to her wont, at the old church of St. George in the Via Ricasoli, and forthwith fell into ecstasy. Thinking that she had been suddenly taken ill, her mother and sisters carried her home in their arms and laid her on a bed. A physician, who was hurriedly called, at first sight exclaimed: "Ah! She has passed away", but on a closer examination he pronounced that this was no ordinary sickness. Day after day she lay there upon her bed, motionless, and, as all believed, at death's door. Good Friday came, when suddenly between two and three o'clock she rose up on her knees with outstretched arms, a dazzling ray like lightning flashed through the room, a sharp loud clap as if of thunder was heard, and with a piercing cry, Passitea, her face radiant with some unearthly glow, fell swooning in utter collapse. Her two sisters who were in the room, alarmed, ran to lift her up when to their astonishment they saw that blood was pouring from her hands, her feet, and her head, whilst her white night-rail was crimsoned all down the left side with blood welling through as if from a deep wound. As quickly as they could they mopped up the stains with towels and ewers of fresh water; they changed the coverlets which were all spotted with blood, and even scoured the floor round the bed. The chaplain of the famous thirteenth-century hospital and church, Santa Maria della Scala in the Piazza del Duomo, a Sicilian Father, Domenico Marchi, a priest of much experience in mysticism, was urgently sent for. Upon his arrival he at once recognized that Passitea had received the stigmata. In reply to his questions, which if delicately and gently put were searching and exigent, as so extra-ordinary an occasion demanded, Passitea under obedience described that she had seen as it were in a vision, Christ crucified, livid and bruised, and covered with wounds streaming with red blood. She heard the words "Daughter, drink of My Chalice", whereupon there darted out rays of transparent glory which struck her hands, her feet, her side, and for a second's space encircled her head. The pain was so acute that she lost all consciousness. The wounds in her hands and feet did not pierce through those members, but were deep round incisions in the palms and on the upper part; her side was gashed in three distinct places; her head was ringed with a series of punctures from which trickled drops of blood. In the course of a few days the suffering was much mitigated, and there was no extravasation, but all the skill of the physicians did not avail to close these wounds, although they experimented with every healing balm, unguent, and cataplasm known to pharmacy. Four years later, in 1593, on Spy Wednesday, when Passitea was rapt deep in contemplation before the altarino in her own room, there appeared a Seraph aureoled with light, but crucified, and covered with wounds. The vision came quite close to her, when suddenly with a loud noise like a thunderclap flames of fire darted forth and pierced her hands and feet completely through, at the same time stabbing her left side and lacerating her head. At the noise, which re-echoed in every corner of the house, her two sisters ran quickly to Passitea's room whence it seemed to come, and there they found her in a swoon, covered with blood. These stigmatic wounds, inflicted a second time, marked her all her life long, and whereas the former stigmata sometimes appeared to be only on the surface, the second stigmata was very deep, boring right through the hands and feet, so that the openings on either side reached one another. On certain days in the year and during Holy Week they bled profusely, and caused her agonies of pain. At other times the effusion was staunched, and they throbbed less achingly.

The Ecclesiastical authorities more than once insisted that these stigmata should be examined by the most skilful doctors and surgeons of the day, and that Passitea should submit to any course of treatment the faculty might prescribe. In this respect she obeyed implicitly and without a murmur all that her superiors commanded. Otherwise, in her profound humility she endeavoured to conceal as far as possible these supernatural manifestations even from the nuns, her closest companions, whilst if any secular extern, of whatever rank or dignity, ventured to question her, or show an indiscreet curiosity, she would abruptly break off the conversation and withdraw, evincing the greatest displeasure.

None the less, both during her life and immediately after death, the stigmata were seen on her body by numerous witnesses, the most con-siderable of whom gave their official testimony to the fact and set their hands to all necessary formal documents. The blood which flowed from the wounds was on various occasions, for example, Good Friday, the

Friday in Passion Week, on the Feast of the Stigmata of St. Francis (17th September), carefully collected in phials of various shapes and sizes, which were hermetically fastened, sealed, and which have been preserved intact. This was done entirely without her knowledge, since generally at the extravasation of blood she passed into ecstasy and was absolutely unconscious of her surroundings.

The phial which I have had every opportunity of inspecting is in height two and a quarter inches, of thick clear crystal glass, authenticated, stoppled, having the stopple covered with parchment which is tied down and sealed, air-tight. The cruor, which does not occupy an eighth of an inch, normally lies at the bottom of the phial. It is desiccated, dark in colour, and resembles minute particles of grit. On occasion this blood has been known to liquefy, and in a fluid state of a roseate hue almost to fill the small phial. Precisely the same phenomenon is recorded in the case of other vessels containing the blood which has flowed from the stigmata of the Venerable Passitea.

Although an enclosed nun, a sublime contemplative, and a mystic of a very high order, Passitea Crogi, who in this as in many other ways closely resembles St. Catharine Benincasa and St. Teresa of Ávila, proved herself an admirable organizer, and an excellent woman of business, and became the trusted counsellor of Popes and Kings. In 1599, after encountering many difficulties, she founded at Siena under the strictest rule of the Capuchinesses and following the primitive observance of St. Clare of Assisi a convent, of which she was the first abbess. In this she was strongly supported by the Archbishop of Siena, Cardinal Tarugi, one of the first companions of St. Philip Neri, and by St. Giovanni Leonardi, a fervid soul who was canonized as lately as Easter, 1938. Very soon after she was called upon to make a foundation of Capuchin nuns at Piombino, and in other towns. In 1602 she was summoned to Florence by the Grand Duke Ferdinand I [8], and here she learned with dismay that his sister, Maria de' Medici, who had been married less than a couple of years previously to Henri IV of France, was beseeching her to visit the French court. The royal request it was impossible to refuse. Moreover Christian charity obliged her to consent, since the poor Queen stood sadly in need of comfort and cheer. Even in so short a time the King had not only proved openly unfaithful, assigning without regard to the barest appearance of common decency a rich suite of apartments in the Louvre to his *maîtresse en titre*, but was treating his consort with a cold neglect, if not with actual contumely.

Passitea, as was becoming a religious, travelled in a closed litter, accompanied by a nun of the convent, her own sister, Maria Francesca. The Grand Duke provided a suitable escort of gentlemen, guards, out-riders, and grooms. "Altezza," she protested, "this is too much, this is unfitting for a poor nun." "Nay, nay, Mother," he pleasantly replied, "you must remember that the poor nun is my ambassadress to a great Queen." One of the suite kept a diary of the journey, which is full of piquant and familiar passages. Being mid-July it was suffocatingly hot, and "we two" said Maria Francesca, "are baked in our litter like two loaves in an oven". As they drew near Modena they were refreshed by grateful showers. When they were approaching Turin the rain came down in drenching sheets. The nuns were about to commence the recitation of Divine Office, and as they opened their Breviaries Passitea, hearing the drops splashing and pattering on the roof of the litter, said with a smile: "Well, well, Heaven is sending us plenty of holy water." At Paris, where they stayed several months, Passitea was received with the greatest honour and respect, and the Queen found infinite consolation and support in her company and counsels. But her heart all the while was with her beloved convent at Siena. "My body is in Paris; but in spirit and in desire I am with you, Sister Felix," she wrote to the nun who was acting as Superior in her absence. On one occasion, when some very complicated business had to be decided, and Sister Felix felt sadly perplexed which course to adopt for the best, as she was sitting all alone, after a long weary day, worrying over her responsibilities, she murmured with a sigh, "O, dear mother, if only you were here to tell me what to do!" The door opened, and the abbess entered. She took a chair at the table, and calmly discussed the difficulties with Sister Felix, pointing out the best line to take, what papers to sign, and how to set about it. Not until she had withdrawn did the Sister realize that Mother Passitea was in Paris. It was all so natural that she did not feel the slightest surprise or fear.

On several occasions, whilst she was absent in France, Mother Passitea was seen by nuns of her Siena house kneeling in the chapel, in the choir stall, or walking down the corridors. In the Lives of the Saints such instances of bilocation are not uncommon. Many examples of this phenomenon are recorded in occult writers, and Mrs. Crowe has an important chapter *"Dopplegängers*, or Doubles". Double-ganger is defined by the *Oxford English Dictionary* as "The apparition of a living person; a double, a wraith".

With much reluctance Maria de' Medici parted from Passitea during the late autumn, and to her joy the Abbess was back in Siena in November, 1602. But she was not allowed to remain in the seclusion of her loved cloister. The Duke and Duchess of Bavaria dispatched a pressing invitation, tantamount to a command, requesting her presence. She was also sent for by the Duke and Duchess of Lorraine. In 1609, she found herself unable to refuse the entreaties of Maria de' Medici to visit Paris a second time, when (it is said) her firm, but perfectly respectful remonstrances brought Henri IV to a very lively sense of his dissoluteness. Two Popes, Clement VIII (1592–1605) and Paul V (1605–1621), received Passitea in private audience and gave her much encouragement in her work of founding convents of Capuchinesses. To Paul V she was introduced by a very great lady, the Duchess Leonora Orsina Sforza, shortly before she set out on her second journey to Paris. The Pope held her in conversation more than half an hour, asking her many questions and when he dismissed her it was with the kindliest words and a warm blessing. After she had retired, he said to the Duchess: "Of a truth here we have a humble and holy soul."

Passitea died at Siena on the 13th of May, 1615. She was surrounded by her weeping nuns to whom until the last with a smiling face she spoke words of comfort and cheer. When the body was laid out in the conventual chapel the Archbishop, Monsignor Alessandro Petrucci, with all his Chapter and a long train of priests came to pray by her bier. He himself saw and touched the stigmata with which she was marked and in order that no question should be raised at any future date he gave instructions to have the body examined by the most skilful physicians and surgeons of the city, under whose directions a memorial, which all signed under oath, was drawn up by two notaries. These papers are still preserved in the archives of the convent.

The two cases of stigmatization of St. Clara of Montefalco, and the Venerable Mother Passitea of Siena, are so complete, so amply authenticated and attested beyond any doubt or question, so fully recorded, and I may add, comparatively speaking, so little known, that it has seemed worth while to consider them in some detail, more especially as both present the unusual feature of the liquefaction of blood which has flowed and been collected from the stigmatical wounds.

The Capuchin Order, founded by Fra Matteo da Bascio in 1524, originated in the ardent desire of that holy man to return to the primitive observance in all its simplicity, in all its austerity, of the Rule of St. Francis of Assisi. Throwing himself at the feet of Pope Clement VII [9] he pleaded: "Holy Father, it is well known to you that in these days of the Rule of St. Francis is not strictly observed; but I yearn to observe it most rigidly, yea, to the very letter." The Pope was much moved, and graciously answered: "That you may observe the Rule to the very letter, as you so greatly wish, we grant you all you ask of us" [10].

The Capuchins maintained, and one may well say, rejuvenated the Serephic Tradition, that system of prayer and meditation, which St. Teresa says, is the foundation of the Contemplative Life, and which must precede and prepare for those higher mystical graces which heaven bestows as and where and when it will. The Capuchins went back to mediæval sources, to St. Bernard with his burning love of Mary, to the Seraphic Doctor, St. Bonaventura, to the *Meditationes Vitae Jesu Christi* and the *Stimulus Amoris*. They were the specialists in the Interior Life. The note of Capuchin mysticism was love before learning. They threw wide the gates of mysticism to all. "La spiritualité franciscaine," writes the Abbé Henri Bremond, "paraît plus affective . . . plus libre, plus épanouissante" than that of many others. Others, I hasten to add, of the highest excellence and indeed of perfection. "Come unto the Marriage", the King invites. He even sends forth His servants, saying, "As many as ye shall find bid to the marriage". But, when the wedding is furnished with guests, among the company is found a man "which had not on a wedding garment".

It is no exaggeration to say that the zeal and fervour of the Capuchins swept through Europe, one might write through the known world, resistlessly like a great prairie fire. At the age of twenty-four, in September, 1587, Henri de Joyeuse, Comte de Bouchage, the handsomest youth and most brilliant star of the luxurious court of Henri III of France, who loved him tenderly, threw off his soft silks and satins, his lace of Valenciennes and his three-piled velvets; cast aside his jewels and his gems, his sweet pomanders and pouncet-boxes of gold, his rings of diamond and emeralds, his collars of balas rubies and orient pearls, to don the rough brown frieze frock, to gird himself with the harsh knotted cord, and wear the hard tanned sandals of a Capuchin, thenceforth to be known as Père Ange. It is said that the King swooned away when they broke the news to him, and whispered that Henri de Joyeuse had gone. Père Ange became an angel indeed. He advanced far along the way of "la vie unitive et extative" [12].

Behind the towering figure of His Red Eminence, Armand Jean Duplessis Richelieu, there stands in the shadow the Capuchin Père Joseph le Clere du Tremblay, "the grey Cardinal" of history, moulding the destinies of Europe. "That Père Joseph aspired to sanctity and the life dedicated to the holiest purpose none can doubt", writes a great authority [13]. He founds the Order of the Daughters of Calvary. He writes *Traités, Exercices spirituels, Constitutions.* For all his politics, for all his power, crumbled to dust and lost in forgetfulness, Mysticism is his sole achievement.

Names less generally known, but of far greater importance in the study of Mysticism are the Capuchins Fra Mattia Bellintani da Salo [14] who wrote the *Practica dell' orazione mentale, ovvero Contemplativa*; Fra Constantine de Barbaçon, Guardian of the Cologne convent, who published at Cologne in 1626 the treatise *Amoris Divini Occultae Semitae* [15], and whose precept was "Do not be anxious for many rules provided than canst love much". In 1637 Zacharie de Lisieux, printed his *La Philosophie Chrestienne* with a Dedication to the consort of Charles I of England, Queen Henrietta Maria, one of whose chaplains he had for a time been. In the last chapter of his work he describes how a soul striving after higher things can so spiritualize the body, that it actually becomes a sharer in the spirituality of the soul. *La Théologie naturelle* of Père Yves de Paris has been praised as a masterpiece for "profundity of thought and sheer beauty of style". We have here a spiritual classic written by a spiritual genius. The great Bonaventuran, Valeriano Magno, great by name, and great by fame, an encyclopædic author [16], published at Vienna in 1645, his *De Luce mentium*, which (it has been shrewdly observed) gave the Capuchins a unique opportunity of reinstating Bonaventuran teaching as a dynamic force in the intellectual world, an opportunity too unhappily let slip by. In 1658, at Paris, Père Paul de Lagny issued his *L'Exercise méthodique de l'oraison mentale en faveur des âmes qui se retrouvent dans l'état de vie contemplative.* The tradition was maintained. In 1680, at Paris, Alexandrin de la Ciotat publishes his *Le parfait Dénuement de l'âme contemplative.*

One name, although earlier in time, I have, as perhaps the greatest of all, kept unto the last. William Fitch of Canfield in Essex, where he was born in the third or fourth year of the reign of Queen Elizabeth, was a country gentleman of a good estate, and as gallant young squires with comely faces and full pockets wont, he soon made his way to London town. "Alas! alas!" he cried, in the very speech Greene or Dekker used, "how oft was I an idle lounger, ruffling it through the streets, how prone was I to run after all manner of games and pleasurings, how gladly did I frequent the theatres, how many times did I brave it up and down the middle walk of Paul's—pity, pity, for the profane desecration of London's cathedral church!—how swiftly did my feet bear me right nimbly to the schools, schools forsooth! schools of vaulting and fencing, of music and the dance, the brawls, the galliard, and light lavolta."

The chance—if chance it can be called—the chance reading of a mystical treatise struck to his very soul. In a lightning flash he realized the worthlessness of the world. From England he crossed to France, and there he found the haven where he would be. With the Psalmist he cried: "Lord, I have loved the beauty of Thine house, and the place where Thine Honour dwelleth." In 1586 Squire William Fitch was professed as a Capuchin at the Paris house, thenceforth to be known as Père Benoît de Canfield. His supernatural life was extraordinary. Even as a novice he passed into ecstasies so exalted and so prolonged that the good fathers were amazed and knew not what to think. One of his ecstasies endured uninterruptedly for two whole days. Physicians were called in who after the somewhat rough usage of the time, when all their remedies availed nothing thrust great pins into his arms and legs "to bring him back to life". But he remained utterly insensible to any cut or wound. It has been said that "the cloisters were the true field of his garnering, and it is known to God alone how many religious, monks, friars and nuns attained the highest perfection under his guidance" [17]. The Master of the Masters, as he was named, Benoît de Canfield was the spiritual director of such chosen souls as Cardinal Pierre de Bérulle, Founder of the French Oratory; of the Benedictine abbess Marie de Beauvillier; of the Carmelite, Madame Acarie, beatified in 1791, as Blessed Marie de l'Incarnation, foundress of the Discalced Daughters of St. Teresa in France. Benoît de Canfield died in Paris in 1611.

The bibliography of this great mystic is intricate, due to the fact that manuscript copies of his works were used in convents, and often transcribed, perhaps sometimes none too faithfully, and given to others. His masterpiece, however, was published by the author in Latin, French and English (Latin, Cologne, 1610), *The Rule of Perfection . . . reduced to this only point of the Will of God*, a treatise which served as a manual for generations of mystics [18]. Benoît de Canfield regards the sum and whole of Christian Perfection as consisting in one thing, the conformity of man's will with the Will of God. As revealed in external law it is the exterior Will of God; as indwelling in man it is the Interior Will of God. But over and beyond, far beyond these, there is yet another and completer conformity, the life of contemplation, the mystery of the divine union of the human soul with God, which is the most intimate possible union with God to which man upon earth can attain. It is, in fact, the Mystic Marriage. The earliest editions of the *Rule of Perfection* contain an allegorical frontispiece, the centre of which is a luminous Sun, the Will of God, to which are attracted and in which are absorbed symbolical figures or faces in three circles, of which the outer and furthest represents those souls who are engaged in an active life for God; in the second circle, nearer the Sun, are those who are in their degree contemplative; in the third circle, inscribed lĕhoüa, are those caught up and enraptured by God. But the eyes of all are fixed intently on the Sun, which according to the due measure of their proximity, irradiates all.

"The Rule of Perfection," comments Father Cuthbert, "is not easy reading, hardly the book for the novice in the spiritual life" [*18*]. Very truly said, but he to whom the teaching of Benoît de Canfield does not grow clearer and clearer as he studies it more closely and absorbs it will always remain a novice in the spiritual life. As Father Faber [*19*] so admirably writes: "The spiritual life is quite a cognizably distinct thing from the worldly life; and the difference comes from prayer. . . . To pray always is to feel the sweet urgency of prayer, and to hunger after it. . . . The peculiar trial of hard work is that it keeps us so much from prayer, and takes away the flower of our strength before we have time for prayer, and physical strength is very needful for praying well." There must be a certain uninterrupted gravitation of the mind to God. The Carthusian, Dom Beaucousin, a great master of the spiritual life, gave it as his considered opinion that Benoît de Canfield's *Rule of Perfection* was "especially helpful and suited to all those who wish to tread the path of perfection, whether they be but beginners, or those who have advanced a little way, or those who have reached the goal." The treatise may not be easy reading at first. What mystical book can be easy reading? The point is that the novice must ask himself whether he finds it becoming more easy, more simple, more plain as he reads on. If not, assuredly there is something wrong somewhere. We cannot read it as some light volume of mere entertainment. If rightly read, the difficulties soon disappear, and all is clear in the light of the central Sun.

Sébastien de Senlis in his *Philosophie des contemplatifs contenant toutes les leçons fondamentales de la vie active, contemplative et suréminente,* Paris, 1621, went so far as to say that "if the duty of charity or of obedience calls us to any external activity at a time when Ecstasy would lift us into the third heaven, we must leave all and quickly descend." This seems to me highly debatable, I hesitate to say that it is a temerarious proposition. God must come first.

Few, of course, few indeed should venture to pronounce the vows made by St. Teresa and the Theatine St. Andrea Avellino—always to do what is most perfect.

We must not try to run before we can walk. The very attempt means failure and discouragement, and sometimes in the dejection hope is abandoned, and the battle lost ere begun. Let us walk warily, slowly, but surely, step by step. The exercise of humility is necessary at every step and nothing is more invigorating than humility.

Those who are beginning a devout life, that is to say a life of more than ordinary devotion, those in fine who aspire to the mystical way, cannot at the very first moment of this resolution expect to find themselves transported to the summit of Carmel. The novice must wean himself gradually from the world—there have, of course, been sudden and altogether exceptional cases, but nobody has a right to expect miracles—and the world has its just and lawful claims in their degree. For instance, no religious Order would admit a subject who had an aged parent depending upon him as a sole support. The aspirant may truly live the interior life, and yet in so far as is lawful, quite laudably conform to the duties of that state in which God has temporarily set him for such time as is necessary. He should endeavour not to be singular in his conduct. There is a sentence of Father Faber's which at first sounds rather startling, but which is profoundly true, "What is all very well for Camaldoli can hardly be the thing for Piccadilly" [20].

A pure and perfect love of God may be independent of any particular station or form of life. Thus whilst Giuliano Adorno and his wife Catharine were still living outside the hospital of the Pammatone in their little house at the junction of the Via S. Guiseppe and the Via Balilla, they were on one occasion visited by Fra Domenico de Ponzo, an Observant Franciscan of great repute for sanctity. This good man, either to test her spirit or else because he was truly mistaken in his argument, during their talk observed that, since she was in the secular state and a married woman, it was impossible for her to love God so perfectly as a religious, as himself for example, who belonged to an Order and who had accordingly renounced the world. So long as he contented himself with showing the undoubted superiority of the religious over the secular state Catharine agreed with him and listened dutifully, but when he began to argue that the love of God was more free to a Religious and must necessarily be experienced in far greater degree by a monk or a friar than a secular, the Saint springing to her feet with sparkling eyes and a joyous countenance, so that she seemed almost in ecstasy, warmly opposed him, saying, "Father, if I thought the habit you are so blessed as to wear could add one tenth to the love of God I would strip it from you and wrap myself in it. That the religious state may well enable you to acquire far more merit than myself I do not dispute, I gratulate you on your privilege and great happiness therein, but that I cannot love God as much as you is a thing you will never never be able to make me understand. For verily such is not the case." And the Saint spoke with such force and fire, enraptured with love, that her beauteous hair came undone, and falling down, was scattered upon her shoulders so that she looked like a bride rejoicing upon her nuptial day [21].

Upon which Baron von Hügel comments: "There is probably no scene recorded for us, so completely characteristic of St. Catharine of Genoa at her deepest: the breadth and the fulness, the self-oblivion and the dignity, the claimlessness and the spiritual power—all are there" [22].

We are reminded how Saint Bonaventura said to the humble old cottager's wife: "My daughter, believe me, a poor ignorant woman can love God as truly and every bit as well as Fra Bonaventura."

In his *The Scale of Perfection* [23], addressed to a nun in the cloister,

Walter Hilton the Carthusian mystic, instructs his votaress: "Worship (*i.e.* respect) in thy heart such as lead active lives in the world, and suffer many tribulations and temptations which thou, sitting in thy house feelest nought of; and they endure very much labour and care, and take much care for their owne and other men's sustenance: and many of them, had rather, if they might, serve God as thou dost, in bodily rest and quietnesse. And nevertheless they in the midst of their worldly businesse, avoyd many sins, which thou, if thou wert in their state, shouldst fall into; and they do many good deeds, which thou canst not do. There is no doubt that many do thus; but which they be, thou knowest not; and therefore 'tis good for thee to worship (respect) them all, and set them all in thy heart above thyselfe as thy betters, and caste thyselfe down at their feet." Thus strongly does the good monk urge humility. It is, he practically says, a question of vocation. The contemplative life is the highest of all, but it is not everyone who is bidden to the mystical estate, and if a man in whatever walk of life he be placed loves God perfectly, the same is a perfect man in the sight of God.

Guigo, the fifth Prior of the Carthusians, in his brief *Meditations* makes it clear that Peace sought, and it may be found in temporal things, is as transitory and fragile as they are. Man's real Peace is only to be found in those things which are eternal. Herein is the spirit of the Carthusian Order, which Pius XI praised as the "most perfect life", and in every deed that "better part" chosen by Mary of Bethany. There can be, a learned Benedictine observes, commenting upon the Apostolic Constitution of 10th August, 1924, no more perfect way of life than is to be found in the silence and solitude of the cloister, where dwell those who seek for an intimate union with God and strive after the highest degree of interior sanctity.

That many should very mistakenly deem a wider and more liberal exercise of active virtues more suited to the present day is an error condemned both by Leo XIII and Pius XI, the latter of whom does not hesitate to say that "This mistaken idea is harmful and destructive to the theory and practice of Christian perfection."

It is hardly to be expected that the world can or will see this. We are not surprised to find that a man of bastard culture such as Matthew Arnold, in his *Stanzas from the Grande Chartreuse* under the guise of pseudo-romantic verse, betrays and lays quite naked and unashamed his utter lack of spirituality, without which quality no poetry can be written. He prattles dryly of himself as

> *Wandering between two worlds, one dead,*
> *The other powerless to be born.*

In fact he is a waif and stray, he confesses himself "forlorn", he is just a nonentity. He tells how "rigorous Teachers seiz'd my youth" and "shew'd me the pale, cold star of Truth". Was he truly deceived? Did he not at times suspect, yet fear to acknowledge that this "pale cold star of Truth" was a vain and empty lie? Had he no questionings, no doubts?

146

Another romantic writer, Robert Louis Stevenson, in similar fashion betrayed himself as lacking the supreme quality of spirituality. He writes himself down unmystical. In *Our Lady of the Snows* he shouts somewhat brazenly for action. The Carthusians to him are life's malingerers. Whereas they are life's victors. Is there not something hectic, something morbid, in this cry for the "the uproar and the press"? Is not Stevenson the sick man trying to boast his superlative health? In contradiction how truly does Ernest Dowson sum up the Carthusian ideal:

> *O beatific life! Who is there shall gainsay,*
> *Your great refusal's victory, your little loss,*
> *Deserting vanity for the more perfect way,*
> *The sweeter service of the most dolorous Cross.*

> *Ye shall prevail at last! Surely ye shall prevail!*
> *Your silence and austerity shall win at last:*
> *Desire and mirth, the world's ephemeral lights shall fail,*
> *The sweet star of your Queen is never overcast. . . .*

> *Move on, white company, whom that has not sufficed!*
> *Our viols cease, our wine is death, our roses fail:*
> *Pray for our heedlessness, O dwellers with the Christ!*
> *Though the world fall apart, surely ye shall prevail.*

NOTES TO CHAPTER IV

1. The Feast of the Stigmata of St. Francis of Assisi, 17th September, is a Universal Feast, kept by the whole Church, and in the General Calendar. The Augustinians keep the Feast of the Stigmata of St. Clare of Montefalco on 30th October; the Carmelites on the 27th August, keep the Feast of the Transverberation of the Heart of St. Teresa; the Dominicans on 1st (formerly 3rd) April keep the Feast of the Stigmata of St. Catharine of Siena. In various offices of Saints and Beati, proper to their several owners, mention is made of the Stigmata which they bore, e.g. among the Domicicans, St. Margaret of Hungary, 19th January; St. Catharine de Ricci, 13th February; Blessed Stephana de Quinzani, 2nd January; Blessed Osanna of Mantua, 18th June; Blessed Lucia da Narni, 19th November; and many more. Among the Augustinians, St. Rita of Cascia, 22nd May; among the Carthusians, Blessed Béatrix d'Ornacieu, 13th February; among the Mercedenians, Blessed Marianna de Jesús, 17th April; among the Trinitarians, St. Miguel de los Santos, 5th July. These are only a few examples from many.

2. Such is the case with the relics of stigmatical blood of the Venerable Passitea Crogi of Siena, as will be noticed below.

3. There is an account of St. Clare of Montefalco in the *Acta Sanetorum*, *B. Clara de Cruce, virgo prope Montefalconem in Umbria*, under 18th August. *The Life of St. Clare of the Cross*, by E. A. Foran, O.S.A., 1935, is a popular, but useful, little book. An American priest in 1886 adapted for general reading from a French version, Fr. Lorenzo Tardy's *Vita di Santa Chiara*.

4. *Vita di Santa Chiara di Montefalco, O.S.A.*, scritta dal Rmo. Maestro Lorenzo Tardy, Roma, Tipografia della Pace, 1881.

5. Reprinted in the various editions of J. A. Symonds' collected *Sketches and Studies in Italy and Greece*. New edition, 1898, Second Series.

6. 1316–1344.

7. *Vita della Ven. Madre Passitea Crogi Senese Fondatrice del Monasterio della Religiose Cappuccine nella Città di Siena*, scrita da Lodovico Marracci Lucchese, Sacerdote professo della Congregatione de' Chierici Regolari della Madre di Dio. In Roma. Nella Stampa di Filippo Maria Mancini. 1669. *Con Licenza de' Superiori*.

8. Ferdinando I, Grand Duke of Tuscany, born 18th July, 1549. Created a Cardinal, 1563. Abdicated 1608. Henri IV of France married Maria de' Medici, his second wife, October, 1600.

9. Clement VII (Giulio de' Medici) reigned 1523–1534. It was his niece, Catharine de' Medici, who encouraged the Capuchins to make a foundation in France. Actually, under her influence, they had come to France at the invitation of her son Charles IX, who died 31st May, 1573. Pending the arrival of Henri III from Poland, Catharine, Queen-regent, most warmly received them, and gave them a house in the suburb Saint-Honoré.

10. There was, of course, opposition, and technical difficulties had to be smoothed. See Mario da Mereato Seracino, *Delle Origini dei Frati Minori Cappucini Descrizione Seconda*, edited by P. Giuseppe da Fermo, Ancona, 1927.

11. *Histoire Littéraire du Sentiment Religieux en France*. II. *L'Invasion Mystique*. Paris, Bloud et Gay, 1925. Chapitre III. La Tradition Séraphlique.

12. For further details see *La vie du R. P. Ange de Joyeuse* . . . by M. Jacques Brousse, Paris, 1621.

13. *The Capuchins*, by Father Cuthbert, O.S.F.C., 2 Vols. London, 1928. Vol. II, p. 307.

14. 1534–1611.

15. It is probable that *The Secret Paths* originally appeared in French. Before 1657 an English translation had been made by Dom Anselm Touchet, O.S.B.

16. He died 25th July, 1661. His life was harassed and sad, and darkened with the most intricate and difficult problems.

17. Brousse, *op. cit.* p. 593.

18. *The Capuchins*, II, p. 424.

19. *Growth in Holiness*, 1854. Fourth Edition, 1872, p. 257.

20. *Ibid*, p. 98.

21. *B. Caterina da Genova* . . . *illustrata*. By Giacinto Papera, Oratorian. Genova, 1682.

22. *The Mystical Element of Religion as studied in Saint Catherine of Genoa and her Friends*. Second Edition, London, 1923; Vol. I, p. 141.

23. Dom Walter Hilton died in 1396. I quote from the old edition of *The Scale of Perfection*, London, 1659, pp. 21–22. There is a more recent edition, edited with an introduction by Father Dalgairns, London, 1908.

CHAPTER FIVE

*The Spiritual Diary of St. Veronica—Dominican Mystics—The Sufferings of Anne
Catharine Emmerich—The Stigmaticas of the Tyrol—Miss Collins—St. Gemma
Galgani—The Saint of the Impossible.*

"CONVOLATE ad urbes refugii, ad loca videlicet religiosa, ubi possitis
de praeteritis agere poenitentiam, in praesenti obtinere gratiam et fidu-
cialiter futuram gratiam praestolari." Those are the profoundly wise
words of St. Bonaventura in his tractate *On the Worthlessness of the
World (De Contemptu Mundi).*

The Seraphic Tradition as taught by the Capuchins, is essentially
one of contemplation. We find it therefore in its fulness in the strictly
enclosed convents of Capuchin nuns. The Capuchinesses, a branch of
Poor Clares, were instituted by the Spanish noble lady, Maria Lorenza
Longo [1], and originally developed from a community of Tertiary Sisters
of St. Francis, at Naples. The nuns were approved by Paul III, who on
10th December, 1538, appointed Capuchins to serve the convent as
chaplains and spiritual directors.

The glory of the Capuchin nuns—may we not say of the whole
Capuchin Order?—is that sublime ecstatica St. Veronica Giuliani. We
are fortunate enough to possess her *Diario* written under obedience, one
of the world's great spiritual masterpieces [2].

Born on 27th December, 1660, at Mercatello, a small township in
the ancient Duchy of Urbino, Ursula—for thus she was named on the
following day at the font of the Collegiate Church—came of a gentle
house. Her parents, Francesco Giuliani and his wife Benedetta Mancini
of San Angelo in Vado, a lady much revered by her friends and neighbours
for her simple piety and tender charities, were persons of position and
no little distinction. From her earliest years Ursula, who lost her mother
when she was but a child of three, showed every sign of an altogether
remarkable and forceful character. She something resembles St. Teresa
of Ávila, since her surpassing holiness was never separated from that
dignity which derives of true nobility, both of soul and of race. Whilst
yet quite young, Ursula Giuliani read a Life of St. Rose of Lima [3],
and as she read she marvelled, half-afraid, at the mortifications of "The
Flower of the New World". She lifted her eyes from the Book, scarce
daring to turn the page, and then suddenly her heart burned within her
with a fire of flame, and she whispered, heard only by the Angels, "If
this Peruvian maiden did thus, why may I not also do the same?"

Wherefore secretly she penanced herself, and a smile always on her
lips she trod the path of pain. In 1669, her father was appointed to an
office of great honour and responsibility, at Piacenza, whither he went
taking his little daughter with him. Her two elder sisters, Anna Gertrude

and Lodovica, were left behind. They had taken solemn vows, and wore the habit of Poor Clares in the convent of Santa Chiara at Mercatello.

Presently Francesco plans a splendid match for his daughter, little knowing that she was already spoused to a Heavenly Bridegroom. He could not read the secret which lay in those sweet clear eyes that met his so lovingly. He did not know the inscrutable thoughts behind that pure white forehead. He saw his daughter, dressed as became her station in velvet petticoat or rich brocade, wearing the jewels he fondly lavished on his darling, and he rejoiced to think of her as the wife of some wealthy noble, for already many a knight had offered for her hand. And at his bidding she braided her hair with pearls, and robed her body in satins and silks he bought her from the mercers, but he little kenned that beneath all the rough hair-shirt chafed and rasped that delicate skin. "For whilst in my father's house," she writes with sweet simplicity, "I thought it my duty to be obedient to my father, and cheerfully to do his will in all things."

One morning, then, Francesco called his daughter to him—she was only sixteen—and told her of the nuptials which were preparing and of her many suitors, bidding her choose him whom best she could love. And so he would live to see his grandchildren clustering around his chair, and the house of Giuliani would be continued in the world. Tenderly she embraced him, and standing there on the loggia in the hot Italian sunlight, she spoke then of another Lover to whom she was promised, a Lover for whom she must forsake all, even her own people and her father's house. His head fell upon his breast, and as the tears rained down his cheeks, she fell upon her knees before him, when laying his hand in blessing upon her lovely hair, he said with a deep sad sigh, "The Will of God be done."

She had chosen, that lovely patrician girl, one of the most severe, one of the most humblest, one of the poorest, of all Orders. "Farewell, sweet world, I leave you for ever!" she cried. Genoa velvet with purfling miniver were cast aside for the habit of course brown frieze girt with knotted cord; a thick black choir mantle covered the head in lieu of gemmed coif or golden coronet; three grates with a dark curtain between shut off all externs; for the rule was uncompromisingly taut, similar to that of the Farnesiane nuns of the Rione Monti at Rome, the *Sepolte Vive*. On 28th October, 1677, she made her profession into the hands of a holy Carmelite, Monsignor Giuseppe Sebastiani, Bishop of Città di Castello [4], and vowed herself as a barefoot Capuchiness of the strictest observance in the Convent of Santa Chiara of Città di Castello.

As I remember it, this Convent of Capuchin nuns is an austere building, remote and recluse. The little baroque church is singularly attractive.

Because of her burning devotion to the Passion Ursula Giuliani in religion took the name Veronica, in memory of that holy woman, who gave her linen napkin to comfort the Christ and wipe the sweat and blood from His eyes as He passed on the way to Calvary.

But convent life is not a bed of roses for God's chosen souls. He did not intend it to be. There are crosses and chagrins. Veronica found that the Abbess, a good and even holy woman as she was, often showed herself strangely capricious, in temper uncertain and often indiscreet. The Novice Mistress, a Florentine lady of high rank, Suor Teresa Ristori, seemed reserved even to moroseness, unhelpful in difficulties, slow of understanding. The nuns were unsympathetic and cold; her fellow novice—there was only one—proved openly inimical to the "bambina" as the community, half in scorn, used to call Veronica. "My only hours of peace," writes St. Veronica, "were those spent in choir whilst we psalmodied the Office." Heaven strewed thorns in her path. It is often thus. We may compare the convent trials of St. Margaret Mary Alacoque, and of many another, made perfect in the furnace of frets, and antagonism, petty jealousies, maybe, and bitter tongues.

However, as the years passed the sweet patience of Veronica was amply recognized by the whole community, who grew to love her dearly. She was elected Abbess on 5th April, 1716, and she died 9th July, 1727.

The greatest of spiritual experience of her life, the Mystic Marriage and the holy stigmata which she received on 5th April, 1697, must be told in her own words, or at least summarized from the *Diario*.

Upon the night of 3rd April, 1697, Veronica, some little while before going down to choir for the Office of Matins, was praying in her cell, when on a sudden there seemed to fall upon her soul a great darkness, a darkness of Egypt which could be felt. She was drenched and saturated with sorrow. After a short space she beheld Our Lord crowned with thorns, who said to her: "I am come to ask somewhat of thee, yea, and to give thee a gift of much price, but thou must accept it not only willingly, nay more, with joy and gladness. Thou shalt be crowned with this My crown." At these words I burned with exceeding fierce desire to be crowned with the Holy Crown of Thorns. And our Saviour said "What dost thou thus yearn for, Veronica? What dost thou ask of Me? What wilt thou?" And I made reply: "Lord, I seek only to do Thy will, I am ready, Lord, to suffer all with Thee." Whereupon there stood by me my Guardian Angel, radiant as the sun. With awful reverence he took in his hands the Crown of Thorns. Our Lord, then, Himself with His own hands pressed the Crown upon my brow, and I felt an agony of pain, not only in my head, but an ache which thrilled throughout every limb, so that I was nigh to swooning. And the Divine Voice said in accents of tenderest love: "All this is nothing to the anguish I felt when they crowned Me with thorns. The agony that racks thee is but a shadow of My sufferings. If thou lovest Me, needs must thou suffer all with Me, so shalt thou be transformed wholly and gathered unto Me." Veronica could but whisper, "Lord, Thou knowest I love Thee." And the Vision faded from her sight. But when she would have risen to her feet, she tottered and nearly fell, so great was the pain of the Crown of Thorns which encircled her head. But she offered to the Eternal Father the Blood and Passion of Christ, and cried aloud: "Blessed be God! More pain! A heavier cross to çome!" She trembled in every limb, and tears streamed from her eyes. Yet she went her way to choir, and performed every duty of the day. And that night, when after Compline, she had returned to her cell, there appeared to her Our Lord and Our Lady in great glory, with a choir of Angels who sang *Victory! Victory!*

Thus St. Veronica Giuliani in mystic wise was crowned with the Crown of Thorns.

During the evening of 5th April, two days later, St. Veronica passed from contemplation to the heights of ecstasy, in which supernatural state she was entranced for above two hours. When her senses returned from the rapture she beheld a glorious vision of the Risen Lord and Our Lady with Angels, upon which she cried aloud: "Lord, have mercy upon me, for I am a miserable sinner!" It seemed to be that miraculously assisted by the Angel choir she made a confession of all her sins, and then Our Lord Himself absolved her, and showed her the red wounds in His hands, feet, and gashed side. "Oh God! Oh God! Such were the raptures of divine love which consumed me that I can neither speak nor write of my burning desire." "Thou also shalt be wounded as I am wounded with five wounds," said the Divine Voice, as the Vision faded away. "Oh, Spouse of my heart, my one and only love," cried Veronica, "crucify me with Thyself." With these words she flung herself on her knees before the Crucifix and taking it in her hands she gently kissed the wounded hands, the feet, and side, saying, "Oh, Spouse of my heart, my one and only love. Thou didst suffer and wast nailed to the Cross for love of me, vouchsafe that I may suffer and be crucified for love of Thee."

She then replaced the crucifix on the altarino, and was lost in prayer, when she saw Our Lord nailed to the Cross, at the foot of which stood Our Lady, just as She had once stood on Calvary. St. Veronica, remembering the words: "Needs must thou suffer all with Me, so shalt thou be transformed wholly and gathered unto Me" [5] besought the Blessed Virgin, the Addolorata, that through the sword which pierced the Immaculate Heart and the infinite merits of Her Sorrows, the promise might straightway be fulfilled. There immediately ensued an extraordinary psychological crisis preceding the physical phenomena. The Blessed Virgin fixed Her gaze more intently upon Her Son, and as their eyes met there came into the field of consciousness of Veronica, as though energized by some irresistible force [6], a conviction profounder far than any intellectual concept or persuasion, that outside God nothing had any existence at all. Veronica had in that instant sensibly contacted the Ultimate Reality.

At that moment God drew her soul to Him (*all' unione amorosa con Essolui*) in that most intimate and divine Union, that sublime state in which, as St. Teresa of Ávila explains, God and the soul are knit together in mystic marriage, and mutually enjoy their corresponsive love in the depths of silence, since such nuptials are not to be expressed in words, and can at best only be vaguely described by the metaphor of the closest and most indissoluble of human relationships.

Our Lady then said to Her Son: "Let Thy bride be crucified with Thee."

"In an instant I saw five brilliant rays of light dart forth from the

Five Sacred Wounds, and all seemed to concentrate their force upon me. And I saw that these rays became small flames of burning fire. Four of them appeared in the form of great pointed nails, whilst the fifth was a spear-head of gleaming gold, all a-quiver as thrice heated hot. And this, a levin flash, lancing upon me, pierced my heart through and through, and the four sharp nails of fire stabbed through my hands and my feet. I felt a fearful agony of pain, but with the pain I clearly saw and was conscious that I was wholly transformed into God [7]. When I had been thus wounded, in my heart, in my hands and feet, the rays of light gleaming with a new radiance shot back to the Crucifix, and illumed the gashed side, the hands and feet of Him Who was hanging there. Thus My Lord and My God espoused me, and gave me in charge to His Most Holy Mother for ever and ever, and bade my Guardian Angel watch over me, for He was jealous of His honour, and then thus He spake to me: "I am Thine, I give Myself wholly unto thee. Ask whatsoever thou wilt, it shall be granted thee." I made reply: "Beloved, only one thing I ask, never to be separated from Thee." And then in a twinkling all vanished away.

"When I came to myself I found that I was kneeling with my arms wide outspread, benumbed and sore cramped, and my heart, my hands and my feet burned and throbbed with great pain. I felt that my side was gashed open and welled and bubbled with blood. I tried to open my habit and see the wound, but I could not because of the wounds in both my hands. After a while, with much suffering, I succeeded in loosing my habit, and I then saw that the wound in my side purled forth with water and blood. I wished to trace a few lines but I could not hold the quill in my hand for very agony. Whereupon I prayed to my Spouse, begging Him that my fingers might at least have power to guide the pen, since being under obedience I wished to write a screed for my confessor, and for him alone. And with the ink of my blood I wrote upon a paper the name Jesus. Then again I tried to lift the quill, and I found I was able to do so and to inscribe fair letters upon the virgin parchment."

St. Veronica proceeds to tell of other wonderful and mysterious experiences. She has, in fact, in her unfolding of the spiritual life few equals among the Saints, and she takes her place with the greatest, with the Gothic Princess, St. Birgitta of Sweden, with St. Teresa and St. Maria Maddalena de' Pazzi, St. Catharine of Siena, St. Gertrude, Blessed Angela of Foligno, Anne Catharine Emmerich, Heaven's most radiant stars.

The successive stigmatization in the case of St. Veronica, who first received the Crown of Thorns and a couple of days later the imprint of the five Sacred Wounds can be not infrequently parallelled in the accounts of other stigmaticas. Thus, Blessed Osanna Andreasi of Mantua [8], a votaress of the Third Order of St. Dominic, being mystically espoused to Christ on 24th February, 1476, received from His hands the Crown of Thorns which He placed on her head saying: "Receive, my beloved, the gift I give thee, this heavenly and most worshipful Diadem, for which thou hast besought Me so instantly and so long. Shrink not from the pain thereof, for thus I give thee a sure token that shalt be one of the virgin quires in Paradise." The Beata made reply: "Sweetest and secret Lover of my soul, not only do I not shrink from the pain Thy adorable gift must bring me now, for certes, cruel is the anguish of Thy thorny Crown, nathless 'tis that for which my heart craveth and burns exceedingly." As she knelt the Divine Hands encircled her forehead with the Crown whose thorns dripped with great gouts of Blood like rubies set there, and such was the agony that she fell into a deep swoon and lay stretched lifeless on the cold ground.

In the following year, upon the 5th June, when a holy woman, her friend Margherita Serafina, was present Osanna was rapt in ecstasy. Upon returning to herself she cried: "I have been raised up, ay, unto the seventh heaven, and there I saw Our Lord in exceeding great glory, and the Wound in His side shone with a light like unto the sun at hottest noon." At that same moment she had received the wound in her left side, as though it had been pierced by a spear.

A year later, on Friday in Passion Week, during which sacred season Osanna had withdrawn to her little country house, Bigarello by name, not far from Mantua, in order that she might spend all Passiontide and Holy Week in absolute seclusion, whilst she was praying fervently in her oratory and weeping over the sufferings of Calvary, there appeared to her Our Lord, the Wounds in whose Hands and Feet were as four radiant crimson jewels, and as He said "My spouse, beloved spouse, fear not the pain; the more thou dost suffer on earth the nearer shalt thou be to My Heart in heaven," lo! from the four red Wounds there darted four forked flambent rays which pierced through, like the thrust of white hot daggers, her feet and hands. She swooned, half-dead, moaning piteously, "like the lament of the turtle-dove" says the old chronicle. All her life long the stab of the stigmata endured. On Wednesdays and Fridays she felt as if huge twopenny nails were being remorselessly hammered through the tender flesh, whilst during Holy Week so fierce was the agony that she herself declares, "Had I not been miraculously holpen of Heaven I had surely died." Under the tenuity of the skin the four wounds crimsoned and flushed as if about to pour forth a great gush of blood, nor could they be concealed from her servants and those who were her familiar friends.

Blessed Osanna died on 18th June, 1505. Her body still remains showing the marks of the holy stigmata, for it is miraculously preserved incorrupt throughout the centuries.

The Dominicaness, Blessed Stefana Quinzani [9] of Soncino (near Bergamo), who lived 1457–1530, on every Friday experienced the agony of the sweat of blood in Gethsemane and the pains of the Cross of Thorns which was often plainly seen encircling her head. Joanna Maria della Croce [10] (1603–1673), a Poor Clare of Rovereto (Italian Tyrol), received the Four Wounds and the Crown of Thorns, which latter she used to conceal beneath her veil. When her body was exhumed many years after her death it was found that not only was it incorrupt but that the wound in the side was fresh, and blood issued thence. In an earlier instance,

St. Christina of Stommeln [*11*] (1242–1312), the wounds both in her hands and her feet were seen by many, and on Good Friday, 1269, whilst she was in ecstasy the maidens who tended her saw rivulets of blood running down from her forehead, and some days later they remarked that her shift was stained on the left side in the region of the heart with a large patch of newly-shed blood. She had received the stigmata for the first time in 1268, and year by year during Passiontide and Holy Week they dripped with blood. It was thus the wounds were discovered, for the Saint expressed her displeasure by silence when any reference to them was attempted or any hint injudiciously thrown out. The skull of the Saint which is venerated at Nideck is surrounded by a curious formation in the bone, which about a finger's breadth at the back sensibly increases as it is carried on towards the ears. There are a series of regular marks which seem as though they must have been made in life, and would be accounted for by a number of wounds made by a nail or sharp thorns piercing the flesh.

In 1879, Teresa Helena Higginson (1844–1905) joined the school staff at St. Alexander's, Bootle, and at first lodged with a Mrs. Nicholson, whose little daughter entering the kitchen one day said: "Oh, Mother, there is blood trickling from the lady's head and hands, and she seems in a kind of trance." When later Teresa joined the Misses Catterall and some other teachers at No. 15, Ariel Street, the marks of blood could not long escape their notice. One morning Miss Catterall met her coming out of church and saw that her white scarf was stained with the blood that dripped from a number of little marks like thorn-punctures round her brow. Often the school-children would say: "Oh! Teacher, you must have hurt your forehead and your hands. Oh! how you have scratched your forehead!" She used to try to cover up her forehead with a veil, but the blood welled through.

Among those ecstaticas who have received the stigmata severally, that is to say after a lapse of time and at intervals occurring between the woundings, which may be first, the diademing with the Crown of Thorns, and then the piercing of one hand or one foot, or the lateral wound, or, perhaps, in some varying order until stigmatization is complete, is the Dominicaness Blessed Helen of Hungary of the Convent of St. Catharine at Veszprim [*12*]. So many extraordinary, one might say unique, phenomena, all most certainly verified so far as human evidence is worth anything at all, are chronicled in regard to Blessed Helen that she assuredly claims special notice.

The Convent of St. Catharine was of the Second Order, that is to say contemplative and most strictly enclosed. St. Dominic desired that his daughters should be totally separated and cut off from the world. Himself, he erected grilles in the Church and locutory. The rule of the enclosure was most rigid and absolute. Only Cardinals, Bishops, reigning Kings and Queens, might enter without desecration, and even for these permission from the Supreme Pontiff was deemed desirable. In the cases of urgent necessity, an approved doctor, "a grave man of reverend years", and the confessor might be admitted. Once a year the Master-

General, the Provincial or his Vicars, were allowed to pass in for their Canonical Visitation. So high are the walls built which surround Dominican Convents of the Second Order that the nuns are frequently spoken of as "Immured" or "Enwalled"—Pope Innocent IV (1243-1254) describes these convents as "fortified citadels, having neither egress nor regress."

Little wonder, then, that these enclosed Dominican Convents became centres and schools of the highest mysticism. In the Lives of the Dominican Sisters of Unterlinden, near Colmar in Alsace, which was one of the most fervent of all the Second Order houses, it is related that not merely two or three nuns but the whole were mystics who had attained to the highest contemplation. "Their hearts burned with the most ardent love, their thoughts were never for an instant diverted from God. Unterlinden was a house of rapture and joy." Unterlinden, indeed, was known as "Heaven begun".

The date of the birth of Blessed Helen of Veszprim and the date of her death are not exactly known, but Père Lechat, an authority of the first class, in the recent November volume of the *Acta Sanctorum* (Bollandists), where Blessed Helen is given under the 9th of that month, argues almost to demonstration that she must have died at some date shortly before 1250 [*13*]. The manuscript Life of Blessed Helen, which the Bollandists now print, is transcribed from a copy of the early fifteenth century, but it is certain that it must have been originally written at Veszprim before 1260, at the latest, and this little biography was composed by nuns who were her contemporaries, who lived with her in daily and intimate intercourse. The ninth of November has been assigned to her on account of an entry under that day in a work of immense and most carefully sifted research by two eminent Dominican scholars Jean Baptiste Feuillet and Thomas Soueges of Paris, *Année Dominicaine, ou les vies des Saints et Bienhereux, des Martyrs et autres personnes illustres, recommandables par leur piété, de l'un et de l'autre sexe, de l'Ordre des frères Prêcheurs*, 13 vols., quarto. Paris, 1678 [*14*] *et seq.*

It may be remarked that although Blessed Helen is so termed, and justly, on account of cultus immemorial there has not yet been any official beatification nor a formal recognition, *confirmatio cultus*, by the Holy See. Her feast is not kept in the Order, but immediately after her death she was honoured as "Beata Helena" in the convent of Veszprim, her relics were preserved there and venerated with episcopal approval, and what is a very important point [*15*], she was depicted with the halo amongst other saintly Dominicanesses, as she appears in the painting by Fra Angelico in the London National Gallery.

The *Life*, written before 1260 by the Veszprim community, does not follow any methodical arrangement, but begins, somewhat abruptly to our thinking, with an account of the stigmata of Blessed Helen. The good nuns, deeming this the most extraordinary and memorable fact associated with their Sister, commence simply enough by at once recording it without preface or preamble. It is very understandable, and is clear proof of the absolute sincerity of the biographers. Cavil and criticism are completely disarmed.

And so they open their honest self-proven relation: "We, the Sisters of the Convent of St. Catharine of Veszprim relate and place on record all that we have seen with our own eyes touching the Lady Helen, our Sister, and we cannot be mistaken nor err, because for many years did we live most familiarly in her company. She had wounds in both hands, and in her feet, and her breast was also wounded. The first wound was made in her right hand, upon the night of the Feast of St. Francis (4th October). And this maugre her oppugnancy and for all that she resisted crying out: "Lord, refrain; do not this thing my Lord and God." In very sooth we heard her utter these words, although we did not see with whom she wrestled nor unto whom she spoke. The second wound was made at noon, upon the Feast of the Holy Apostles Peter and Paul (29th June). In the wound of her right hand there budded a thread or stalk of fair gold, and this golden filament, intertwining, bourgeoned, and so increased in length. Also we saw a fragrant lily grow with fair white petals and a stem of gold. This we saw, but to prevent them being seen by any other eyes the Lady Helen uprooted and dug them out of her hands. Which flowers were religiously kept by us for a long while after she had passed to Paradise." Moreover there grew from the wound, the ferita, low down in the bosom, a lily of exquisite purity and marvellous perfume. This flower she tore out as from its very roots, but it was carefully preserved by the nuns. Not only did the whole community see this but it was shown to King Bela IV, the father of St. Margaret of Hungary, as also to several other externs.

The stigmata of Blessed Helen gradually assumed the form of golden circles, and it was remarked that at certain times, particularly upon great Feasts, her hands shone with a soft radiant glow.

The stigmatization of Blessed Helen is a very early example. St. Francis of Assisi in retreat on Monte Alvernia, received the stigmata on Holy Cross Day in September, 1224.

He died at sunset on 3rd October, 1226, and, less than two years later, was canonized by Gregory IX on 16th July, 1228. Blessed Helen must have received the first wound, in her right hand, not later than 1237, and probably at an even earlier date. That the phenomena which accompanied her mystical experiences are literally true and most faithfully reported is not open to question. Seek to explain them as some may, the facts remain.

Wherever Blessed Helen went some strange beauty followed and surrounded her. Often flowers would spring to life beneath her feet as she trod the cloister garth. Fresh flowers fell from her scarred and pierced hands. A mysterious and lovely light accompanied her. The Veszprim convent was very humble and poor, too poor for the community to have candles save at Mass. Once when her duties detained Blessed Helen in the kitchen where she had been chopping up kindling wood, she perforce came later to choir, not indeed until Compline was ending and the *Salve Regina* was about to be sung. As she took her wonted place two tapers were seen aglow upon the altar, and these continued to shine until the last notes died away. More than once, in her presence, the altar candles lit of their own accord, and remained burning without being consumed. Not a splash or dropping of wax was lost.

The same phenomenon occurred during the Mass of St. Herman Joseph, the Premonstratensian of Steinfeld. At the consecration he passed into an ecstasy, which lasted an hour, but the candles which were carefully measured and compared did not diminish. Other cases might be cited, for example that of St. Philip Neri.

Clare de Bugny [*16*] seemed to be especially devoted and predestined to the Friars Minor. She was born on 4th October, the Feast of St. Francis, 1471, and she died at Venice in 1514, upon the 17th September, the Feast of the Stigmata of the Saint. A Tertiary of the Seraphic Order, she led a life of extraordinary holiness, preserving a cloistral retirement from the world. Whilst in ecstasy she received the ferita, the Wound in the side. Her experience is remarkable on account of the well-attested fact that from this wound there poured such quantities of gurgling blood that the physicians were baffled and amazed. Professors of the School of Medicine at Padua examined her, and tormented her with every remedy and stringent drug in their pharmacopœia. She suffered all with exemplary patience, until at length they frankly confessed that such a phenomenon belonged to the supernatural order, and was beyond all human skill. Moreover the blood emitted a most delicious fragrance, and not unseldom spiteful gossip accused her of secretly bathing in costly perfumes, a luxury which would have been clean contrary to the austerity of the rule, and have betrayed her as an impostor. She bore the slander cheerfully. Later there was complete stigmatization, but she was so overcome by this signal favour that upon her earnest prayer the visible stigmata disappeared. This was about a twelvemonth or rather more before her death. When she was laid upon her bier a vast concourse of people came to see the Holy Clare, and upon her body the stigmata shone forth with a sort of quiet radiant glow. Popular opinion at once declared her a Saint. Many who had doubted, and even calumniated the gentle maiden went away in tears, sadly striking their breasts.

Maria-Josepha Kümi [*17*] was born at Wollerau, in Switzerland, on 20th February, 1763. At the age of twenty she was professed in the strictly enclosed Dominican convent at Wesen near Lake Wallenstadt, in the diocese of Saint-Gall. In 1803, she received the ferita, her heart being pierced in the form of a cross. A little later her head was encircled with the Crown of Thorns. In February, 1806, during an ecstasy she beheld a vision of Our Lord, Who raised His hands in blessing over her at which moment rays of intense light darted forth from the Sacred Wounds, stabbing through her hands and feet, which effected complete stigmatization. She died on 7th February, 1817.

Incidentally it may be mentioned that the last case of stigmatization among nuns of the Second Order of St. Dominic is that of Mother Dominic Clare of the Cross, foundress of the convent of Limpertsberg in the Duchy of Luxembourg. For nearly thirty years she was rapt in ecstasies of the Passion, and, after her death in 1895, the Stigmata, shining and transparent, appeared upon her body.

In addition to her own *Revelations*, the *Sorrowful Passion*, and the *Visions*, a whole literature surrounds the name of Anne Catharine Emmerich [*18*], perhaps the profoundest and certainly the most widely discussed mystic of the nineteenth century. This "Living Crucifix", as she has been aptly called, was born on 8th September, 1774, at Flamske, a miserable hamlet, about a mile and a half from Coesfeld, a very old insignificant little town in Westphalia. Religion in Germany was then at its lowest ebb. It was a zero time of sore distress. Joseph II had done his bad work thoroughly, and sown the cockle far and wide. "The inscrutable decrees of Divine Providence," writes George Goyau [*19*], "suffered the hierarchy to be lost and disappear." A bitter bureaucracy, the harshest form of tyranny, suppressed the episcopal sees. The Church was looted, and officially robbed of all property. Religious Orders were banished, and their houses one after another closed down. The monastic libraries, the treasuries of centuries of scholarship, had been plundered and dispersed. The Universities were moribund, practically defunct.

Bernard and Anne Emmerich were poor peasants, miserably poor. Their home was but a dreary red brick barn, a mere cabin, where the family and their beasts all huddled up together for shelter and warmth. Even as a saw child, Anne Catharine saw visions and was endowed with extraordinary spiritual graces. God taught her from His own picture-book. From the first her one desire was to enter a convent, but how could she, a mere rustic, hope for admission? She took a post as servant in the house of the organist Söntgen, since she hoped to learn how to play and with this accomplishment more than one community would welcome her. So faithfully did she fulfil her duties—often without wages, and fare of the scantiest—that when the Augustinian nuns of the convent of Agnetenberg at Dülmen wished to receive Clara Söntgen, a clever organist anxious to correspond with her vocation, the girl's father would not allow his daughter to go unless the Sisters would take Anne Catharine as well. With considerable reluctance the nuns consented. They were in extreme poverty and another subject meant another mouth to feed. At last, on 13th November, 1802, both Clara Söntgen and Anne Catharine Emmerich were admitted as postulants. A year later Anne Catharine was solemnly professed. But convent life meant a routine of hard work, which was made all the harder since the novice-mistress, if not actually unkind was at least unsympathetic and distrustful, whilst the community became more than suspicious of their new Sister, who seemed to enjoy extraordinary gifts and graces they could not understand. They felt uneasy in her company, and scarcely cared to conceal their dislike. It is perhaps only fair to remember that they were all living on their nerves. Within there was carking poverty. They were undernourished, half-starved. From without there came, almost daily, news of the gravest kind, first one convent suppressed, then another Order prohibited and compelled to leave their home, driven from the country, penniless and without hope or surrour.

The blow fell on the 3rd December, 1811, when under the government of Jerome Bonaparte [*20*], King of Westphalia, in the convent of

Agnetenberg was suppressed, the church closed, and the community scattered far and wide. Anne Catharine, destitute and ill, was left. A servant, belonging to the nuns, out of charity attended to her, and she was ministered to by an aged emigrant priest, the Abbé Jean Martin Lambert, of the diocese of Amiens. who had officiated as chaplain to the nuns. These three, however, were compelled to vacate the buildings in the spring of 1812, and the Abbé found a lodging with the Widow Roters, in whose house a wretched little room on the ground-floor was given to Anne Catharine.

Her ecstasies were of such frequency and duration that it was impossible they should pass unremarked. She went out of doors for the last time on All Souls Day, 2nd November, 1812, and afterwards was obliged to keep her bed. The fact that she was wounded with the stigmata could now no longer be concealed. They were discovered, almost accidentally, on the 25th February, 1813, by Clara Söntgen, who had returned to her father's house at the dissolution of Agnetenberg, and who was paying her former convent-companion a neighbourly visit. Actually on 28th December, previously, Fraülein Roters had found their lodger in ecstasy, praying with outstretched hands from which fell a stream of blood. The girl thought she had met with an accident and spoke of it to her afterwards, but Anne Catharine begged that nothing should be said about it, and the Fraülein honourably respected her confidence. On 31st December, her confessor, Father Limberg, a Dominican, then living at Dülmen in his brother's house, whilst giving Anne Catharine Holy Communion saw the stigmata in her hands. He sent for the Abbé Lambert. The two priests talked the matter over, and decided to keep it secret. Father Limberg was young. He was untrained in mystical theology, and he appears quite candidly to have been utterly bewildered by what he saw. Nor is he altogether to be blamed. The Dominican Priory had been closed by secular authority some months before, and the routine of studies was thus inevitably broken off and disrupted. Naturally the young priest had not taken the higher course. Nor did the Abbé Lambert care to say much. In the first place he was an *émigré*, and as such he felt it an embarrassing position. Exiled French priests who had refused the oath of allegiance were not over-readily received in other countries. They were.tolerated, scarcely more. The ecclesiastical crisis was acute enough without any complications being superadded by the presence of intruders. Moreover he did not speak German with any fluency, nor did he understand it very well, and the Westphalian dialect was yet another difficulty. He contented himself with the one remark: "Above all my sister, you must not imagine that you are a second St. Catharine of Siena."

This was, at least, discreet. Clara Söntgen was wildly indiscreet and a gossip of the first water. Life was more than a trifle monotonous in a little provincial town such as Dülmen. Here was a chance of some excitement. She flew home to her father's, and with considerable elaboration and surmise most dramatically related what she had seen. Then the next door neighbours would (she felt sure) be interested, and then other friends must be let into the secret, under a pledge of holding their tongues

PLATE V: BLESSED ANNA MARIA TAIGI, A ROMAN MYSTIC

PLATE VI: ST. ROSE OF LIMA

about it, of course. The consequence was that by the middle of March the extraordinary phenomenon was being discussed in every house in Dülmen. It was clacked at street doors; it was scoffed at in the beer-bars; it was debated by the serious; pious folk accepted it most fervently. The local doctor, a youngish man, and full of enthusiasm for his profession, felt that it was high time for him personally to inquire into the matter. On the 23rd March, 1813, Dr. Frantz Wilhelm Westener paid a visit to the little room, and compelled the patient to submit to a close medical examination. He was very formal and starchy, a little overbearing maybe, and determined to put an end to this hysteria or silly imposture. But he had a completely open mind. At the end of his visit he was absolutely convinced of the genuineness of the stigmata. He drew up an official report of what he had observed. He became Anne Catharine's doctor and friend, and he remained so always, defending her from insult and obloquy.

Ecclesiastical authority now took up the matter. The administrator of the diocese of Münster, Mgr. Clement Augustus von Droste-Vischering [21], deputed Dr. Wesener to draw up a yet more detailed memorandum, and colleagued with him an eminent surgeon, Krauthausen, whose special business was to heal up the wounds. Two priests accompanied the doctors, Bernard Overberg, Dean of Münster, and Rensing, Dean of Dülmen. The result of the inquiry proved entirely favourable to the stigmatica. But Mgr. von Droste-Vischering, who has been described as a cold business-like prelate, highly suspicious of anything tending to romanticism, thought it his business to investigate the phenomena himself. The whole business was widely talked of, and if there was any deception, even if it were unconscious deception, the church would be involved. Accordingly on 28th March he visited Dülmen and after a stay of three days, during which he put Anne Catharine through a most searching catechism, he determined, that no loophole might be left, that an even more thorough investigation should be entered upon, an inquiry which lasted from 28th March until 23rd June. During the last ten days twenty doctors were commissioned not to leave the sufferer for one minute, either by day or night. In relays they kept her under observation, and on 23rd June signed a report to certify that during the whole time she had taken no food, and that nobody had touched her wounds.

What the agony of these investigations meant to the poor patient mystic can hardly be imagined. On 23rd October, 1813, she was moved to another and better lodging, yet a very humble little room. But Dülmen was by now infested by a horde of sightseers, curious to gaze upon the poor suffering nun. This in itself became a terrible trial. Then there were bickerings and jealousies among her friends. Her sister Gertrude, a rather rough busy bustling woman appeared on the scene and attempted to take sole charge. Clara Söntgen was more than importunate and arrogant, evidently priding herself on having set the whole business afoot. "Always spied upon and worried and suspected," writes the Redemptorist, Father Schmöger, "Anne Catharine could never keep the door shut, never suffer alone and in peace."

There were some few visitors who came with reverence and respect as pilgrims to a shrine. Hither came the noble Count von Stolberg, and the holy Bishop of Ratisbon, Johann Michel von Sailer. Mgr. Overberg on 29th September, 1813, brought to the bedside the daughter of the Princess Galitzin. This lady of distinguished piety, not only repeated the visit, but later, when she had become Princess of Salm, used openly to declare that Anne Catharine was verily and indeed a Saint.

And hither on Thursday, 24th September, 1818, came the famous poet and romanticist, Clemens Brentano [22], who was to remain at Dülmen for five and a half years as an amanuensis, daily taking down the enraptured visions of a bedridden nun, which visions, be it noted, are no *Dämmerzustände*, twilight states, when the patients imagine themselves elsewhere, since as Görres wrote: "I know no Revelations which are as rich, profound, marvellous, and gripping as those of Anne Catharine Emmerich." Moreover, the great Abbot of Solesmes, Dom Guéranger in 1860 declared that Anne Catharine was fulfilling a Divine mission, and Cardinal Gibbons of Baltimore tells us that the visions were approved by a multitude of holy men and learned theologians, and, what is more conclusive than all, the Supreme Pontiff, Pius IX of blessed and immortal memory, so highly regarded them that he ordered an Italian translation to be prepared which should appear simultaneously with the German original.

The sufferings of poor Anne Catharine increased. The stigmata continually welled blood, whilst her body was racked with indescribable pain. Her spiritual life was one of agony, and yet she was patient, kind, and loving through it all. "The task I have to endure," she herself said, "is to bear the Cross to Calvary."

Towards the conclusion of the year 1819 the blood began to flow less frequently from her stigmata, which disappeared on Christmas Day leaving white scars. But there was no dimunition of the pain. On certain occasions such as Good Friday, 30th March, 1820; 3rd March, Holy Cross Day, 1822; on Maundy Thursday and Good Friday, 27th and 28th March, 1823, blood gushed out of the marks of the wounds, but usually it was staunched. "I have prayed for this," said Anne Catharine, "and it is a forewarning of the end." "About two o'clock in the afternoon on 9th February, 1824," Father Limberg records, "she lay groaning piteously because of the agony caused by the wound in the side. I wanted to shift her pillows and to arrange them so that she should perhaps find a little ease. But looking up with her gentle patient smile, she said: 'What does it matter? There is so little time left'." Dr. Wesener, who was present, says that she did not lose consciousness until the end, and although she could only speak a few words in a whisper she affectionately pressed their hands. The scars, Brentano noticed, were shining with an extraordinary lustre. Eight o'clock struck. Her breathing became more laboured. She murmured the name of Jesus, and with one deep long-drawn sigh she passed to Paradise.

The burial took place on the 13th February. All Dülmen mourned, and the whole population of the town followed in the funeral train.

Some six weeks after her interment the grave was twice opened, once privately, and once officially. The reason for these exhumations was a persistent rumour that the body had been stolen. It was found, however, to be without the least fleck of corruption.

On 6th October, 1856, at the instance of a religious who had a great veneration for the holy stigmatica, for the case was already being discussed in Rome, and at the request of the Vatican, the grave was once more examined, and there was then erected over it the monument which may still be seen in its place there, surrounded by a strong silvered railing.

Having thus briefly sketched the life of one of the most amazing ecstaticas and seeresses of all time, it were well to add a few brief details with regard to the impression of the stigmata, and in what manner she received the mystic charisms of Christ.

In 1798, that is to say some four years before she entered the convent of Agnetenberg, Anne Catharine, one day at noon, was kneeling absorbed in meditation before a crucifix in the Jesuits' church at Coesfeld. Suddenly she felt in her head "a strong but not unpleasant glow of warmth." Then, in her own words, "I saw my Divine Spouse under the form of a young man, gloriously aureoled in radiant light, come towards me from the tabernacle of the altar of the Blessed Sacrament. In his left hand he held a garland of fragrant flowers, in his right a crown of thorns. He bade me take from Him which I would wear. I stretched out my hand to the crown of thorns. He placed it on my head, and as He withdrew, I pressed it firmly on my forehead. At that moment I felt my brows circled with pain. Since the church was going to be closed, I was obliged to leave, and I retired together with one of my friends who had been praying near me. I quietly asked her, in a way not to arouse her curiosity, if she had noticed anything in church, but she merely said 'No, nothing'. The next day my forehead and temples throbbed terribly, and I saw that they were greatly swollen. Several at home remarked on this. The pain and swelling would disappear for a short while, and then return, continuing whole days and nights together. I suffered sadly. A little while after one of my friends said; 'You must put on a clean cap. The one you are wearing is covered with red spots'. After that I took care to arrange my cap and mutch so as to hide the blood which now began to flow in greater quantities from my head. I took the same precaution when I entered the convent. One of the nuns, however, saw the blood and questioned me about it. I answered as best I could, but I think she guessed what had happened. None the less she never betrayed my secret." In later years, when Anne Catharine was bedridden, and when Dr. Wesener and other physicians examined her, the impression of the Crown could not be concealed. Many persons saw blood dripping from her head, and it welled through the linen bandages and her cap. When in ecstasy she was revealing the successive scenes of the Passion and had described the Death upon the Cross she fell inert and blood streamed from her head saturating the pillows and staining the sheets.

In 1812, upon 28th August, the Feast of St. Augustine of Hippo, the founder of the Order, Anne Catharine, ravished in ecstasy, beheld a young man, wounded in hands and feet, with His right hand He signed her with the Cross, and there was marked upon her bosom, as if from a burn, a cross about three inches long and wide. On certain days the skin rose in blisters, which broke, exuding a colourless lymph of extraordinary heat, and in such great quantities as to soak through her nightgown to the very sheets. It was for some time thought that this was due to a violent perspiration, but medical evidence proved such could not have been the case. One Christmas a smaller cross appeared, rather above the previous marking. The smaller cross was red, and on some Wednesdays and most Fridays blood copiously poured from it.

She received complete stigmatization, the Five Wounds, on 29th December, the Feast of St. Thomas of Canterbury, 1812. She was lying, extremely weak and ill, on her bed in the little room at Frau Roters, when about three o'clock in the afternoon she saw a supernatural radiance in the midst of which appeared Our Lord whose "wounds shone like so many furnaces of light". At the moment she felt endowed with supernatural strength. Then triple rays, pointed like arrows, darted from the Hands and Feet, and Side of the sacred Apparition. No word was spoken, but these rays stabbed through her own hands and feet, and lanced her side. She swooned away with blissful agony. When she returned to herself she saw blood flowing from her hands, and she felt a violent pain in her feet and her side. At that moment Fräulein Roters came into the room, and seeing the blood ran to tell her mother, who at once hurried to the bedside, and most anxiously asked what accident had happened. Anne Catharine, however, begged her not to call for help, and was so earnest in her request that they contented themselves with bandaging her hands and feet, and putting fresh linen to her side. Later, when questioned by ecclesiastical authority, she avowed that all the blood in her body seemed to flow to the stigmata. "No words can tell," she said, "what I endure."

The choice of the two crowns can be paralleled in the experiences of many mystics. Primarily, we can cite the case of the Seraphic Mother St. Catharine of Siena. Another Dominicaness of the Third Order. Blessed Catharine of Racconigi [23], who lived 1486–1547, when only a child of ten, saw a vision of Our Lord who offered her a garland of flowers or the Crown of Thorns. Heroically she stretched out her hands to the thorny Cross, but the Saviour gently smiling said: "My child, I am happy in the choice which thou hast made, and thou art all the dearer to My Heart therefor. But thou art as yet a little child, and haply thou canst not measure thy strength with thy exceeding great love. I will not now crown thee with the Diadem of Pain. It shall be laid up for thee until the hour cometh." When she had reached her twenty-fourth year Blessed Catharine on Easter Wednessay did in fact receive the stigmata, the Five Wounds, and the Crown [24].

Gian Francesco Pico della Mirandola, Count of Concordia and Quarantola, platonic philosopher, mystic, occultist, one of the most profoundly learned scholars of the golden age of humanism, who during a short sojourn at Racconigi met and talked with Blessed Catharine, says: "She had, encircling her head, a depression large and deep enough for a child to have put its little finger into it, and this was punctured (as it were) and clotted with blood. She told me that these indents often shed copious blood. I myself saw her suffering agony from this Crown, and her poor eyes even seemed full of blood."

Maria-Domenica Lazzari, the youngest child of the miller Lazzari, who was born at Capriana in the Tyrol on 16th March, 1815, was stigmatized with the Five Wounds on New Year's Day, 1834, and three weeks later was given the Crown of Thorns. The case aroused immense interest, and there took place most detailed and protracted investigations, both ecclesiastical and medical. Professor Leonardo del Cloche, director and senior physician of the Great Hospital at Trent, visited her and used every scientific test, prescribing various courses of treatment [25]. There further followed a searching inquiry by the civil authorities. But all were obliged to acknowledge that the phenomena were genuine and humanly inexplicable. From near and far, as happens at Konnersreuth to-day, crowds flocked to Capriana. Some, no doubt came in a spirit of curiosity, mere sightseers. Others were animated by very different motives. They were serious and reverent pilgrims; dignitaries of the Church, patricians and the optimacy of many lands, all palmers devout. Thus Capriana was visited by John, Earl of Shrewsbury; A. L. M. P. De Lisle, Esq. [26]; the famous Rev. W. T. Allies; and many more. In 1847 this latter gentleman, the Rev. W. T. Allies, who had carefully collected information on the spot, especially from Signor Yoris, a surgeon of Cavalese, the principal town of the district in which Capriana is situated, in 1847 gave the world an account of the phenomena he had witnessed. "In August, 1833, Maria-Domenica had an illness, which, persisting, confined her to her bed. On 10th January, 1834, she received on her hands and feet the Sacred marks of Our Lord's Five Wounds, whilst her left side was gashed as by a spear. Three weeks afterwards her family found her one morning covering her face in a rapture of great delight—a sort of trance. (It seems obvious that she had been in ecstasy.) Upon gently removing the handkerchief, characters were found on the linen inscribed in blood, and her brow showed a complete impression of the Crown of Thorns, in a regular line of small punctures about a quarter of an inch apart, and from these fresh blood was flowing freely. They asked her what had scratched and torn her forehead. She replied: "During the night a very beautiful lady came to my bedside, and set a crown upon my head." From the day (1st January, 1834) when she received the stigmata, to the present time (1847) the wounds have bled every Friday with a loss of from one to two ounces of blood, beginning early in the morning,and on Friday only." Maria-Domenica died at Eastertide, 1848.

This case is particularly interesting, since the Crown of Thorns was bestowed by Our Lady. It may be observed that St. Alphonsus de' Liguori was Maria-Dominica's especial patron and protector, and that his devotional works were her favourite reading.

It may further be observed that after April, 1834, Maria-Domenica rejected and was unable to eat any kind of food whatsoever. This extraordinary and supernatural abstinence is not at all unusual in the case of stigmatized mystics. Thus it is a matter of common knowledge that since September, 1927, Teresa Neumann of Konnersreuth has lived without food or drink. The phenomenon is known as *inedia*, and Benedict XIV laid down some very stringent rules to prove the authenticity of such cases [27]. The mere fact is to be made the subject of a most rigorous canonical and medical inquiry. Not only the duration of the abstinence but the physical effects upon the individual must be established. Then the examiners have to be satisfied that it is not pathological. The Church required there should be health, or at any rate no symptoms of unusual weakness. Then it must be asked whether the one fasting has been sustained by the Blessed Sacrament? Does natural hunger disappear before divine hunger, the longing for Holy Communion, which invigorates, sustains and supports? Further precautions are taken, regulations into which were needless to enter here. If all conditions are proven to have been scrupulously fulfilled, then and then only can the *inedia* be pronounced mystical and miraculous.

To mention but a few cases out of many. St. Catharine of Siena at the age of twenty declined all food, even bread and water. Whenever she was forced to eat anything she was sick with violent retching pains. St. Rose of Lima passed weeks without nourishment, and may be said to have lived on the Blessed Sacrament. In Norfolk, a devout anchoretic maiden, Jane the Meatless, was sustained by her Communions alone for fifteen years. Sister Louise of the Resurrection, a Spanish nun, lived on the Host [28], Louise Lateau (1850–1883), the stigmatica of Bois-d'Haine, took no food after 30th March, 1871 [29]. In 1868 the complete abstinence of Soeur Espérance de Jesus pursuant to a most strict medical examination and six weeks supervision, by day and night, was officially confirmed by the Bishop of Ottawa, assisted by two physicians of the highest repute. Dr. Baubien, a Catholic, and a Protestant, Dr. Ellis. From 25th October, to 7th December, 1877, the abstinence of Josephine Reverdy was similarly tested, and proved to be without doubt genuine and absolutely authentic [30].

A Stigmatica, contemporary with Maria-Domenica Lazzari, was Maria de Moerl, a Franciscan tertiary, generally known as the "Ecstatica of Caldaro". Born at Kaldern, a townlet hidden away in an exquisitely beautiful Tyrol valley on the right bank of the Adige, Maria de Moerl first saw the light on 16th October, 1812, in one of those ancient stone houses which belong to the fifteenth or sixteenth centuries. In those happy days life in Kaldern was simple enough, but almost idyllically peaceful and content. At the age of fifteen Maria was obliged to take upon herself the cares of the household, for her father was left a widower with nine children, of whom the youngest was a babe only ten days old. Father Eberle, who had been parish priest of Kaldern, but who, shortly after the death of Maria's mother, transferred to the rectorship of the largest church in Bozen, an important centre not so many miles away, had always regarded Maria as an example to all his flock. He admired her unfeigned and ingenuous piety, and approved the long hours she spent in meditation and prayers before the Blessed Sacrament. But it seems that it was the Capuchin, Fra Giovanni Capistrano, himself a master of mystic theology, who first recognized how far Maria had advanced along the supernatural path of perfection. He had come to Kaldern in 1825, and was soon the friend and adviser of the Moerl family. Accordingly he was the less surprised when he found her entranced in ecstasy, especially after she had received Holy Communion. In the late autumn of 1833 she received the stigmata, the Five Wounds, and on Thursdays and Fridays her hands, feet, and side often ran with blood. The prudent friar counselled his penitent to keep the secret as far as possible, lest remark should be excited and gossip stir.

She was at the time confined to bed through illness. On Corpus Christi Day, 1834, there took place the usual procession through the streets of Kaldern, where the Feast was kept with great solemnity. Every house was decked with flowers, greenery, and bright bunting; candles and lamps were lighted along the route; the street was strewn with laurel and bay. Cannon were fired; and a military band accompanied the Host on the way. It so happened that from the windows of the Moerl house, and from Maria's bedroom, an excellent view could be obtained of the procession with its groups of winged angels and tableaux of Saints and seraphim. It was high holiday throughout the district. Friends and neighbours crowded the house of the Moerls. Maria's room, as she lay in bed, was full of young girls, laughing, talking, jostling for a place. As the Blessed Sacrament beneath its canopy, in fumes of frankincense, surrounded by myriad tapers, passed the window, one of the company in the room glanced round saying "Poor Maria! She can't see the ——" The sentence was broken by a cry. Maria had fallen into ecstasy. She was levitated from the bed, and transfigured with an angelic beauty radiant as a celestial spirit, her arms extended, her feet not touching the bed, and the stigmata shining with a clear crystal light. All witnessed the phenomenon, which could no longer be kept concealed.

The countryside rang with the story. Groups of pilgrims began to pour into Kaldern. From near and far they came in orderly procession, often led by the parish priest. It was estimated that between the end of July and the 15th September more than forty thousand persons, rich and poor, peer and peasant, had palmered it to Kaldern. The clergy, for the most part held aloof, after the first outburst of enthusiasm, but in November, a great prelate, the Prince-Archbishop of Trent, came in his huge episcopal coach with outriders and a train of chaplains to interview the Stigmatica. For a while he would not formally decide upon the matter, beyond saying that Maria was of exceptional holiness and purity. In this attitude of reticence and reserve Monseigneur merely followed the line of discretion which the Church so warmly recommends. It may be remembered how St. Bernadette was contradicted and opposed, nor was it until four years after the apparition that the Bishop of Tarbes officially issued his Episcopal Letter declaring that the apparition had all the appearances of truth.

That eminent and famous scholar Johann Josef von Görres visited Kaldern and in his *Die Christliche Mystik* [*31*] has given us a long and detailed account of Maria de Moerl. He proves the absolute authenticity of the phenomenon beyond all question of doubt. Maria de Moerl died in 1863.

A little known case of the stigmata is that of Miss Collins (the Christian name is not given) which was described by Father F. Prendergast of San Francisco in 1871. Although actually born in England, Miss Collins at an early age emigrated with her parents to America, and after she had left school, with the consent of her father joined a friend, Miss Armer, and an elderly lady who kept house for them at San Francisco. Miss Collins and Miss Armer entirely devoted themselves to acts of charity, nursing the poor sick, clothing the destitute, rescuing little children, and doing innumerable works of mercy. Although not then bound by vows, they lived a quasi-religious life, as nuns of an active Order. This was approved by the Archbishop of San Francisco, who showed his appreciation of and sympathy with their work in very many ways. They won the respect of all, and did an immense amount of good. During the spring of 1871 Miss Collins was seized with a violent pain in her forehead, which could be traced to no cause and baffled medical skill. These agonies passed away only to return, and then again suddenly to disappear. On Friday in the third week of Lent, the Feast of the Five Sacred Wounds of Our Lord, she was further seized with terrible pains in the palms of her hands, her feet and side, but there was no swelling, and no marks could be seen on her body. However, upon Friday in Passion Week, the Seven Sorrows of Our Lady, the pain, which had been mitigated, was intensified, and the stigmata could now be distinctly discerned in those places, which oozed blood. The next day she was a trifle easier, but on Holy Thursday the same pains began in the afternoon, and continued until the Saturday morning. Blood flowed incessantly from hands, feet, and side. During Good Friday she passed into ecstasy, and seemed to be in Calvary where her anguish was terrible, whilst blood literally poured forth from the stigmata. Several doctors of the highest repute had been summoned to her bedside, but none could suggest any remedy or alleviation. Indeed, an eminent specialist, Dr. Polactri, who remained by the bed taking notes on his patient's condition, frankly confessed that the case was beyond the help of medical science. The agony passed away gradually on Saturday, so that on Easter Sunday she was able to attend an early Mass and received Holy Communion. The marks of the stigmata remained on her hands, feet and her side, but there was no pain, and, wrote Father Prendergast, she "has since been in the enjoyment of excellent health". I have been unable to discover with any certainty details of her later life, but there is reason to suppose that about 1872–3 Miss Collins and Miss Armer entered a contemplative strictly enclosed Order. I give this striking case since it has (I believe) only been recorded by that profound student of supernatural lore and master of mystical theology, Dr. Frederick George Lee [*32*].

When Dorothea Visser, who was born at Gendringen, a town of

Gelderland in the Netherlands, lying about twenty-two miles from Arnheim, in 1820, was some fifteen years old, one forenoon whilst she was praying before the Blessed Sacrament, a young child, a complete stranger came up to her, and said, "You do well to pray, Dorothea, for when a few more years have flown, you will receive extraordinary favours from God." She had not the least idea what was intended, and after puzzling over it for a long while she practically dismissed it from her mind. In 1843, she received the Crown of Thorns, and during the same year at intervals of some weeks the Five Wounds on hands, feet, and in the side. Full details are to be found in *Die Stigmatizirte zu Gendringen*, an exhaustive study by the famous Doctor Te Welscher, which was published at Borken in 1844.

Some mystics were stigmatized only with the Crown of Thorns, or, it might be more correct to say that the Five Wounds were not visible upon their bodies. Such was the case with the Dominicaness Blessed Emilia Bicchieri of Vercelli (Piedmont) who lived 1238–1278; also with Vincentia Ferrer, a Dominican tertiary of Valencia, who died in 1515; Blessed Christina d'Aquila, an Augustinian nun, who died in 1543; the Dominicaness Maddalena Caraffa, in the world Duchess d' Andria, who died in 1615; and Ursula Aguir, a Dominican tertiary of Valencia, 1554–1608. Ursula felt the spasm of the Wounds and the ferita, but only the Crown was visibly marked. A Franciscan tertiary, Caterina Ciaulina, who died in 1619, only felt the Crown. Hippolita of Jesús, 1553–1624, an enclosed contemplative in the Dominican convent of the Holy Angels at Barcelona, was crowned by the Hands of Our Lord in mystic vision. Louise de Jésus, a Carmelite of Dôle, in the world Madame Jourdain, who lived 1569–1628, received the Crown about six months before her death. When she was ill the sister infirmarian and her assistants whilst changing the linen guimpe saw that her forehead was pierced and torn, and blood trickled from the wounds staining the white cloth and the pillows (*33*).

Some stigmaticas received the visible Wound in the side only. A Dominicaness of the Third Order, Blessed Vanna of Orvieto [*34*], 1264–1306, was thus marked. Prudenza Rasconi, a Sicilian Dominicaness of the enclosed Second Order, who died about 1620; and Martina de los Angeles, of the same contemplative Order, a Spaniard born near Saragossa, who died 11th November, 1635, both experienced the ferita [*35*]. Gabriela Pizzoli, a Poor Clare, who died in 1472, had the wound in the side. The same is recorded of a Spanish Franciscan nun, of the enclosed life, Isabel di San Diego, who was born at Montilla, some twenty miles south of Cordova. She died in 1510 [*36*]. Francesca de Serrone, who was born 12th July, 1557, at San Severino delle Marche, the ancient Septempeda, in the Potenza valley, six miles north-west of Tolentino, received the wounds in the side at the early age of fourteen. She was already a Franciscan tertiary, and later entered an enclosed convent. Every Friday the wound gushed forth blood, which was fragrant with the odour of sweetest violets. Moreover the blood was so burning hot that it often cracked the vessels in which it was caught. The same phenomenon is recorded of many other mystics. St. Catharine of Genoa may be cited as a striking example [37]. Every case is fully attested by the sworn depositions of scientists and medical men, and cannot be legitimately disputed. Francesca de Serrone experienced inedia, and was often seen rapt in ecstasy. She died 7th April, 1600 [38].

A Franciscan nun of the Convent of St. Agnes at Foligno, Lucida, was only wounded in the hands. She died in 1440 [39]. Bianca Guzman, who entered the enclosed Dominican convent at Seville, taking in religion the name Sor Maria de la Corona, and who died 13th January, 1564, received the stigmata in the feet. Even after her death blood issued from the two wounds [40]. A Franciscan friar, a native of Scotland, John Gray, who on 5th January, 1589, was martyred at Brussels by the anarchical Gueux, a rabble of revolutionaries well described by Count Berlaymont, as "the veriest scum and offscouring of the filthiest gutter," was stigmatized through the two feet [41].

The Dominican ascetic, Blessed Matteo, of the noble Mantuan House of Carreri, who died at Vigevano in October, 1470, experienced the ferita about a year before. So great was his reputation for sanctity that his cult (confirmed with Mass and Office by Benedict XIV) was almost immediately authorized by the reigning Pontiff, Sixtus IV (1471-1484). When the body of Angolini of Milan was exhumed it was found that the alb under his vestments was stained with blood from his gashed left side. Seventy years after his entombment the body of Blessed Ugolino Zefirini of Mantua, Augustinian, was not only incorrupt, but the ferita was welling with blood. Another saintly Augustinian, Blessed Cherubino of Avigliana, who had during his life concealed the phenomenon from all, was found at his death to be wounded with the lance. A Spanish Augustinian, Melchior di Arazil, of the Valencia convent, also experienced the heart wound, which in life he hid beneath a hair shirt. Leonardo da Lettere, a Dominican of the monastery Santa Maria della Sanità, Naples, whilst in ecstasy was favoured with a mystic vision of Our Lord, Who pierced the heart with a gold spear tipped with flame. Marchese says: "This was no imaginative experience, for when Leonardo died, 12th February, 1621, his heart was found to be transfixed as by a quarrel. The heart, without fleck of corruption, and the deep wound therein may be seen to-day at Santa Maria della Sanità, where it is preserved as a most precious relic." Blessed Carlo de Sezze (the Volscian Setia), a Franciscan lay-brother of the Roman province, who died at Rome, 6th January, 1670, experienced the ferita in 1648. At his death a deep scar was seen on his side, and his heart was pierced by a formation exactly resembling a long nail [42].

A Dominicaness of the thirteenth century, Helena Brumsin of the enclosed convent of St. Catharine at Diessenhofen, was visited with the stripes and weals of one Dolorous Mystery only, the scourging at the Pillar [43]. The daughter of a well-known physician practising at Piazza, a town seventeen miles south-east of Caltanisetta in Sicily. Archangela Tardera, a tertiary of St. Francis, during six-and-thirty years was not unseldom rapt in ecstasy and often favoured with celestial visions. Her bodily sufferings were very great, but she endured all with the most exemplary patience. There was always a smile hovering on her lips, and it was commonly averred that even to be in her company for a short time cheered up the hearts of all who conversed with her. She diffused happiness. "We serve a good God," she used to exclaim, "It is our duty to make others blithe and glad." Another of her sayings was: "We are doing God our humble service if only we lift the burden off somebody's shoulders." During the last four years of her life she lost her sight, but even that did not affect her unfailing joy. She lived in the sunshine of her heart, and refused to be depressed or give way to the dismals. Archangela experienced the Five Sacred Wounds, upon which she cried: "Yes, Lord, but let me also be bound to the Column with Thee." At this heroic demand she fell in a swoon, and her attendants discovered that her body was covered with weals and contusions, with stripes and bruises. This phenomenon took place about 1608. When, several years after her death, her tomb was opened the body was supple and fresh, without decay. The stigmata were plainly visible as well as the marks of the scourging [44].

St. Gemma Galgani, 1878–1903, participated in all the sufferings of the Passion. "Gemma was wont to meditate upon this painful mystery (of the Scourging) with tenderest love; she counted one by one those deep gashes with which she beheld the Body of her Divine Saviour covered, and kept repeating: "All these are the works of love." She often prayed, that if found worthy, she might have some share, however inadequate, in the torment of the flagellation. On the first Friday in March, 1901, when she was contemplating this ineffable Mystery, she passed into rapture and amid scenes of indescribable agony her prayer was granted. It was about two o'clock on a Friday that she felt the blows. That evening her adopted mother, noticing that she seemed to be suffering more acutely, insisted upon examining her arm which was furrowed with wide red stripes. Blood flowed, and the good woman discovered that Gemma was covered with deep gashes and weals, the blood from which saturated her underclothing, so that it was impossible to remove it without tearing open the wounds to which it had stuck, causing terrible pain. All this exactly accords with Anne Catharine Emmerich's visions. In the *Dolorous Passion* she vividly describes how the executioners, six dark swarthy gangsters of giant strength, malefactors from the frontiers of Egypt, who had been condemned to hard labour for their crimes, came bearing whips and rods and ropes, and appeared eager to commence their hideous business. "They resembled wild beasts or demons, and seemed half-drunk." Two atrocious ruffians, having tied Our Lord to the Pillar, tearing off His garments, with horrid oaths and abuse knouted Him from head to foot. Their innocent Victim writhed as a worm under the lashes, and the air was full of their shouts and curses, and the swift hissing of the instruments of torture. The Jewish mob yelled in derision, and several servants of the High Priests not only gave the tormentors money but plied them with hot heady draughts of red wine which quite inebriated them and increased their fury tenfold. Two executioners made use of sticks covered with thorns, and two men wielded scourges of small iron chains and straps knotted with sharp hooks which tore off pieces of bleeding flesh at each blow. This was revealed to St. Birgitta of Sweden, who gives a harrowing picture of this awful scene of fiendish torture and divine agony [45].

St. Gemma, then, in some measure, as far as a human being may (Our Lady always excepted), participated in this profound Mystery of the Scourging on each Friday of March, 1901 [46].

St. Gemma also endured the Wound of the left shoulder caused by the weight of the Cross and the friction of the wood when Our Lord carried His Rood on the way to Calvary. In Gemma's case this particular wound was "very large and deep, and caused her so much pain that she was often obliged to lean to one side when walking." It often bled copiously. To the Cistercian nun, St. Lutgarde, appeared a vision of Our Lord bearing a heavy cross, and whilst she was weeping over the Sorrows of the Son of Man, He said: "Lutgarde, art thou willing?" To which she replied, "Yea, Lord, if Thou dost help me." Whereupon He placed the cross upon her shoulders, and it seemed to crush her to the very earth. That shoulder remained lower than the other, and as if slightly deformed and disjointed [47]. An almost precisely similar mystic experience was the lot of the Dominicaness, Blessed Catharine de Racconigi, one of whose shoulders was so notably lower than the other thereafter that she seemed hunch-backed. Her life, written by Serafino Razzi [48], is included by Domenico Maria Marchese in his great *Diario Domenicano* under 5th September. After the death of Maria Benigna Pepe, a Dominicaness, born at Trapani in 1590, died 1658, there was found (as if branded) on her left shoulder a cross surmounted by the Crown of Thorns [49].

When the body of St. Veronica Giuliani was examined on 10th July, 1727, thirty-four hours after her death, there was discovered "a very considerable curvature of the right shoulder, which bent and bowed the bone itself just as the pressing weight of a very heavy cross might well have done." Gentili, an expert surgeon, who performed the autopsy, stated in his sworn deposition that this abnormal deflexion could not possibly have been brought about by any illness, or any natural means whatsoever [50]. Colomba Trocasani of Milan, a member of the Third Order of St. Dominic, who died in 1517, not only received the Five Wounds when stabbed by five glorious rays of light, but she also endured the agony of the Scourging her body being marked with stripes and weals, and she also suffered the binding of the hands with cords, since on Fridays in Lent her wrists swelled with great pain and turned one over the other, as if fixed and manacled. Any attempt to separate them caused her intolerable anguish, and if held apart by force, directly they were released they at once automatically resumed their previous position [51].

Fra Benedetto da Reggio, a Capuchin from Calabria, who died at Bologna in 1602, used to spend long hours in ecstasy before a Crucifix, whereon the Crown of Thorns was represented in a very realistic manner. On one occasion it seemed to him that a long sharp thorn mysteriously detached itself from the Crown and thrust through his forehead causing him a spasm of intensest agony. The wound, which sometimes bled, could not be concealed and was plainly seen by many, although the stigmatist tried to hide it by wearing a linen coif or band. Physicians were unable to heal it, and after trying every remedy in vain and submitting Benedetto to torturing experiments they were forced to conclude that the phenomenon was supernatural [52].

Among the greatest glories of the Augustinian Order is St. Rita of Cascia, "Sweet Saint of the impossible," as she is called, since her prayers seem to have a particular power of impenetration with God [53]. In Italy, Spain, and France, her statue is to be seen in many churches. At Brussels she is much venerated in the Church of Sainte Madeleine, rue de la Madeleine. Rome keeps her Feast, 22nd May, at her titular church in the Via delle Vergini, and there is a great Solemnity at San Agostino, where she has an exquisitely beautiful side-chapel. But in more materialistic England her shrines are few.

Rita, that is Margherita (Margaret), was born in 1386 at Cascia, a small Umbrian town, of parents, who from their loving habit of composing quarrels and quietly settling differences between neighbours, were known throughout the town by the gentle name "The Two Peacemakers of Christ." From her earlier years Rita was surrounded with the supernatural, and there are lovely legends of the childhood of one whose playmates were the Angels. A Convent was evidently her vocation, and it is strange that, deeply religious as they were, her father and mother should have insisted that she must marry the suitor they had chosen for her. One remembers how peremptory is old Capulet in *Romeo and Juliet*, and he is entirely typical of Italian masters—masters, indeed—of the household in the fourteenth and fifteenth centuries. Rita, in spite of her own heart's longing, obeyed. Her husband, to whom she bore two sons, proved a hot-tempered youth with his hand ever on the hilt of his finely-tempered toledo ready to flash it out in the least provocation, often without any provocation at all. They were hot-blooded reckless fellows in those Renaissance days, gallants whose one argument, often whose one answer, was the swift stiletto and the sword. Within doors too Rita's husband was a domestic despot. How often we meet those husbands in Bandello, in Masuccio, in Giraldi Cinthio, and *Le Cene*! It says much, very much for Rita's gentle love and forbearance that during two-and-twenty years they lived together in perfect harmony. The blow, not unexpected but long feared, fell. Rita's husband was stabbed to death in a sudden street brawl, and lay a corpse upon the cobbled stones 'neath the glare of the golden noontide sun. A vendetta was inevitable, and furiously her two sons, lads in their teens, took up the feud. More bloodshed, more murders, enmity and fatal hate! Overwhelmed Rita fell on her knees and prayed to God. "Dear Christ," she cried, "were it not better that my sons, the children of my womb whom I love so tenderly, were it not better that they died clean of blood, rather than that they took the lives of those who verily have injured them sore, but, Lord, Thou didst forgive, and Thou hast said it, 'Vengeance is mine'. Lord, thou knowest best." Heart-broken she prayed, for whether God heard her or no, nothing but sorrow, bitter sorrow lay before her. Whence it came about that her younger son was suddenly taken with a malignant fever which soon burned in his brother's veins, although no other person in the house ailed or was in any way affected. And as they lay in their chamber death showed them the folly of life. They confessed to an Austin Friar, and passed hence, forgiving their enemies, pardoning those who had slain their father. And so they went to God.

Rita then set in order all her affairs. She made due provision for those who had enjoyed her bounty and alms, and free of the world betook herself to the gate of the Convent of enclosed Augustinian nuns, Santa Maria Maddalena, and humbly begged to be admitted as a postulant. The Prioress, however, in rather cold tones answered that according to their custom widows could not be admitted to the house. Only those who had never married might take the vows. The black curtain was drawn again over the grille, and Rita left, desolate, forsaken, and drenched in tears. Sadly she stumbled through the streets to her own home. All night she prayed, and at dawn there seemed to enter the room three glorious figures, St. John Baptist; a venerable Bishop, St. Augustine himself; and a barefoot friar in the black habit and pendent girdle of the Order, whom she recognized as the sublime ecstatic, St. Nicholas of Tolentino. "Come, my daughter," said St. Augustine, taking her by the hand, and the celestial three, unseen by all, led her through the streets to the Convent. St. Augustine then knocked thrice upon the grating and said, "Daughter, ask." In a few moments the curtain was drawn wide and Sister Portress looked out. "Ah," she said, "Mother Prioress is awaiting you," and opened the door. Rita turned to her companions and found herself alone. Tremblingly she entered, and threw herself on her knees before the Prioress, who raised her with kindliest words of welcome. "So you are come to join us."

Not once did St. Rita falter on her way. Indeed her life may truly be said to have been lived on the supernatural plane. What wonder that in midwinter a rosebush over which she had passed her hands suddenly bore the most fragrant flowers, that a fig-tree, withered and barren, which she touched, was on the next morning, green and sapful, laden with the most luscious fruit.

Her ecstasies were of daily occurrence, and as she was a model of observance and obedience, constant in prayer and mortifications, the community soon realized that a Saint dwelt among them. One day as she was meditating before the Crucifix, a rapture fell upon her, when there detached itself from the Crown a large thorn which pierced through the centre of her forehead, and disappeared leaving an unsightly malignant wound. This stigmatical wound is a unique phenomenon in the history of mysticism. I use that much overworked and misbestowed word "unique" in its true and quite literal signification. The wound of the thorn-spine upon St. Rita's forehead ulcered and suppurated, exhaling a most noisome fetor. *Foeda sanies exhalabat*, says the Breviary. In fact it stank extremely. The Sister Infirmarian and many of the nuns, for all their courtesy and good will, retched when they came near her. So far as possible she was obliged to live apart from the community, to withdraw to her own little cell and be alone, save when the rule and necessity compelled her to mingle with her sisters. (*Unde ne sororibus nauseam moveret solitaria cum Deo versabatur.*) This was yet one more mortification for the Saint, which she accepted most humbly and with exemplary patience. She knew that although she seemed to be alone in her retreat within retirement, she was companioned by God.

The ferita, the wound in the side of the Franciscan Clare de Bugny diffused a most sweet perfume. The same fragrancy was observed in the case of the stigmata of the Dominicanesses St. Catharine de Ricci and Blessed Catharine de Racconigi; of the Franciscans Francesca de Serrone and Giovanna della Croce. In 1497, Pope Alexander VI sent his own physician, Bernardo de Recanati, accompanied by a Franciscan Bishop and the Master of the Sacred Palace thoroughly to examine and report upon the stigmata of Lucia de Narni [54]. The wounds were washed with medicated lotions, bandaged, and the hands enclosed in gloves which were fastened and sealed round the wrists. After a week the doctor opened the seals in the presence of several witnesses. The wounds were found still open, with no sign of peccant humour or fester. Moreover, they exhaled the sweetest perfume. The statement sworn to and signed by the doctor and his coadjutors was the only possible report, the thing was supernatural and of God. However, the very next year, the Pontiff summoned Lucia to Rome that he might himself see her. In March, 1502, Bernardo da Recanati, who had been raised to the hierarchy, with two other Bishops re-opened the case. The deliberations were slower, longer, and (if possible) more meticulous and exact. It was definitely established that the stigmata were divinely imprinted on Lucia, and that they gave off a most sweet, persistent, and lasting perfume. Blessed Bartolo of San Gimignano [55], who lived about 1300, when fifty-two years old, was attacked with leprosy in its most virulent form. The holy man, "the Job of Tussany" as he was called, literally rotted to pieces with the inroads of the horrible disease. And yet there was no contagion. Moreover a most heavenly perfume exhaled from his poor body, the *odor del paradiso* as the Italian phrase goes. When he died his little hermitage became radiant with light, and the air was laden with the fragrance of beds of violets. The pus of St. John of the Cross and of the Blessed Didée gave forth a strong scent of Madonna lilies.

This especial and unique humiliation, then, fell to the lot of St. Rita. Her wound was inflicted in a prominent place, upon the forehead; it was loathly and malodorous. It is difficult to imagine anything more distressing. Such a wound seemed to lack dignity, to be in a sense shameful and abject, almost a personal defilement. We know that Saint Christina of Stommeln was foully persecuted and deluged with ordure by satanic agency, so that her story in its crudity is painful, and indeed in some passages revolting in the reading. But in the case of St. Rita we have an extremely poignant and ashaming stigma inflicted on His loved one by God Himself. It is a profound mystery. Her patience and her gentle acceptance of this suffering, as experience shows, and as was revealed to a very great Servant of God, have won her a particular glory in Heaven. She is the Saint of meekness, of complete and unswerving trust in God. She consoles the lonely and those who are weary and worn. She was so human. She knew sad and desolate days, when she was all forlorn and forsaken. She is the Saint who comforts and cheers in hours of depression and weariness, when the outlook seems so dark and dreary, when tears are in the eyes and the heart is very sick and tired.

During the last four years of her life she was attacked by an illness which caused her excruciating pain, but although her strength failed utterly her patience never. At the last, on 20th May, 1457, there was seen standing by her bedside a Lady of surpassing beauty, Who taking the dying woman by the hand, said: "Daughter, dear daughter, well done. Come home with Me." The room was at that moment filled with an exquisite perfume, the wound upon St. Rita's forehead shone like a star, and (some accounts have it) the sweetest music was heard.

Solitaria inter solitarias. A solitary among solitaries. And now, *gloriosa inter gloriosas.* Among the glorious she is most glorious.

NOTES ON CHAPTER V

1. St. Cajetan openly proclaimed that this holy woman was a Saint. She died, a strictly enclosed Capuchin nun in 1542, aged 79.

2. *Un Tesoro Nascosto ossia Diario di S. Veronica Giuliani, Religiosa Cappuccina in Città di Castello, scritto da Lei Medesima, pubblicato e corredato di note dal P. Pietro Pizzicaria, D.C.D.G.* Vol. I, Prato. Tipografia Giachetti, Figlio e C., 1895; II, 1897; III, 1898, etc. Nine volumes printed. The *Diario* was written under the obedience imposed upon the Saint by Mgr. Luca Antonio Eustachi, Bishop of Città di Castello, and his successor in the see, Mgr. Alessandro Codebò. There are several lives of St. Veronica, e.g. *Vita della Venerabile Serva di Dio, Suor Veronica Giuliani, cappuccina nel monastero di S. Chiara di Città di Castello, scritta da Gio. Francesco Strozzi della Compagnia di Gesù,* Roma, 1763. An anonymous *Vita* was published the same year, 1763, at Piacenza; and in 1777 at Florence, another *Vita* appeared, the author of which was Canon Anton Francesco Giovagnoli. In 1776 had appeared at Rome a *Life* from the pen of the Postulator of the Cause for Beatification, the Capuchin Padre Francesco Romano. In the year of the Canonization of St. Veronica, 1839, the Oratorian P. Filippo Maria Salvatori gave to the Press, Rome, his *Vita della S. Veronica Giuliani.*

3. St. Rose was canonized by Clement X in 1671.

4. A city of some 7,000 inhabitants. In the fifteenth century it belonged to the Vitelli; and afterwards to the Estates of the Church. The city is built in the form of a rectangle, and still surrounded by the walls erected in 1518. There are many churches and convents. The present Cathedral of S. Florido was begun in 1480, and finished sixty years later.

5. "Il Signore mi ha detto, che veniva, per transformarmi tutta in Lui, e per segnarmi coi sigilli delle sue piaghe." *Diario,* Anno 1697, III, p. 662.

6. "Mentre Ella (La Vergine) ha pregato per me, mi è venuto un lume e conoscimento sopra il mio niente; e questo lume facevami penetrare e conoscere che tutto ciò erano opere di Dio." *Ibid.*

PLATE VII: St. Clare of Montefalco, O.S.A.

PLATE VIII: BLESSED BÉATRIX D'ORNAGIEU, CARTHUSIAN NUN

7. Thus St. Teresa writes that in the Seventh Mansion "The soul is entirely transformed into the likeness of its Creator—it seems more God than soul." "In such a one," that is one who has attained to this state, says Blessed Henry Suso, 1300–1365, "God is the very essence, the life, energy, and vital force. The man is a mere instrument, a medium of God." Most mystics use the same or very similar terms in describing their experiences. The Benedictine abbess, St. Mechtild of Hackeborn (c. 1240), exclaimed: "My soul swims in the Godhead like a fish in water." She was literally absorbed in God, and God had so closely united Himself with her that she saw through His eyes, heard with His ears, and spoke with His mouth. St. John of the Cross teaches us that "the soul must wholly lose all human knowledge and all human feelings in order to receive in fulness Divine knowledge and Divine feelings." Further, the same holy doctor quite definitely says that God grants the soul "the favour of attaining to being deiform and united in the Most Holy Trinity, wherein she becomes God by participation." This state, which is known as *Deification* was foreshadowed in some sort in the Orphic Mysteries. Johann Tauler of Strassburg (c. 1300–1361), the Dominican, speaks of man abandoning use of self and flung deep down into the Divine Abyss, when God transforms the created soul, absorbing it into the Uncreated Essence, so that the soul becomes one with Him. Thus Teresa Helena Higginson describes how Our Lord appeared to her (at Sabden in 1878) and Himself gave her the Blessed Sacrament. This effected a complete annihilation of self, and "When I had received Him He drew me so entirely into Himself that I was lost in His immensity and love." Delacroix, *Études d' histoire et de psychologie du mysticisme. Les grands mystiques chrétiens*, Paris, 1908, calls this "the theopathetic state", which is perhaps not altogether a happy term. Of course the mystical doctrine of the Deification of the Soul must be carefully safeguarded, and rightly understood.

8. *Acta Sanetorum*, 18th June. *De B. Osanna Andrasia Virgine, Tertii Ordinis S. Dominici, Mantuae in Italia.*

9. Feast, 2nd January, Steill, *Ephemerides dominicanosocrae, der ist, Heiligkeit und Tugenden voller Geruch der aus allen Enden der Welt Zusammen getragenen Ehe-Blumen des himmlisch-Fruchtbaren Lust-Gartens Prediger Ordens.* Dilligen. 1692.

10. Fortunatus Hueber, *Menologium sen brevis et compendiosa illuminatio relucens in splendoribus Sanctorum, Beatorum, &c. ab initio Minoritici instituti usque ad moderna tempora.* 2 vols., folio, Monachü, 1698. See also Greiderer, *Germania Franciscana*, 1781. René Weber's study of Joanna Maria has been translated into French by Charles Sainte-Foi, *Vie de Jeanne-Marie de la Croix, traduite de l'allemand*, Paris, Poussielgue Rusand, 1856.

11. Wollersheim, *Das Leben der ekstatischen . . . Jungfrau Christina.* Also, *Acta Sanetorum*, 22nd June.

12. 60 Miles S.W. of Buda (Ofen)—Pest, and five miles from Platten Zee (Balaton Lake).

18. 1270 has hitherto been given as the date of the death of Blessed Helen. But, for some months at least she trained St. Margaret of Hungary, who was born in 1242, and at the age of three and a half was sent to the Veszprim convent, where she shortly received the habit. Actually St. Margaret took solemn vows in the convent of St. Mary of the Isle, founded by her father and mother, King Bela and Queen Maria Lascaris. St. Margaret, who was canonized in November, 1943, by Pope Pius XII, received the stigmata, and is thus depicted by Fra Angelico in a painting now in the National Gallery. She died 18th January, 1270.

14. The date 1670 has been assigned to the first Volume of this work into the rather intricate Bibliography of which space is lacking to enter in any detail. It may be that some title-pages carry 1670 or that a preliminary compendium was issued in this year. The copy of the *Année Dominicaine* which I have used is that cited in the text.

15. One may compare the pictures of English Martyrs which Gregory XIII caused to be painted for the English College, Rome, a fact which was accepted as quasi-beatification by Leo XIII who formally beatified the Martyrs on 29th December, 1886.

16. Luke Wadding, *Annales Minorum*, 8 vols., folio, Lugduni, 1647, *sqq.*, and Hueber, *Menologium, ut cit. supra.*

17. *Die Gottselige Josepha Kümi Klosterfrau zu Wesen in Gaster.* Biographie von P. Justus Landolt. Saint-Gall, 1868. A 12mo brochure of 76 pages.

18. See particularly, Father K. E. Schmöger, C.SS.R., *Life of Anna Catharine Emmerich*, English translation; and French translation by Mgr. E. de Cazalès, Vicar-General, and Canon of Versailles, *Vie d' Anne-Catharine Emmerich*, traduite de l'allemand, Paris, Bray, 3 vols., 8vo., 1868–1872. Also, Father Thomas Wegener, O.S.A., *The Miraculous Inner and Outer Life of the Servant of God, Anne Catharine Emmerich, of the Order of Saint Augustine* (English translation), Tournai, 1896.

19. *L'Allemagne religieuse. Le Catholicisme*, 1800–1848. Tome II.

20. 1784–1860. The youngest of the Bonaparte family, and the latest survivor of the original stock.

21. Afterwards Archbishop of Cologne. Being opposed to the rule in Westphalia of Jerome Bonaparte, he was regarded with open hostility by the French. In November, 1841, the Prussian troops occupied Cologne and imprisoned the Archbishop at Minden on a charge of too faithfully obeying the mandates of Pope Gregory XVI, and refusing to admit civil jurisdiction in ecclesiastical affairs.

22. 1778–1842.

23. Twenty-three and one-half miles from Turin.

24. *Compendio delle cose mirabile della B. Caterina da Racconigi.* Torino, 1858. Marchese, *Diario Domenicano*, t. iv.

25. Il Signor Dottore del Cloche wrote a long article discussing this phenomenon, *Annotazioni intorno*, etc., which appeared in the *Annales de médicine universelle* of Milan, Number, November, 1837.

26. De Lisle wrote a pamphlet, published London, Dolman, 1841, with etchings by J. R. Herbert, R.A., giving an account of his visit to the Ecstatica. See also, John Talbot, Earl of Shrewsbury: "Letter from the Earl of Shrewsbury to Ambrose Lisle Phillips, Esq., Description of the Ecstatica of Caldaro and the Addolorata of Capriana . . . to which is Added the Relation of Three Successive Visits to the Ecstatica of Monte Sansavino in May, 1842." London, 1842.

27. *De Canonizatione Sanctorum*, IV, pars 1, c. xxvii, n. 14.

28. Faber, *The Blessed Sacrament*, 1855; Third Edition, 1861, pp. 530–534.

29. Dom Francis Izard, O.S.B., M.R.C.S. Eng., L.R.C.P. London, *Louise Lateau*, pp. 20–22: "The Complete Abstinence of Louise."

30. *Apparitions de Boulleret*, ch. v. There were, of course, impostors. James Ward's "Some account of Mary Thomas of Tanyralt in Merionethshire, Who Has Existed Many Years Without Taking Food, and of Ann Moore, the Fasting Woman of Tutbury," London, 1813. Alexander Henderson wrote "An Examination of the Imposture of Ann Moore, called the "Fasting Woman of Tutbury . . ." London, 1813. Again there have been 'professional' fasting men, Tanner, Succi, Merlatti, and others who for money have undertaken extraordinary abstinences, and who have been scandalously exhibited in great European capitals. In most cases these degrading experiments broke down, Succi's 'fastings', for example, ended in dementia.

There are also cases of exceptional illnesses. "Twenty-one-year-old Kenny Swanson, of Oren, Utah . . . swallowed lye (a form of soda) which his mother was using for laundering when he was a baby. After that he had to be fed artificially. But now an operation at a Chicago hospital has opened a way from his upper to his lower food passage, and enabled him to swallow normally. Before the operation he had no memory of the taste of food and drink." *Sunday Dispatch*, 11th May, 1947.

31. 5 Bände, Regensburg, 1836–1842. French translation, by M. Charles Sainte-Foi, Deuxième Edition, 1861, tome II, pp. 287–306. See also Léon Boré, *Les Stigmatisées du Tyrol*, Paris, 1840; Veyland, *Les plaies sanglantes du Christ reproduites dans trois vierges chrétiennes vivant actuellement dans le Tyrol*, Metz, 1844,

32. *The Other World; or, Glimpses of the Supernatural.* 2 vols., London, 1875. Vol. I, pp. 108–113.

33. Blessed Emilia, *Acta Sanctorum*, 3rd May. Her Feast is kept on 19th August.

THE PHYSICAL PHENOMENA OF MYSTICISM

Vincentia Ferrer, Steill, *Ephemerides dominicanosacrae* . . . 18th April. Blessed Christina, O.S.A., *Acta Sanctorum*, 18th January. Feast, 3rd October. *Histoire de la vie de Notre Père Saint Augustin, des Saints, Bienheureux et hommes illustres de Notre Ordre*, par le Père Simplicien Saint-Martin, O.S.A., folio, Toulouse, 1640–41. Maddalena Caraffa, Marchese, *Diario Domenicano*, 29th December. Ursula Aguir; Steill, *ut cit, supra*, and Marchese. Caterina Ciaulina, Hueber, *Menologium*, 27th January. Hippolita of Jesus, Marchese, 6th August; Louise de Jésus, *Chronique de l'ordre des Carmélites de France*, Troyes, 1850. Tom. II, p. 526; and Henri Bremond, *Histoire Littéraire du Sentiment Religieux en France*, Paris, 1925, II, pp. 308, *sqq*.

34. Vanna (Giovanna), Jane. There is a *Vita* by the Dominican Fra Giacomo Scalza. See also *Acta Sanctorum*, 23rd July.

35. Prudenza Rasconi, Marchese, 5th April. Martina de los Angeles, Marchese, 11th November; and P. Lopez, *Vida prodigiosa de la venerabile Sor Martilla de los Angeles*, Madrid, 1687. This *Vida* largely draws from a previous *Life* by the Dominican Fra Maya. Both Maya and Lopez incorrectly write 'Martilla' which should be 'Martina'. See further *Acta capituli generalissimi Romae* . . . *in conventu S. Mariae supra Minervam*. Tornaci, 1645.

36. Gabriela Pizzoli, Hueber, *Menologium*, 19th June, Isabel di San Diego, Hueber, *op. cit.*, 7th November. See also, Arturus a Monasterio *Martyrologium Franciscanum*, folio, Parisiis, 1653; and Luke Wadding *Annales Minorum*.

37. *Vita e Dottrina* (first edition, Genoa, 1551), thirteenth Genoese edition, a reprint of the 1847 edition. "In proof that this holy woman bore the stigmata interiorly a large silver goblet with a stem and a shallow bowl was brought to her. Now the cup was full of ice cold water for laving her hands, in the palms of which, because of the great fire which consumed her, she felt an agony of pain. And when she had dipped her hands into the bowl, the water became boiling hot, so that the stem and the shallow bowl were scalding to the touch." Baron von Hügel's attempt to explain away this passage and his subsequent rejection are unscholarly, and strike one as completely out of place and factitious in so learned and detailed a work as *The Mystical Element of Religion* (vol. I, p. 214 and p. 452). The Venerable Orsola Benincasa (1547–1618) dipped her hands in water to cool them and the water actually boiled, steam coming from it, whilst the vessel itself became so hot that it was hardly possible to hold it. This phenomenon was witnessed by so many as to be beyond any question. *Novissima Positio super Virtutibus*, an official document of the Beatification Process.

38. *Memorie del'origine, fundazione, avanzamenti, successi ed economi illustri in lettere e santità della Congregazione de'Clerici Regolari di S. Paolo, chiamati volgaramente Barnabiti*. P. Barelli da Nizza. Bologna. 2 vols., folio, 1703.

39. Arturus a Monasterio, *Menologium*, 12th July.

40. Marchese, *Diario Domenicano*.

41. *Historia ecclesiastica de martyrio fratrum Ordinis S. Francisci de observantia, qui partim in Anglia, partim in Belgio, et partim in Hybernia tempore Elisabethae, ab anno 1536 ad hunc annum 1582 passi sunt*. Parisiis, 1582. By an English Franciscan, Thomas Bourchier.

42. Feast 7th October. Marchese, *Diario*, under 5th October. Angolini of Milan, Görres, French trans., *ut cit. supra*, II, p. 231. Blessed Ugolino, O.S.A., Feast 22nd March. Blessed Cherubino, O.S.A., Feast 17th December. Avigliana is a mediaeval town fourteen miles west of Turin. Melchior d'Arazil, O.S.A. For these three Augustinians see *Tempio Eremitano dei Santi e Beati dell' Ordine Agostiniano*, folio, 1628, by Ambrogio Staibano; *Elogia virorum illustrium ex Ordine Eremitarum S. Augustini*, 4to, Antverpiae, 1658, by Cornelius Curtius; *Historia de los Augustinos Descalzos de la Congregacion de España y de las Indias*, folio, Madrid, 1664, by Andres de San Nicolas, O.S.A.; and Père Pierre de Sainte Hélène, *Abregé de l'Histoire des Augustins Dechaussés*, 12 mo, Rouen, 1672. Leonardo da Lettere, Marchese *Diario*, 12th February. The Observant Blessed Carlo de Sezze, Hueber, *Menologium*. Blessed Carlo was beatified by Pius IX. Feast 19th January. Sezze, among the Volscian Mountains is some 35 or rather more miles from Rome.

43. Steill, *Ephemerides dominicanosacrae*, 28th October and 31st May. Helena

Brumsin died about the year 1285. The relics of the Sacred Column are preserved in the Chapel of that name in Santa Prassede, Via di S. Prassede, Rome, and here on the Fourth Sunday in Lent the Commemoration is observed with great pontifical solemnity.

44. Luke Wadding, *Annales*, also Hueber, *Menologium*, 19th September.

45. *Revelationes Caelestes Seraphicae Matris S. Birgittae Suecae . . . olim ab Eminentissimo Domino Joanne Cardinale de Turrecremata Recognitae et approbatae. A Reverendissimo Consalvo Duranto Episcopo Feretrano . . . eruditissimae illustratae.* Folio. Mönachii, 1680. Liber I, c. x, pp. 16–22, and Liber IV, c. lxx, pp. 289–295. St. Vincent Ferrer, Ludolphus, *De Vita Christi*, Para, II, c. 58, and Lanspergius, Homily L, *On the Passion*, say that Christ at the Scourging was wounded with more than 5,000 blows, and He must have expired, were it not divinely decreed that He should suffer death on the Cross. Ludolph of Saxony, the Carthusian, a most prolific writer, died 13th April, 1378. He is one of the several authors to whom *The Imitation of Christ* has been attributed. The Carthusian Lanspergius (family name Gerecht) was born in Bavaria 1589, and died at Cologne 1539. He was a very copious writer and a mystic of a high order.

46. *Life of Gemma Galgani*, by Padre Germano di S. Stanislao, C.P., translated by Dom O'Sullivan, O.S.B., Sands (London and Edinburgh), and Herder (St. Louis) 1914, Chapter VIII, pp. 67–76.

47. *Lilia Cisterciensia, sive Sacrae Virgines Cistertienses et earum Vitae,* folio, Duaci, 1633. By Chrysostom Henriquez. (16th June, *De Beata Lutgarde*.)

48. *Vite de' primi Santi e Beati dell' Ordine dei Predicatori, cosi uomini come Donne.* 4to, Palermo, 1605.

49. Marchese, *Diario*, 25th December.

50. *Vita di S. Veronica*, Rome, 1839. By Filippo Maria Salvatori. *Ut cit. supra.*

51. *Vite degli huomini illustri dell' Ordine di San Domenico.* 2 vols., Bologna, 1620. By Giovanni Michaele Pio.

52. Hueber, *Menologium*.

53. *Vita della B. Rita di Cascia*, Cardi, Foligno, 1805. *Breviarium Ord. S.P.N. Augustini,* 22nd May. *Breviarium Romanum*, Desclée, 1909. Pars Aestiva, "Officia pro Aliquibus Locis," die XXII. Maii. *Acta Sanctorum*, 22nd May, *De Beata Rita vidua, Ordinis Eremitarum S. Augustini, Cassiae in Umbria.*

54. 1476–1544. *Vita della Beata Lucia virgine di Narni*, 1711, by P. Domenico Ponsi, O.P., 1711. In the Office of Blessed Lucia, 16th November, granted by Benedict XIII, 1724–1730, the Pope sanctioned a special memorial of her stigmata.

55. Feast, 14th December, Hueber, *Menologium*.

CHAPTER SIX

Great Names—St. Francis of Assisi—St. Catharine of Siena—St. Teresa d' 'Ávila—
The Mystics' Mystic—On the Border-Line—The Curious Case of Georges Marasco—
A Miraculous Cure—Simulated Stigmata—The Pretended Miracle.

IT is generally accepted that the first recorded stigmatic was St. Francis
of Assisi. There is, however, in the Epistle to the Galatians [*1*] (VI, *17*)
a very important passage which must be carefully considered in this
connexion. St. Paul writes: "For I bear the stigmata of Jesus [*2*] in my
body." In the first place, it is to be observed that the Greek word translated "bear" is singularly emphatic, and indeed is not unaptly rendered
by the phrase of the Revised Version "I bear branded". St. John Chrysostom draws attention to this, and writes: "Note, he does not merely say
'I bear' but 'I bear impressed', just as if it were somebody who was
proudly vaunting a token or some trophy." Secondly, the Greek word
"stigmata" in its original sense means a brand, or indelible mark of
ownership and identification. Such branding was employed among the
Greeks and Romans in the case of slaves, but it was very seldom resorted
to, except as regards such rascal bondmen who had repeatedly endeavoured
to escape or who had actually run away, or who it might be, had
committed a crime. Thus the Romans often branded slaves who were
notorious thieves on the forehead with the letter F, the initial of *Fur*,
the Latin word for a Thief, and those punished so ignominiously were
known as "three-letter men", which became a scurril term of abuse [*3*].
The brand was also occasionally employed in the case of captives, although
this was disapproved of as having something of a barbarous complexion.
In a fit of enthusiasm, soldiers would not unseldom brand the name of
their general on some part of their body, which is practically equivalent
to tattooing.

Branding, and a branding which carried with it an honourable, even
a mystic significance, was very frequently used in the case of slaves
devoted to the service of a particular deity, to whose sanctuary in some
one numerical hallowed spot they were attached. These "Sacred Slaves",
as they were technically known, and the phrase occurs in a Galatian
inscription [*4*], were often not slaves at all in the ordinary sense of the
word, but self-dedicated votaries and ministers of the shrine, "voteens",
as the Irish would say.

The Galatians of Asia Minor, recent converts, to whom St. Paul is
writing, were a mixed race of Phrygians, Gauls, and Greeks, and being
an intensely "passionate and ritualistic" folk, as Bishop Lightfoot well
describes them [*5*], they were given to the darkest occultism and the
most extravagant superstition. Here in Galatia, at Pessinus, a very ancient

and almost legendary city, the modern Bala Hissar, dwelt with his flamen college, Attis—for so the title ran—the high pontiff of the Idaean mother, turret-crowned Cybele. Here, in its chariot drawn by tawny lions [6] stood her famous image; here was the primal home of her exotic impure cult with its effeminated priests and their acolyths, the kedêshim [7]. It was a worship of orgiastic rites, of mad dances to the clashing of cymbals and the tinkle of tambourines, of a frenzied ceremonial, of hideous mutilations [8], of slashing with steel and branding with hot iron. Lucian of Samosata, who was born about A.D. 120, in his treatise *The Syrian Goddess* [9] describes how all the ministers at the temple of the lady Cybele "are branded with a holy mark, some bearing it in the palms of the hands or the soles of the feet, some again in the neck. Now all the clerks and clergy who serve the Syrian goddess are branded with these sacred stigmas."

There can be little doubt that the Galatians, when St. Paul's letter was read to them, hearing of the stigmata of Jesus branded upon his body, would have at once thought of the priests with whom they had been so well acquainted, and the cult they had abandoned not so very long ago. Nothing could be more obvious than the parallel, and they would immediately understand that St. Paul was marked by and for his Lord and God in a very especial manner. It was almost a ritual technicality, we might say.

How St. Paul received the stigmata, we do not know, but one might hazard the suggestion that it was when he was "caught up to the third heaven, caught up into paradise" [10].

It is plain from the reference to and application of the passage in Galatians, as quoted by St. Bonaventura in his *Life of St. Francis* [11], that this great Doctor believed St. Paul to have been stigmatized. St. Thomas Aquinas does not pronounce an opinion. Commentators have conjectured other explanations such as [12]: "The brands of which the Apostle speaks were doubtless the permanent marks which he bore of persecution undergone in the service of Christ", which seems singularly weak, and a wresting of the sense. Ramón Nonnato [13], who died in 1240, whilst engaged upon the work of ransoming Christian slaves in Barbary, was seized upon by the Moors and terribly tortured. The scars and deep wounds of his multilations were indelible, but nobody has ever thought of speaking of him, hero and saint that he was, as stigmatized.

A remarkable revelation of the Bavarian ecstatica, Theresa Neumann of Konnersreuth, confirms the belief that St. Paul was the first stigmatic. Dr. Fritz Gerlich, editor of the *Münchner Neuesten Nachrichten*, relates how one day when she was in rapture she was asked: "Who was the first person to receive the stigmata?" The entranced girl at once replied: "Saint Paul." Whereupon Dr. Frantz Wütz, a professor of Munich University, who was present, listening intently, whispered to the priest who was putting the questions: "Let her tell us if anybody ever saw the stigmata of Saint Paul." To which the answer was: "No, nobody ever saw them. The exterior marks were not visible on his hands and feet, but he felt the pain of the Five Wounds."

"How curious that is!" was the comment of Dr. Wütz. "You know it is a point which is much disputed among theologians and Biblical commentators. There is a famous passage in the Epistle to the Galatians where St. Paul speaks of bearing the stigmata impressed on his body." Dr. Gerlich adds, "Myself, I had never heard of anything of the sort. I always believed that the Poverello of Assisi was the first person who received the stigmata."

On the occasion of another visit, Dr. Gerlich, who could not forget this, was in the church at Konnersreuth with Theresa. They were standing before a statue of St. Francis, and he inquired: "Theresa, do you know? Tell me, who was the first person to receive the stigmata?" She looked at him with her clear candid eyes, and then turning towards the statue, replied: "It was St. Francis, of course." "No, no, Theresa. Don't you remember? That's not quite right. Give it a moment's thought. St. Francis was not the first." "Not the first! What do you mean, Doctor?" "You know, Theresa. You know somebody received the stigmata long before him." "I am sure I don't know of anyone else, Doctor. Who could it be? I have always been told St. Francis was the first." "But a month ago, Theresa, when you were in an ecstatic state, you said St. Paul was the first person to be stigmatized. Possibly in his case the Five Wounds were not visible, or at any rate, not always visible. He felt them in his body, none the less. Does he not speak of them in one of his Epistles?" Theresa Neumann was startled, and a troubled perplexed look came over her face. She pressed her hand wearily to her forehead. "I don't know," she murmured. "I can't tell. I recollect nothing at all about that" [14].

It was early August, 1224, that St. Francis, longing to devote a season to tranquil contemplation, withdrew with certain of his friars in his company to the solitude of Monte Alvernia, that remote mountain which more than ten years before the Lord of Chiusi, Orlando dei Cattani, had bestowed upon the brethren. Distant from the loneliest villages and hamlets, Alvernia, although clothed on its lower slopes with a hem of greenery and foliage, soon towers up into a bare and rocky aerie wholly cut off, and far from the haunts of men. The air is nipping, rare and keen. There is the unbroken and awful silence of the heights of the Apennines, of vast skies which canopy cliffs and dizzy craigs.

It was in this loved spot, among the grottoes of Alvernia, dwelling in the little rude huts they had built, that Francis and his companions designed to keep the great feast of the Assumption, 15th August, and to prepare by a feast of forty days, "Angelic Lent", for Michaelmas, the solemnity of the gonfalonier of the hosts of Heaven, as he has been picturesquely called, Monseigneur St. Michael.

Every morning, very early, Francis assisted at the mass said in their cave-oratory on a mere ledge of rock, by Brother Leo, "the little lamb of God", but when the fifteenth day of August was passed he withdrew to the furthermost hermitage of all, a little hut under a lone beech tree, and hither Leo was to come twice only in the four-and-twenty hours, once to bring him a pittance of bread and water, and again at midnight so that they might recite matins together, and when Leo drew near he was to give a signal by crying aloud the words that commence that office: *O Lord, open thou my lips*, and Francis would respond *And my Mouth shall show forth Thy praise*. If there was no reply, Leo must turn and discreetly depart.

Many beautiful and mysterious things are told of what happened in that lone retreat, but the most wonderful of all took place upon the Feast of Holy Cross in September [*15*], the fourteenth day of that month. Whilst it was yet dark, Francis, who had been meditating profoundly upon those words of St. Paul which are the refrain of the liturgy of that day, "God forbid that I should glory, save in the Cross of Our Lord Jesus Christ, by Whom the world is crucified unto me, and I unto the world", came forth into the open air and kneeling on the hard flint, with arms outstretched and hands lifted up, turned towards the east to await, rapt in prayer, the breaking of the dawn. And his heart, says the old chronicle, was all aflame with the love of Him who deigned to be crucified for us, and he yearned to suffer the agony of the Passion of the Cross.

And as he prayed, there came towards him a very strange and wonderful thing, which struck his soul with awe. Full swiftly did it glide through the clear aurorean air. No delay or hovering, and upon a stone just above Francis stood one who had the form of a Man Crucified, and Who yet was a Seraph with six most radiant wings. Two wings were raised on high about His head; two wings were extended as poised in flight, and two covered His body. The face of Christ was of aspect gracious and benign as He looked at His servant. Moreover it was exceedingly beautiful; but unearthly sorrow mingled with the unearthly loveliness. So St. Francis was filled with great joy as he beheld that face upon which Angels scarce dare to look [*16*], that Face fairer than all the children of men; and yet he was full of sadness and of a pity passing all words to tell when he saw the anguish and the divine compassion of those eyes. Suddenly in a moment of vehement rapture, a moment which seemed a long space of time, it was made known to him that in sort he was to be transformed into the similitude of the Crucified, and that to him was it given to suffer, so far as man may, the bitter agony of the Cross and become a partaker of the Passion.

It was at this mystic moment that the whole range of Monte Alvernia lit up with a glorious splendour, as it were the sun in his power at hottest noon, so that certain shepherds who were watching their flocks questioned one another what this might be, and were sore afraid. Likewise a company of muleteers who were going to Romagna, rose from their sleep at the radiance of the light which shone through the windows of the hostelry where they were lodged that night, and all made haste to saddle and load their burden-beasts and pass on their way. Now they had not gone far before the light waned, and presently the sun began to rise over the hill-tops.

The vision faded, and Francis was left in ecstasy, kneeling upon the rock. When he came to himself he stood up [*17*], and began to ponder what the Celestial Vision could mean. Then in the flesh and body of Francis appeared the very marks and imprints of the wounds as he had seen them on the body of the Crucified Christ Who visited him in the form of a Seraph aflame with the fire of love. For the Saint's hands and feet were bored through the middle with nails, just as nails had pierced Him who hung upon a Tree. The round heads of these nails, black and protuberant, were plainly visible in the palms of the hands and on the insteps of the feet; whilst on the backs of the hands and on the soles of the feet were the clinched and bent back points of the nails, penetrating straight through and recurved. His right side, moreover, was pierced as if by the thrust of a lance.

For a while St. Francis was minded to conceal this marvellous sign, this sealing of his hands and feet and spearing of his side, from all. But a little reflection showed him that it was impossible. And so, very shyly and under constraint he related (in great part, at least), to the brethren who had borne him company to Monte Alvernia the Vision he had seen. None the less he kept hidden, as well as might be, the marks in his hands and feet, covering them up with his tunic. It was to Leo alone, Leo "the little lamb of God", that he told his secret without reserve, since because of the pain and the blood which flowed from the wounds they needs must be swathed in bandages [18].

The gentlest touch caused the stigmata to throb with agony, whilst the constant loss of blood often exhausted him. The wounds in the feet and the nails wrought in his living flesh lamed him. To walk but a few steps was agony [19]. In order to relieve the pain of his pierced feet St. Clara herself made a pair of sandals, which are still preserved at San Damiano, Assisi.

When Francis died at sunset on 3rd October, 1226 [20], crowds came all night long to venerate the body, and it was there that many (even of the brethren) first saw the Stigmata. In fear and trembling they kneeled there, for it has been truly said that it seemed as though they were gazing upon the very Body of Christ. The Saint, less than two years after, was canonized by Gregory IX. The Stigmata of St. Francis is a fact so amply attested and proved again and again that it were superfluous to discuss this phenomenon any more fully here [21]. The Church has appointed the 17th September in the General Calendar as the day upon which the Feast of the Stigmata of St. Francis is universally observed.

It is authoritatively stated that the record of stigmatization next in time is that of a recluse in Frisia, Blessed Dodo of Hascha, a Premonstratensian Anchorite. Little is known of this Beato, but it is chronicled that at his death in 1231, it was discovered that his hands, feet, and side, were marked with the Five Sacred Wounds. He must, accordingly, have been a contemporary of St. Francis, since he died (at what age is uncertain) only five years after the Saint of Assisi. The learned Domenico Maria Marchese, writing in the seventeenth century, includes Blessed Dodo as a Dominican, but he is certainly at fault here. The Bollandists, *Acta Sanctorum*, 30th March, "of Blessed Dodo of Hascha, of the Order of Prémontré, a hermit in Frisia", clearly establish the fact that he was a

Nobertine. That he is not in the Nobertine Calendar is nothing, since there are many Saints and Beati of the Order who are not liturgically commemorated. The Bollandists, indeed, comment with some surprise upon the fact that there are so very few saints and Beati of this ancient Order solemnly honoured with Mass and Office. It is certainly to be wished that a public cult was restored to many Nobertines now not officially observed. Nor is Abbot Augustine Wichmans' *Epigrammata de Viris Sanctimonia Illustribus ex Ordine Praemonstratensi* (*Epigrams on the Praemonstratensian Saints and other Illustrious Sons of St. Norbert*), a book in which Blessed Dodo does not appear, of any significance in this respect. Abbot Wichmans only eulogizes a few of the more famous names. There were many Premonstratensian hermits, who dwelt as solitaries, far from the path of men. Such a one was St. Gerlac who was born in the twelfth century at Houthem (now called Houthem St. Gerlac), a village five miles from Maastricht. A nobleman in high favour with the Emperor, he abandoned the world for a hermitage, and passed many years in a secluded and almost inaccessible spot at some little distance from the very castle where he was born. He died 5th January, 1171, and his feast is kept on the Monday after Ascension Day, the anniversary of the Translation of his Relics. So blessed Dodo is by no means exceptional in his rigid anchoretism.

Throughout the century following the death of St. Francis, more than twenty mystics—probably the number might wellnigh be doubled—received the overwhelming favour of the divine stigmata. In a brief survey it is not possible to name more than a few. Some, in fact, have already been mentioned, for example, Blessed Helen of Hungary, Blessed Emily Bicehieri, Helena Brusmin, Blessed Vanna of Orvieto, all five Dominicanesses; Blessed Angela of Foligno, the Franciscan; and that wondrous ecstatica, the glory of the Order of Holy Father Augustine, St. Clare of Montefalco.

A Dominican contemporary of St. Francis is Walter, Prior of the Strasburg and Colmar houses, both in Alsace-Lorraine. This holy man who died in 1264 had the complete stigmata [23]. A Friar Minor, Blessed Phillipe d'Acqua, who was born at Aix in Provence in 1269, and who lived to be a centenarian, dying at Naples, 8th May, 1369, during an ecstasy saw a vision of the Crucified and received the Five Sacred Wounds [24].

The Magdalen of Tuscany, the Poor Little Child of Christ, the Pearl of Pearls, whose legend has been so simply and so beautifully told by her confessor, Fra Giunta, St. Margaret of Cortona [25], she who to expiate spring-tide love of but a little while, lived long days of penitence in a poverty past belief, days of abject humiliation and shuddering austerity, whilst once half-distraught with compunction and self-reproach (only too little deserved!) she lay prostrate on the bare earth before the Crucifix, heard a Voice which comforted her saying that as she had shown great mercy so also she should receive great mercy, yea, more, hers was the reward of the poor in spirit, hers was the kingdom of heaven. And it seemed as though Our Lady Herself comforted her, for she was one of those who mourn, and in that moment Margaret in some sort mystically felt the stroke of the sword which pierced the Immaculate Heart and experienced some shadow of the suffering of the Seven Dolours. She died on 22nd February, 1297, but she lives forever in the hearts and on the lips of the dwellers in and around Cortona. They love her to-day, and they call upon her to help them as she was so ready to help their forbears all those centuries ago. In the quiet streets of the town as they go to and from their business, in the country lanes and in the Tuscan fields softly they sing to her:

> O Lily of our fields,
> O Violet of humility,
> O little Sister of the Seraphim,
> Ora—ora pro nobis!

Dignified and gracious, a very great lady, as well becomes the Benedictine tradition, a very great Saint and supreme Mystic, St. Gertrude stands before us [26]. In that spiritual classic the Revelations [27] she relates how she felt in her burning heart the impression of the Sacred Stigmata, and throughout all her Works her intimate intercourse with Our Lord is amply apparent. An ancient hermit, to whom heavenly secrets were revealed, once said to her, "Daughter, know that thy heart is so pure it might well be venerated among the Holy Relics on yon Altar." A recent biographer quite definitely tells us that in 1281 "she received from our Lord the impressions of the stigmata—His Five Sacred Wounds. These were imprinted interiorly on the heart and thus, unlike those of St. Francis and many other Saints were invisible to others; nevertheless, they united her intimately to the sufferings of Christ and hence forward she was to tread the Way of the Cross" [28]. Gertrude loved all living creatures, and when she saw animals in pain or sick she would tend them as a mother tends her child, and she would pray for them and comfort them. This is, assuredly, not the least attractive trait in one who was all gentle and loving and sweet.

"A mystic, with a genius for politics", such is the admirable description one, himself a mystic, has given of Caterina di Benincasa, the dyer's daughter of Siena, "the greatest of all Tuscan saints, and one of the greatest women of all time". And yet politics were thrust upon her Heavenly Dream, invading the depths of her contemplation. But little she recked of that, for "God had taught her to build in her soul a private closet, strongly vaulted with Divine providence, and to keep her always enclosed and retired there. He bade her know that by such means she would find peace and perpetual tranquillity within her soul, a repose which no stress nor storm could disturb." And he showed her who longed so much for utter seclusion the neediness of the world. She addressed these four requests to the Supreme and Eternal Father [29]. The first prayer, in all humility, was for herself. Now the reason she first made petition for herself was simply this, because the soul cannot do any great thing for her neighbours or perform true service, unless she first serve herself, and do a great thing for herself, to wit the acquiring and being stablished in solid virtue.

Secondly she asked for the reformation of Holy Mother Church. For indeed those were evil days.

The Pope's residence was at Avignon—"the Babylonish captivity" as Petrarca proclaimed it—and although when Clement V [*30*] (Bertrand de Got, Archbishop of Bordeaux), established himself in the French city it may at the moment have been a prudent and even necessary precaution, in consequence great abuses and perils had grown up and were on the increase. The States of the Church were governed by Papal Legates, some of whom in the absence of the Pontiff, proved tyrants, hard and implacable, although perhaps no sterner than the state of things demanded. Rome itself was the prey of three princely houses; the Orsini, the Savelli, and the Colonnesi. Of these the Orsini and Colonna became so furiously impious and overbearing as to demand the allegiance of the Holy City. Other powerful nobles lorded it over Papal cities. Thus the Malatesti were the despots of Rimini and Pesaro; the Varani of Camerino; the Manfredi of Faenza; the Alidosi of Forli, and so on. The traditional sovereignty of the Pope was lip-acknowledged, but he dwelt far away in Avignon. Unless he was established in Rome itself—at what danger to his own Sacred Person—it seemed as though Christendom itself might crumble. Even such men as Cardinal Egidio Albornoz and the doughty Robert of Geneva could scarce curb the impetuosity and ambition of these tyrants. In fact it was not until the days of Sixtus IV and Alexander that they were brought to heel.

Catharine, then, had much to pray for when she sought the domestic Reformation of the Church. Her third prayer was for peace and the reconciliation of the rebels without. There were grave anxieties here. The subtle and subversive preaching of Wycliffe; the foul doctrines of the Beghards and Patarini were corrupting thousands. Her fourth and last prayer was general, with particular petitions for a business in which she was concerned. "Her desire was very great and ever increased, yea, it grew far more when the First Truth showed her the neediness of the world, and in what a whirling tempest of offences against God it was storm-tossed and like to be wrecked."

St. Catharine of Siena saved the social order, she saved Christendom.

Born on Lady Day, 25th March, 1347, she was one of a numerous family, and her mother, a notable good housewife, seems to have loved her above the rest, whilst her father called her Euphrosyne, his "little joy". When she was but seven years old she resolved to devote herself wholly to God, and so promised her maidenhood to Christ. But Ser Giacomo and Monna Lapa his wife were already discussing some good match for their daughter, as Italian parents will. Giacomo was more than a bit of a Capulet, and Monna Lapa ruled her home in autocratic fashion. Catharine was twelve years old—it will be remembered that Juliet was wed before she was fourteen and Lady Capulet talked of time wasted,

> *Younger than you*
> *Here in Verona, Ladies of Esteem,*
> *Are made already Mothers. By my count*

*I was your Mother much upon these Years
That you are now a Maid.*

Monna Lapa already had a suitor in her eye, one of her own family, a
di Puccio di Piagente, an excellent alliance. The youth had every
recommendation. He was good-looking, bore a fair fame in Siena, and
was (or would be) wealthy. Could any prospect be better? Ser Giacomo
agreed. So with many a glad smile and tender caress her parents bade
Catharine to prepare herself for her marriage. It was all nicely settled.
The girl absolutely refused. Most firmly and unequivocally she utterly
rejected the idea of a husband. To say that her father and mother were
amazed is little. They were stunned and horrified. That their daughter
should venture to question their will, to disobey, shocked them beyond
belief. Their anger was terrible. Nevertheless their modest and quiet
little daughter, their darling, their joy, remained unmoved by threat
or argument, and Monna Lapa's tongue when let loose could be tart and
biting enough. At last they appealed to a great friend of the family, a
Dominican, Fra Tommaso della Fonte, a pious and austere man, to
come and deal with the froward hussy. He talked to Catharine of the
duty she must pay to her parents. He was stern and hard. But when
he saw how she answered his arguments, and that she was resolute,
he was convinced. Nobly had she come through the trial when he was
testing her vocation. "My daughter," he said, "pursue your own way.
Wait upon the will of God. This is of God."

Ser Giacomo and Monna Lapa, however, proved unyielding, and were
not to be moved. Catharine patiently endured what is one of the most
difficult things in life to put up with, an organized family persecution.

Presently her father relented, and with his blessing bade her follow
the Will of God. In 1363 she received the habit of the Third Order of
St. Dominic from a friar of that religion in the Cappella della Volta in
San Domenico. For three years she led the life of an anchoress in her
own home, dwelling apart in one room, wrapt in prayer and contemplation,
mortifying herself and fasting with the most rigid discipline. She spoke
to none save to God only and her confessor. In 1366 her public life began,
loath as she was to leave her seclusion. Siena was in a state of something
like anarchy. But Catharine went up and down, composing quarrels,
ending feuds, bringing a great peace with her. Then other cities, Pisa
and Arezzo appealed to her, crying out, "Come over and help us." The
Florentines, who had been ready to rise against the Sovereign Pontiff,
called upon her, and when she came to them the Chief Magistrates met
her with all honour at the very gates of the town. Then follows the most
incredible happening, a miracle in all truth, beyond thought, beyond
belief. Alone, the ambassadress of Italy, she travelled to Avignon. Humbly,
yet without fear, she faced Gregory XI, and kneeling at his feet she
bowed, she bent him to her inflexible will. The whole College of Cardinals,
diplomats, interested statesmen are against her, determined to thwart
her purpose, and yet she with God prevails. The Pope echoes that sweet
word which was ever on her lips, *Peace.* "I leave the whole affair entirely

in your hands," he said, "only I commend to your good keeping the honour of the Church." Sending her before him to Genoa, he meets her there and with her returns to Rome. Her words are always echoing in his ears: "Be a brave man, and not a coward," words she could only have spoken if she herself had not first been brave.

But, save for the sake of that Christendom which she had saved, all this means less than nothing to her. She now turned to her own business, and, as has been admirably said, "her whole life became a continual miracle absorbed in a Divine contemplation." Hers was the supreme experience of the Mystical Marriage [*31*], when in the presence of His Immaculate Mother, with St. John the Evangelist, St. Paul, St. Dominic, assisting, Our Lord placed upon her finger a ring of gold, and King David made music of Paradise upon his harp of celestial strings, as we may see in Professor Franchi's painting in the Saint's house at Fontebranda [*32*].

On a Sunday morning, when she was twenty-eight years old, Catharine received the Sacred Stigmata. The phenomenon was, so to speak, simple, which sounds a paradox, but then her whole life was on the surface simple, and yet she was the greatest force in the political world of her day, and she reached the highest heights of mysticism. Being at Pisa, Catharine was present at the mass of the Dominican, Blessed Raimondo da Capua, who offered the sacrifice in the church of Santa Cristina, which is on the Lungarno Gambacorti. After receiving communion she went to kneel before the crucifix and passed into ecstasy [*33*], when those present noted that after a short space her face was radiant with light and her hands outstretched. For a moment she remained thus as they gazed in awe, and then, as if struck by a mortal blow, she collapsed and fell prone upon the pavement.

The good Sisters ran to raise her, and support her in their arms, not a little affrighted, since they realized some marvellous thing had happened. Thus Blessed Raimondo related the event: "Catharine came to me and said in a low voice, 'Father, know that I bear in my body the Five Wounds of Our Lord Jesus Christ', Whereto I made reply, 'Certes, my daughter, thy ecstasy was so admirable and so prolonged I felt assured some great gift had been granted thee. But, tell me, if it may be told, how didst thou receive this mystic grace of God.' She answered: 'I saw our Blessed Lord aureoled with exceeding glory. He was nailed to the Cross. At which sight my soul fainted within me and my heart burned with love. Forthwith I saw five brilliant crimson rays dart from the Five Wounds, and sharp as a spear, they severally pierced my hands, my feet, and my side. But I cried aloud, My God, my Lord and King, I beseech thee that these wounds of mine betray me not, and show that I have been found worthy in some sort to share Thy Passion. At my words the rays changed from crimson to a golden glow, and these five golden rays of lucent light transpierced my hands, my feet, and my side.' And I asked her: 'Did this ray wound the right side, my daughter?' To which she replied, 'No, father, it is my left side which is wounded, it is my heart which is wounded, for the spear of radiant light, shooting forth from

190

the side of Our Lord, struck me unswerving in its course.' 'Dost thou, then, feel grievous pain therefor?' Catharine with a deep sigh made answer, 'O my father, so great is the agony that unless Our Lord sustain me I shall surely die.' With which words she slowly passed out of the chapel."

Upon returning to the house where she lodged, Catharine went into her room, and falling on the bed, swooned away. Those who had followed her, and were ministering to her, burst into tears, and fell on their knees, praying that she might not be taken from them. "Not yet, Lord, not yet," they lamented. "Lord, give us our mother for a while longer, if it be only a little while." But anon Catharine gently rebuked them, saying, "Pray rather that God's will be done." So she lay sick and ill. But when the Saturday evening came she sent for Fra Raimondo, to whom she whispered: "Father, God has heard your petition. Presently I shall be well again. My wounds indeed are wounds of suffering. But God will give me new strength and new courage." The next day she insisted upon rising, she heard Fra Raimondo's mass at Santa Cristina, and communicated when "health poured into her body and the blood was warm and young again".

St. Catharine died at Rome on Sunday, 29th April, 1380. Her last thoughts were of the welfare of the Church. She foresaw the agony that was to come. Her last words were those of Christ Himself, "Father into Thy hands I commend my spirit." Immediately upon her death the five wounds, which (at her prayers) had not been visible during her lifetime. could be clearly discerned. The Prior of the Minerva Convent [34] in a letter to Fra Raimondo tells how not only he himself and the religious plainly saw the stigmata on St. Catharine's body when it was placed on an open bier in the church, but that the multitudes who came to honour her exclaimed aloud when they perceived that she bore the Wounds of Jesus. Moreover the stigmata appear upon her relics, and are impressed there in such a way that it is impossible the marks should have been made (by some erring if pious devotee) after death. Medical evidence attests this. The fact is beyond dispute. In the famous Dominican church at Venice, San Zanipòlo (St. John and St. Paul [35]), is preserved a famous relic, the foot of St. Catharine in which the wound is quite visible. The relic of the hand, also, venerated at Rome in the ancient Dominican convent of San Sisto, on the Via Appia and opposite the Baths of Caracella, can be seen to be pierced with a wound [36].

On Sunday, 4th May, 1940, the present Holy Father, Pius XII, amid scenes of unexampled splendour, at Santa Maria Sopra Minerva crowned the statue of St. Catharine with a gold and jewelled diadem, presented by the ladies of Rome, and proclaimed her Patroness of Italy. Making a departure from the usual ceremonial the Pope preached not from his throne, but from the pulpit, a glowing panegyric of the Saint. The Pontiff made this change so that he might be better heard by the majority of the vast congregation. This was a fitting climax to the celebrations which had begun on 28th April. Upon the Feast Day itself Cardinal Tisserant pontificated at High Mass at the Saint's altar-tomb.

On 27th August the Carmelites keep the Feast of the Transverberation of the Heart of their Holy Mother St. Teresa of Ávila. For the most part the stigmata, or it may be the wound in the side alone, are given instantaneously, as one might say with a single sharp blow. Professor Allison Peers draws attention to the fact that the most famous of the mystical experiences of St. Teresa, the phenomenon known as the Transverberation of her heart, which may certainly be dated in 1559, was not a single and isolated vision, but one which was many times repeated, extending over several days. Teresa saw standing close to her, on the left hand side, an angel. He "was not tall, but short, and very beautiful, his face so aflame that he appeared to be one of the highest Orders of angels who seem to be all afire. They must be those who are called Cherubim" [*37*]. This vision she was aware of not once nor twice, but again and again. In his hand the angel held a long spear with shaft of gleaming gold, which was tipped with red-hot iron. Time after time he thrust at her with this Celestial lance, piercing her heart, and penetrating her very entrails with a pain so excruciating that she moaned aloud [*38*]. Although her body suffered keenly, this agony of the wounding was psychical, though very real, and (the Saint writes) "so excessive was the sweetness caused me by this intense pain that one can never wish to lose it, nor will one's soul be content with anything other than God."

St. Teresa adds how "during the day that this continued I went about as if in a stupor; I had no wish to see or speak with anyone, but only to hug my pain" [*39*].

The heart of St. Teresa, a most holy Relic, is still preserved with great veneration at Ávila, where her body remains incorrupt to this day. P. Francisco de Ribera in his *Vida de Santa Teresa de Jesús* gives a very detailed description of the perfect preservation of the body and its marvellous fragrance in 1588. Fray Jerónimo Gracián confirms this. Various relics were distributed to Carmelite houses and others. Thus on 15th October, the Feast of the Saint, the Relic of the right foot is venerated at Santa Maria della Scala (where there is celebrated a Pontifical High Mass), Rome. This distribution of relics may seem a little strange, perhaps, to those who are ignorant of the full tradition of Relics, and it would require too much space to explain and defend it here. It must suffice to note that it is very amply dealt with by St. John Damascene, *On the Orthodox Faith*, and by later writers such as the learned Alban Butler, Ribera, *Vida*, v, i, ii, iii, deals with the heart phenomena of St. Teresa. On occasion, under episcopal sanction, and with all due precautions, the Reliquary has been formally unclosed to be sealed again by the Bishop after scrupulous examining. The heart is thrust through as if by a keen blade, the wound being about an inch and a half across. The edges of the wound are burned and charred as if by a red-hot iron.

Vel pati vel mori, to suffer for Love's sake, or to die, thus St. Teresa exclaimed; whilst another Carmelite who, to my thinking, stands by the side of St. Teresa and St. John of the Cross, exclaimed *Pati, sed non mori*. To suffer for Love's sake, to suffer but not to die. There is no greater mystic in the whole history of mysticism than the Florentine nun, St. Maria Maddalena de' Pazzi. She is, it is true, not so well known in England as the Seraphic St. Teresa, and St. John, Doctor of the Church. This is practically due, I think, to the fact that she has not met with such scholarly and eloquent interpreters as the two great Saints of Carmel, but assuredly in the sublimity of her vision she falls no whit behind them. Hence it is, perhaps, her raptures and ecstasies, her visions and revelation, are far above the ken of ordinary folk. Her eyes are ever fixed upon the stars; her face is ever turned upwards to Heaven. She is a mystic for mystical souls [40].

"We have St. Maria Maddalena de' Pazzi, that ecstatically voluble Carmelite, whose work is a series of apostrophes and divine eloquence. She shows herself a rhapsodically enraptured ecstatica, her inspiration can only express itself in similitudes and adumbrations, she is on the rarest heights. Her pages are embroidered with metaphor and hyperboles. There is no medium, nor mediety; she talks directly with God the Father, the ineffable, the First Person of the Trinity, and so far as human tongue may in ecstasy she stammers out explanations of mysteries, which are revealed to her by the Ancient of Days. Her revelations contain one sovran passage upon the Circumcision; another magnificent passage, built up of antitheses, upon God the Holy Ghost; others, which to any but a mystic soul, seem exceeding strange, upon the Deification of the human soul, the closest and most intimate connexion with Eternal God, upon the union of the soul with Heaven, and on the essential part played in this supernatural phenomenon by the Wounds of the Only-Begotten, the Word.

The Wounds are abiding-places and nests wherein Christ dwells; the Eagle, type of soaring faith, has his home in the eyrie of the left foot; in the wound of the right foot, sighs the melancholy sweetness of the gently cooing turtle-dove; symbol of completest trust and self-surrender, the dove is homed in the wound on the left hand; whilst in the wound of the right hand dwells enharboured the pelican, emblem of perfect love.

These birds wing their way, softly hovering from their nests, and come forth to seek the soul that they may lead her to the nuptial chamber which is the wound that gushes with the Precious Blood, the Wound in the side of Christ" [41].

It was this Carmelite who was so interpenetrated and overwhelmed with grace that she desired not but despised that certitude which comes from the evidence of the senses. It was she who said to God: "Lord, if I saw Thee always with mine eyes here on earth I should lose the sovran gift of Faith, because Faith must cease to be when certitude is attained, and that soothly is in Paradise."

St. Maria Maddalena de' Pazzi with her Dialogues and Contemplations sees horizons, nay, surveys boundless vistas the mere human eye cannot reach. The ordinary soul, even the soul of one striving to do better, yet limed and clogged with sin, cannot follow her up the slopes of Carmel to those dizzy heights which she treads with foot unfaltering and unafraid. Where she stands and whence she gazes upon eternity only the greatest

M   193 of mystics can stand by her side, and look forth unwinking with clearest sight. The air upon the summit is too radiant and rare for us to breathe. We may but lift our longing eyes to the goal, as in our weakness we stumble even on the lowest rises and acclivities of the mystic mountain.

It was in 1585, on 24th March, after First Vespers of the Annunciation had been sung, that the full flood of supernatural experience and supernatural suffering inundated and resistlessly overflowed both soul and body of the Saint. In a vision, a vision poignantly true, there appeared to her St. Augustine of Hippo who wrote upon her heart in letters of crimson and gold the words *Verbum caro factum est*. The Word was made flesh. It was on the 11th April that she participated in the sufferings of Calvary and first received the stigmata. So intolerable was her anguish that she cried aloud: "Ah, my God, surely if Thy Passion is so bitter to me, I must die!" On the Monday in Holy Week the stigmata were more deeply impressed, and on Shrove Thursday "I felt all the sufferings of Christ," says the Saint. Her face was deadly pale, her lips white, her person bowed to the ground, every limb ached with an immense fatigue, whilst she broke out in a sweat of blood, and seemed about to swoon away to death.

A few days later she beheld in a supernatural way all the sins of the world and the malice of them, in some measure as Christ beheld the offences of mankind as He prayed in Gethsemane. St. Maria Maddalena was drowned in tears, which could not be staunched until the glorious appearance of St. Augustine and St. Catharine of Siena, to whom she had a particular devotion, turned her sorrow into joy. On 4th May, Our Lord Himself crowned her with the Crown of Thorns, whilst Our Lady Who appeared with Her Son held a coronal of dazzling light and said, "Lo! this, and more than this, shall be thy crown in Heaven."

St. Augustine, St. Catharine of Siena, and St. Angelo the Carmelite, were present at this mystery. Thenceforth, on every Friday, St. Maria Maddalena suffered the agony of the Crown.

On the following 7th May the Saint was absorbed in contemplation meditating the descent from the Cross and the Burial. Suddenly she saw Our Lord and Our Lady. She was instantly rapt in ecstasy, when occurred the supreme mystery of the Change of Hearts. Our Lord taking His sacred Heart from His breast placed it within the bosom of the Carmelite, and exchanged her heart for His own. So ineffable a Union cannot be described in any words which are aught but simple and shadowy, indirective and analogical. *Cor ad cor loquitur.* For sheer delight her breath was stifled, and she sighed most tenderly. Then the Eternal Father looking with the utmost complacency upon the Sacred Heart enshrined within her bosom, spake and said: "Bride of the only Begotten Word, My Son, ask of Me whatsoever thou wilt."

"The Five Red Wounds of Jesus are my sure anchor of salvation amid the stress and shipwreck of the world, they are my shadow of a great rock where I rest me and cool in the burning heat and sirocco winds that sweep the arid Saharas of temptation." These are the words of St. Maria Maddalena. But how inadequately have I presented her beauty, mistress

194

of mystical science! Her life was one long ecstasy. On 25th May, 1607, she passed from Paradise on earth to Paradise in Heaven.

The astounding phenomenon of the Exchanged Heart, although very rare, is not unique in the history of mysticism. It is recorded of San Miguel de los Santos (St. Michael of the Saints). San Miguel, whose family name was Argemir, was born at the little town of Vich in Catalonia on 29th September, 1591. Before he had reached his twelfth Birthday he entered the Order of the Most Holy Trinity for the Redemption of Captives (Discalced Trinitarians), which had been founded by the royal hermit, St. Felix de Valois, and St. John de Matha, and approved by Innocent III by a bull in 1198 [42]. San Miguel is one of the most amazing ecstatices in the whole range of mysticism. It has been truly said of him that throughout all his days he seems never to have passed out of the state of rapture. It will be understood that this mystical experience ebbed at times, very infrequently, and seemed less vehement than at others, since he perfectly performed every obligation of his religious life. He was, for example, assiduous in the confessional. But, as an old writer has it, even whilst he dwelt on earth Heaven was Miguel's home. He appeared an angel not a man. "Wherefore Our Lord was pleased to bestow a very great and singular grace upon His faithful servant, and on a day when Miguel was in ecstasy He deigned to make the mystical Exchange of his Most Sacred Heart with the heart of the Saint." Miguel de los Santos died at Valladolid on 10th April, 1625. He was canonized by Pius IX on Whit Sunday, 8th June, 1862, and his Feast is kept upon the fifth of July [43].

The exact number of mystics who have received the stigmata, whether it be the complete stigmata, or the Crown of Thorns alone, or the heart wound, or the shoulder wound, cannot be precisely computed. There are very many difficulties in attempting any list which could be presented as statistically accurate and comprehensive. A painstaking and very researchful recent investigator, writing in 1933, says "in the history of the Church, there are reckoned up to the present three hundred and twenty-one known cases of stigmatization." I am confident that at least thirty more cases could be added, and then I am very sure that the tale would yet be far from complete.

For example, I have never met in any catalogue of Stigmatization the Venerable Serafina di Dio [44], the Carmelite nun of Capri. Born on 24th October, 1621, at Naples, she passed most of her life at Capri, where she built with her own fortune a convent, San Salvatore (generally called Santa Teresa), which in 1678 was solemnly blessed by the Archbishop of Benevento, Cardinal Orsini, afterwards to be raised to the Chair of Peter as Benedict XIII. Other foundations were at Massa Lubrense in the Sorrento Peninsula in 1673, and here is still venerated the Crucifix which spoke to her, whilst she was in ecstasy. Two years later a convent was opened at Vico Equense, a small town on the road from Castellmare to Sorrento. In 1680, another house was founded at Nocera de' Pagani, where to-day sleeps St. Alfonso de' Liguori. In 1683, a larger convent was built at Anacapri, and dedicated to St. Michael. Torre del Greco, near Pompeii, was the next site. The seventh and last convent Serafina raised was in 1691 at Fischiano, hard by the city of Salerno. This great and holy woman died in the attitude of one crucified on 17th March, 1699. She was seventy-eight years old.

The Venerable Serafina received the stigmata, which were clearly to be seen by all on her hands and feet, whilst her heart was pierced through by a golden dart lanced by a vision of the Divine Child, Who appeared as if about twelve years of age. She participated, it seems, to some little extent in the agony of the Third Dolour, the loss of Our Lord in Jerusalem. On one occasion when the Madre Serafina was kneeling enraptured before the Cross, a little novice had crept close, croodling to her, and prayed for some spark of fervour. Doubtless the novice, whose name we are not told, had advanced far on the mystic way for thereupon darted forth five rays of radiant light from the Five Wounds of the figure on the rood, and these five rays mingling in one as a lance tipped with golden fire pierced her heart, so that she felt "as if she had passed out of a great shadow of darkness into a fair champaign bathed in sunshine, where it was most excellent and healthful to be".

I do not venture to say that the Venerable Serafina is not included in the list of Stigmaticas which some diligent author has compiled, but to the best of my recollection I have not met with her name in such a mystic poll, and although her memory is green in Capri she is so little known elsewhere that this case may well have escaped enumeration. There must, one feels sure, be many similar exceptions.

Another such instance is that of Blessed Béatrix, who was born at the Château d'Ornacieu, Dauphiné. At the age of thirteen she entered the Chartreuse de Parménie, Isère. Her life, which was truly hidden with God, was distinguished by humility, obedience, charity, and above all by a fervent devotion to the Passion. Blessed Béatrix was stigmatized with the Five Wounds. With two other nuns, Louise de Graisivaudan and Marguerite de Sassenage, she was sent to found a Convent near Valence. Here she lived most holily, dying on 25th November, 1303. Blessed Béatrix is painted [45] in company with the other Carthusian Saints in fresco upon the walls of the Charterhouse of St. Hugh, Patridge Green, Sussex, and she is figured in other Certosas, but I think outside her Order, and where her Relics, which are very miraculous, are preserved at Parménie, the Beata is very little known [46].

It is obvious that any list of stigmaticas which omitted the names of Blessed Béatrix the Carthusian, the Venerable Serafina di Dio of Capri, and the Carmelite novice of San Salvatore, would be far from complete.

Again, another factor which militates against an entirely comprehensive tale of stigmatization is that many cases are under consideration, and have not been definitely pronounced upon by authority. Moreover cases are continually becoming known as occurring in various parts of the world, and scrupulously careful investigation is made into each one of these. Such official processes naturally take time, and so meticulous is the caution employed, so searching the inquiry, that months and years go by whilst the matter is in abeyance, and should there be the least particle of doubt judgement may be almost indefinitely suspended. There is medical evidence to be weighed, and often specialists are consulted, physicians from quite other towns and countries, so that there cannot possibly be any prepossession, however involuntary and unconsciously shown. Again, a case is not unseldom put back, to be resifted from the very beginning. Just this brief outline may serve to indicate how prudent and how guarded is Rome in pronouncing upon a case of stigmatization.

Be it well borne in mind that I am not speaking of canonization. That is another thing, and hedged about with even more elaborate investigations. The best way to gain some idea of the proceedings entailed is to consult the Encyclopædic and authoritative work of Benedict XIV, *De Servorum Dei Beatificatione et Canonisatione* [47]. It may be remarked that before his accession to the Papal Throne in 1740, Cardinal Prospero Lambertini (1675–1758) was Promotor Fidei, commonly known as the "Devil's Advocate", that is to say the official whose duty it is, when the Cause of a holy person comes under consideration, to advance any arguments which may tend to show that the subject of investigation and inquiry is not so pre-eminently holy, and has not exhibited the "heroic virtues" (a technical term) to such a degree as to be raised to the Altars of the Church, the supreme honour. The "Promotor Fidei" under obedience performs a difficult and in some sense an invidious task. He is arguing against a person who is, no doubt, extraordinarily holy and gifted, and yet who may not be on purely technical grounds "a candidate for canonization". When all that he advances, that it has been his duty to advance, falls to the ground nobody is more rejoiced than himself.

Doubtless many cases of divine stigmatization have occurred through the centuries and occur to-day which are not recorded. It may be some innocent country girl in a remote district, the Swiss valleys or Calabria, who in wonder and shame has concealed the Sacred Marks, never deeming herself worthy of the Seals of Christ. She has lived and died unknown. If, after her death, the Wounds were seen, the family and friends, the simple priests of the hamlet, unwitting, would not speak of the phenomenon. They did not understand how a spouse of Christ could have dwelt in their midst. Thus whilst the cause of Blessed Anna Maria Taigi, who died in 1837, was being officially commenced in 1852, among the witnesses examined was her aged husband Domenico Taigi, who when various questions were put to him could only answer: "She was a very good wife, an excellent wife, but a Saint! Oh, no, I never guessed she was a Saint."

It may be it is the case which has never been chronicled of some enclosed ecstatica, a Poor Clare, a Dominicaness of the Second Order, a Carmelite, a Benedictine, the mystery of whose stigmata was never known to any save her Superiors and perchance her sisters, whose name is only written in the annals of her convent, for ever sheltered from the world.

Very difficult, far-reaching and intricate problems are raised by what we may call "the border-line" cases of stigmatization. In this field we encounter those examples of stigmatization which may quite probably be in the origin of divine impressing; and at the other extreme instances of stigmata, or rather pseudo-stigmata, which prove upon investigation to be altogether fraudulent and fictive markings, artificially imitated by some agent, or deliberately self-inflicted; or, to plumb the lowest and darkest depths of all, made by satanical operations, consequent upon a diabolical contract and agreement with hell.

Accordingly the most scrupulous care must be employed in discussing "border-line" cases, and any pronouncement has to be made with diffidence and the nicest reserve.

About five-and-twenty years ago a great sensation was caused by an extraordinary case in Brussels, which gave rise to considerable discussion and was the subject of many articles, both in Belgian and other journals and newspapers. Bertha Mrazek was born in Brussels on 11th December, 1890, her father being a Czechoslovak and her mother a Belgian. During the war of 1914–1918, Miss Cavell, with whom she worked and who was her firm friend, aptly suggested that she should adopt a somewhat less unusual name in Belgium, and accordingly Bertha Mrazek called herself "Georges Marasco", the nom-de-plume under which she had contributed verses and some short articles to various newspapers. It may perhaps be as well to emphasize that this alteration of name, the idea of which came from so wise and admirable a source, was in the circumstances a prudent and wholly laudable precaution.

The first time that Georges Marasco came before the public was on 27th July, 1920, when the *Libre Belgique* printed a long account of "A Cure at the Shrine of Our Lady Hal". Briefly, on Monday 19th July, 1920, a very sick young lady, scarcely thirty years old, living at Forest, a suburb of Brussels, was brought in a motor-car to the Church of Our Lady of Hal [*48*], where is venerated the Miraculous Statue. There accompanied the sick girl the Parish Priest of Forest, a nurse, and a soldier who had fought in the war. It was feared that she would die on the way, but without any sign of life she was lifted on to a stretcher, carried in, and laid before the shrine. All joined in fervent prayer, when the invalid, who had been paralysed for a year and blind for a couple of months, after a little struggle rose up, mounted the steps leading to the altar unaided, and kneeling down prayed earnestly. Turning to her parish priest she cried in a voice of thrilling joy: "I am cured! I am cured! I can see!" M. le Curé in thanksgiving intoned the *Magnificat*. The whilom sick girl, Georges Marasco, left the church with a firm step, and her arrival at her home caused an immense sensation among the neighbours who had seen her carried out in a state of utter collapse. None were more surprised than the specialists and doctors; who had been attending her and who had pronounced the case incurable, declaring that it must inevitably have a fatal ending since both hands and feet were affected by creeping paralysis, bones were dislocated, seven vertebræ were out of place, and the jaw injured and awry.

So far, so good. That the cure was miraculous was proved beyond any manner of doubt, but it does not in the least follow that a person who has been miraculously cured at some shrine, Hal, or Lourdes, or Fatima, or Beauraing, is in any sense a saint, or anything like a saint. The *miraculé* or *miraculée* is generally speaking a pious person, or at any rate one who decently fulfils the religious duties of his (or her) state. Yet even this may not be the case. Thus, Benito Pelegri Garcia, an avowed anarchist of Barcelona, who had married a Belgian wife, was a red-hot revolutionary and an infidel of the most aggressive and inimical extreme. Exceptionally skilful and a great strong man, he earned high wages, but on the explosion of a boiler at the factory in November, 1931, his right arm was so severely injured that thenceforth he was utterly incapacitated, and so thrown out of employment. Compensation was, of course, awarded him, yet this did not go very far, especially when in hopes of a complete cure he drained it to undergo medical treatment, not only at home, but also in Italy and Germany. He trusted before long to be able to resume work again, but in the end the case was declared to be hopeless, and the family were left in poverty with no outlook for the future. It is little to be wondered at that he became cankered at heart and broken down, a mere wreck. At the age of thirty-six his life was finished. Where could he turn?

His good wife, who in spite of her husband's atheism, had always preserved her simple faith, in 1933 heard of the apparitions of Our Lady at Banneux [*49*], an inaccessible and sequestered hamlet in the diocese of Liège, but at no very considerable distance from Dolhain, a modern place in the valley of the Vesdre, on the site of the lower part of the ancient city of Limburg, under the heights, whereon towers the Castle of Limburg, the ancestral seat of the Dukes of that name. Now Dolhain was Señora Garcia's native town, so she was especially interested in these Apparitions by whose healing power, invoked as *La Sainte Vierge des pauvres*, so many cures had been wrought through the little spring which ran there. *Je viens soulager les malades*, the Lady had said. Would she not heal her husband also? Inspired with a new hope the pious woman entreated him to have recourse to Our Lady of Banneux. At first he was enraged at the very idea. But she persisted, and he was worn down with pain and grief. Yet he held out. "Well, then," his elder daughter said, "if you will not make this one effort—and we will ask no more—I must go into domestic service, or to anyone who will take me as a drudge, since we have no other way to live." The man gave way. "I don't believe a word of it," he cried, "not a word. But I am a mere useless log. Carry me where you will."

The children being left in a neighbour's care, the pilgrimage was undertaken by Garcia and his wife in two very different kinds of spirit. She prayed, and as they went knitted little things which she could sell for a trifle to purchase bread. He grumbled and cursed the weariness, the privations, the heat, for they had set out on 4th July, and the way was long and toilsome. They went on foot, and their bed was often under the hedges, or at best a truss of rotting straw in an empty barn. When they drew near Banneux, the man's anger blazed out: "I am just being fooled," he bawled, "you have made a fine ninny-noddy out of me. Trapesing here like a couple of priest's mugs! And we get there I'm going to plant you down in your dear old home, and cut." Within half a mile from Banneux he actually slipped away, and it was only by the aid of the police that his devoted wife discovered him. With much difficulty she persuaded him that he would be making a far greater fool of himself to have come all this way and not bathe in the water. That at least seemed common sense, so muttering and frowning he took his place and waited his turn among the pilgrims by the spring. A doctor, a materialist, who was standing by and taking notes, when Garcia came up examined his arm, and said: "If you go putting that in the pool we shall have your wound even more septic. Come along, let's have a fresh bucket of water. We don't want to run any risks." The bucket was brought, and Garcia immersed his arm. He drew it out quickly with a cry. "Whew!" he exclaimed, "Oh! Ouch! The water's boiling hot!" The doctor smiled, and Garcia seeing this felt the water in the bucket with the tips of the fingers of his left hand. The water was icy cold. Amazed and quite dumbfounded, he dipped his right arm into the bucket again. "Here I am," he said, "a poor fellow who has tramped all the way from Spain. If you are, 'the Virgin of the poor', prove it!" A tinkle was heard. The tube which was inserted by the doctors in the suppurating arm had fallen out, and there and then before the eyes of all present the wound healed. A medical examination was at once held, every test was applied, and presently inquiry was made of all the doctors and specialists whom Garcia had consulted. No vestige of doubt remained. There is no possible explanation except that a miracle had taken place [50].

Garcia returned to Barcelona a whole and sound man, in perfect health. Unflinchingly he confronted his former associates. He openly told how he was cured, and thenceforward there was no stouter champion of *la Sainte Vierge des Pauvres*, Our Lady of Banneux, Immaculate.

From this we see that the favours of miraculous cures are granted, as the sun rises "on the evil and on the good", to the just and to the unjust alike. Hence we cannot argue that any person who has been supernaturally healed is particularly pious or devout, although humanly speaking, unless there be circumstances out of the ordinary, it may without rashness be surmised that only those who believed would seek Heaven's aid at some holy shrine.

Georges Marasco [51] (Bertha Mrazek), then, was miraculously cured at the church of Our Lady of Hal. It was inevitable that she should become "a centre of attraction", so to speak; that visitors, some out of pity, some out of curiosity, some (no doubt) in a spirit of unbiased yet scrutinizing inquiry, should flock to her little villa in the Avenue De Nayer, Forest. A number—if not of disciples—at least of devoted admirers began to gather round her; it was said on excellent authority that many conversions had been the result of her admonitions, and that through her sufferings and prayers many cures had been obtained. The highest mystic phenomena exhibited themselves. She received the stigmata, the Five Wounds, and also the Wound in the side. She was believed to be the victim of mystical substitution [52], which is to say that she could vicariously take the mental sorrows, the anguish and distress, even the physical pains of others upon herself, and suffer in their place. There is nothing new, and, to a student of mysticism, nothing startling in this. 'Cette substitution d'une âme forte débarrasant celle qui ne l'est point, de ses périls et de ses craintes, est une des grandes règles de la Mystique." St. Teresa d' Ávila took upon herself and bore without flinching the temptations of a priest wellnigh driven to despair. Blessed Maria Bartolommea Bagnesi, the Florentine Dominicaness of the sixteenth century, was well known throughout the city for relieving, by taking on herself, the illnesses and troubles of her neighbours and of the wretched who had recourse to her. She became a complete invalid, and died, a victim of love, in 1577. Blessed Anne Maria Taigi, the Roman matron, who was, perhaps, the most illumined seer of the nineteenth century, often bore the sufferings both interior and physical of those who sought her aid. During several weeks every symptom of consumption, the racking cough, continual sputation, excessive sweats which drenched her whole bed, and unintermittent fever, tore the wasted body of Anne Catharine Emmerich. Her death was hourly expected. Suddenly she said to one who was in the room: "Let us say the prayers for those in their last agony." A little later there came in a neighbour to ask her to remember his sister who had just expired. He related the details of her illness, which exactly resembled in every minutest particular the sufferings of Anne Catharine herself. "But, thank God," he added, "during the last two weeks and more, she was, although slowly sinking, free from pain, and made her peace with any she might have offended, and passed away in perfect tranquillity." The profuse sweating, the constant cough, the fever within an hour had left Anne Catharine. A good priest, who was attending her, divined the truth. "Ah, daughter," he said, "this is all your doing. You took this sick woman's agony on yourself, and so she died quietly, in good dispositions." The holy nun did not deny it. She merely bowed her head and whispered gently: "Father, we are all one body in Christ." So Sœur Bernard de la Croix, who died in 1847, and Barbara of St. Dominic, a Spanish votary, who in 1872 offered her life for the cure of a sister, an important member of the community, long confined to bed by a complication of agonizing disorders, were both wont to take upon themselves the mental anguish and miseries of others [53].

Mystical substitution is a very high claim, and by the end of the year 1922 the stigmatized Georges Marasco was regarded by increasing numbers of pious people as a figure of something like extraordinary sanctity, one who received constant revelations from Heaven, who had almost uninterrupted intercourse with the Angels, one to whom a mysterious message had been entrusted by God, a message which she must announce to the world. Moreover, these individuals who so entirely believed in her surpassing holiness were by no means simple peasants and blind enthusiasts, but persons of high social standing, men and women of the world, as the phrase goes, not likely to be deceived, and themselves in absolutely good faith. A distinguished French abbé, who held an important position in his home diocese, and who had long been a student of mystical theology, was approved as her Director. He was satisfied that she was indeed a chosen vessel, one guided from on High. Most of the Belgian clergy, it was observed, rather markedly declined to express any view, save in one or two instances, a prelate and several canons, who did not hesitate to voice their grave suspicions.

The stigmata of Georges Marasco have been photographed, the wounds in hands and feet, the gashed side; and one thing is very certain, they were not in any way artificially made, they were not, in colloquial English, "a fake".

None the less curious rumours were afloat. It was hardly to be expected that a stigmatica who had been so widely discussed in the public streets should not meet with malice and detraction as well as reverence and respect. But something more than mere gossip and scandal-mongering seemed to be bruited. It was (as far as may be ascertained truly) said that the parents of Georges Marasco were loose-living and disreputable, that they harshly drove her from home at a very early age. A number of people distinctly remembered how she appeared as a performer, a lion tamer, in the circus of Van Been frères. Further she gave a very skilful contortionist turn. She also sang in more than one café-chantant, at the "Chat Noir" and at the "Minerva" in the Rue Haute. All this is quite possible, and it may even be in some measure praise-worthy; a young girl's gallant attempt to earn an honest livelihood under extraordinarily difficult conditions. That the little girl, aged about eleven (in 1924), who lived with Georges Marasco and who was called Irène Adèle Mrazek was not her sister, as she universally declared, but her daughter, she was eventually compelled to admit. Again, it may be urged that St. Margaret of Cortona, the Franciscan Ecstatica, was the unmarried mother of a son [54]. St. Margaret, the Magdalen of Tuscany, the "lily of the Valleys", attained to heights of supreme sanctity.

During the War, 1914–1918, and it must be recorded to her credit, Georges Marasco rendered splendid service to Belgium. She was, as has been mentioned elsewhere, a co-worker with Miss Cavell, whose death proved a heavy blow. Herself, twice she only escaped being executed by a clever ruse which both times deceived the enemy. After the Armistice she continued her patriotic work, and made more than one expedition into Germany to report upon conditions there. It was this twittery life of perilous excitement that broke down her health, until after she had passed through several hospitals and the hands of many doctors she was cured at the shrine of Our Lady of Hal.

None the less, it is quite certain that soon after 1920 the higher ecclesiastical authorities were regarding her with mistrust, which, as various circumstances came to their knowledge, dictated some very severe measures amounting in fine to insistence upon a complete sub-mission on her part, and a pledge no longer to exhibit herself in such culpable extravagances, which were giving and had given much scandal to the faithful. The French abbé who was her director was instructed to withdraw and informed that he must for the future hold no further communication with her either by letter or by word of mouth, a pro-hibition he loyally obeyed, for needless to say the discipline required was more than amply justified.

A proceeding which appears to have been by far from the least injurious to her good fame and to have seriously damaged her integrity of purpose, was the fact that she systematically levied from her admirers, many of whom quite honestly believed in her claims to a mystic sanctity and eagerly swallowed her revelations and prophecies, large sums of money, and since the persons who thronged around her, hanging on her words, were for the most part cultured and very wealthy, she was soon able quietly to make up a pretty comfortable purse for herself. Perhaps, over-confident, she screwed too tightly, for in the late winter of 1924, Bertha Mrazek (Georges Marasco) was arrested on a charge of obtaining money by means of a trick. It was then that under a searching cross-examination by the magistrate many of the incidents in her life, as I have related them, were brought to light. An extraordinary hubbub ensued, for she was still supported by the majority of her clientèle who obstinately refused to believe her guilty, whilst others in anger at having been so gulled (as they declared) turned round to assail her with boundless rancour, and heaped upon her virulent abuse, which mere decency, not to mention Christian charity, would have refrained from hurling at an unfortunate, blameworthy though she must have been.

The climax of the whole matter came when she was pronounced to be mad, as a Brussels newspaper flared out in great headlines, "Bertha-Georges Marasco est folle". But the pronunciamento of the specialists cannot be summed up quite so crudely. The doctors, after a long and most careful investigation, gave it as their opinion that it was a marked case of schizofrenia complicated by acute mythomania. She was undoubtedly, they said, in a state of inculpable aberration when the acts upon which the prosecution was instituted took place. It was advised that she should be placed in a home, and accordingly she was removed to an asylum near Mons. *La Libre Belgique*, 4th December, 1927, remon-strated with some vigour. Specialists, it said, have attested that she is on occasion not a responsible agent. But this state is only intermittent, and she unquestionably enjoys long periods of normal lucidity. She is a sick woman and should be treated as such. To confine her in an asylum can only result in exciting the frequency of any morbid crises. She will be reduced to sheer lunacy. It is a barbarous and most pitiable doom.

Without further comment we ask in what category are we to place the stigmatization of Georges Marasco? That she did not bear divine stigmata is certain. It is equally certain that in this case the stigmata was not artificially produced, a fake. When we review the facts of her career, so far as they are known to us, we cannot disguise that there is much evidence of eccentricity, of foolishness, of irregularities, and forward-ness and cunning. I am quite willing to accept the fact that her cure by Our Lady of Hal was miraculous. Indeed, I do not see how this can be questioned. But instead of amending, or at best regulating her life, the unhappy woman fell into the snare of excess of spiritual pride. Some very ugly traits begin to be exhibited, traits in comparison with which the frivolities—to use no harsher name—of her appearance in café-chantants, as a lion-tamer, as a contortionist, the illegitimacy of her child, and whatever else, are nothing at all. She became a false prophetess, a pretender to sanctity; she laid claim to the gift of mystical substitution; she had mysterious revelations; she was marked with the stigmata. She trafficked in these things, collecting around her a numerous clientèle whom she blackmailed, if they did not voluntarily give. What is all this but the sin of Simon Magus? Moreover, "witchcraft is as the sin of rebellion", and Georges Marasco certainly did rebel in refusing to listen to the admonitions and obey the counsels of the Church. Here, then, we have the clue. Here the cloven hoof is plainly to be seen.

She certainly was not mad. The verdict of the specialists was admittedly unsatisfactory. It was, as we are not at all surprised to learn, much criticized. There is one obvious explanation. To me it appears quite plain that she must have entered into a formal or tacit compact with the fiend. Her stigmata then were demoniacal. I am the more confirmed in my opinion since, as I took especial note at the time, the lower pseudo-occult and spiritistic press made loud lament concerning the persecution and martyrdom of Georges Marasco.

A simulation of sanctity aggravated and advertised by a pretence to revelations, mimic visions, the exhibition of the stigmata, and the like, Holy Church regards in the gravest light and deals with very severely. There are recorded a number of such cases, which inevitably have in their day given most unhappy scandal. It will amply suffice to mention but a few.

John Gerson [55], the famous Chancellor of the University of Paris and mystical writer, in his *De Examinatione Doctrinarum, Consid*, vi, mentions the case of a woman who gained a very ample livelihood, by falling into ecstasy and asserting that by her intercession she could release souls not merely from purgatory, but from hell. She also promulgated certain revelations, which (she claimed) were granted her by Heaven in extraordinary circumstances. In 1424, she was living at Bourgen Bresse, Savoy, and this became a centre of much resort.

Such extravagances were soon dealt with by ecclesiastical authority. Upon interrogation she was remanded to be medically examined, and the verdict came that she was an epileptic, with distressing delusions. Whereupon the tribunal, which had at first and with reason regarded the whole business very seriously, relegated her to a fitting hospital, adding that, if possible in order to atone for the scandal she had given, it were well she should undertake certain mild penances to show her contrition.

In 1591, the Holy Office at Toledo sentenced to a condign punishment Maria de Morales of Alcázar for feigning ecstasies, divine revelations, and practising all kinds of trickery to acquire the reputation of a saint. The Inquisitor-General, Andrés Pacheco, sometime Bishop of Cuenca, at a Seville auto of 1624, put an abrupt end to the profane performances of Juan el Hermito, who claimed to heal the sick, to have released by his prayers thousands of souls from purgatory, to dwell continually in the unveiled presence of God, to have celestial revelations, and a great deal more. It will hardly be credited that he had an immense following in the city, and was welcomed, nay, entreated to the houses and tables of blue-blooded grandees. When this lewd impostor was unmasked he was sentenced to be soundly scourged, to be confined for life in a monastery or a hospital, where he was to work for his board, and to recite daily five decades of the rosary [56].

In 1618 the house of Sor Lorenza Murga of Simancas, a religious tertiary, who dwelt at Valladolid, began to be a centre of pilgrimage. Her clientèle increased as the years went on, and since none visited her without a gift in hand, sometimes even of jewels and gold, from the most grinding poverty she rose to a state of considerable affluence. In fact she was an oracle and a power in the city. Ecstasy succeeded ecstasy, and she was always ready to reveal the secrets of Heaven. The higher the fee, the more wonderful the revelation. In the winter of 1633 all this attracted the attention of the Holy Office. When Sor Lorenza was arrested on the following 20th April, Vallodolid seethed with excitement. At first she stoutly maintained that she was a saint, but the inquisitors soon convicted her of fraud, and after a while she confessed. It was further proved that she had been leading an impure life. It was a bad business, but she was dealt with lightly, her sentence including six years banishment from any place, town or village, where she had ever lived [57].

Grandelot in his *Histoire de Beaune*, 1772 (p. 191), relates how at Autun in 1674 an impostress, Jeanne Gros, in penitential sackcloth, made a solemn and public confession in the porch of the Cathedral before the Bishop and Chapter. She openly acknowledged that a sweat of blood which she feigned to have experienced on Good Friday, three years before, deluding many people, was mere cozenage; that the blood-stains, supposedly supernaturally produced, which appeared on her shift had been smutched on the garment with the blood of an animal; and that the stigmata which she had exhibited in her hands, feet, and side, were cunningly contrived by herself, false and fraudulent.

At Seville on 18th May, 1692, Ana Raguza, a Sicilian, was sentenced to seclusion in an enclosed convent, and two years exile. This is very lenient treatment since she denied the efficacy of Masses and Fasting. Moreover she termed herself the Bride of Christ, declared that she could detect sinners by the sense of smell, and prated of her visions and revelations [58].

When Doña Agueda de Luna entered the Carmelite convent of Lerma in 1712 she already enjoyed the reputation of a saint. A crowd of devotees told of her miracles; her ecstasies were repeated several times a day; and each morning the chapel was thronged by nobles and their ladies who besought her intercession. Happy was the person who might speak a word with her at the grille. Soon a convent was founded at Corella, of which house she was elected Prioress. A manuscript life of Madre Agueda was in circulation and copies were multiplied. It was full of the most extraordinary happenings, and it was this which first roused suspicion on account of the unorthodox and even impious relations. Close inquiry was made, and with difficulty a terrible record of malpractices and licentiousness, not unmixed with sorcery, was unripped. The Holy Office did not spare to strike sweepingly, far and wide, to eradicate the evil. Madre Agueda died, but the tribunal of Logroño prosecuted her disciples and accomplices with the rigour their criminality deserved. The convent of Corella was shut down. The community was dispersed singly, one by one, to other convents throughout Spain. All copies of the manuscript *Life* were ordered to be destroyed, as well as such periapts as medals, papers, little pictures and the like which had purportedly been blessed by the Prioress, and distributed to be venerated almost as Holy Relics [*59*].

During the reign of Benedict XIV, 1740–1758, a girl named Vittoria Bondi acquired a considerable reputation for sanctity, and was much venerated by those amongst whom she dwelt. She was supposed to fast for weeks and months together, living only on the Host which was brought her by an angel. Moreover she exhibited the stigmata impressed during one of her frequent ecstasies. There were other phenomena, and not only poor folks but persons of rank and wealth declared their belief in her surpassing holiness. Ecclesiastical authority stepped in, and she was soon convicted of imposture and delusions. The girl made ample confession of her tricks, and was dealt with very mercifully by the Holy Office. After she had performed certain very mild and salutary penances, absolution was granted her, the Pope himself directing that she should be treated thus leniently (*Annali Universali di Medicina*, Vol. cxxiii, pp. 541–2).

One of the most notorious cases of the eighteenth century was that of María de los Dolores Lopez, whose career as a feigned Saint commenced when she was only twelve years old, and continued until she was well over thirty. At Seville, where she resided, supported in luxury by a large clientèle, it seemed almost an open secret that she was leading a life of flagrant immorality under the cloak of religion. She widely boasted of her familiar conversations with Our Blessed Lady, and declared herself to be truly the Bride of Christ, to Whom she had been wedded in Heaven whither she was transported in ecstasy. The witnesses were St. Joseph and St. Augustine of Hippo. There was a good deal more shocking blasphemy, and it seems certain that the woman was a witch. At last the Holy Office was compelled to act, since one of her confederates denounced himself to the Seville tribunal. In 1779 she was put on trial and interrogated, but confronted her judges with the utmost impudence. For nearly a couple of years the pious Fray Diego de Cádiz laboured to bring her to a sense of shame and guilt. It proved a bootless task, and very reluctantly on 22nd August, 1781, the Inquisitor declared that the law must take its course. Almost to the end she yelled out her blasphemies, but at the last moment penitence touched her heart. She confessed, was absolved, and then as justice demanded she was strangled by the executioner, her body being thrown into the flames [*60*].

In his valuable study *Critique et Contrôle médical des Guérisons surnaturelles*, Paris, 1920, Dr. Le Bec, sometime Director of the Bureau des

Constatations at Lourdes, relates how with three other doctors, at the especial request of the then Archbishop of Rennes, Cardinal de Bonnechose, he had a few years previously examined into the case of a reputed stigmatica, living near Dieppe, who claimed to enjoy extraordinary favours from heaven. This girl told long tales of celestial visions and divine voices. There were wonderful revelations. The stigmata with which she was marked bled every Friday night. She was very frequently to be seen rapt in prayer in a side chapel of the village church, and so often would she pass into ecstasy that it became quite a regular thing for numbers of people to assemble and watch her admiringly. The parish priest was greatly embarrassed, since such publicity in itself proved that all was not right.

The committee of four specialists arrived rather late one Friday evening, but as the girl was in bed and asleep they decided not to awaken her, but adjourn. This they did, going no further however than the next room. Before dawn they heard murmurs and deep drawn sighs, upon which, returning to the bedchamber they discovered the girl apparently entranced, with blood upon her hands, feet, and side, and encircling her head. No very searching examination showed plainly enough that the marks had been made with her own fingers, upon which she was questioned closely and soon brought to confess her tricks. The blood she obtained by scratching her left side deeply with a pin, and thus she counterfeited the stigmata. On the whole of the left side of her body she suffered from a complete anæsthesia.

In 1849, the year after the foul murder of Count Pellegrino Rossi, when Pope Pius IX had retired to Gaeta, Caterina da Sezze, a peasant girl from Caselvieri, Sora, appeared in the rôle of a prophetess, and predicted that the Holy Father would soon return in triumph to Rome. The Supreme Pontiff was persuaded to admit her to a private audience, but although he dismissed her with his blessing he said to those about him, "Up till now there is no harm done. But that girl will need to be carefully watched." In 1850 Pius IX re-entered his City, and many who should have known better began to regard Caterina as inspired. Amongst these was Commandatore Filippani, steward to the Papal household, who was perhaps rather too much under the influence of his wife, a highly imaginative and enthusiastic woman. She took Caterina to live in the house, and lost no occasion of proclaiming the girl's heavenly gifts. Her head turned with vanity, the wench secretly entertained a lover, who scenting that money might be made, with two or three confederates began to tutor her in all sorts of pseudo-phenomena. She allowed herself to be "discovered" rapt in ecstasy; declared that she saw visions; acted as a clairvoyante; and carried the thing off with such adroitness that the Roman aristocracy began to flock to her receptions. She netted quite considerable sums, but her revelations became so extravagant and so bizarre that not a few of her admirers were startled and even alarmed. The thing was reported in detail to the Holy Office, and searching inquiries began to be made into these extraordinary proceedings with the result that in February, 1857, Caterina was sentenced to twelve years imprisonment. The charge runs: "For studied inventions of Apparitions of the

Most Blessed Virgin Mary and of Our Lord Jesus Christ; for professing to have the spirit of prophecy; and for claiming to be a saint, whilst she was living in very gross immorality."

Holy Church is rigid, it may appear, in these matters, and most scrupulous, but as a little consideration will show, they are of the gravest and indeed fundamental importance. Sin being in its essence an intellectual act, spiritual sins are quintessentially evil in a degree of which other sins do not partake. The sin of Satan in the beginning was spiritual.

Pride, it has been said, is "the most corrupt and corroding, the most hideous of all sins". The great test, then, that Stigmatization is divine, is humility.

In his authoritative *Il Direttorio Mistico* (published 1574), Gianbattista Scaramelli lays down that the source and place of origin of the Divine Stigmata is the soul. The wounds are primarily spiritual, and simultaneously produce their effect upon the body visibly marking it. The tests by which any case of true Stigmatization can be appraised are, first: That a notable spiritual progress along the mystic path should have been made, and hence that the subject should have endured the purgation of the senses, which, broadly speaking, consists in aridity and desolation, a dry and sandy desert to cross; natural troubles, illness, misunderstandings, the loss of friends or money, ill-treatment, obloquy and defamation, whence scandals arise and there results persecution even from well-meaning and good-intentioned persons, ay, even from authority itself, since all these things cause a supernatural detachment from the world. There may also be diabolic assaults and a regular besiegement by Satan. All men, of course, are liable to attacks from the demon, but for the most part such are intermittent, and not so intensified.

The second test of true stigmatization is that some degree of infused contemplation must have been attained, and infused contemplation depends solely on the will of God, although we presuppose a certain disposition thereto, for example, an intense love of divine things, a vocation, as we might term it. Thirdly, true stigmatization is inevitably accompanied by great physical pain, which, however, is absorbed in a far intenser spiritual delight. Without suffering, the Five Wounds would be little more than empty symbols, and even, perhaps, conducive to pride.

Fourthly, the pain and the heavenly joy as constantly as they recur must result in interior recollection and an extraordinary elevation of the mind to God, which gives a supernatural strength enabling to endure the physical anguish and to partake to the full of the gladness of God.

So far Scaramelli [*62*]. It surprises me that he omits a fifth test of true stigmata, a test which seals all—Humility.

Not one of these five tests must be wanting. To return to Georges Marasco, it is evident that although one or perhaps two of these tests may have *seemingly* been exhibited others were certainly not to be observed. Above all, the crowning grace of humility was conspicuously absent.

Contrariwise, in the case of that sublime mystic the Venerable Orsola Benincasa [*63*], treated with merciless severity and even brutally handled by her antagonists and detractors, who were many, high-placed, and powerful, throughout the long period of incredibly harsh testing, when she was openly assailed as an impostor so that a rumour bruited abroad how she had been discovered to be a witch and was going to be sent to the stake, the holy ecstatica manifested from first to last a degree of resignation, perfect obedience, and humility, which cannot but have been of God.

In July, 1937, Padre Raffaele Codipietro, parish-priest of the tiny village of Paganico Sabina, a few miles from Rome, was visited with severest penalties, being excommunicated and unfrocked, for "an act of sacrilege and simulation". On Wednesday, 23rd July, 1936, the feast of San Apollinare, Padre Codipietro asserted that during Mass, when after the *Agnus Dei*, he proceeded to the fraction of the Sacred Host, breaking It into three pieces, blood flowed from the smallest particle, eight drops falling upon the corporal, whilst some sprinkled the altar-cloth, and the veil of the tabernacle. He unvested in due course but without leaving the altar, and remained there until the arrival of the Bishop of Rieti, Mgr. Massimo Rinaldi, who was immediately requested to come to the church. The Bishop placed the linen marked with the red spots in the tabernacle, of which he himself retained the key. When he had heard a full account of what had occurred from Padre Raffaelle and also from others present, he submitted the whole matter to the Supreme Pontiff, who directed the Holy Office to institute a strict inquiry into this alleged miracle. The Inquisitors after a long and patient examination of every detail, and hearing the various witnesses, delivered into the hands of the Holy Father their unanimous verdict, and when ratified by the Apostolic authority sentence was pronounced [*64*].

From these, and many other examples could be cited throughout many centuries—I cannot insist upon the point too often—we see how closely and with what meticulous care the Church watches the manifestations of any unusual phenomena, generally held to be indicative of an extraordinary holiness of life, how searching are the inquiries made, how severe the test, with studied discouragement and calculated disappointments to mortify the least spark of pride and to purify as if in a refiner's fire so that the gold may shine the brighter and be more esteemed in the end.

We see, moreover, that any simulation, or traffic in supposed spiritual gifts, is utterly condemned and abhorred, judged worthy of severest penalties and swift punishment. Ecclesiastical authority indeed, is rarely cognizant of any darker offences than so deliberate and devilish a mockery of the Most High God.

NOTES TO CHAPTER VI

1. Bishop Lightfoot argues against the commonly received view that this Epistle was written from Ephesus, and is of opinion that it is to be dated in the winter or spring of the years A.D., 57, 58 in which case it would be dispatched from Macedonia or Achaia. *Saint Paul's Epistle to the Galatians*, with Introductions, Notes, and Dissertations by T. B. Lightfoot, D.D., D.C.L., LL.D., Bishop of Durham. First Edition, 1865. Twelfth Edition, 1896, pp. 36–56, "The Date of the Epistle".

2. Vulgate; Domini Jesu. Douai, A.V., "the Lord Jesus." R.V. "the marks of Jesus". The majority of the older MSS. read τοῦ Ἰησοῦ not τοῦ Κυρίου Ἰησοῦ.

3. Thus Plautus, *Aulularia*, II, IV, 47.
      tun' trium litterarum homo
      Me vituperas? fur, etiam fur trifurcifer,

4. ἱερὸς δοῦλος. Téxier, *Asie Mineure*, I, p. 135.

5. Lightfoot, *op. cit.*, p. 16.

6. Catullus, *Attis*. Cybele to her lion: "Rutilam ferox torosa cervice quate jubam." "And fiercely toss thy brawny neck that bears the tawny mane." Burton.

7. T. A. Dulaure, *Des Divinités Génératrices*, Paris, 1805, Ch. ix. Dr. S. R. Driver, *Deuteronomy*, Third Edition, Edinburgh, 1902, pp. 264–65. See also Apuleius, *Metamorphoseon*, XI, the procession of Isis, edition, Lugduni, 1614, Vol. I, p. 1022, the excursus of Philip Beroald.

8. Catullus, *Attis*: "Devolsit ilei acuto sibi pondera silice." Apuleius, *Metamorphoseon*, VIII, has a vivid description of a wandering company of priests of Cybele.

9. *De Dea Syria*, 59.

10. 2 *Corinthians* XII, 4. Lightfoot, *op. cit.*, pp. 44, 49, 64, emphasizes the similarity between the Epistle to the Galatians and the Second Epistle to the Corinthians.

11. XIII, 4.

12. Lightfoot, *op. cit.*, p. 225, note.

13. Life by Pinius the Bollandist, for which see the Bollandists under 31st August; Vol. VI, August; p. 729, Hélyot, *Histoire des Ordres Monastiques*, ed. 1715, Vol. II, pp. 282–3. Alban Butler, *Lives of the Saints*, 31st August.

14. *Die Stigmatisierte Th. Neumann von Konnersreuth Erster Teil: Die Lebensgeschichte der Theresa Neumann*, von Dr. Fritz Gerlich. Munich, 1929.

15. The *Fioretti* distinctly says: "Vieni il di sequenetè, cioè il di della santissima Croce." This seems decisive, although St. Bonaventura (*Legenda Major* XIII, 3) writes "circa festum Exationis sanctae crucis."

16. I follow St. Bonaventura (*Legenda Major*). He says it was Christ *sub specie Seraph* Who appeared to St. Francis.

17. Thomas of Celano, *Legenda Prima*, 1229, is emphatic that the Marks of the Stigmata appeared after St. Francis had risen from his knees and was meditating upon the mystery.

18. *Fioretti:* "Being compelled thereto by necessity, he chose Brother Leo, the most single-minded and most pure in heart of the companions, and to him Francis revealed all that had befallen; and so he suffered him to see and touch those holy wounds of love and to wrap them round with kerchiefs to assuage the pain and staunch the blood which welled there from and ran down in abundance." See also *Glassberger's Chronicle*, written about 1508, and published in *Annales Franciscanae*, III, p. 68. It may be noted that the pictures of St. Francis receiving the stigmata which show Brother Leo gazing with wonder at the mystic event, such, for example, as the extremely fine canvases by Domenichino and Badalocchi, although artistically justifiable, are actually incorrect.

19. Thomas of Celano, *Legenda Secunda*. The *Tractatus de Miraculis*. See also Salvatore Vitalis, *Chronica Seraphica Montis-Alverniae*, 4to, Florentiae, 1630.

20. According to our computation of time. According to ecclesiastical usage, reckoning from vespers, 4th October.

21. The Franciscan literature is, of course, enormous, and to be really useful a very long note would be necessary here. There are many quite recent translations, for example, of the *Fioretti*. The Italian text in a convenient form was published *Milano*, 1907, *I Fioretti di S. Francisco e il Cantico del Sole*. There are English versions, *The Little Flowers of St. Francis*, by Cardinal Manning, 1864, 1887; by the Upton Fathers revised by T. Okey, 1894, 1899, 1905, 1909, 1910, 1912, 1917; by T. W. Arnold (Temple Classics), Sixth edition, 1903. St. Bonaventura's *Life of St. Francis* was translated 1904 (Temple Classics), English translation of Thomas de Celano, by A. G. Ferrers Howell, 1908. The Nuncio Apostolic to Eire, Archbishop Paschal Robinson, O.F.M., has given us a very valuable *A Short Introduction to Franciscan Literature*, 1907. The *Life of St. Francis of Assisi*, by Father Cuthbert, O.S.F.C., 1912; 6th edition, 1925, is an admirable biography of the Saint, with notes and appendices for those who wish to follow the Franciscans further.

22. He died 11th February, 1661.

23. Steill, *Ephemerides dominicanosacrae*. Dilligen. 1692, 27th March.

24. Arturus a Monasterio, *Martyrlogium Franciscanum*, Paris, 1653; Hueber *Menologium*, Monachii, 1698, Luke Wadding; and the *Acta Sanctorum*, 18th May.

25. *Acta Sanctorum*, 22nd February. Capuchin Breviary, 23rd February. A *Tuscan Penitent*, by Father Cuthbert, O.S.F.C. In his *Siena and Southern Tuscany*, 1910, Edward Hutton has some delightful pages on St. Margaret.

26. *Revelationes Gertrudianæ ac Mechtildianæ*. 2 Vols. Poitiers & Paris, apud Henricum Oudin. 1875. *The Life and Revelations of St. Gertrude*, by a Religious of the Order of Poor Clares: London, 1865. *Ste. Gertrude*, by G. Ledos, Paris, 1901.

27. *Legatus Divinæ Pietatis* II, iv, *ed. cit.* pp. 66–8. "De Impressions Sanctissimorum Vulnerum Christi."

28. Wilfred H. Woollen, *St. Gertrude, A Saint of the Sacred Heart*, n.d. (1927). St. Gertrude is given among the lists of stigmaticas both by Rayssius and d'Alva. The Office of St. Gertrude for Catalonia, where the Feast was kept as a Double of the Second Class, 17th November, has: "Coelestis sponsus in ejus purissimo corpore delicias suas collocavit, cui suorum etiam stigmata igneo amoris stylo divinus Coelator inussit," Matins, Second Nocturn, Fifth Lesson.

29. See the beginning of the *Dialogo*.

30. His immediate predecessor, Blessed Benedict XI, O.P. (Nicolas Bocassini di Treviso, formerly General of the Dominicans), was poisoned at the instigation of Philippe le Bel.

31. The date of the "mistico sposalizio" is 1364.

32. The painting is modern, 1896.

33. The crucifix is a painting on panel by Giunta Pisano, about 1260. Mrs. Jameson in her *Legends of the Monastic Orders* notes that by a special decree of the Pope it was removed to Siena, and (she adds) "placed in the Oratory of St. Catharine of Siena, where I saw it in 1847."

34. The great Dominican church in Rome in Santa Maria sopra Minerva, so called because it stands near the site of a temple dedicated to Minerva by Pompey. The body of St. Catharine lies under the high altar.

35. The martyrs St. John and St. Paul were officers in the service of Constantia, daughter of Constantine. They were put to death by Julian the Apostate in A.D. 362.

36. In art St. Catharine of Siena is always represented with the stigmata, as should rightly be the case. It has been foolishly, and a little profanely argued that since the stigmata were invisible during the Saint's life they should not be depicted. But St. Catharine's contemporary and disciple, the painter, Andrea Vanni, depicts her with the stigmata. The literature dealing with St. Catharine of Siena is immense. (She even figures in fiction.) First, there are her own writings, *L'Opere della Seraphica Santa Caterina da Siena*, Lucca, 1721; and N. Tommaseo's edition of the Letters, *Le Lettere di Santa Caterina de Siena*, 4 Vols., Firenze, 1860. Two useful collections. There is no satisfactory English translation as Algar Thorold's versions are tampered with and incomplete. A scholarly and unabridged version is badly needed. The Life, auctore F. Raimundo Capuano, is given in the

Acta Sanctorum, Aprilis, Tom. III. There is also a *Vita sanctae Catharinae Senensis et Philippi Beroaldi*, per Joannem Pinum, 4to, Bononiae, 1505. The work of P. Chavin de Malan, Italian translation by Pietro Vigo *Storia di Santa Caterina Da Siena*, Siena, 1906, is valuable. Edward Hutton has delightful sketches of the Saint in his *Studies in the lives of the Saints*, 1902, and *Siena and Southern Tuscany*, 1910. Among the older Lives *The History of St. Catharine of Siena and her Companions*, 2 Vols., 1887, by Mother Francis Raphael, O.S.D., is highly esteemed. Amongst the more recent biographies Edmund Gardner's *St. Catherine of Siena*, 1907, is generally considered the best. Benedict XIV warmly commends a *Vie de Ste Catherine* by F. Touron. Giovanni Lombardelli's *Diffesa delle sacre stimate di Santa Catarina da Siena*, 4to, Siena, 1601, is an excellent treatise on the stigmata of St. Catharine. Various interpolations made in the Saint's Works and unauthentic passages which were fraudently inserted are dealt with and exposed by Hippolytus Maraccius in his *Vindicatio Sanctae Catharinae Senensis a comentita revelatione contra Immaculatam Conceptionem B.M.V.*, 4to, Puteoli, 1663. A work dealing with the Dominican Rule of the Third Order, with especial reference to St. Catharine, is *La Regla que professan las Beatas de la Tercera Orden de Predicadores, item la vida de san Catalina de Sena y ostros deste stado*.

37. The radiant Cherubim, says the Archdeacon of Evreux, Henri-Marie Boudon, in his great work *Devotion to the Nine Choirs of Holy Angels* (English translation, 1869), are among the highest angelic intelligences. Divine light is especially attributed to this Order. Two cherubim shadowed the mercy seat with their wings. The prophet Ezechiel had visions of the cherubim. The Old Testament Hebrew is *K'rūb, K'rūbīm*. In early Christian art these angels were coloured a lovely red.

38. In the left transept of the Carmelite church, S. Maria della Vittoria, Via Venti Settembre, Rome, is Bernini's exquisitely beautiful group of St. Teresa and the angel.

39. E. Allison Peers, *Mother of Carmel*, S.C.M. Press, 1945, pp. 27–28.

40. So far as I am aware there is (recently at any rate) no study of St. Maria Maddalena de' Pazzi in English. *The Life of St. Mary Magdalene of Pazzi a Carmelite Nun, newly translated out of Italian, by Vincent Puccini, by the Reverend Father Lezin de Sainte Scholastique, Provincial of the Reformed Carmelites of Touraine, Paris*, 1670. *And now done out of French, London*, 1687, is a scarce book. This has an appendix, *A brief discourse about discerning and trying the Spirits whether they be of God*, pp. 85–134. The Oratorian *Life of St. Mary Magdalen de' Pazzi* is not altogether satisfactory. *La Santa di Firenze . . . da Una Religiosa del Suo Monastero*, Firenze, 1906, is an excellent and most informative little work.

41. J. K. Huysmans, *En Route*, Première Partie, Ch. x.

42. *Annales Ordinis SS. Trinitatis* by the Minim, Bonaventura Baro, folio, Rome, 1684. *Compendio Historico de las vidas de San Juan de Mata y San Felix de Valois Patriarcas y fundadores de la Orden de SS. Trinidad*, by Gil Gonzalez Davila, 4to, Madrid, 1630.

43. On 17th July, 1862, a proper Office was granted for San Miguel de los Santos, the feast ranking as a Double of the Second Class with an Octave. Lections iv, v and vi, of the Second Nocturn of Matins give a short life of the Saint. Since the Trinitarians have no house in England San Miguel is not very generally known here.

44. *Vita di Venerabile Serafina di Dio*, Napoli, 1723, and the authoritative documents, *Positiones supra dubio . . .* which were compiled in connexion with the beatifacion of Venerable Serafina di Dio.

45. Only one other Carthusian nun has been raised to the altar, St. Roseline des Arca de Villeneuve, who lived 1263–1329. Feast 16th October. A useful study of this Saint, *Sainte Roseline des Arcs de l'Illustre Famille des De Villeneuve*, Aux Arcs (Var) and Avignon, 1913, is from the able pen of Le Chanoine A. Arnaud.

46. Feast 13th February. Collect: "O God, Who in imitation of the Passion of Our Lord Jesus Christ, did cause Blessed Béatrix to be so conformed thereto as to be made a victim of love; grant, we beseech Thee, that by her intercession and example, we may so become partakers of the Passion of the same Thy Son whilst we are now here on earth, that we may be found worthy to receive the guerdon of eternal happiness in heaven. Through the same. . . ."

47. There is no English translation. It is well to emphasize this since *Heroic Virtue*, 3 Vols., 1850, 1851, 1853, respectively, Thomas Richardson, London, Dublin, and Derby, however useful commences with Book III, c. xxi, and concludes, Vol. III, c. xiv, with the chapter "Of Revelations". *Heroic Virtue* is frequently (but erroneously) spoken of as though it were a complete version, which misleads. Moreover *Heroic Virtue* is a little old-fashioned. Annotations are required. A full translation with commentaries of the *De Canonisatione* is badly needed.

48. Hal is about nine miles from Brussels. The Church of Notre Dame de Hal was begun in 1341, and consecrated in 1409. The wonder-working statue of Our Lady is celebrated throughout Belgium and the whole world.

49. *Les Apparitions à Banneux*, by Armand Gérardin. Editions Rex, Louvain, 1933.

50. Full details of the pilgrimage, and the incontrovertible evidence of the cure, can be read in *La Libre Belgique*, 24th August, 1933; and in *Les Annales de Beauraing et Banneux*, 1st November, 1933.

51. In a note I should state that my knowledge of the Georges Marasco case is mainly derived from Belgian newspapers, which at the time were sent over to me from Brussels by friends residing in that city, and also from private letters that gave me such details of the affair as were being much discussed. I cannot claim to have known any "followers" of Georges Marasco, or any who came in contact with her. From the very first I received the impression that there were features connected with the case which seemed, to say the least, suspicious.

52. See "Mystical Substitution," pp. 159–165, *Essays in Petto*, by Montague Summers, 1928.

53. Both Sœur Bernard and Barbara of St. Dominic were stigmaticas.

54. He became a Friar Minor, and died a martyr's death.

55. 1363–1429.

56. Bodleian Library, Mss., Arch. S., 130.

57. Cartas de Jesuitas, *Mem. hist. español.*, XIII, 42, 51, 457.

58. MSS. of Archiva municipal de Sevilla, Seccion especial, Siglo XVIII, Letra A. Toma. IV, n. 52, cited by H. C. Lea, *Inquisition of Spain*, ed. 1922, vol. IV, pp. 69–70.

59. Juan Antonio Llorente, *Histoire critique de l'Inquisition d'Espagne*. . . . Traduit de l'espagnol par Alex. Pelliez, 4 Vols., Paris, 1817–18. Cap. xl, art. ii, n. 1–14.

60. Menéndez y Pelayo, III, 405.

61. 1687–1752.

62. Scaramelli is incorrect when he writes that the vision of an Angel, or a celestial messenger, or of Christ Himself, inflicting wounds which mark the body is merely symbolical of that which is taking place in the soul. This is a very temerarious and ill-sounding suggestion, and can be shown to be definitely erroneous. The vision, whatever it may be, is an intense reality. One is justified in this comment when we note how, as is remarked, Scaramelli omits so important a test as humility —perhaps, the most important test.

63. *Vita della Madre Orsola Benincasa, Fondatrice delle Monache Theatine* per il Padre Francesco Maria Maggio, folio, Rome, 1655. Also *Compendium ejusdem vitae*, Brussels, 1658. See further, Ponnelle and Bordet's *St. Philip Neri and the Roman Society of his Times*, English translation. Later the attitude of Mgr. Charles Erskine (1759–1811), who in 1803 received the Red Hat from Pius VII, as Promotor Fidei when the cause of the Venerable Orsola was under discussion, is very remarkable, and, speaking with all respect, I for one find his conclusions unwarranted and distasteful, as was indeed felt and expressed by many of the Sacred College at the time.

64. The case was noticed in *The Universe*, Friday, 16th July, 1937.

Simulated sanctity is truly a heinous and horrid thing, yet even a
lower, a far lower depth is plumbed in the cases of diabolic or satanical
stigmatization for it is not to be supposed that the demon will stamp
the imitative marks of the Sacred Wounds upon his creature unless
indeed the wretch is already bound to him by some compact, and is
already the sworn slave of hell. So here we trench upon witchcraft, which
may be aptly called the mysticism of evil.

Satan is the ape of God. And as God has delighted to seal His most
favoured servants with the signature of His own Five Wounds, so the
adversary, the demon, in foul travesty and bitter deceit will seek to
seal his bondslaves with a miraged semblance of those Founts of Mercy
whence Redemption was poured forth so bounteously upon the human
race.

Far back among the Gnostics we already catch some whisper of
these horrid mysteries.

Cardinal Bona (1609-1674), General of the Cistercians, in his celebrated treatise *De discretione spirituum* (*On the discerning of Spirits*),
Rome, 1672, Chapter VII, says that "Persons who assert and noise it
abroad that they have in a vision received crowns of roses, or necklaces
studded with rich gems, or golden wings, from the hands of Our Lord
Himself or from His Most Blessed Mother, or else have been given such
gauds by a radiant Angel, ought to be sharply reproved as victims of
a too lively imagination, or, worse still, as foully deceived by a diabolic
illusion, unless indeed they are persons of most rigid life, of proven
humility and holiness, lovers of retirement, contemplatives, shunning
the world, in which case of course, they will be the last to speak of such
charismata, heartily endeavouring to conceal the secrets of Heaven,
deeming themselves utterly unworthy." The Cardinal continues: "The
same rule applies to stigmatists and stigmaticas, since the marks of the
wounds can be imitated and impressed by the fiend, as many sad examples
too painfully have proven."

In the year 1533, Father Reginald, a Dominican learned in mystical
theology, a very grave and revered religious with a great reputation
for holiness of life, who was then Prior at the Convent of San Domenico
at Bologna, came to Rome for the express purpose of consulting St.
Ignatius in regard to a nun of the Second Order, of which he was spiritual

director. This nun was completely stigmatized in hands, feet, and side. She also had the Crown of Thorns, and frequently blood flowed from these wounds. She suffered much, and was very often rapt in ecstasy, when she spoke of wonderful and most profound things. While she was thus entranced she was absolutely unconscious, and any attempt that was made to arouse her failed. Feathers were burned under her nose; doctors applied blisters, and even lanced and cauterized. She felt nothing. Yet, under obedience, when the Prioress or a Superior commanded, she at once came out of her ecstatic state. "Father Reginald," answered Ignatius, who had listened with close attention to the good friar, "of all the signs and phenomena you have related to me, there is one, and one only, I count at a penny's worth. That is, her obedience. This in truth argues that the rest may be, I do not say *are*, of God." And so the Dominican went away, confirmed and much comforted, for so also had been his own private judgement in the matter. Ribadaneyra who relates this (*Acta Sanctorum*, in Vita S. Ignatii, 31st July, p. 767) goes on to say that afterwards when they were alone he questioned St. Ignatius concerning these mysteries. To whom the Saint replied: "Whilst it is very true that God may endow His chosen souls with especial graces, yea, and fill them even to overflowing so that what is within erupts, as it were, and cannot be hid, unmasking itself and being made manifest visibly imprinting itself upon the body, yet this is a rare gift of God, who bestows it as He will. Let us always bear in mind that Satan, although he has no power over the soul may yet perplex and disturb the imaginative faculty of man, yea, and sorely bewilder and distress us, insomuch that he will lead astray the best, and tempt them into his own sin, spiritual pride, in which once enmeshed and englued he will danger them yet more by visible and exterior signs, feigning such to be the very Wounds of Christ. So subtle is the fiend; so nice his craft. I have alas! known many fallen into this snare."

And, says Ribadaneyra. "I have heard that this very nun of Bologna, being rebuked and humbled by good Father Reginald for her greater edification, rebelled and was so puffed up with pride that in the end it was seen to be no brightness of divine fire that enlightened her, but rather was she suffocated in the blackness of a demoniacal smoke."

That very acute and learned physician Paolo Zacchia, chief medical attendant of Pope Innocent X, in his *Questiones medicolegales*, first edition, 1630; third and complete edition, folio, Amsterdam (1651), a book which Benedict XIV quotes with warm approval, cautions exorcists, directors, and others that it is a far easier thing to simulate an ecstasy than it is to simulate such disorders as apoplexy and epilepsy and carry it off well. Zacchia speaks of a Sicilian girl who would have been taken for a saint, and who deceived many by her feigned ecstasies and raptures, which she acted with such effect and with such attention to detail that a crowd came to see her, and asking her prayers made offerings and presented her with gifts. So that she did famously, and happy was the devotee who might touch her garments, and leave a gold or silver ducat behind him, all unaware that she was laughing up her sleeve at his simplicity. But the doctor observed her shrewdly for a while, and exposed the cheat.

In France, during the turmoil caused by the League, impostors flourished. A girl who came to Paris from Rheims, by name Nicole Tavernier, acquired an extraordinary reputation for sanctity. Daily she passed into a trance when she spoke at great length, her words being taken down as divine revelations. She was supposed to have the spirit of prophecy, and it was widely bruited that her predictions were infallibly true.

On one occasion when in the Church of the Capuchins at Meudon, she was kneeling not far from Madame Acarie (Blessed Mary of the Incarnation), this latter remarked that Nicole had withdrawn, and remained absent for nearly an hour. Madame Acarie did not notice her return, but saw that she was in her former place. After Mass the saintly woman asked: "Where did you go, Nicole, and remain away so long?" To which Nicole mysteriously replied: "I have been to Tours to warn certain noblemen who were met to plot and cabal that they must abandon their projects, since their intentions are very hurtful to the true faith, and, if carried into effect, will work terrible mischief." At Paris Nicole was indeed daily consulted by statesmen even and patricians, as well as by priests and religious.

Two prominent persons, however, Madame Acarie and the Cardinal de Bérulle, placed no faith in Nicole Tavernier. Madame Acarie openly said that she feared that the girl was terribly deluded and deceived, that it must be an evil spirit who had taken possession of her and was simulating all kinds of mystic phenomena to draw many into error, and hence the prediction could be very well explained. The sudden voyage to Tours was far from being proved to be a fact, and even if it were, it is well known that these aerial transvections are by no means impossible to the demon, as so many witchcraft trials have shown times without number. Moreover Nicole was found out in a good many lies and some cozenage. So she was questioned by two Capuchins, experts in these matters, and they found the whole thing was trickery and obsession. When the girl was freed from these dark influences and the devil cast out, she proved to be in herself a rather stupid and ignorant rustic. In spite of all persuasion she married a low churl, and soon entirely ceased to practice her religion. All Paris was scandalized and deeply shocked at such an exposure. However, eventually, Nicole was reconciled by Pére de Lingendes. A detailed account of these extraordinary events is given by the Bishop of Orleans in his study *La Bienheureuse Marie de l'Incarnation*, new edition, Paris, 1854.

One of the most notorious cases of diabolic stigmata, a case upon which it is not necessary to dwell in detail so often has the history been repeated, is that of Magdalena de la Cruz, which has been admirably summed up in his full-flavoured Caroline English by the pious Richard Baxter, who more than once tells us of "the Witch *Magdalena Crucia*, who got the reputation of a Saint". In his *Historical Discourse of Apparitions and Witches*, 1691, pp. 102–103, he writes: "The Story of

Magdalena Crucia (cited elsewhere by me, and by Dr. *H. More*) was, saith *Bodin*, famous through the World, cited by many; who being suspected, to save her life, went to the Pope himself (*Paul III*) as a Penitent, and confessed her Sins, that at twelve years old the Devil solicited her, and lay with her, and that he had layen with her thirty Years; yet she was made the Abbess of a Monastery, and counted a Saint. And she confessed that the Devil, among all the people, brought Christ's Body (the Wafer) to her Mouth, none seeing what carried It; whereby she was taken for a Saint, as done by some good Spirit." It was not, of course, the Consecrated Host which the demon conveyed to the wretched woman, but an unconsecrated host (as Baxter duly distinguishes, 'the Wafer') which he had privily filched. Those who witnessed this marvel would have been entirely deceived. "De fraische memoire l'an 1545", Bodin tells us, "Magdelaine de la Croix, native de Cordove en Espagne, Abesse d'un monastere, se voyant en suspicion des Religieuses d'estre Sorciere, & craignant le feu, si elle estoit accusee, voulut prevenir pour obstenir pardon du Pape, & confessa que des l'aage de douze ans un malin esprit en forme d'un More noir la sollicita de son honneur, auguel elle consentit . . . Elle obtint pardon du Pape Paul 3. estant repentie comme elle disoit. Mais i' ay opinion qu'elle estoit dediee à Satan par les parens des le ventre de sa mere . . . Ceste histoire a esté publiee en toute la Chrestienté." [*1*].

Magdalena de la Cruz, whom Benedict XIV calls a *saga famosa* "a most notorious witch-woman," was born of poor parents at Aquilar in 1487. According to her account at five years old she attempted to imitate the Crucifixion by nailing herself to a wall, but she fell and broke two of her ribs [*2*]. She soon professed to see visions of angels, and her trances began to be more and more frequent. In fact when at the age of seventeen, in 1504, she entered the Franciscan Convent of Santa Isabel de los Angeles she already enjoyed a great reputation for sanctity. For thirty-nine years Magdalena successfully exhibited a series of pseudo-mystical phenomena, ecstasies, apparitions and prophesyings, which deluded practically all Spain, and caused her to be regarded as a saint by the highest and the lowest in the land. She was stigmatized, and lost few opportunities of showing her visitors the bleeding wounds. St. Ignatius Loyola, however, entirely distrusted these exterior signs, and rebuked her ardent followers with unwonted severity. Blessed Juan d'Ávila, one of the directors of St. Teresa and a profound master of the interior life, never faltered in his opinion that these trances and the stigmata were of no heavenly origin. In 1543 Magdalena fell dangerously ill, and was given over by the physicians. She then made a long and terrible confession. Her seeming sanctity was not only a feint, but from the first she had been aided by and acted under the influence of two demons, Balban, a familiar of the fifth order of evil spirits, "the Deluders", and Patorrio (or Python), to whom she had delivered herself over at the early age of twelve, sealing her bondage with the black pact of hell. Magdalena recovered, and the Holy Office inquired into these abominations. It was not until 1546 that judgement was given, so numerous were the witnesses to be examined, so complicated and detailed the evidence which had to be sifted and weighed.

At the auto-de-fé in the Cathedral of Córdoba on Holy Cross Day, 3rd May, 1546, the public recital of her crimes and her sentence, announced by relays of officials, occupied from six o'clock in the morning until four o'clock in the afternoon. The sacred building was thronged. Magdalena, meanwhile, was exhibited on a scaffold, her mouth lightly gagged, a halter round her neck, and a burning taper in her hand, as signs of true repenting and public shame. This unhappy woman was most mercifully consigned to perpetual seclusion in the convent of Santa Clara, at Andujar, where she passed her days in the most exemplary penitence. She died, full of sorrow and deeply contrite, in 1560. It may be remarked that on her confession of imposture and guilt, seventeen years before, the demoniacal stigmata disappeared [*3*].

It is very doubtful whether at this date the truth can ever be known about the case of the Dominican Madre María de la Visitacion of the Convent of La Annunciada at Lisbon. That she was vilely calumniated seems certain. Superficial historians have been only too eager to repeat the alleged scandals, without pausing to inquire upon what actual foundation these stories were bruited. That she was condemned and penanced by an Ecclesiastical Commission is in the circumstances not of itself sufficient to be proof positive. It is known that many of the assessors were politically prejudiced, and we may recall processes which (to me) seem very similar, for example, the trials of and judgement delivered upon St. Joan of Arc.

Born in the year 1556, María, at the age of eleven entered the Convent of La Annunciada. and since she showed every sign of a fervent vocation she was professed some five years later. In 1572 her mystical experiences were already profound. About 1580 there appeared to her a marvellous vision of the Crucified Christ, His Wounds all glorious. A ray of fire suddenly lanced from the Wounds in the side and pierced her bosom, leaving a deep wound from which on Friday there trilled drops of blood. This caused her exquisite agony. In 1583 María for her very holiness was elected Prioress of the Convent, an office she was obliged to accept, although she knew she was opposed by a small but obstinate party of the older sisters who could scarcely conceal their mortification and jealousy. The following year upon 7th March, the Feast of St. Thomas Aquinas, another radiant vision of the Crucified comforted her, and four red rays darting from His pierced hands and feet transfixed her hands and feet. There also appeared to her Dominican Saints, St. Dominic, St. Thomas, and above all St. Catharine of Siena, who, María averred always looked upon her with a sorrowing face and eyes full of tears. Such phenomena could not be hid, and the fame of the saintly nun was noised abroad, not only up and down the Peninsula, but throughout Europe as well, and as far as the Indies.

In 1584 Albert, Archduke of Austria and Cardinal of Santa Croce in Gerusalemme, addressed a detailed account of the Spouse of Christ to the Supreme Pontiff, Gregory XIII, who replied saying that he indeed blessed God for what he heard of this holy Dominicaness, and that he prayed Heaven to fulfil her with its grace to the edification of the faithful and the confusion of all enemies of the Church. He also wrote to the Prioress herself, bidding her in spite of all difficulties to be strong and of good courage, to press forward upon the mystic way without faltering or pause in her path. About the same time the Portuguese Provincial, Fray Antonio de la Cerda, addressed two letters respecting Madre María to his delegate in Rome, Fray Hernando de Custro, O.P., who was to lay them before the Pope. Gregory read them with indescribable joy.

That sublime mystic, the Venerable Fray Luis de Granada, also wrote a long letter, detailing his close observation of these phenomena, to the Patriarch of Valencia. These letters (as the custom then was) were printed in Italy, and immediately translated into French by the Dominican scholar, 'Etienne de Lusignan, who incorporated them in a mystical treatise which he dedicated to the pious consort of Henri III, Queen Louise de Lorraine, *Les grands Miracles et les Tressainctes Playes advenuz à la R. Mere Prieure auiord' huy 1586 du Monasteire de l'Anonciade en la ville de Lisbonne, au Royaume de Portugal, approuvez par R. Pere Frere Loys de Granade et autres personnes dignes de foy, côme se verra à la fin du discours.* A' Paris, par Jean Bressant, 1586. A contemporary Italian study is *Relatione del Miracolo delle Stimmate, venute nuovamente ad una Monacha dell'Ordine di S. Domenico, in Portogallo, nella Città di Lisbona,* Rome. 1584, also printed at Bologna and Venice. These two works are by far the best, and (as I think) the only reliable histories of Madre María de la Visitacion.

Fray Luis de Granada investigated the stigmata with much care and gave it as his opinion that they were divinely imprinted. He further states how on every Thursday, at the hour of Ave Maria, two-and-thirty punctures which extravated blood appeared surrounding the head of the Prioress, and this which was accompanied with intense pain endured until Ave Maria on the Friday. Christ had bestowed upon her the Crown of Thorns. When she prayed the community not unseldom saw her raised in ecstasy from the ground. Pieces of linen which she had pressed to her wounds and which were stained with stigmatical blood, often mystically assuming the form of a cross, were sought for as gifts by grandees and their noble ladies, and from the application of these illnesses were cured in an extraordinary way. The most pious Countess of Urrea, wife of the Viceroy of Sicily, the Conde d'Alba, treasured such a cloth which she had obtained from La Annunciada. A lady of very high estate had suffered long from a gangrened lip, and her physicians decided a surgical operation was necessary. The day before Doña Vincenzia gave her a small piece of linen stained with blood from the stigmata of Madre María. The invalid placed it over her mouth, and on the following morning when the doctors came, to their amazement they found the flesh whole, and firm, and well. There was but one explanation. It was a miraculous cure. This was attested by a notarial certificate. The Holy Father himself accepted one of these cloths. The evidence is so ample and so convincing that I cannot believe these things are fictive, delusions, cogging, or clever sleights. It is impossible. Ugo Buoncompagni, before he ascended the Papal throne as Gregory XIII, was renowned as one of the shrewdest of Bolognese lawyers. On account of his extraordinary keen knowledge of canon and civil law he had been appointed by Pius IV, the uncle of San Carlo Borromeo, as jurisconsult to the Council of Trent. The author of *Introducción del Simbolo de la Fe*, Fray Luis de Granada, was an acknowledged master of the spiritual life. Such men are not deceived.

The political situation in Portugal and Spain was critical to a degree. 1588 was the Armada Year. Philip II was heartbroken, overwhelmed. He distrusted every counsellor. He distrusted himself. Men in Spain were living on their nerves. At such an hour of tension, strange inexplicable things can happen. Her enemies—and holiness always makes enemies—seized the opportunity. There was a party, small but full of rancour, within the cloister of La Annunciada itself. Curious gossip was retailed, exaggerated, and repeated again. Scandal sought a victim. It was said that the sanctity of Madre María was a sham, that her stigmata were faked. An Ecclesiastical Commission was appointed to inquire into these phenomena. Not only the Peninsula but all Europe was stunned by their findings. They gave their verdict that Madre María was an impostor. They even professed to explain how the miraculous effects had been produced. To my mind their proceedings are obviously impregnated with the most vicious political bias, their judgement reeks of falsity and abuse. We know they threatened Madre María that the devil would carry her off. We know she was unmoved by their menaces. We know little more. We are told that she made a long and full confession of deceit. I do not believe a word of it. This sort of thing has happened before and since, when a pack of politicians—men frightened for their own lives—were in full cry. To me the vaunted *Relazion de la santidad y elagas de la Madre María de la Visitacion*, Seville, 1589, bears the hall-mark of falsity. It is obviously written to order.

It so chanced that Fray Luis de Granada died about this time, and it was instantly rumoured that he had been unable to survive the agony of finding how he had been imposed upon and deceived. This is the veriest canard. Later it was reported that the discovery of the feigned sanctity and the exposure was due to the Carmelite Fray Jerónimo Gracián, the sometime Vicar-General of the Discalced Province and counsellor of St. Teresa of Ávila. "An able young man of exceptional precosity whose charm and apparent saintliness delighted the woman of nearly sixty," says Professor Allison Peers. There is, so far as I can find, not the least foundation in fact for Mármol's assertion in his *Vida del P. Jerónimo Gracián*, but the business had to be bolstered up somehow.

It is a sad story, and on 6th December, 1588, the sentences of the Commissioners was read to Madre María, being published two days later from the Cathedral pulpit at High Mass. She was relegated to perpetual seclusion in an enclosed convent, but—be this carefully noted—not in the house of her own Order. Various penances were added in the harshest spirit, and it is to say the least incongruous that, even supposing she were culpable, her sentence should be so much more cruelly severe than that of an avowed and notorious witch, if happily repentant, as was Magdalena de la Cruz.

Lodovicus de Paramo *De Origine et progressu Sanctae Inquisitionis ejusque dignitate et utilitate,* Libri tres, Apud Joannem Flandrum, Matriti, folio, 1598, says that Madre María died a most blessed death, a saint indeed.

A modern historian writes: "The Dominicans had not been much given to mystic extravagance, but in her [María de la Visitacion] they had a saint whom they exploited to the utmost, and the disgrace in which her career ended served them as a salutary lesson to preserve them in the future from similar erratic zeal." It would not be easy to parallel so misleading and so misunderstanding a sentence. The writer quite evidently had an entirely erroneous preconception of what is meant by Mysticism, and indeed throughout his pages he seems to imagine that the Dominicans are professedly inimical to Mysticism. It were a lengthy task and, perhaps, labour lost to put him right in every detail. Let it be sufficient to quote a great authority and a great mystic. Father Faber, the Oratorian, tells us (*The Blessed Sacrament,* Third Edition, 1861, p. 568): "Father Squillante, of the Naples Oratory, [wrote] the life of the Sister Mary of Santiago, of the Third Order of St. Dominic, which rivals Carmel as a mystical garden of delights to the Heavenly Spouse." He further adds: "We possess now the Third Order of St. Dominic in England. Those who are conversant, indeed who find the strength and consolation of their lives, in the Acts of the Saints, well know that there is not a nook of the mystical paradise of our Heavenly Spouse where the flowers grow thicker or smell more fragrant than this Order of multitudinous child-like Saints. Nowhere in the Church does the Incarnate Word show His 'delight at being with the children of men' in more touching simplicity, with more unearthly sweetness, or more spouse like familiarity, than in this the youngest family of St. Dominic." To revert—I believe the only trustworthy book dealing with Madre María de la Visitacion is the study by 'Etienne de Lusignan, O.P., and upon the available evidence I feel convinced that this stigmatica was the victim of a great wrong and terrible injustice, so that her name and her memory are even to-day calumniated and sadly traduced.

During the first half of the nineteenth century the quiet little cathedral city of Agen was what may be termed a tranquil backwater of piety, lapped in peace, unruffled and undisturbed by the storms which raged abroad. A number of religious associations were formed by persons living there, the members of which obeyed a few simple rules, and from time to time met to discuss various charities, to edify themselves by mutual conversation on holy things, or to listen to spiritual reading and instruction. One of these associations had as its secretary and leading spirit Mme. Jeanne Belloc, a doctor's widow, who after the early death of her husband had led a most secluded life, entirely devoting herself to the education of her son and to good works. Naturally she was the friend of the wretched and the poor to whom she was always ready to give a helping hand, and her name was daily pronounced with blessings by hundreds of lips. One afternoon in 1835, a stranger, a woman of about thirty-five, who must be known as Virginie, since the surname does not appear to be recorded, asked for and was granted an interview by Mme. Belloc. Virginie who exhibited the utmost distress, mingled with terror, unfolded a terrible tale that appalled her hearer. In floods of tears and with moans of anguish she confessed to Mme. Belloc that for more than twenty years she had belonged to a secret band of Satanists, who under the guise of religion, made Agen their headquarters, and who were actively engaged in every abomination of devil-worship. In a secret chapel a renegade priest celebrated black masses for this gang, whose unspeakable orgies included the profanation of the Host stolen from various churches. To Virginie and some few others was assigned the blasphemy of procuring Hosts for this fearful ceremony of hell. This was done by the satanical women receiving Communion every morning at various churches, and then slipping the Host from their mouths into a handkerchief, and carrying it to the infernal rendezvous. Virginie declared that not infrequently she visited four or five churches of a morning, assisting at the early masses for this horrid purpose. At last she realized the enormity of her guilt, and had resolved to break for ever with the diabolic crew.

Mme. Belloc well-nigh swooned at so fearful a recital. "But why come to me?" she asked. "Would not a good priest help you in the confessional. M. l'Abbé——" "Madame," answered Virginie, "I have never even been baptized. If the diabolists discover I have betrayed them—and they will discover—and I fall into their hands, they will kill me. That is the penalty for 'traitors'." "Remain here. You will be safe", Mme. Belloc assured her, for the woman trembled like a hunted animal. "Meanwhile . . ." But she felt stunned. She summoned to her aid the Abbé Degans, a priest who was reputed a master of mystic theology. He heard the tale with amazement. Yet nothing was beyond Satan's malice and cunning.

In her anxiety to save the poor woman from the toils Mme. Belloc took Virginie under her especial care, whilst the abbé visited her daily. Virginie was baptized, whereupon she fell ill with a complication of strange disorders which the doctors pronounced beyond their skill to cure, and which, it was concluded, were caused by black magic. In the course of her sickness the stigmata appeared on her body. She avowed that these wounds which drenched her in blood, had been made by the archfiend himself who materialized under a visible human form, like a tall black man of menacing aspect. This apparition further had the effect of paralysing her in every limb, whilst she suffered the most excruciating pains. The Abbé Degans proceeded to exorcism, and after a long and painful struggle, extending over many months, into the details of which it is not necessary to enter, she was freed on the 15th August, the Feast of the Assumption, 1838. Ecclesiastical authority now took action. It was not to be supposed that these extraordinary revelations did not cause an immense commotion throughout the city. Everyone was asking: "Where is the rendezvous of these Satanists? Who may not be secretly one of the gang?" Something like a panic reigned. The Bishop of Agen, who had privately received a full series of reports on the case from Abbé Degans ordered that Virginie should be closely examined and tested by two of the leading members of the Chapter, Canon Sérougne and Canon Pierre Deyche, two priests of great experience and solid learning. Their report was scarcely favourable, but the Bishop watched without making any gesture or uttering any word.

Virginie now set up as a kind of clairvoyante, one who, wrested from Satan's clutches, was as a reward especially favoured by Heaven. In 1840 she announced that she enjoyed frequent visions of Our Lord; she could exhibit the stigmata; and large numbers of devoted followers were most lavishly supporting her with presents of no inconsiderable value, and regularly contributing sums of money, "alms", in return for her prayers, her good word with Heaven. She was gifted with prophecy, and her "Revelations" were taken down by her admirers. It seems to have been in August, 1839, that she established relations (secretly, at first) with that enigmatical and, as it proved, impious figure, the pseudo-prophet Pierre-Michel-Eugène Vintras, whose performances at Tilly-sur-Seulles gave rise to such grave scandals that his teachings were condemned by the Bishop of Bayeux upon the 8th November, 1841, and by a Brief of Gregory XVI two years later, 8th November, 1843.

In the matter of Virginie, the Bishop of Agen, a prelate of a great name, was slow to move. It was not until 1846 that Mgr. Jean Aimé de Levezon de Vezins issued his weighty and solemn admonitions, in which he thoroughly exposed the folly and deceptions of Virginie and condemned her as an impostor and common cheat. An impostor, yes, but a diabolic impostor. That Virginie had belonged to a coven of Satanists is hardly to be disputed; that her "confessions" and seeming repentance and the wild stories she related were merest flummery wickedly to mislead and deceive a number of good-living and religious persons, to involve them in error, is attested by the Bishop of Agen. She was deeply concerned in a diabolic plot. The demon helped her throughout. It was he who inspired her "Revelations", who marked her in bitter travesty with the stigmata [4].

The celebrated writer upon occult subjects, Marie-Victor-Stanislas, Marquis de Guaita, [5] in his *Essais de Sciences Maudites* [6] has a note of some fifty lines upon "L'affaire Rose Tamisier" which occurred in 1850 at Saint-Saturnin-les-Apt, Vaucluse.

Rose Tamisier is not mentioned by so encyclopædic a writer as Canon Ribet in his authoritative *La mystique divine distinguée des contrefaçons diaboliques*, 4 volumes, 1879–1883, and subsequent editions. Neither is there any reference to her in Gougenot des Mousseaux, *Mœurs et pratiques des Démons*, "nouvelle edition", 1865, "ouvrage très documenté"; nor yet in Père Joseph de Bonniot, S.J., *Le miracle et ses contrefaçons*, 1888, and other editions, 1889, and 1895; nor in l'abbé Lecanu, *Histoire de Satan, sa chute, son culte*, 1861, and reprint, 1882; nor in the six vast volumes ("cet enorme travail") of Joseph Bizouard's *Des rapports de l'homme avec le Démon*, 1863–4; nor in Eliphas Lévy.

Neither J.-K. Huysmans nor Jules Bois knew the strange history of Rose Tamisier.

M. Maurice Garçon, after immense research, was able to trace the source of de Guaita's note. He says: "Une brochure quasi introuvable nous parvint entre les mains." This pamphlet is *Affaire Rosette Tamisier, précédée d'une notice sur Pierre Michel Vintras et sa secte*, par l'abbé J. F. André. Carpentras, Imprimerie de L. Devillario, Septembre 1851, in–18, 151 pages. He then looked up the files of such contemporary newspapers as *L'Univers, Le Charivari, La Gazette des Tribunaux*, and *le Droit*, where full accounts of the case were given. Moreover, the Archbishop of Avignon, Mgr. de Llobet, permitted him free access to the diocesan archives, and here he discovered a quanity of material, letters, reports, medical certificates, official findings, and the like, which were of the utmost value to him in writing his study, *Rosette Tamisier, ou La Miraculeuse Aventure*.

The Abbé André's *Affaire Rosette Tamisier* is so rare and unknown that it is not even listed in the Bibliographies of Caillet and Yve-Plessis.

There is, however, a contemporary English account of Rose Tamisier, which appears to be entirely overlooked. It is detailed and occurs in *A Tour of Inquiry through France and Italy, illustrating their present Social, Political, and Religious Condition*, two volumes, London, 1853, by Captain Edmund Spencer.

Captain Edmund Spencer was a fairly prolific writer of travel-books, which had a well-deserved popularity in their day, although now they seem altogether forgotten. He gives a very ample account of "The Saint of St. Saturnin", as he dubs her, and he relates how "by the intensity of her devotion she caused the representation of a cross, a heart, a chalice, a spear, and sometimes the image of the Virgin and Child, to appear on various parts of her body, at first in faint lines, and afterwards so developed as to exude blood thereby exciting the amazement and pious admiration of every beholder".

On Thursday, 1st September, 1853, *The Leisure Hour*, a very widely read journal, under the title *A Miracle of Modern Times!* printed a lengthy article upon the subject.

Captain Spencer, it is interesting to note, had a copy of and quotes from the Abbé André's rare brochure, which is also referred to by the writer in *The Leisure Hour* as the "life" of Rose Tamisier, "written by the Abbé André", and which "continues to be circulated".

Rose Tamisier was born at Saignon, Vaucluse, in 1818. Her parents were in very modest circumstances, none the less they gave their five children of whom Rose, generally known as Rosette, was the eldest, a good education, sufficient indeed for the girl when she was fifteen to open a small kindergarten for the village children. As many as forty to fifty attended her classes, which did not go beyond reading, writing,

224

PLATE IX: THE VENERABLE MADRE SOR JOANNA RODORIGUEZ DE
JÉSUS MARIA

"Poor Clare", from an old print

PLATE X: BENEDICT XIV

and a little arithmetic, with sewing and plain embroidery. Towards
the end of the year 1836, when Rose was eighteen, some Presentation
nuns [7] came to Saignon to take charge of the local hospital, and at once,
giving up her school, she applied for admission as a postulant. She was
allowed to assist the sisters in their work, but the Mother Superior for
some reason chose to postpone any form of admittance to the Order,
however preliminary. She remained merely a lay helper. Perhaps a little
suspicion was aroused since she began to complain of unusual pain in her
hands and feet, and more than once she spoke of the Wounds of Christ
when she mentioned the throb and smart she was experiencing. After
a period of six months she was transferred to the house of the Presentation
at Salon, and here she fell ill, whilst she appeared to be the subject of
extraordinary phenomena. A sharp watch was kept, unknown to her,
but nothing suspicious could be detected, although at the end of eighteen
months, acting upon medical advice, she decided to give up the idea
of entering the Order. Her father was sent for and took her back home
with him to Saignon, where she lived quietly for the next eight years,
entering into a kind of partnership with her sister who was a dressmaker,
but who specialized in vestments and church linen. She was thus brought
into continual contact with priests and sacristans, and she showed such
fervent piety that l'Abbé Sabou, one of the clergy of the parish church,
was heard to remark of her, "Here we have in Saignon a young woman
of most edifying life. I believe that her example will effect many conversions. Indeed it would not surprise me if one day she went far, and
was a shining light of faith."

In 1845, Rose's brother, François, a handsome young fellow, won by his
good looks the hand of Delphine Jean, who with her sister Thérèse
kept an excellent inn at Saint-Saturnin-les-Apt, a hostelry which did a
pretty brisk business. Rose often used to visit her brother, and one day
when she appeared ailing it was suggested that she should pay them a
prolonged visit. The air at Saint-Saturnin was particularly good, "and",
remarked the prudent Delphine, "if she can help us in the house, and
Heaven knows we can do with an extra hand, it will amply pay for her
board and bed." So the arrangement was made. Rose only wanted to go
out once in the day, first thing in the morning, to the earliest mass,
after which she was content to stay indoors and do any job she was
asked to undertake. She won golden opinions from l'Abbé Caire, the
parish-priest, and there were few in Saturnin who did not look upon her
as an exceptionally holy person. She was attractive enough with her
chestnut hair, soft brown eyes, and clear complexion, but she would
not so much as listen to a word from any of the young men. The only
fault that her sister-in-law had to find was that often on her return from
mass she would be taken with strange fits of illness which obliged her to
keep her room for four-and-twenty hours.

It seems to have been one day in the summer of 1850 that Delphine
in great distress sent a lad to ask l'Abbé Caire to call at the house as soon
as possible. The good priest lost no time in hurrying to the inn, but he
could get nothing out of the hostess save "Rosette is in bed, and I don't

O   225 know what ever is the matter." "Why not send for the doctor?" asked the Abbé. "No, mon père, she said a priest." "Ah! She is indeed a chosen soul. Do not be alarmed, my daughter, I will go up to her."

Rose was in bed, and when the Abbé gently questioned her without much difficulty she replied: "I am stigmatized. My feet are pierced through and my hands. I have the wound in the left side. There are other wounds which seem to picture a chalice, a cross, the Heart of Mary, the Heart of Jesus, and also the Heart of Mary transfixed with seven swords. When I press pieces of linen to these wounds the white linen is stained with the blood that drips from them." The good priest could not hide his astonishment, but being a very discreet man he said little, and after a few words of caution withdrew. This did not suit Rose's book. She felt sure he would have fallen on his knees in rapture and declared her a saint. She was piqued, and determined on a new move.

She returned for a time to Saignon, but here too she found the parish priest by no means so sympathetic as she had hoped. The fact was that l'Abbé Caire had sent him a private word of warning, advising him to be very cautious. None the less in order to convince himself that she was really a stigmatica he tested her in several ways, not very thoroughly, perhaps, and when he saw the chalice, the cross, and a crown of thorns, imprinted upon her body he was profoundly moved. The assistant-priest M. Lucas, could not entirely rid himself of some lingering doubts, but he was afraid lest he should be culpably incredulous and seem to doubt the supernatural charismata of Heaven.

On the 2nd November, Rose returned to Saint-Saturnin and resumed her usual duties at the hostelry. She learned that a priest, l'Abbé Grand, in charge of an old gothic chapel, built in 1050, a short walk from the town, having heard the story of the stigmata and being informed on every hand of her edifying life, had constituted himself her champion, and almost openly contradicted l'Abbé Caire who went so far as to say: "If it is not all a clever trick I suspect it is something worse, in fact I fear the devil himself may be mixed up in it."

In company with a friend, a firm believer in her sanctity, one Joséphine Imbert, Rose visited the old chapel, which had once been the chapel of the Castle of Vaucluse, a mighty fortress, now a heap of picturesque ruins. The two girls knelt down before the High Altar, the reredos of which was formed by an ancient picture depicting the Descent from the Cross, not a masterpiece, but very realistically and strikingly painted. The wounds on the hands, feet, and side of the Christ were most vividly portrayed. Their prayers ended, Rose went up to the altar, and mounting the steps, pressed her lips in fervent devotion to the hands of the Crucified. She uttered a cry! Her lips were wet with blood! She beckoned to Joséphine, who advanced timidly, and bade her kiss the picture. She did so with awe, and started back. Rose then took the white kerchief from her head, and touched the wounded side. The linen was stained with blood. After a few moments of stupefaction the two friends hurried to the presbytery and told l'Abbé Grand what had happened. He hastened to the church, and at once exclaimed "A miracle! a miracle! But my children," he added, "we must go slowly. My old friend Dr. Bernard, shall examine this prodigy." Dr. Bernard, a most pious physician, was summoned. He collected and analysed the liquid, and declared it was unmistakably human blood. On the 13th December following, Joséphine again fetched l'Abbé Grand to the chapel. Rose was in ecstasy before the altar, gazing at the picture in which the wounds were undoubtedly covered with fresh blood. In order to be reinforced by a second opinion they sent for a clever young practitioner, Dr. Clément, to examine the phenomenon and give his written opinion. Dr. Clément, taking a piece of spotless linen, put it to the painted wounds, and analysed the stains on the linen. In his report he states that it was undoubtedly human blood, but he asked, "How did it get there?" He would not say that he considered it a miracle.

A tremendous sensation followed, for l'Abbé Grand soon spread the astounding news. It was the talk of the whole countryside, and hundreds of pilgrims thronged the chapel. The civil authorities were obliged to take cognizance of these happenings. Rose was everywhere acclaimed a saint, and a great saint. Happy were the favoured few who might speak to her, and kiss her stigmatized hand, or even the hem of her dress. The most extraordinary scenes of frantic emotion and the wildest enthusiasm took place. Offerings were rained upon the chapel, and upon the saint.

On Thursday evening, 19th December, His Grace the Archbishop of Avignon with his chaplains arrived at the presbytery. A man of prompt action Monseigneur resolved to investigate the matter for himself. He first ordered everyone to leave the chapel. When it was empty the doors were locked, and the keys brought to the house. All night long, crowds were praying outside, and at dawn there began to arrive in coaches, carriages, tax-carts, hay-wagons, priests and people from near and far. About half-past seven in company with Joséphine Imbert there appeared Rose Tamisier, walking slowly with her eyes nearly closed as if almost in ecstasy. The crowd reverently made way for her, and hundreds knelt. She prostrated herself in prayer, and then said she must be allowed to enter the chapel to intercede at the very altar. When l'Abbé Grand was informed of this, he entreated the Archbishop to grant her request. For a few minutes Monseigneur, who had not as yet left the presbytery, seemed to hesitate, and then, as several priests pleaded earnestly with him, he yielded. The key was handed to Rose who entered and closed the door behind her. Joséphine remained in the porch.

M. Grave, the *sous-préfet* of Saint-Saturnin, was present on behalf of the civil authorities to regulate with his gendarmes the huge concourse. Everything, however, was perfectly orderly and quiet. Himself, he firmly believed in Rose Tamisier's divine inspirations. When the chapel was opened to the public all entered without scuffling or noise. Rose was seen kneeling entranced before the altar. In a very few minutes the solemn procession of the Archbishop and his train appeared. Monseigneur knelt at the faldstool and surrounded by his household engaged in prayer. At a sign from His Grace one of the chaplains ascended to the altar and held a piece of fair linen to the wound in the side as depicted on the reredos. He drew it away, and handed it to the Archbishop, who perceived

227

there were seven or eight distinct blood-stains marked on it. They folded it, and gave it in charge to another chaplain. All engaged in prayer. During this time Rose seemed rapt in a trance. After some fifteen minutes, the chaplain applied in the same way a fresh piece of linen to the canvas. The stains were now very faint, hardly visible. This was shown to M. Grave, who rising to his feet began in a clear voice: "I can explain why——" A gesture from the Archbishop stopped him, and realizing the impropriety he had committed he sat down in some confusion. "She seems tired. Take her home and let her rest," said Monseigneur, turning to Rose, who was accordingly led out, half-swooning and hardly able to walk. The Archbishop then took his place upon an improvised throne, and to the surprise of all, two carpenters with their workmen entered and proceeded to remove the picture from the wall. It was carried away through the Sacristy, and the prelate with his procession withdrew.

At eleven o'clock High Mass *coram pontifice* was celebrated, and the Archbishop addressed the overflowing congregation. It was noticed that although he took for his text the words *Memoriam fecit mirabilium suorum* (*He hath been mindful of the Miracles which He wrought of old*), his sermon dealt almost exclusively with the Blessed Sacrament.

Later, the Archbishop granted Rose an interview of some thirty minutes. He was kindly but entirely non-committal, although he remarked that it was a mistake for her to have insisted upon visiting the chapel alone that morning. "There should be others present," he observed. And so he dismissed her. Just as he was on the point of departure Mr. Grave came hurrying up, but Monseigneur entering his coach with his chaplains rather dryly declined to hear any more. "What we have seen and heard to-day will amply suffice for us to form our judgement," he said. And so he drove away.

After the visit of the Archbishop of Avignon the whole countryside seemed divided into two camps. The majority regarded Rose as one of God's most favoured souls. A minority declared that it was all cunning imposture. L'Abbé Caire and a few feared it was diabolical. An Ecclesiastical Commission of five dignitaries was appointed to inquire into the alleged miraculous phenomena. Rose herself, Joséphine Imbert, and Delphine Jean were closely interrogated. Authorities in mystic theology visited the district, examined witnesses, consulted with other experts. The Abbé Grand was privately warned that some very ugly facts had come to light, and he was instructed to use the utmost circumspection in his dealings with Rose Tamisier. The Bishop of Rochelle, a prelate of great learning and a keen intellect, did not hesitate to write as follows to the Archbishop of Avignon: "Having thoroughly gone into the whole business I am convinced that the alleged miraculous phenomena are at best absolutely fraudulent. I recognize Rose Tamisier as none other than a cunning impostor. We only have to call to mind how she insisted upon being left alone in the church before the 'miracle'; how after the wounds in the picture had been lightly touched with a piece of linen two or three times the blood ceased to flow; with what pride and anger she spoke when anyone ventured to doubt the 'miracle', which she asserted would occur yet again to humble her enemies, as though a miracle were ever worked for so unworthy a reason. God does not act thus. Nor must we forget the harvest her sister-in-law has been reaping through the immense concourse of strangers, many wealthy and generous, from all parts, who have literally besieged the hostelry. Their profits have been enormous. One cannot blind oneself to these facts, and there are other more than dubious circumstances in the case."

Mgr. Caval, rector of the diocesan seminary, and an important figure among the commissioners, gave his opinion even more plainly. "I firmly believe," he declared, "that all these bizarre phenomena are demoniacal. Rose Tamisier, as I have discovered, belongs to a secret society whose aim is to astound and mislead the faithful by the exhibition of miracles, miracles which are, I say, worked by the Prince of Darkness. In fact this society is a coven of satanists. The members are nothing other than Manichees although they may go by a different name."

There can be no question, then, that the stigmata of Rose Tamisier were demoniacal. It was further proved beyond a doubt that Rose belonged to the followers of the pseudo-prophet Vintras, with whom, as was noticed in the history of the Agen sorceries, the satanist Virginie was allied. The Ecclesiastical Commissioners delivered their report to the Archbishop. Although, in order not to arouse more scandal it was couched in very moderate terms, their decision could not but be most damnatory. They glanced, as lightly as possible, at the ill repute of the person principally concerned, they emphasized the exaggerations and eccentricities of the whole business, and gave as their opinion that the events were not miraculous in any true sense of the word, that is to say they were not of Heaven. In a phrase they hinted at something evil which so to speak counselled and conducted the imposture, there were phenomena which at the moment they preferred to leave unexplained. A far fuller and more detailed report was sent by the Archbishop of Rome, to the Holy Office, in order that it might be submitted to the Holy Father. The text of this naturally is not available.

The *procureur de la République*, the Public Prosecutor as we may term him, now stepped in since there had been a serious offence. Rose Tamisier was committed on two charges. Firstly, she had acquired considerable sums of money by means of a trick, that is to say by deluding a number of persons in the belief that she was the recipient of divine favours. Secondly, she had by her conduct gravely offended and outraged by her roguery and dishonesty both morals and religion. It was necessary for the preservation of social order and decorum that such knavery should be punished, and it was in fact punishable by the law.

On the 10th February, 1851, she was brought before the local magistrate, who cross-examined her at great length. He treated her with much kindness and forbearance, encouraging her to make a full acknowledgement of her guilt when she would be leniently dealt with, but she stuck to her story. However, there was forthcoming most incriminating evidence. It was proved, for example, that on two separate occasions Rose and her brother François had been seen slipping out of the house long before dawn and walking stealthily in the direction of the chapel. A neighbour, who happened to be looking out of his window since he was about to rise on some early business had caught sight of them, and again a chance traveller, staying one night at the inn, who was aroused by a door softly closing, saw the brother and sister steal out, but as it was none of his business he thought nothing more of it at the moment. A few minutes later Delphine Jean followed them. Other witnesses deposed that long before sunrise, Rose had been seen within a few yards of the chapel. It was certain that she had procured a set of false keys. It may well be that a coven of diabolists met in hellish rendezvous within those sacred walls. Incidentally, it should be remarked that Joséphine Imbert, an impressionable girl, was a simple dupe throughout the whole black business.

Upon the 13th February, 1851, the Pope who had instructed Cardinal Lambruschini at once to inform him of every new detail of the *affaire* Rose Tamisier, wrote with his own hand to the Archbishop of Avignon, whose prudence and cautious conduct he praised in the highest terms. This, said His Holiness, will be an excellent lesson to many, and serve to show them with what circumspection and mistrust even, the Church regards the report of any miracle or supernatural phenomena. We propose to publish, if not officially, at least with our sanction and good-will, a report pointing out how ready the laity were to accept these happenings as miracles of God, whilst Ecclesiastical Authority wholly repudiated any such explanation. Upon the next day, the Holy Office, acting upon the Pope's direction, formally transmitted to the Archbishop the conclusions arrived at, and suggested the course which at any future date might be followed should repercussions of the scandal ensue.

Rose Tamisier had meanwhile been medically examined by a couple of specialists who found no sufficient reason to advise any departure from the usual proceedings. Her trial took place at the Assize Court upon the first of September. All night long, crowds poured into Carpentras, and in the Court itself which was packed to suffocation many persons of high rank and great distinction were glad to find any inch of room were it but a stool or an old chair brought in from outside. The charge may be summed up as common swindling aggravated by sacrilege. The Abbé André proved the connexion of the accused with the followers of Vintras who had been prosecuted and punished by the Assize Court of Caen on 23rd November, 1841. In the witness-box the Abbé Caire maintained that these "miracles" were diabolic from first to last, an exposure which struck terror to the heart of the wretched woman and fearfully alarmed her fellow satanists.

Eventually Rose Tamisier was sentenced to fifteen months imprisonment and amerced in costs of 882 francs. She was gaoled at Carpentras, and since she declared herself unable to pay the money, her release did not take place until 30th November, 1852, under the edict of Louis Napoléon, which abrogated the further detention of those who having fully served their sentence could not discharge additional costs or fines.

She returned to Saignon, to find herself completely ignored and forgotten. Her day of hectic excitement was over. But the Church remembered still. It might well be that the diabolists would again make use of her to arouse fresh scandals, fresh bedevilments. On 16th December, 1852, the parish priest of Saignon wrote to the Archbishop, informing His Grace that on the previous day Rose Tamisier had taken up her residence there. He asked for detailed instructions, which were promptly transmitted. Briefly, as Canon Law required, until such time as the unhappy wretch had made open and ample acknowledgement of her impostures and her wickedness to the Archbishop himself, humbly begging pardon and receiving such penance as might be assigned her, in a humble and contrite spirit to attest her sincerity, she was to be deprived of the Sacraments.

Every day Rose haunted the church, and shadowed the parish priest uttering protestations and reproaches. Her defiance became unbearable. There was something inhuman, something of abnormal malice in that figure which glided to and fro the aisles, suddenly confronting the Curé and his assistants. She refused, absolutely refused to submit. "The miracles were true—true—true——" was her constant cry, "they were miracles." Miracles, yes, but of hell. In April, 1853, the Archbishop deemed it necessary in a private letter to warn all the priests of the provinces against her, and a year later he was obliged to re-iterate his charge. The only concession he would or could make was that if she were mortally ill the priest might administer the last Sacraments, provided that in the presence of two or three witnesses, she acknowledged her impostures. If she were unable to exert herself so much, absolution might be given *sub tacita conditone*. What more could Monseigneur concede?

In 1858 Rose wrote a letter of remonstrance to the Archbishop, who returned no reply. She knew her duty if she really wished to be reconciled. At the very same time there was some trouble brewing at Saignon in regard to a Relic, which she was suspected to have stolen. The matter was quietly cleared up, but the good parish priest remarked that it bitterly grieved him to learn that she had confederates at Saint-Saturnin who seem to be prompting her and furnishing her with funds.

A little later, in 1862, Rose Tamisier was living at Villeneuve-les-Avignon. There was some gossip to the effect that she was distributing pieces of linen stained with blood. A canon of the cathedral inquired whether this was the case. The parish-priest of Villeneuve-lés-Avignon wrote to say that so far as he can discover, and he has made searching inquiries, the rumour is untrue. She was leading a very retired life in utter obscurity, seemingly anxious not to attract attention. And so she disappears from sight.

I have given these two cases of diabolic mysticism, Virginie of Agen and Rose Tamisier, at some length for the following reasons. Firstly: although all the great authorities upon Mysticism, for example, Schram, Görres, and Canon Ribet, deal in detail with diabolic mysticism, too many of the more recent English writers upon the subject have entirely ignored the darker aspects, and hence their surveys cannot but be halting and lame. One author, indeed, no undistinguished name, goes so far as to parade his cowardly avoiding of what he is pleased to term "debased supernaturalism" as meritorious and a virtue. Such an ostrich-attitude in these writers appears to me self-illusory. Is there to be no warning-post of danger? There are few, if any, among the Saints and mystics who have not been attacked, it may be with open violence, it may be insidiously, by the demon and his angels. We know of the satanical persecutions of St. Antony the Great, St. Hilarion, St. Pachomius, and other holy anchorites. Blessed Christina of Stommeln was bruised by fiends, and subjected to almost incredible outrages and assaults. The Seraphic Mother, Catharine of Siena, wrested with and overcame immense forces of evil. Blessed Eustochium of Padua is hailed by her biographer the Augustinian Giovanni Maria Giberti as "L'Invitta Guerriera trionfante di Satanasso", "the Invincible Heroine who battled with and triumphed over the Archfiend" [8]. The Curé d'Ars, St. Jean Baptiste Vianney was sorely plagued by the poltergeist phenomena of the *grappin*, a foul goblin [9].

In the Life of St. Paul of the Cross it is recorded how the devil was permitted to torment the Saint with terrible disturbances, horrid hissing, and frightful noises, as if many pieces of artillery had been discharged, and often awoke him thus in the night to his terror and dismay. Hideous fiends in the shapes of monstrous deformed cats leaped suddenly upon his bed. They often appeared as great black grimalkins with hellishly intelligent staring green eyes, or mastiffs of giant size, and frightful birds of prey, all of which shrieked and yelloched and yowled in mocking human voices [10].

St. Gemma Galgani, too, who died in 1903, was so hateful to Satan that he waged a continual war against her, and tortured her by bruises and blows, attempting the most abominable deceits to entrap her. Padre Germano, her spiritual director, relates how once when she lay ill in bed, after having prayed by her side, he seated himself to recite his Office. Suddenly there brushed past him an enormous dark-coloured cat which furiously leaped on to the bed and crouched there with savage looks. "I felt my blood curdle at the sight, while Gemma remained quite calm. She said: 'Don't be afraid, father; it is the vile demon who wants to annoy me.' I approached her trembling, with holy water and sprinkled her bed. The demon vanished away" [11].

In view, then, of these satanical assaults and artifices a writer on mysticism cannot ignore the darker side, and the devil is never more dangerous than when disguised as an angel of light, when he is counterfeiting the supernatural gifts of God such as ecstasies, the stigmata, levitation.

Secondly: the cases of Virginie of Agen and Rose Tamisier seem to be little, if at all, known in England. They are fully documented, and very instructive in detail. We note that even pious and well-intentioned persons were deceived by these impostures.

The greater the grace the more necessary it is that the utmost prudence should be used. All mystical theologians of authority are insistent in

PLATE XI: THE TRANSVERBERATION OF THE HEART OF
ST. TERESA

Les Œuveres de la Sainte Mère Terèse de Jésus. Paris: 1050

emphasizing this. Holy Church shows extreme caution before pronouncing upon the nature of these phenomena.

It has been stated that during the nineteenth century at least thirty cases of true stigmata were recorded, but as has been already pointed out it is not possible to reach any exact estimate of the subjects of this divine phenomenon, and I feel sure that the number thirty could be doubled, or very nearly doubled, without any exaggeration. An arid list of names and dates is not very inspiring, and accordingly two or three typical examples must stand for many, nor is it possible to deal with these at any great length. The fact is that each stigmatist or stigmatized ecstatica demands a separate and detailed study.

Maria Elisabetta Cecilia Gertrude Canori [12] was born at Rome on 21st November, 1774, some three months after the death of Clement XIV and a little before the election of Pius VI, *sede vacante* as the technical term goes. Her parents, Tommaso Canori and Teresa *née* Primoli, came of good old stock, a house ranking just below aristocracy. As a child, Elisabetta attended the school of Santa Eufemia, where she was distinguished by the quickness of her ability, her clear grasp of the subjects taught, and above all, as the good Sisters used to delight to report to her mother, by her natural piety, "That little girl will go far," said the Superioress, Mother Riggoli. When she was eleven years old circumstances obliged her father to withdraw her from the school and place her to complete her education with the Augustinian nuns of Cascia, the glory of whose cloisters had been Saint Rita. Elisabetta longed to take the vows, and the house she ardently desired to join was that of Montefalco where sleeps the incorrupt body of St. Clara. She already showed so extraordinary a knowledge of things mystical, an intuition far beyond her years, that one day the spiritual director of the nuns asked her in surprise: "Little girl, how did you learn all this? Who has been talking to you?" Looking up with her clear limpid eyes Elisabetta replied in two words: "Jesus Christ."

But her wish was not destined to be accomplished. Her father came to Cascia to bring her back home. She was through obedience to her parents obliged to mix in society, and Rome at that time was the city to which all the great and pleasure-loving members of society in Europe naturally gravitated. It has been truly said that the Papal Court in its most brilliant days was unique in Europe. Many princesses shone like stars, but the leader of them all was acknowledged to be the Princess Santacroce, whose palace was the centre wherein collected all the fashionable and all the noble visitors to the eternal city. This lady delighted in receiving her friends with boundless hospitality. It was said that the Princess Altieri received on Sunday evenings, Princess Massimi on Wednesday, Don Marco Ottoboni on Thursday, and so on, but la Santacroce was at home every day in the week. The entertainment at such gatherings consisted of recitations, music by the best masters, singing by the most admired voices, and a good deal of conversation where the finest wits and keenest intellects in Europe struck fire. In those salons might be seen Cardinal de Bernis; Cardinal Zelada, the

Secretary of State; the sometime Nuncio at Paris, Cardinal Bernardino Giraud, one of the most influential of the Consistory; Cardinal Giovanni Battista Rezzonico, and his brother the Cardinal Camerlingo. The Queens of Bosnia, Cyprus, Hungary, Sweden, Poland, Spain, Sardinia, Sicily, and Etruria, were entertained with the utmost magnificence, almost exceeding the splendour of their own courts, by the great hostesses of Rome. Many and many a foreign monarch found in these truly regal drawing-rooms the lavish welcome which etiquette precluded the Holy Father himself from offering them.

There were also the literary clubs, or *accademie*, frequented by the *élite* of society. The "Arcadia" confined its membership to the highest nobility, although visitors were allowed on special occasions, which were not a few. The "Aborigines" met at the Villa Giustiniani with the Prince as its President. The "Forti" was an assembly under the patronage of Duke Sforza Cesarini. The "Colleges of Poetry" were thronged by young gallants of the first families since nobody could take any place in society who was not an accomplished *littérateur*.

Performances of sacred music, the *Oratorio* introduced by St. Philip Neri, were given in the oratory attached to the Chiesa Nuova, S. Maria in Vallicella, in San Girolamo, Via di Monserrato; and at the Caravita. Often the music was illustrated by scenic representations, and invariably these gatherings were thronged with notables.

This, then, was the social life to which Elisabetta Canori was presented. But it must be remembered that Rome was also (as ever) a City of deep spirituality, and it was here that Elisabetta's heart was fixed. She had no care for dazzling diversions, the galas, the banquets, the conversazioni, the soirées and receptions, whereat in obedience to her parents' command she must needs from time to time appear and play her part. It was all, had she realized it, in the Divine plan, and she was acting according to the Will of God, since it brought home to her with intenser conviction that such a life could never satisfy the longing of her soul. Amid those brilliant fêtes she was the only reality in a world of shadows.

There were many suitors for her hand, since she was very lovely. But she refused offer after offer, until when she was one-and-twenty her father grew impatient at this "nice procrastination" as he termed it, and she was constrained to betroth herself to Cristoforo, the son of an eminent and very wealthy physician, Dr. Francesco Mora. Her fiancé was young, cultured, handsome, much admired for his talents and charm. He was deeply in love. And yet her mother had a presentiment that the match would not be for her daughter's happiness. She could give no real reason for this foreboding. Her husband's word in the household was law. Cristoforo and Elisabetta were married on 10th January, 1796.

Teresa Canori had feared only too truly for her daughter. The intuition of a mother's love did not deceive. Cristoforo complained that his bride did not seem to appreciate the fine suite in the Palazzo Vespignani to which he had brought her. She took no delight in presents of rich dresses and jewels. She was reluctant to mix in society. She was silent and solitary, always retiring and shy. He had not bargained to marry a nun. So against her own will she strove to do her best to please him. Then he changed his tune. Why did she talk so long to so-and-so last night? Why did she keep all her good humour for such-a-one? He became insanely jealous.

After the birth of their first child, a daughter who died, Cristoforo treated his wife with the utmost coldness, and now openly neglected her. The reason for this, as she soon discovered, was that he had indulged in a shameful intrigue with a common woman who was, leech-like, draining him of his estate. He seemed in fact to have lost all sense of decency, and did not trouble to disguise his infidelity from the patient and long-suffering Elisabetta. Never a word of reproach fell from her lips, but when this low trull demanded more and more money he vented his ill-temper at home. Things, indeed, came to such a pass that Dr. Francesco Mora insisted upon his son and daughter-in-law removing to much more modest apartments, in the same house as he himself resided, hoping that this would at least prove some check on his profligate son, whose depleted purse did not allow him to refuse the new arrangement. But Cristoforo, of course, laid the blame on his wife's shoulders. She must have gone with some whining tale to his father or hers he declared, and her life was rendered miserable. As she afterwards avowed, she must have succumbed had it not been for her infinite trust in God.

A second child had died in babyhood, but a third daughter, Marianna was born, and on 5th July 1801, was born her fourth daughter, Maria Lucina. In their two daughters she found much consolation, herself undertaking their education, the first lesson they learned being to love God. Thus her husband's neglect she turned to advantage. It enabled her to withdraw completely from society and to lead a secluded life. She was always willing and ready to share in the labours of the house, nay, cheerfully to do the work of all, so that she became a great favourite with Dr. Mora who appreciated her worth, and was the more angry with his recalcitrant son, whom nothing seemed able to divert from his evil courses.

Almost unknown to herself, Elisabetta in her patience, her meekness and humility, had already far advanced along the mystic path to perfection. It was early in the morning of the 7th September, the Eve of the Nativity of Our Lady, for which Feast she had prepared by fervent prayer, that she beheld a vision of the Mother of God. The radiant figure smiled upon her as well-pleased. In Her hands the Madonna held a snow-white dove, whose wings were marked with the Five Sacred Wounds aglow with crimson light. From one of these wounds there detached itself a nail, flaming with fire, which pierced like a sharp lance the heart of Elisabetta, overwhelming her with love, so that she passed into ecstasy.

Her confessor, Don Gian Giacomo Pegna, a man of great prudence, said little to her when she related what had occurred, beyond encouraging her to persevere, but it came about that he was shortly leaving Rome,

235

at least for a time, and meanwhile she must needs seek another spiritual director. Being one day in San Carlo alle Quattro Fontane, the church of the Discalced Spanish Trinitarians, she felt impelled to open her heart to a priest in a confessional there. This was none other than Padre Ferdinando di San Luigi, a mystic of the highest order. He questioned her closely, and at once recognized that she was far advanced in grace, one of God's holiest souls. From October 1807, he was her spiritual father and guide. "It was Heaven," she said, "that directly sent me to him." We may remember a similar circumstance in the life of St. Teresa of Ávila, who was completely misunderstood by at least five or six priests to whom she related her mystical experiences. They were "all great servants of God," she says, but adds distressingly "they were all against me." They left her, in fact, "quite upset and worn out, with not the least idea what to do". And then she was encouraged by St. Peter of Alcántara, the Franciscan contemplative, with whom she had "many talks", and her Jesuit directors were full of sympathy, and above all there came into her life "the father of her soul", that "Spirit of Flame"- whom the world knows as St. John of the Cross.

Padre Ferdinando the Trinitarian moulded and directed the soul of Elisabetta Canori Mora until she attained the highest realms of mysticism. She truly needed a strong helping hand. Cristoforo, her husband, seemed to be going from bad to worse. He had already impoverished his family, his wife and daughters, by his licentiousness, gambling, and other depravities, and when his father died, heart-broken in 1813, he did not hesitate to try to embezzle a considerable sum of money. His sisters not unnaturally refused to help him unless indeed he completely altered his ways, and Elisabetta, deprived of her father-in-law's kindly aid, was obliged to move to a small house at a very low rent.

In 1819, on Whit-Sunday, whilst she was rapt in prayer before the High Altar of San Carlo she heard a voice which said: "It is My Will that thou shouldest become a Tertiary of the Order of Barefoot Trini- tarians." When, in fear lest she should be refused—for the rule was of the strictest—she falteringly spoke of this to Padre Ferdinando, to her surprise he answered that he also had received an inspiration that she must be enrolled, and he was but waiting for her to approach him with the prayer that she might be clothed in the habit. After the usual period of probation and testing, early in the following year she was solemnly invested and took the Tertiary name of Joanna Felix of the Most Holy Trinity. It may be explained that the Tertiary habit is generally worn only at the formal assemblies, and that at death the Tertiary is buried in the full robes of the Order. During life a scapular is worn under the ordinary dress, but it is enjoined that the clothes of a Tertiary, whilst fitting his or her station in life should be as far as possible simple and neat, without any superfluous ornament, and subfusc in hue.

It is from this time that Elisabetta was especially devoted to Our Lord under the title Jesus the Nazarene. This is one of the great Feasts of the Trinitarians.

The world treated Elisabetta hardly, but she overcame it with patience

and humility. She suffered, as the Saints have done, demoniacal persecutions and assaults of the evil one. She suffered and was silent. Great
was her reward, for she was granted the supreme mystical experience
of the Spiritual Marriage, when Our Lord appeared to her with His
Mother and St. Joseph amid a radiant company of Angels. Upon the 2nd
July, 1823, the Feast of the Visitation of Our Lady she received the
stigmata. Her life, it was said, was none other than one long ecstasy.
In church, at San Carlo, in the house, in her own room, at table, even
in the street the divine rapture would entrance her and her soul flew
heavenwards on the wings of love.

Modest, retiring as she was, such gifts could not be hid. Often and
often her neighbours, if a child were ill, if they were anxious or in trouble,
in the event of loss or any calamity, would say "Let us ask Signora
Elisabetta to pray for us, and all will be well." She was known to be
gifted with the spirit of prophecy, whilst the mysterious colloquies, full
of mystic wisdom, which she uttered whilst in ecstasy were carefully
committed to paper and are now being examined by experts in mystical
theology in view of her beatification which is confidently awaited.

She died upon the 5th February, 1825, and is buried in her much-
loved church, San Carlo alle Quattro Fontane, hard by the altar of San
Miguel de los Santos. Padre Ferdinando wrote the epitaph which is
graven on her tomb.

The cause for beatification was introduced on 22nd June, 1876, and
formally approved by Pius IX, whose successor Leo XIII on 22nd June,
1892, declared that the official Process in the case of the Venerable
Elisabetta Canori Mora was valid and good.

Elisabetta Canori Mora is an example of a mystic who was compelled
by circumstances not only to live in the world rather than in the cloister
she would have chosen, but as a girl to mix in society, to marry, to endure
the martyrdom of an unhappy domestic life. She was the wife of a bad
husband, a reckless and disloyal profligate, she was the tender mother
of two daughters. Such was her exterior life. It was very commonplace,
and often very sad. In one way she may seem the nearer to us therefor;
she is more understandable, more ordinary.

So this mystic has a marvellous message for ordinary people, for
those who are weighed down by the dull burden of domestic care. Her
interior life was lived on the highest plane.

An entirely different figure from the Roman matron and mother was
the "Little Arab", Marie Baouardie, in religion Sœur Marie de Jésus
Crucifié. Born at Abellin, a little village of Galilee near Nazareth, in
1846, she died in the Carmelite convent of Bethlehem at the age of thirty-
three. It was obvious from the first that Sœur Marie was a mystic of a
very advanced order. Her austerities and mortifications were ever concealed under a radiant smile. The Carmelite nuns of Pau, where she
spent much of her cloistered life, declared that she was a ray of sunlight
in the house. She was a true daughter of St. Teresa who liked her nuns
to be cheerful and detested gloomy faces. The sayings of Sœur Marie,
whilst rapt in ecstasy, were carefully taken down, and as recently as 15th

July, 1924, the Congregation of Rites at Rome pronounced a favourable judgement after a meticulous examination of those writings.

Sœur Marie died at 5.10 in the morning, and five hours later an eminent surgeon, Dr. Carpani, removed the heart from her body. He at once perceived on this organ, a deep wound, triangular in shape, and appearing as though it had been inflicted by a broad sword. The monks and priests who were present carefully observed the cicatrice, whose two lips were dry, showing that it was impossible for it to have been inflicted during the post-mortem operation. "But might not some malady have caused it?" inquired Dom Belloni. "That is out of the question," replied Dr. Carpani, "the heart is perfectly healthy and sound." On 24th May, 1868, Sœur Marie, who was then living in the Carmelite convent of Pau, passed into ecstasy. It seemed to be even more extraordinary than her wonted raptures. She was thrilled by indescribable delight, and endured Love's completest martyrdom. Suddenly, addressing herself to St. Teresa, she cried out: "O Mother Teresa! Jesus has pierced my heart!" This, then, was the ferita, discovered ten years later, immediately after her death. The heart is treasured at Pau, but shut away until such time as the Little Arab has been beatified by the Supreme Pontiff. On 13th May, 1929, the Bishop of Bayonne assisted by two of the leading doctors of Pau made official inquiry into the condition of the heart. The cicatrice could be plainly seen, and both doctors signed a certificate to that effect [13].

Dr. Imbert-Gourbeyre speaks of a holy stigmatica of Ardèche, Victoire Claire of Coux, who died in 1883. Only a few details are told. She is also mentioned by Eugène-Auguste-Albert de Rochas d'Aiglun in his *Recueil de documents relatifs à la lévitation du corps humain*, Paris, published P. G. Leymarie, 1897. Victoire Claire was frequently seen levitated in ecstasy. There is no published life of this mystic since that written by Père Roussett, S. J., has not been given to the press. The Abbé Combes, who was parish-priest of Coux during Victoire Claire's lifetime, carefully noted in a diary many of the phenomena, and gave an account of the stigmatica. But this also remains in manuscript. Victoire Claire suffered greatly from demoniacal persecutions, and seems to have reached a very advanced state in the supernatural life since she was (we believe) divinely comforted and sustained during the attacks of the fiend.

It has been said of Louise Lateau of Bois-d'Haine that "Lapse of time has for the most part made the recollection of this interesting case of stigmatization a dim memory only, but Louise Lateau does not merit this oblivion, both on account of her unassuming, simple and captivating personality, and from the fact that all the supernatural phenomena in her case were subjected to the most rigorous investigation . . . she was a very tower of strength for the existence of the Supernatural, not only with regard to Belgium, her native country, but also for many who flocked to Bois-d'Haine to see her from France, Germany, and England."

It is, I think, hardly true to say that Louise Lateau is "a dim memory only". She is a very striking figure in the history of mysticism, the more especially so since her case was so rigorously investigated by specialists and doctors from practically every European country. There was not a test which was not applied, and amplest opportunity was given for the most scrupulously exact examinations, not once or twice, but repeated, again and again.

Dr. Lefebvre, one of the most distinguished medical men of the day, and a professor of the University of Louvain, undertook a thorough and prolonged examination of the case. During the autumn-winter of 1868 and throughout 1869 Dr. Lefebvre paid many visits to Bois-d'Haine, often (on purpose) arriving quite unexpectedly, and most minutely investigating the several phenomena of the ecstasies and the stigmata. He filled many note-books, and after most careful deliberation he published the results in Vol. XXVIII (1869) and Vol. XXIX (1870) of the *Revue Catholique*. In 1870–2, these important articles were collected in book form as "Louise Lateau of Bois-d'Haine. Her Life, her Ecstasies, her Stigmata. A medical Study. Louvain, Charles Peeters." During the fall of 1872 the Belgian Royal Academy of Medicine sent a commission to report the facts and their findings.

At two o'clock on 21st January, 1875, Dr. Warlomont and Dr. Duwez, before there was the slightest sign of bleeding from the stigmata, enclosed the right arm of Louise in a glass apparatus, which was carefully placed and bound by bandages hermatically sealed. Canon Hallez of Tournai and the Abbé Niels, parish priest of Bois-d'Haine, were present but touched nothing. The next day the seals being found intact the apparatus was taken off by Dr. Warlomont and Professor Dr. Crocq, who was an agnostic. The stigmata had bled as usual. The doctors' report ran: "The hæmorrhages appear most certainly to have been spontaneous and it seems that they must have occurred without the intervention of any exterior agency": *Bulletin d l'Académie Royale de Medecine de Belgique*, 1875. Tome XV, No. 2, pp. 176–79.

Already in October, 1868, the celebrated Dr. Imbert-Gourbeyre of Clermont-Ferrand had visited Bois-d'Haine, and in 1873 he published a most exhaustive study—perhaps the completest study—of the case. His conclusion was exactly that of Dr. Lefebvre: "The Stigmatization and Ecstasies of Louise Lateau are real facts, devoid of any suspicion of fraud, and Science can furnish no explanation of the phenomena."

When the famous German Professor Virchow, an obstinate freethinker, was consulted with regard to the stigmata of Louise Lateau he gave much care and attention to the case. At last he pronounced his verdict: *It is either trickery—or a Miracle*. Not another word could be got out of him. We know that there was no trickery.

The biography of Louise Lateau [*14*] has been written several times and there are so many studies of this amazing ecstatica it will (I think) suffice briefly to say that she was born of honest working class parents at Bois-d'Haine on 20th January, 1850. From 1861–1864, with the exception of a couple of months when she was engaged in domestic service in Brussels, she took situations on small farms near her home. In April, 1865, she joined her two sisters who were needlewomen, and showed herself an admirable sempstress. During the epidemic of cholera which devastated Belgium in 1866, and severely attacked Bois-d'Haine, Louise gave up her time to nursing the sick, who often were deserted even by their nearest relatives, so awful was the panic that prevailed. She certainly exercised heroic charity, and (as she herself acknowledged) divine illuminations flooded her soul. The stigmatical pains endured by Louise date from 3rd January, 1868, although they were not exteriorized with bleeding until the following 24th April, a Friday. After that date, with two exceptions, they bled every Friday, in all 800 times. The widow Lateau and her daughter at first considered the phenomenon as a nuisance. They shunned the publicity which inevitably ensued, and regarded the concourse of visitors as a punishment. Other phenomena were what is known as the "Recall", that is to say however profoundly she was rapt in ecstasy, when no physical force had any effect, at the command of an ecclesiastical superior the trance immediately ceased. Extraordinary changes in her weight were recorded by the various specialists who examined her. She had a knowledge of languages whilst in ecstasy. A Belgian peasant girl, she could converse in Latin and English, whilst Mgr. d'Herbonnez, Bishop of British Columbia, who visited her in 1869, as a test, spoke in the tongue of the natives of his diocese, which she perfectly understood. There was superadded the phenomenon of complete abstinence from food. She lived on Holy Communion alone, a recognized fact in divine mysticism. From 1879 until her death on 25th August, 1883, the sufferings of Louise sensibly increased. Times of peril for the Church always augmented her agony, although she did not know the cause. In 1871, during the funeral of the notorious atheist, Monteschi, and on Good Friday of that year when a banquet was held with diabolic rites, she lay as if at the point of death. The same week during the terrorism at Paris those who were watching thought that she had actually passed away in paroxysms of intolerable anguish. Her obsequies, which she desired should be as simple as possible were attended by more than five thousand persons. She was buried very plainly in the churchyard of Bois-d'Haine.

It is interesting to remark that Louise prophesied the First Great War and said that Holland would be the only neighbouring country not involved. She further declared that Bois-d'Haine would be untouched, unharmed. The village escaped the forced deportation of men; no troops were ever quartered there; and whilst the surrounding country was terribly damaged by aviators Bois-d'Haile remained unscathed.

From Belgium we pass to Spain to consider the case of a stigmatica, who was no less wonderful than Louise Lateau, who was misrepresented and reviled, whose story has (to my knowledge) never been truly told in English.

María Rafaela Quiroga [15] who, upon taking the veil, was known in religion as Sor María Cipriana del Patrocinio de San José was born in 1809–10. After the deaths of her father and a brother, when she was thirteen years old, she was placed by her newly widowed mother in a convent, and the community soon recognized that here was a child of no ordinary piety. They were careful not to betray the least sign of this impression. She was not in any way favoured, but rather the reverse. Nevertheless her vocation irresistibly manifested itself, and in January, 1829, she took the cloistered vows in the house of San José, known as *del Caballero de Gracia* (*Our Protector in Heaven*), in Madrid. Shortly it was whispered that the saintly nun was an ecstatica, who in her raptures voiced mystic revelations. Upon a day Sor Patrocinio, entranced, beheld a vision of Our Lord Whose Five Red Wounds streamed with blood and shone with golden light. At that moment there darted forth five iridescent rays which lanced her feet, hands, and side. In great confusion and abashment she endeavoured to conceal the divine stigmata, but since she needed fresh linen to staunch the flow of blood this proved impossible. She revealed her wonderful secret to the spiritual director of the convent, a Capuchin profoundly versed in mystical theology, Fray Firmin de Alcaráz, who to her surprise did not seem in the least degree astonished or perturbed. He knew even better than herself, how far she had advanced in the spiritual life. He counselled discretion and obedience. It was not many days afterwards that she received the Crown of Thorns. Her Superior, who had recognized that something extraordinary was happening, now questioned her, tactfully but searchingly, and in all humility she was obliged to avow the truth. The Prioress then consulted Fray Firmin, and was soon assured that in his opinion which carried no little weight, the stigmata of Sor Patrocinio were divine. He recommended prudence. But somebody, it may have been an extern sister, talked. It may have been a whisper through the grille. Madrid learned that in the Convent of San José del Caballero de Gracia there was cloistered a saintly nun, whom Christ Himself had marked with the Five Sacred Wounds and crowned with His diadem of thorns. The devotion of the people could not be restrained. Ladies of the highest rank, princesses and duchesses of the royal family; privileged prelates; the cardinal and bishops; crowded the parlours of San José, and begged for even the smallest pieces of linen stained with her stigmatical blood. These they regarded (and truly) as curative. Such dignitaries were not to be denied.

Fernando VII died on 29th September, 1833, and Spain was almost immediately plunged into a welter of internal revolts and anarchy, upon the details of which it is fortunately not necessary to enlarge. Suffice to say that the anti-clericals conceived and carried through a most daring plot. The very audacity of their conspiracies reached such a height of diabolic effrontery that for the moment it seemed as if they swept all before them. Sor Patrocinio was regarded by the subversives with especial dislike, and they had determined that at any cost, by perjury, by bribery, by bullying and deception, she must be got rid of, relegated to eternal obscurity and oblivion. A process was commenced, and in November, 1835, a partisan judge, well-primed and well-paid, with a posse of constables, made a sudden descent on the convent, forced his way in, and proceeded to interrogate the community. With the exception of one young sister who was half driven out of her wits by the confusion and the torrent of questioning and abuse so that she did not know what she was saying, the nuns, one and all, solemnly attested that the ecstasies and stigmata of Sor Patrocinio were supernatural; on one occasion it was proved that the gush of blood from her hands filled two coffee cups, nor in spite of all his menaces could the judge induce the sisters to be forsworn. In an access of rage he ordered his officials to drag Sor Patrocinio away, but by this time the news of this sacrilegious incursion had got abroad, and so threatening a crowd collected in the street that the ruffian and his gang were glad to escape as best they could. None the less a second visit was made more secretly, and Sor Patrocinio was taken off to a private house where she was kept prisoner. It was sedulously reported that she was under the care of her mother and a priest of great integrity. This, of course, nobody believed except those whose object it was to do so. Three physicians, corrupted by very considerable sums of money, Diego Argumosa, Mateo Seaone, and Maximiano Gonzalez, purported to have made a close examination of the stigmata, and unblushingly set their names to a lying certificate which declared in very considerable detail that there was imposture. Meanwhile, Sor Patrocinio, who was allowed no communication with anyone save perjured officials was conveyed to the Convent of Santa Maria Magdalena, the *Recojidas*, an enclosure which was complete. The authorities, without any fear of contradiction, were now able to publish a statement to the effect that she had confessed her mystical experiences were play-acting, the stigmata a fake. Even in nineteenth century politics there have been few more scandalous and shameless perjuries and intrigues.

A prosecution was pompously initiated against Sor Patrocinio, the Prioress and Vicaress of the convent, and a chaplain Andrés Rivas. Padre Firmin, who was denounced by the lawyers employed as *fanático é ignorante en sumo grado*, "an ignorant and crazy fanatic", had been warned in time, and in obedience to the Capuchin Guardian had withdrawn to a retreat which could not be discovered. His name and fame, however, were covered with all the scurril obloquy a refinement of fiendish malice could invent. A mock trial was carried through, and he was condemned *in contumaciam*. In order to give more publicity to the affair it was dragged out and advertised, sentence not being pronounced until 25th November, 1836. The counsel for the defence entered an appeal, upon which the sentence was gloatingly increased in severity. The Madrid house was suppressed, the chaplain, Andrés Rivas, was banished from Madrid for eight years; Sor Patrocinio, the Prioress, and Vicaress, were relegated separately to three distant convents of the most rigorous observance of their Order.

Public excitement was intense. It was, indeed, not until 27th April, 1837, that, at five o'clock in the morning a closed carriage drew up quietly at the gate of the *Recojidas*, and Sor Patrocinio was quickly hustled into it. She wore a secular dress, and was bidden on the journey under a heavy penalty only to answer to her secular name, María Rafaela Quiroga. The next day at eight in the evening her guards delivered her to the charge of the community of the Madre de Dios house at Talavera. She was to be forgotten, extinguished. Evil triumphed.

242

Seven years passed. Governments rose and governments fell. Often a state of revolt and semi-anarchy prevailed. Later in 1843 a Cortes was elected, and on the 8th November of that winter the young Queen Isabel II was declared to have attained her majority, which is to say that she was called to play an impossibly difficult part. "Few sovereigns," it is said, "have been so popular as Isabel II in the early years of her majority." Among her first acts was to build in Madrid in 1845 the Convent of Jesús, of which Sor Patrocinio was elected Abbess. The Queen felt that she could have no better adviser than the saintly nun, who, the royal command insisted, was to be received at the Convent with all the dignity befitting her rank. On the 10th October, 1846, the Queen married Don Francisco de Asis, whose confessor Padre Fulgencio had always been a staunch supporter of the holy stigmatica. The King-Consort appointed Manuel Quiroga, Sor Patrocinio's brother, a groom of the Royal Bed-chamber. The Minister General of the Capuchins bade Fray Fermin Alcaráz come forth from his retirement, and the good friar was conse-crated Bishop of Cuenca. The notorious Dr. Argumosa was justly prose-cuted for his venality and malfeasance.

In 1849, the Duke of Valencia, General Narváez, a ruthless and brutal swashbuckler, was openly aiming at a dictatorship, when the Queen would have become a mere puppet in his hands. Barricades sprang up in the streets of Madrid, and the gutters ran with blood. On the morning of St. Ursula's day, 21st October, he caused Sor Patronicio whose influence would (he feared) counteract his despotism, to be hurried into a postchaise and driven off to a convent in Badajoz. Fortunately his plans received a timely check, and Queen Isabel insisted upon the return of her best adviser. In 1850, Narváez was succeeded as Prime Minister by Brabo Murillo, a hard harsh man, full of schemes for his self-aggrandize-ment. He also was fearful lest Sor Patroncinio should see through his designs, but he went more warily to work. He persuaded the Nuncio Brunelli to send the saintly nun to Rome in order that she might have an audience with the Holy Father, hoping that there might be alleged some specious reason for detaining her in Italy until he had found time to gain a secure footing and well feather his nest. The scheme failed miserably. Pius IX indeed welcomed Sor Patrocinio with most fatherly kindness, and warmly gave her his blessing, but he whispered at the last audience, "My daughter, do not tarry here with Us overlong. Your place is at home."

In 1868, the revolution which swept Spain, drove Queen Isabel to seek refuge in France, whilst her faithful subjects wept bitterly for the woe to come, and kneeling kissed the hem of her dress. It was a moment of poignant tragedy. Sor Patrocinio retired to the convent of Guadalajara, of which she was Abbess, and never again passed beyond the quiet cloister walls. She felt that her work was done, and at last she could give herself wholly to God. Yet even now calumny and lies pursued her. In his book *La physique des miracles*, Paris, Dentu, 1872, Dr. Wilfrid de Fonvielle, an unscrupulous but pretentious dabbler in third-rate journalism, had the audacity to assert that when Queen Isabel exiled herself from Spain

Sor Patroncinio also hurriedly crossed the frontier, and was there established as a tobacconist at Montmorency, Seine-et-Oise. Such fabrications were continually exposing this humbug de Fonvielle to some very severe handling by the critics, and Charles Richet in a leading article said: "It is plain enough that M. Wilfrid de Fonvielle has complete confidence in his own knowledge of the subjects concerning which he writes with such vapid fluency, but it may be as well for him to learn and, if he can, realize that this confidence is not shared by his readers." He was, in fine, summed up as an ignorant and bumptious charlatan [16].

In her convent at Guadalajara Sor Patrocinio lived her life of the highest mysticism. She died most happily, surrounded by her sorrowing daughters, on 27th January, 1891, comforted in the last moments by the Apostolic Blessing of the Supreme Pontiff, Leo XIII [17]. There are few mystics who have been subjected through the years to such systematic and deliberately engineered persecution. Her genius had something of St. Catharine of Siena, something of St. Teresa of Ávila.

Early in March, 1945, there died at the Dominican convent of Sondrio, the capital (with some 4,000–5,000 inhabitants) of the Valtellina, Suor Tomassina Possi, who was described [18] a little incorrectly as "the last woman known to have been marked with the stigmata". Suor Tomassina, who was thirty-four years old, had received the wounds on hands and feet, and the ferita, the wound in the side.

There are known to be other stigmaticas of the twentieth century, several of whom are still alive. Of these, several are nuns belonging to enclosed Orders, but the contemporary stigmatica who has been most widely discussed is without doubt Theresa Neumann of Konnersreuth. It is not too much to say that "the living crucifix" of Konnersreuth has attracted the attention of the whole world, and Theresa Neumann is already the subject of a library of books, mystical, theological, medical, critical, written by the most diverse pens from the most diverse points of views. Any account of the phenomena of Konnersreuth to be useful would have to be very full indeed, and it must not be taken that because I touch upon Theresa Neumann briefly (and inadequately) here that I fail to recognize her immense importance in the history of stigmatization. It is merely because there are easily accessible so many authoritative and indeed exhaustive studies of the case.

Konnersreuth is a small village of about 1,500 people in the Bavarian mountains on the borders of Germany and Czechoslovakia. Life is—or was—very tranquil and remote in this far-away place, where the telephone, and the radio had not penetrated, and a motor-car in the little streets and squares used to be a thing to be gazed at as something novel and strange. It has been said that "daily toil forms the recreation and amusement of the people". The houses are grouped round the church, and a spirit of simple piety reigns supreme. It is the usual thing, not a mere Sunday or holyday observance, for everyone to assist at Mass every morning of the week. Simplicity, peace, and a profound piety are the characteristics of Konnersreuth.

The Neumanns themselves are nothing more than plain peasant folk.

The father is a farmer and a tailor; Frau Neumann an honest hard-working country woman. Born on 8th April, 1898, Theresa is the eldest surviving child. When twelve years old she entered domestic service, helping after school hours at a neighbouring farm, where, upon leaving school two years later, she was permanently engaged. As she herself says, "I learned long ago what a long day's work means." In 1918, whilst engaged in her duties, she unfortunately met with a couple of accidents which necessitated medical treatment, and eventually she was compelled to take to her bed, which distressed her deeply, since she felt that she was a burden on the poor household. Dr. Seidl of Waldsassen gave it as his opinion that no adequate medical explanation could be found to fit this baffling case. None the less Theresa was cured, as she believes miraculously, by her patron, the Little Flower, St. Teresa of Lisieux.

The stigmata were impressed upon her during Lent, March, 1926. She had visions of several incidents of the Passions and felt the agony of the scourging, the carrying of the Cross, culminating on Good Friday with the whole drama of the crucifixion, the wound in the side, the wounds piercing hands and feet. Later the Crown of Thorns was given, and the wound on the right shoulder. On ordinary Fridays blood flows from the head and the eyes. On the first Friday in each month the ferita also gushes with blood. The stigmata of the hands and feet bleed regularly during Lent, and on each Good Friday the deep crimson weals of the scourging appear with intense pain. The blood which exudes has been analysed in a University laboratory and has been proved to be blood, pure and healthy. With the exception of the weals of the scourging, which appear on Good Friday only and shortly after fade, the stigmata are always visibly impressed upon her and can be plainly seen by anyone. Hence she always wears fingerless gloves on her hands, loose easy slippers on her feet, and is mantillaed in a thick black shawl.

Theresa Neumann is also gifted with mystical *inedia*, that is, as has been explained in Chapter V, supernatural abstinence from food or liquid nourishment. On 5th January, 1940, *The Universe* noted: "Theresa Neumann, the stigmatized peasant woman of Konnersreuth, has declined to accept the German ration cards, pointing out that she does not need any food. Only the Blessed Sacrament passes her lips." This was the same with the Carmelite St. Maria Maddalena de' Pazzi, whose only food was the Host. For more than twenty years the Dominicaness, Blessed Colomba de Rieti, lived upon the Eucharist alone, "a banquet", she was wont to say, "in which I taste every delight". By order of Pope Innocent VIII a judicial inquiry was made into this case, and the *inedia* was proved beyond all doubt. The Holy Father expressed himself as very greatly edified, and sent the saintly woman his especial Blessing.

Many other cases might be cited.

Visitors, doctors and scientists, and priests and pilgrims have crowded to Konnersreuth, but they were not encouraged, on the contrary they were rebuffed. Ecclesiastical authority has acted with what may seem to many, who are unthinking and unwise, an excess of caution. On 4th May, 1926, Father Josef Naber, the parish-priest of Konnersreuth at

245

the request of the Bishop of Ratisbon submitted a report upon the phenomena concerned with Theresa Neumann. The Bishop did not approve the conclusions arrived at, and the German hierarchy forbade any further visits to the village. In September, 1927, their Lordships sent a notice to the Press, asking that no opinions should be expressed with regard to the Theresa Neumann stigmata and other mystical experiences. Previously, the Cardinal Archbishop of Munich, Michael de Faulhaber, who had seemingly ignored the whole thing, publicly admonished his people from the Cathedral pulpit that no judgement must be passed on Konnersreuth. It was not until August, 1928, that the Cardinal paid his first visit to Theresa Neumann, and it is not concealed that he was profoundly impressed by her candour and simplicity. Pope Pius XI, it is believed, privately instructed Father Gemelli, the Director of the Sacred Heart University of Milan and an acknowledged Expert in mystical theology, to investigate and report on the phenomena. Father Gemelli visited Konnersreuth on 23rd March and 6th April, 1928. He made most searching inquiry into every detail. Upon leaving the village he went directly to Rome and had more than one audience with the Holy Father, who a few days later signed two special Apostolic Blessings and sent them, through Cardinal Faulhaber, to Theresa Neumann and to Father Naber. More cannot be said. The Church has made no definite statement.

The Bishop of Ratisbon still regulates very strictly any visits to the Neumann household. In fact nobody is admitted without his authorization, which is far from easy to obtain.

Scientists now honestly confess that they are baffled. Those who will not accept a supernatural explanation take refuge in silence. Indeed what else is there for the poor fellows to do? It may be useful to mention a very few of the numerous books which under various aspects treat in detail of the stigmatica Theresa Neumann and the phenomena of Konnersreuth. The editor of the *Müncher Neuesten Nachrichten*, Dr. Fritz Gerlich, has published (Kösel and Puster, Munich), *Die Stigmatisierte Th. Neumann von Konnersreuth* and *Die Lebengeschichte der Theresa Neumann*. In 1928 appeared Dr. Karl Keifer's *Konnersreuth im Lichte des Christmums und der Wirklichkeit Prüfende Überlicke*. An important work is Freidrich Ritter von Lama's *Konnersreuth Kronik*, 1928–1929, *sqq*. The theological point of view is examined by a Doctor in Theology, Martin Mayr, who has written *L'Enigme de Konnersreuth*. *Le Stigmatisée Thérèse Neuman*, Mulhouse, 1928. In the same year was issued von Lama's *Thérèse Neumann, une Stigmatisée de Nos Jours*. There is also *Thérèse Neumann, 'Etude Critique* by Father Dorsaz, Saint-Maurice, 1930. This study sums up the phenomena thus: "Konnersreuth is a divine message sent to the world." Kaplan Fahsel issued in 1931 *Konnersreuth*. *Le Mystère des Stigmatisés*, Paris, 1933 (English translation, 1934), by Jeanne Danemarie gives an interesting and detailed account of visits to Emmerich-haus at Dülmen and to Konnersreuth. In English there is a very useful book, first edition, 1936; reprinted, 1940; *Theresa Neumann of Konnersreuth* by two priests, Father Charles E. Roy of Gaspé, Canada, and Father William A. Joyce of London. Dr. R. W. Hayneck wrote *Konnersreuth,* "A Medical and Psychological Study of the Case of Teresa Neumann", translated and adapted by Lancelot W. Sheppard. Friedrich von Lama was also translated by Albert Paul Schimberg, *Further Chronicles of Teresa Neumann,* Bruce Publishing Company, Milwaukee.

Some twenty or more years ago Mgr. Count Franciscus de Campos Barreto, Bishop of Campinas, Brazil, founded in his diocese the "Institute of the Crucified Jesus for Women Missionaries". One of the original eight sisters is Sister Amalia of Jesus Scourged, who has so faithfully trodden the mystic path to God that she bears upon her body the miraculous imprint of the Five Wounds of Christ. It was to Sister Amalia in 1929–30 that a vision revealed the Rosary of the Tears of Mary, whose milky white beads (it has been beautifully said) encircle the world [*19*]. A contemporary stigmatica, who suffered much and was long misunderstood, was the Breton peasant woman, born about 1853, Marie-Julie Jahenny of La Fraudais, near Nantes, who lived to be an octogenarian.

Several cases of stigmaticas, now living, and who have beyond all doubt divinely received the Five Wounds of Christ, are known to me, but it will be appreciated that the utmost reticence is desirable, and these histories have been told to me in the strictest confidence and under promise not to divulge them, even if only initials and pseudo-place-names were given. In fact without the evidence of a full theological and medical investigation it might prove useless, were it allowable, to give any details, and therefore, I must content myself with recording these facts, which in the future no doubt, in many instances, will (when it is authorized) be made known to the world.

I have not sufficient data to offer any opinion upon the case of the Jesuit novice in the Sicilian province who in 1885–6 was stated by trustworthy witnesses and his own superiors to have been completely stigmatized whilst in ecstasy, and to have partaken in measure of all the sufferings of Christ's Passion. A Letter, dated 26th April, 1886, and written from the College of St. Ignatius, Malta, by the Rector, Father Henry Martin, S. J., has been printed, and a few details may accordingly be given. At the time extraordinary precautions were taken to guard against any publicity, and Fr. Martin's letter is addressed to the Provincial. Already some rumour had leaked out, and "the young scholastic novice is now all the talk of the island (Malta)". I saw the five wounds, says the Rector, and upon Good Friday, when they were open and gushed with blood, the stigmatist was carefully examined by no less than twelve medical men. Whenever the youth received Holy Communion, blood poured copiously from the ferita, drenching linen cloths and kerchiefs. Great pain was suffered, and the lad was obliged to walk as best he could, upon his heels. The weals of the Scourging at the Pillar were plainly seen on his back. The novice showed true humility, and shrank from notice. When questioned, he answered under obedience with modesty and reluctance, evincing considerable distress and constantly declaring he was no saint. "It is," wrote Fr. Martin, "a very extraordinary case which is a source of great anxiety to his Superiors.

Our enemies are saying that it is all a piece of Jesuit cunning to deceive."

That the phenomena were genuine there can be no question. No suspicious circumstances occurred, and the lad was watched closely. Beyond this nothing appears to be known. It seems probable that the stigmatized youth was transferred to some distant house, where no doubt he lived and died—for one may presume that at this date he is dead—in obscurity. Gossip whispered that he left the Society, and under the conscription laws was recruited into the Italian army. But this sounds remarkably like some fabrication to injure the Jesuits.

Five-and-twenty years ago much discussion was aroused by the case of Fra Pio Pietrelcina, the saintly Capuchin friar of San Giovanni Rotondo in the diocese of Foggia. A short article in the *Daily Mail*, 19th June, 1920, excited considerable comment and curiosity. "Extraordinary scenes," it said, "are being witnessed in Foggia from day to day." In the same year, 1920, it was authoritatively stated that Fra Pio "is a man of remarkable sanctity". Miracles had been worked by his intercession; his ecstasies were frequent and prolonged; several instances, proved beyond all doubt, of bilocation were recorded. Moreover, since September, 1918, he had been stigmatized with the Five Wounds. Entirely convincing and of great weight is the evidence of the Most Rev. A. J. Kenealy, O. S. F. C., Archbishop of Simla, who in 1922, writing in the *Simla Times*, gave an account of personal interviews with Fra Pio. "I have seen," wrote the Archbishop, "and spoken privately with Fra Pio. The Stigmata came *in un colpo*, that is, all at once, like a sudden and unexpected blow, during his thanksgiving after Mass. The marks on the hands are like dried blood. In the palm the perforation is perfectly circular with rays of dried blood going from one side to the other, and is about the size of a penny. It looks much redder than the palm. It is precisely as if a big nail had been driven right up to its head into the palm, and the point had come out on the other side, where a hole, which can be seen quite clearly is covered with a pink skin." The Archbishop goes on to say, "I did not press him to show me the wounds in the feet as he assured me they were exactly like those in the hands. But I really did wish to see the mark—the *ferita*—in the side. I failed. He did not refuse, but said with indescribable meekness and dignity '*mi dispensi*', '*I beg you to excuse me*'. I made another effort, but. there was something in his face and eyes so strong and yet so humble, so remote and yet so friendly, that I simply had not the courage to insist."

As the fact of these phenomena got known there was a rush of visitors and pilgrims to see the good Capuchin, who only desired to be left in solitude and peaceful retirement. The publicity was more than unwelcome, it distressed him exceedingly and embarrassed the whole community. Actuated doubtless by the best motives, many religious persons and persons of eminence came from Rome, dignitaries whom Fra Pio was forced to receive with humility and respect.

The Pope ordered a most searching inquiry into these manifestations. It is interesting to remark that on more than one occasion the clinical

248

thermometer used in medical investigation proved unable to register the high temperature of the young Capuchin, and was broken by the abnormal expansion of the mercury in the tube. The Holy Office now stepped in to prevent these intrusions upon Fra Pio. In the *Acta Apostolicae Sedis*, 31st May, 1923, this supreme tribunal under the Holy Father published a statement to the effect that the phenomena had not been definitely shown to be supernatural and divine. Wherefore it was injoined that no rash and unfounded statements should be bruited abroad to be mischievously exaggerated, moreover all sorts or kinds of pilgrimages whether undertaken by an individual alone, or by a palmer band, must cease. There was not the least censure of Fra Pio, he was merely protected from publicity and the importunities of the crowd. This judgement, be it noted, was given after the publication of a couple of reports signed by two distinguished doctors, who had been requested by the Capuchin Superiors to examine the stigmatist. One of these specialists was a free thinker, Professor A. Bignami of the Roman University, who, signing his certificate on 26th July, 1919, attempted—but signally failed—to explain the stigmata as having a neurotic origin. The second report issued later in the same year, signed by Dr. Giorgio Festa, is very cautiously worded, but it emphasizes the flow of blood from the wounds. When Fra Pio says Mass, those who are near the altar can plainly see the stigmata on the hands, and that he suffers from the wounds in the feet is evident from his painful and laboured gait. He was, in fact, compelled to wear soft felt slippers instead of sandals. I have known the case of another religious who, being stigmatized in the feet, was similarly obliged to wear felt slippers. He also belonged to a discalced Order, that is an Order whose members are sandalled.

Yet so difficult is it to guide and counsel that on 24th July, 1924, the Holy Office felt obliged to repeat the former admonitions in even more forcible terms [*20*]. Those who had not conformed to the ruling of the previous year, 31st May, 1923, were now admonished absolutely to abstain from visiting Fra Pio for any devotional purpose, as also forbidden to continue any correspondence with him, writing long letters and beseeching direction and mystical instruction. The fact is that in the unquiet and turmoiled world of to-day there is such fantastic and itching curiosity, such morbid inquisitiveness and fevered newsmongering, which boils over in scandalous and scatter-brained stories, all too eagerly swallowed and with grotesque additions irresponsibly broadcast in the cheapest catchpenny press [*21*], that it is to-day necessary for ecclesiastical authority to be doubly diligent, to be ever cautious and slow, and prudent in a degree which perhaps never before was needful. To have any effect prohibitions must be underscored; warnings must be peremptory and insistent. We should, then, be all the more careful not to read too much into the formal and meticulously considered language of the decrees. There is no reprimand, no condemnation. But circumspection there decidedly is. Years go by, and no pronouncement is forthcoming. As has been well said, the mysteries of mystical phenomena are often "left to the implacable intervention of time, that acid which

Q

separates the authentic from its contrary". There, then, the matter rests.

It is instructive and significant to remember how St. Bernadette was reprimanded, menaced, and (we may well say) bullied by M. Jacomet, the local Commissaire de Police, whom some still regard as "a very worthy and conscientious functionary", a man who was only doing his duty; how the Procureur Impérial, M. Dutour, interrogated her with the utmost harshness and threatened her at the very first official examination that if she were found to be romancing or if it were discovered that either she or her family benefited by one penny through her story of the apparition, the law would surely intervene, and a severe sentence would follow. He did not disguise the fact that he disbelieved her and was of opinion that her father and mother hoped to reap considerable benefit from these visions, "even though they be no more than dreams, or, worse still, falsehoods" [22]. One of the Sisters at the Convent, where she was being prepared for her first Communion, told St. Bernadette that her story was all imagination, and added very tartly, "if you have seen Our Lady you had better ask Her to help you to learn the simple catechism which you do not seem able to grasp". The Curé of Lourdes, M. l'Abbé Peyramale, was at first, at any rate, most discouraging and unsympathetic. For some while Mgr. Laurence, the Bishop of Tarbes, and the high ecclesiastical authorities maintained an unbroken silence.

The way of the mystic is hard. It is not a path of flowers, but of thorns.

We must remember, too, how often in his serene wisdom Benedict XIV insists that the phenomena of ecstasies, stigmatization, bilocation, levitation, are nothing, unless the fact of heroic virtue be first established beyond all question. The fact of heroic virtue is not established by wonderful happenings, but by testimony of quite another kind. Where this is proven, then the phenomena of mysticism are accepted in confirmation. They are recognized as outward manifestations of sanctity. They do not prove sanctity. But it is certain there cannot be divine stigmata without heroic virtue.

The Physical Phenomena of Mysticism are a visible radiation of sanctity.

"I promise to make you happy, not in this world, but in the next," said Our Lady to St. Bernadette, and this is Her promise to all mystics.

As St. Bernadette triumphed, so will all true mystics triumph in the end.

I very well remember that a well-known scholar engaged upon some points of historical research in order to verify certain references read several passages from the great work of Benedict XIV, the *De servorum Dei Beatificatione et Canonizatione*. He was bewildered and amazed. "Upon my word," he cried, "I always took it for granted that it only needed a miracle or two, and that miracles were accepted practically at their face value without much examination, or questions asked. If there have to be these rigid investigations, this weight of evidence,

I am beginning to wonder how you accept the fact of any miracles at all!"

"A Miracle," says St. Augustine, "does not happen in contradiction to nature, but in contradiction to that which is known to us of nature [23].

Mystical theology deals with those Physical Phenomena of Mysticism which are miraculous. They cannot be explained in any other way. Once more to quote Canon Ribet, "Mystical Theology is the science which treats of the supernatural phenomena, either interior or exterior, which prepare, companion, or follow the passive attraction of souls towards God and by God, which is to say Divine Contemplation; which classifies and justifies them by the authority of Scripture, the Doctors, and reason; distinguishes them from parallel phenomena due to the dark action of the devil, and from analogous facts which are purely natural; and which, finally, traces out practical rules for spiritual guidance in these sublime but perilous ascents" [24].

"L'Eglise reste sainte, immortelle, infaillible" [25].

"Si quis dixerit miracula nulla fieri posse, proindeque omnes de iis narrationes, etiam in Sacra scriptura contentas, inter fabulas vel mythos ablegandas esse: aut miracula certo cognosci nunquam posse, nec iis divinam religionis christianae originem rite probari: anathema sit."

NOTES TO CHAPTER VII

1. *De La Démonomanie des Sorciers,* Lyon, 1593, pp. 243–4. The first edition of Bodin's *Démonomanie* is Paris, 1580. Paul III reigned 1534–1549.

2. During the horrible mania of the *convulsionnaires* of St. Médard at Paris, an outbreak, doubtless of demoniacal origin, which followed upon the death of the Jansenist François de Pâris, who was buried behind the high altar of St. Médard in May, 1727, la Sœur Françoise in 1759 underwent the test of a crucifixion for three and a half hours. The details are very blasphemous and revolting. See the *Correspondance Littéraire, philosophique et critique,* by Grimm, Diderot, etc., Paris, 1877 . . . IV, p. 379. Dom Bernard de la Taste, O.S.B., in his *Lettres Théologiques,* 1740, recognized that the St. Médard mania was clearly satanical. At Fareins, near Lyons, during a similar epidemic of evil fanaticism, on 12th October, 1787, a peasant girl named Etienette Thomasson was for the space of three minutes actually nailed in the attitude of crucifixion to a wall. A resounding scandal resulted. See A. Dubreuil, *Etude historique sur les Fareinistes,* 1775–1824, Lyons, 1908, pp. 96 *sqq.* Cases of self-crucifixion are recorded such as that of Matteo Lovat, 9th July, 1805. Such happenings are reported to have occurred at Turin in 1910 and at Berlin in 1927. A similar case was recorded in 1943.

3. The British Museum has a MSS. account (Egerton 357) of the process of Magdalena de la Cruz, *Sucesso de Madalena de la Cruz, monja professa del Monasterio de Santa Isabel de los Angeles de la orden de Santa Clara, y natural de la villa de Aguilar, y su sentencia dada por el Santo Tribunal de la Inquisicion de Cordoba en 3 de Mayo de 1546.* Another MSS. is to be found in the Bibliothèque Nationale, and there are many printed sources. See the contemporary, Simone Maiolo, Bishop of Asti (1520–97), *Dies caniculares,* ed. Moguntiae, 1610. Also Johann Weyer (1515–88), *Histoire, Disputes et Discours des illusions et Impostures des Diables* . . .

Genève, 1579; *Acta Sanetorum*, 31st July, in Vita S. Ignatii (p. 767), by Riba-daneyra; Martin Delrio, S. J. (1551–1608) *Disquisitionum magicarum Libri sex*, Louvain, 1599; Francesco Torreblanca *Daemonologia*, Moguntiae, 1623, and *Epitome delictorum, Sive de magia*, Hispali (Seville) 1618. Many other demonologists, e.g. De Lancre, Paris, 1612, p. 215; Collin de Plancy, *Dictionnaire Infernal*; mention the case in more or less detail. Of recent date see Montague Summers, *The History of Witchcraft and Demonology*, 1926, pp. 69–70; also the same author's *The Geography of Witchcraft*, 1927, pp. 605–612, where the history is discussed at some length; and further the same author's *Witchcraft and Black Magic*, 1946, p. 104.

4. The case of Virginie and the demoniacal scandals of Agen is little known. M. Maurice Garçon in his *Trois Histoires Diaboliques*, Paris, 1929, has given an excellent account of the proceedings, deriving his information from original documents, which he discovered at the Bibliothèque Nationale, a long and detailed MS. entitled "L'Affaire d'Agen," F.R. nouv. acq. 11,053. This MS. which M. Garçon identifies as having been written by a Sieur Albouys, who was living at Cahors in 1842, well repays a full and intensive examination.

5. Born 6th April, 1861, at the Château d'Alteville, Lorraine. He died at the Château on 18th December, 1897. His library of occult works is authoritatively stated to have been the largest and richest in rarities (including many MSS.) of any known private library, at least during the last century and a half. See Charles Berlet, *Un Ami de Barrès, Stanislas de Guaita* (640 copies only), Grasset, Paris, 1936. The *Catalogue de la Bibliothèque occulte de Stanislas de Guaita*, Dorbon, Paris, 1899, a reference work of great value does not appear in the Bibliothèque Nationale.

6. *Le Serpent de la Genèse*, livre I, Chamuel, 1891; and Durville, 1916: livre II, Chamuel, 1897; and Durville, 1915. For Guaita's note on Rose Tamisier see the édition Durville, p. 448.

7. Sisters of the Presentation of Mary, a Congregation founded on 21st November, 1796, by the Venerable Mère Marie Rivier, whom Pius IX called "the Apostolic Woman". The Congregation is numerous in France and Belgium. The Sisters are an Educational Order, and also undertake such active works of charity as nursing and superintending hospitals.

8. This is the title of Giberti's biography of Blessed Eustochium, published at Venice, 1672.

9. *Life of the Blessed Curé d'Ars*, with a Preface by Henry Edward Manning, Cardinal Archbishop of Westminster, n.d. (1906), Chapter VIII, "The sufferings inflicted upon him by the devil". This *Life* is a translation of *Le Curé d'Ars*, par l'Abbé Alfred Monrin, 2 v., Paris, 1861.

10. *The Life of the Blessed (Saint) Paul of the Cross*, 3 Vols., London, Richardson, 1853. Vol. II, Ch. XXIV, "Of the Vexation of Devils", pp. 296–305.

11. *The Life of Gemma Galgani*. Father Germanus, C. P. 1914. Ch. XIX.

12. Material for the Biography is to be found in the Processus, that is to say the official sworn documentary evidence for the Cause of Beatification. A useful work is *Compendio della Vita Ammirabile della Serva di dio Elisabetta Canori Mora, Romana, Terziaria dell' Ordine de' Trinitari Scalzi*, Rome, Tipografia degli Artigianelli di S. Giuseppe, 1896.

13. There are several lives of the "Little Arab". The latest, *Vie de Sœur Marie de Jésus Crucifié*, by the Abbé Buzy was published in 1927 with the approbations of Cardinal Camassi, Patriarch of Jerusalem, and Cardinal Sevin.

14. There is a French biography by Madame Maria Didry, Religious of the Cross in collaboration with the parish-priest of Bois-d'Haine, A. Wallemacq, S.T.B., the second edition of which was translated into English by Dom Francis Izard, O.S.B., M.R.C.S. Eng., L.R.C.P., London. Dom Izard has also written a short but useful biography, n.d. (1932), *Louise Lateau*. Earlier works are, an important article, *Louise Lateau, a biological study* by Dr. George E. Day, *Macmillan's Magazine*, April, 1871; *La Stigmatisée de Bois d'Haine* by M. l'Abbé de Menneval, Dillet éditeur, Paris, 1871; *Louise Lateau, the ecstatica of Bois-d'Haine* by J. S. Sheppard, London, pub. Richardson, 1872: *Louise Lateau von Bois-d'Haine, een studiebeeld voor de positieve wetensvhap* by A.J. Riko, pub. van Langenhuysen,

Amsterdam, 1872, a study strongly emphasizing the divinely supernatural character of the Stigmata; *Excursion à Bois-l'Haine* by M. X., i.e. M.l'Abbé Edmond Jaspar, Ducoulombier éditeur, Lille, 1872; *Biographie de Louise Lateau* by H. V. L., serialized in *La Bonne Lecture*, Paris, 1873–4, by Père Séraphin, C.P. of Erelez-Tournai, one of the two theologians of the Ecclesiastical Commission. See also Rohling, *Louise Lateau, her Stigmas and Ecstasy*, New York, 1884.

15. I have been fortunate enough to be able to avail myself of notes made by contemporaries, as also of private information. Such monographs as *Extracto de la Causa sequida à Sor Patrocinio*, Madrid, 1865, are bitterly inimical to the holy nun, and are quite unscrupulous in their inventions.

16. Wilfrid de Fonvielle, born at Paris in 1828. His writings include *Les Saltimbanques de la Science*, Paris, Deyfrons, 1884, which treats of the "convulsionnaires" of St. Médard, Mesmer and his followers, the divining-rod, Allan Kardec, i.e. Hippolyte-Léon-Denizard Rivail, the spiritist and prophet of reincarnation; *Les Endormeurs*, Paris, du Parc, n.d. (1887), which prattles of hypnotism, hysteria, and modern sorcery. Scholars regarded de Fonvielle's output with distrust and contempt.

17. *Revista Cristiana*, Marzo-Abril, 1891, Madrid. In *The Times*, 16th December, 1885, there is a reference to Manuel Quiroga and "his sister the famous stigmatic Sor Patrocinio".

18. A Milan dispatch to the German overseas news agency, quoted by Reuter. *Oxford Mail*, 19th March, 1845.

19. *Our Lady of Tears* by Fr. Gereon Stach, C.M.M. published Detroit, Michigan, with the Imprimatur, 5th December, 1936, of Mgr. Michael J. Gallagher, Bishop of Detroit.

20. *Acta Apostolicae Sedis*. September, 1924, p. 368. *The Tablet*, Saturday, 20th September, 1924.

21. With such headings as "Miracle Monk" that gave great offence.

22. *Histoire de Notre-Dame de Lourdes d'après les Documents et les Témoins*, By Père L. J. M. Cros, S.J. Tome 1, "Les Apparitions", Paris, Beauchesne, 1925. p. 195. See also Henri Lasserre's *Notre-Dame de Lourdes*.

23. *De civitate Dei*, XXI, 8.

24. *La mystique divine*, Vol. I, p. 15.

25. *Les Stigmatisées*, Dr. A. Imbert-Gourbeyre, éd. Palmé, Paris, 1873; II. p. 258.

INDEX

D

E

G

F

Ingram Content Group UK Ltd.
Milton Keynes UK
UKHW012059220323
419005UK00003B/247